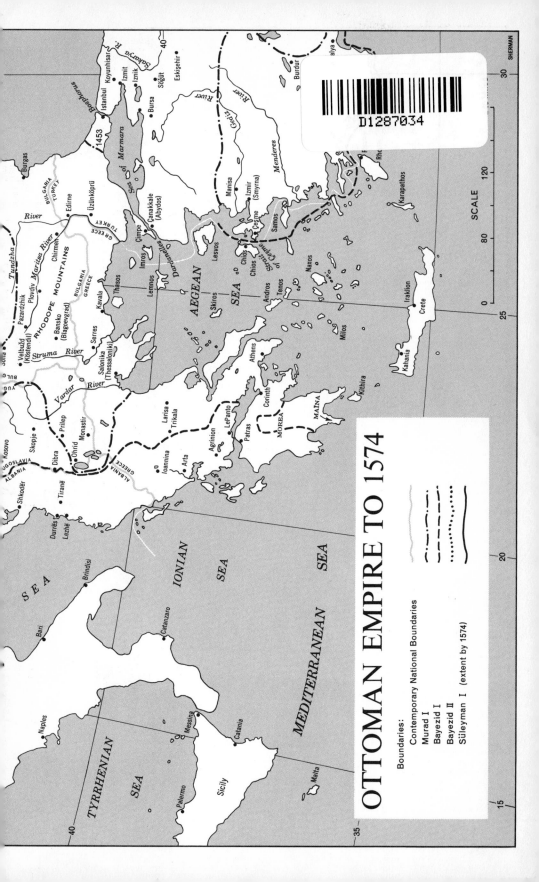

OTTOMAN EMPIRE TO 1574

Boundaries:

Contemporary National Boundaries
Murad I
Bayezid I
Bayezid II
Süleyman I (extent by 1574)

SCALE

0   25   80   120

SHERMAN

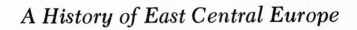
A History of East Central Europe

VOLUMES IN THE SERIES

VOLUME V

Southeastern Europe
under Ottoman Rule, 1354-1804

A HISTORY OF EAST CENTRAL EUROPE

VOLUME V

EDITORS

PETER F. SUGAR
University of Washington

DONALD W. TREADGOLD
University of Washington

Southeastern Europe under Ottoman Rule, 1354-1804

BY PETER F. SUGAR

UNIVERSITY OF WASHINGTON PRESS
Seattle and London

PJK4
S93
vol 5

Library of Congress Cataloging in Publication Data

Sugar, Peter F

    Southeastern Europe under Ottoman rule, 1354–1804.

    (A history of East Central Europe, editors, Peter F. Sugar, Donald W. Treadgold; v. 5)

    Bibliography: p.

    Includes index.

    1. Balkan Peninsula—History. 2. Turks in the Balkan Peninsula. I. Title. II. Series: Sugar, Peter F. A history of East Central Europe; v. 5.

DJK4.S93 vol. 5 [DR36]   949s   [949.6]   76–7799

ISBN 0–295–95443–4

For Steven, Klári, and Karen

Foreword

THE systematic study of the history of East Central Europe outside the region itself began only in the last generation or two. For the most part historians in the region have preferred to write about the past of only their own countries. Hitherto no comprehensive history of the area as a whole has appeared in any language.

This series was conceived as a means of providing the scholar who does not specialize in East Central European history and the student who is considering such specialization with an introduction to the subject and a survey of knowledge deriving from previous publications. In some cases it has been necessary to carry out new research simply to be able to survey certain topics and periods. Common objectives and the procedures appropriate to attain them have been discussed by the authors of the individual volumes and by the coeditors. It is hoped that a certain commensurability will be the result, so that the eleven volumes will constitute a unit and not merely an assemblage of writings. However, matters of interpretation and point of view have remained entirely the responsibility of the individual authors.

No volume deals with a single country. The aim has been to identify geographical or political units that were significant during the period in question, rather than to interpret the past in accordance with latter-day sentiments or aspirations.

The limits of "East Central Europe," for the purposes of this series, are the eastern linguistic frontier of German- and Italian-speaking peoples on the west, and the political borders of Russia/the USSR on the east. Those limits are not precise, even within the period covered by any given volume of the series. The appropriateness of including the Finns, Estonians, Latvians, Lithuanians, Belorussians, and Ukrainians was considered, and it was decided not to attempt to cover them systematically, though they appear repeatedly in these books. Treated in depth are the Poles,

Czecho-Slovaks, Hungarians, Romanians, Yugoslav peoples, Albanians, Bulgarians, and Greeks.

There has been an effort to apportion attention equitably among regions and periods. Three volumes deal with the area north of the Danube-Sava line, three with the area south of it, and four with both areas. Four treat premodern history, six modern times. The eleventh consists of an historical atlas and a bibliography of the entire subject. Each volume is supplied with a bibliographical essay of its own, but we all have attempted to keep the scholarly apparatus at a minimum in order to make the text of the volumes more readable and accessible to the broader audience sought.

The coeditors wish to express their thanks to the Ford Foundation for the financial support it gave this venture, and to the Institute of Comparative and Foreign Area Studies (formerly Far Eastern and Russian Institute) and its three successive directors, George E. Taylor, George M. Beckmann, and Herbert J. Ellison, under whose encouragement the project has moved close to being realized.

The whole undertaking has been longer in the making than originally planned. Two of the original list of projected authors died before they could finish their volumes and have been replaced. Volumes of the series are being published as the manuscripts are received. We hope that the usefulness of the series justifies the long agony of its conception and birth, that it will increase knowledge of and interest in the rich past and the many-sided present of East Central Europe among those everywhere who read English, and that it will serve to stimulate further study and research on the numerous aspects of this area's history that still await scholarly investigators.

PETER F. SUGAR
DONALD W. TREADGOLD

Preface

THE editors of the series, *A History of East Central Europe,* asked their collaborators to "aim at producing volumes that will deal with all major aspects of history. Political, social, economic, institutional, and religious aspects are to be treated . . . and each author will endeavor not to weight his volume too heavily on any single aspect." The same memorandum, dated March 23, 1963, also stipulated that "scholarly apparatus is to be kept to a minimum," with the exception of the bibliographic essay.

As one of the two editors making these requests, I followed these guide lines as closely as I could in writing this volume. To fit roughly five-hundred years of Albanian, Bulgarian, Greek, Romanian, and Serbo-Croatian history within the limits set, and at the same time cover some aspects of and periods in the lives of Hungarians and Turks and write a book conforming to the accepted forms of the historians' craft exceeded my abilities. While the chronological framework has been retained, the material has been organized topically or geographically into chapters, which tell specific stories. It was my intention to present a chronologically organized series of descriptive pictures that in their totality depict life in Southeastern Europe under Ottoman rule. If what was done succeeded in satisfying this requirement, my purpose will have been achieved. The entire series, including this volume, is aimed at the beginning graduate student or the historian who is not an area specialist but is interested in learning something about Southeastern Europe. It seemed more important to meet the needs of these potential readers than to follow accepted norms of organization. The circumstances and explanations just presented determined the organization of this volume.

Names and expressions taken from a great number of languages appear on the following pages. Unless they have an equivalent in English that has practically become part of our language (e.g., vezir, sultan) or are known in a certain form (e.g., Vienna, Belgrade), they are rendered in the contemporary spelling of the language from which they are taken. Cities are cited by the name used at the time they are mentioned (e.g., Constantinople before 1453 and Istanbul after that date), but when they first appear in the following pages all alternate names are also given in parentheses. The glossaries of foreign expressions and geographic locations supplied at the end of the volume should help the reader to identify them without difficulty.

It is with great pleasure that I turn from these technical explanations to a much more pleasant task and acknowledge the help of many without which I could not have produced this study. Financial support for research was generously made available by the Guggenheim Foundation and by the Institute for Comparative and Foreign Area Studies of the University of Washington. A grant from the American Council of Learned Societies gave me the needed time to produce the first draft of this book. My warmest thanks go to these organizations.

The list of persons who helped me in archives and libraries is much too long to permit individual mention. I wish to thank all those who generously placed their time and knowledge at my disposal in the following places: the British Museum and the Library of the School of Slavonic and East European Studies at the University of London; the Bibliothèque Nationale in Paris; the National Library, the University Library, the Haus,- Hof, und Staatsarchiv, the Historical Institute, and the Institute for East and Southeast European Studies in Vienna; the National Archives, the National Széchenyi Library, and the Historical Institute of the Academy of Sciences in Budapest; the National Archives, the National Library, the Historical Institute "N. Iorga," and the Institute of South-East European Studies in Bucharest; the Historical Institute of the Bulgarian Academy of Sciences, the "Kliment and Methodius" Library, and the Library of the Bulgarian Academy of Sciences in Sofia; the Library of the Historical Institute of the Serb Academy of Sciences, the Public Library, and Archives of the Republic of Serbia in Belgrade; the Library of the Yugoslav Academy of Sciences in Zagreb; the Public Library, the Archives of the Republic of Bosnia-Hercegovina, and the libraries of the university and the Territorial (Zemaljski) Museum in Sarajevo.

I wish that this list of places could be extended, but unfortunately my inability to read Greek and the refusal of the Turkish authorities to let me work in Istanbul precluded extension of my research.

Last but not least, I wish to thank two people without whose help and understanding this volume would never have been written. My wife, Sally, showed much understanding for my numerous absences and for the long hours spent at home that might as well have been spent hundreds of miles away as far as her needs were concerned. Her tolerance went far beyond that expected from an academic wife. My colleague and friend, Professor Donald W. Treadgold, helped me considerably with his understanding, patience, and the inspirational example that association with him provided.

PETER F. SUGAR

Contents

Contents   xvii

Maps

Part One

THE OTTOMANS

CHAPTER 1

The Early History and the Establishment
of the Ottomans in Europe

1. THE BASIC MUSLIM AND TURKISH FOUNDATIONS OF THE OTTOMAN STATE

IN THE middle of the fourteenth century the Balkan Peninsula was in turmoil. The second Serbian empire was disintegrating, and the Byzantine
Empire, which in previous centuries had always been able to fill the
vacuum left by similar collapses in the area, was too weak to play this
role. Political chaos was paralleled by social and religious controversy.
The lower classes were trying to shake off the rule of the traditional noble
ruling element, and heresies, which often represented social class differences, flourished. Members of the Slav ruling families were fighting each
other, and a similar struggle for the throne was in progress in the Byzantine Empire. It was the latter struggle that brought a new force, the Ottomans, into the Balkans.

Between 1341 and 1355 the corulers of the Byzantine Empire, John V
Paleologos and John VI Cantacuzene, were fighting for sole possession of
the throne. Being short of support and troops, the latter called on Orhan,
the ruler of a rising Turkish principality on the eastern shores of the Marmara Sea, to come to his aid. Thus, in 1345 the first warriors serving the
House of Osman crossed the Dardanelles and a new chapter began in the
history of Southeastern Europe.

A little more than a hundred years later, in 1453, the House of Osman
conquered Byzantium for which the two Johns had fought so desperately
and made it the capital of a large state that stretched roughly from what is
today central Yugoslavia to eastern Asia Minor. That state, known in the
West as the Ottoman Empire, was called "The divinely protected well-
flourishing absolute domain of the House of Osman (Memālik-i mahrūseh-
i maʿ mūreh-i ʿosmāniyeh)." The two basic elements of the empire, the Islamic and Turkic, are indicated by this curious name. Neither can be fully
explored in this volume, but a few important aspects must be mentioned
to explain the system that determined the fates of Europeans under Ot-

3

toman rule. The House of Osman was a latecomer in the Near East and created a state based on pre-existing principles that justified its rule. Throughout the six hundred years of rule they clung to these principles, which they believed represented the divine and laic justifications for everything that they and the empire undertook. For that reason an understanding of these principles is essential.

In order to introduce the Islamic features that played a role in Ottoman thinking, one must begin with a few remarks about the origin of Islam. The Muslim lunar calendar begins with the year of the *Hijra* (migration) in 622 A.D. when the Prophet Muhammad moved from Mecca to Yatrīb (Medina). The strictly monotheistic religion preached by the prophet included Jewish, Christian, and traditional Arabic elements together with some original additions. Islam, while morally and ethically lofty, is theologically much simpler than other monotheistic creeds. Therefore, it was perfectly suited for the people to whom the prophet addressed his message. It was equally well suited then, as it is now, for peoples who had reached a stage in civilization demanding a higher level of religious and metaphysical beliefs as well as a moral code regulating the activities of society, but who were not yet ready to cope with the theological difficulties and complications of either Judaism or Christianity. The Turks were such a people.

Muhammad recognized the common bond of monotheism between the religion he preached and Christianity and Judaism. Verse 62 of Chapter (*sūra*) 2 of the *Qur'ān* clearly links all montheists in a common fate until and including the Day of the Last Judgement:

> Lo! those who believe (in that which is revealed unto thee Muhammad), and those who are Jews, and Christians, and Sabaeans—whoever believeth in Allah and the Last Day and doeth right—surely their reward is with the Lord, and there shall no fear come upon them neither shall they grieve.[1]

This recognition went beyond mere statements. Muhammad was willing to use Christian and Jewish tribes as allies, and when his realm expanded he incorporated them in his Islamic state without demanding their conversion. We have several treaties dating from the time of his rule that spell this out quite clearly. One treaty with the city of Najrān in Yemen, dating from 631, lists the obligations and taxes of the city and then states that

> Najrān and their followers have the protection of God and the *dhimmah* [guarantee of security] of Muhammad the prophet, the Messenger of God, for themselves, their community, their land, and their goods . . . and for their churches and services [no bishop will be removed from his episcopate and no monk from his monastic position, and no church-warden from his church-wardship]. . . . On the terms stated in this document [they have] protection

---

1. Mohammed Marmaduke Pickthall, *The Meaning of the Glorious Koran; An Explanatory Translation* (New York: Mentor Books, 1953), p. 38.

of God and *dhimmah* of the prophet for ever, until God comes with His command, if they are loyal and perform their obligations well, not being burdened by wrong.[2]

In these passages we find the first Islamic element that became fundamental for the life of the people of Southeastern Europe under Ottoman rule. Any monotheist who accepted the political supremacy of Islam and was willing to live in a Muslim state under stipulated conditions became a *zimmi*, a protected person. This protection extended beyond the religious freedom made explicit in the above passage. It involved a sort of self-government that under the Ottomans became institutionalized and known as the *millet* system, which was basically a minority home-rule policy based on religious affiliation. We can trace the origin of that system to the following lines of the treaty mentioned above:

> If any of them asks for a right, justice is among them (i.e., in their own hands) [To see that they are] not doing wrong and not suffering wrong; it belongs to Najrān.[3]

The protectors were the first-class citizens and the protected *zimmis* had to carry special burdens. Of these the oldest used throughout the Ottoman period was the poll-tax (*cizye*). There were other tribute-taxes and obligations dating from early Muslim days that the Ottomans retained; these will be discussed in later chapters.

This distinction among the Muslims, the "people of the book" as the other monotheists were called, and the pagans who theoretically had to convert or die rested on a basic world view. This view is fundamental in understanding the "divinely protected" part of the Ottoman state's official name, and its reasons for existing in the eyes of those who ruled the empire. Islam, like Judaism and Christianity, believes that humanity can live happily only if it follows God's command. God made his will known by repeatedly speaking through prophets. According to the Muslims, Adam was the first and Muhammad the last prophet. Sinful man always twisted God's word to suit himself, thus forcing the divinity to send more and more prophets. Because God is eternal, perfect, and unchanging His commands were always the same; therefore, all "people of the book" received the same message. The difference between the Muslims and other monotheists is simply that the former accepted the last, and therefore uncorrupted, message while the others stuck to their erroneous versions of divine revelation. The Muslims' perfect understanding of God's commands makes them His chosen people, whose duty it is to spread the true word to all mankind.

The basic Muslim beliefs concerning the *Qur'ān* cannot be discussed

2. W. Montgomery Watt, *Muhammad at Medina* (Oxford: The Clarendon Press, 1956), pp. 359-60.
3. Watt, p. 360.

here, but it must be pointed out that the book is considered to contain not the words of the prophet, but those of Allah. Therefore, it is neither subject to interpretation nor translatable because translations distort God's meaning. The *Qur'ān* contains everything a man must know to live righteously and save his soul.

It soon became clear, however, that additional legislation was needed when the small Muslim-Arab community grew into a world-wide empire. First the community turned to the traditional sayings of the prophet, then to those of his immediate successors, and finally to the utterances of the first caliphs. Those statements that were considered genuine were collected and codified in the *Hadiths* (traditions). The *Hadiths*, together with the consensus of the learned (*ijma'*) and their rulings based on analogy (*qijās*), and naturally the *Qur'ān*, formed the Muslim law code, the *shari'a*. The splits that occurred in the Muslim community stemmed from diverging views concerning the acceptability of certain *Hadiths*, but the great majority of Muslims followed the four so-called orthodox legal schools and were jointly known as the *Sunnis*. The Ottoman were *Sunnis* and followed the *shari'a*. Because this law applied only to Muslims, a system had to be introduced for the non-Muslims, and it had to follow confessional lines because religious differences were the only ones that the Muslims understood. That system was the above-mentioned *millet* system.

Law was very basic to all Muslim, including the Ottoman, states because religion, law, and administrative structure and, therefore, correct behavior and salvation were closely tied together. The Muslims did not distinguish between secular and sacred or religious law; to them law meant *shari'a*. In practice, however, a distinction did exist, and the *shari'a* was by no means the only law. The second excerpt from the Najrān Treaty indicates quite clearly that local laws and customs were respected and even reconfirmed. Later, local laws were confirmed in the Ottoman-ruled parts of Southeastern Europe at the time of conquest. In addition they were frequently incorporated into subsequent Ottoman laws, the *kanuns*, issued by the sultans for use in their provinces.

Kanuns were secular laws, provided we consider the *shari'a* sacred or religious law, something that would not be quite correct but comes nearest to our western concepts of what it really was. That such laws were needed, both in the earlier Islamic and later the Ottoman empires, to deal with a great variety of problems that did not face those who codified the *shari'a* is obvious. Nevertheless, in a religious-legal community whose basic law theoretically covered all the needs of mankind, the issuance of these additional laws had to be justified.

By definition inferior to the *shari'a*, these additional laws were based on *urf* (*adat*, *örf*), which is best translated as customary law. According to early jurisconsults, this was the law that princes were to follow in regulating the affairs of the country. Closely related to *urf* was *âmme*, general or public law, which regulated state-to-state and state-citizen relation-ships. After the Turkish element became dominant in the eleventh cen-tury, the old Turkish principle of *törü* was added, which recognized the rights of the ruler to issue decrees. Because *törü* was closely related to the Islamic *urf* concept, it was easily absorbed into the Muslim legal tradition. These principles were the legal basis for the issuing of the numerous *kanuns* that became very important for the European people under Ot-toman rule. Most *kanuns* were nothing else but the old laws of any given region which the Ottomans confirmed in areas they conquered.

The *kadis* (judges), who administered both the *sharī'a* and the *kanun* laws, and the *müftis* (juriconsults who interpreted the former) were also old Muslim officials whose offices the Ottomans had taken over from the former Islamic states and brought intact into Europe. They belonged to the *ulema* (plural of *âlim*), the class of learned men who were the educa-tional, legal, spiritual, and often scientific and cultural leaders of the Muslim community. They played an important role, as will be seen, in Ottoman life.

What must be obvious from this sketchy outline of Muslim-Ottoman law is that Ottoman law was not centralized-territorial, but practically territorial-individual, because every individual's religion, occupation, place of residence, status in society, and sex determined the law that was applicable to him or her. This produced important variations that will be discussed later.

Brief mention must be made of one more Islamic aspect that became crucial for the Ottoman state and its inhabitants: the "Five Pillars of Faith," the basic duties of a Muslim. These duties are very simple: Prayer, Almsgiving, Fasting, Pilgrimage, and Profession of Faith. Naturally the Ottomans followed these basic rules. Every Ottoman tried to live up to these commands, and the numerous public buildings, hospitals, roads, and so on that were built in Southeastern Europe were the result of these en-deavors. More important for the Ottoman state's well-understood mission are verses 190-93 of the second chapter of the *Qur'ān:*

Fight in the way of Allah against those who fight against you, but begin not hostilities. Lo! Allah loveth no aggressors.

And slay them wherever ye find them, and drive them out of the places whence they drove you out, for persecution is worse than slaughter. And fight not with them at the Inviolable Place of Worship until they first attack you there, but if they attack you (there) then slay them. Such is the reward of dis-believers.

But if they desist, then lo! Allah is Forgiving, Merciful.

And fight them until persecution is no more, and religion is for Allah. But if they desist, then let there be no hostility except against wrongdoers.[4]

4. Pickthall, p. 50.

Literally, these lines speak of defensive war, condemn aggression, and appear to address themselves to a religious group subject to persecutions. Only one line, "fight until persecution is no more, and religion is for Allah," can conceivably be read to mean the spreading of the word of God by the sword. Yet, on these lines was based the concept of *jihād*, holy war, against unbelievers. In its Ottoman version, *gaza, jihād* became the official *raison d'être* of the Ottoman Empire.

One of the earliest accounts we have about Osman, the founder of the dynasty, describes how his future father-in-law, Şeyh Edebali, the leader of a mystical fraternity, ceremoniously hands him the sword of a *gazi*, a fighter for the Faith. Osman won his first major battle against the Byzantines as a *gazi* chieftain at Baphaeum (Koyunhisar) near Nicea (Iznik) in 1301, for which the Seljuq sultan gave him the title of *bey* (*beğ*). Although the Ottoman rulers added a long list of impressive titles to these first two, including those of sultan (the holder of authority), *hudavendigâr* (emperor), *sultan-i azam* (the most exalted sultan), and *padişah* (sovereign), they always kept *gazi* as their first title.

The extension of the realm of the *dar al-Islam* (the domain of Islam) at the expense of the *dar al-harb* (the domain of war, the domain of those who fought Islam) was the Ottomans' duty. When the empire ceased to expand and especially when it began to shrink, the Ottomans began to feel that they had failed in their divinely ordered mission.

The above Islamic aspects of the Ottoman Empire, while not complete, give the most important features affecting the lives of the people of Southeastern Europe and are sufficient to explain the Muslim nature of the state that was "divinely protected." This state was also the "domain of the House of Osman." In the various states of Europe, the Far East, and even the Arab-Muslim domains, a change of dynasty was a frequent occurrence, but in a Turkic-Turkish state this was impossible. The existence of the Ottoman Empire was closely tied to the rule of a single dynasty, the Osmanli (Ottoman). This is the first important Turkish feature that must be noted, and it can be explained by the development of Turkish states prior to that of the Ottomans.

The original home lands of all Turkish (Turkic) people were the plains of southern Siberia and the endless expanses between the Caspian Sea and the Altaic range. The early Turkish "states" were at best tribal federations put together by strong men whose death usually meant the end of the "state." This society was dominated by a warrior aristocracy, the *beys*; not only was it stratified, but it also had the beginning of a vague legal system. Everybody had his place, but the entire structure hinged on a common loyalty to a supreme chief and possibly to his family. By the beginning of the eighth century the Turkish-inhabited areas bordering on Iran had been subjugated by the 'Abbāsids and had supplied them with

an endless stream of slaves, many of whom became important functionaries in Baghdad.

Toward the end of the tenth century a confederation of Ghuz and
Oghuz tribes established itself in the region of the Aral Sea. Known after
their conversion to Islam as Turkomans, these peoples were led by a chief
called Seljuq. The descendants of Seljuq had expanded their realm south
and westward as far as Isfahan by the middle of the next century. In 1055
the weak caliph Al-Qa'im (1031-75) wanted to free himself from the tyrannical tutelage of another Turk, the chief of his body guard al-Basasiri. He
turned to the leader of the Seljuq state, Tughril, for help and made him his
chief officer. For the next hundred years, until 1157 when the caliphs reasserted their power, the Seljuqs were the real masters of the ʿAbbāsid state.
Their title was sultan.

When they were finally expelled from Baghdad, the Seljuqs had already
established other power centers. One of these was in Asia Minor (Anatolia, Anadolu). There were reasons for this development. Turkish warriors
were always looking for strong chiefs to follow, and once the Seljuqs were
firmly established in Baghdad there were more followers than could be
usefully employed. Since the newcomers were able and willing to fight,
the Great Seljuqs, as those ruling in Baghdad were called, sent them to
border regions to fight for faith, honor, advancement, and booty. They
were equally eager to get rid of certain members of their family who had
either the ability or the inclination, and sometimes both, to strive for the
sultanate. The Byzantine border was the ideal place for unwanted relatives as well.

There Muslim *gazis* and their Christian equivalents, Greek *akritoi*, had
developed a rough frontier society. This society was the result of centuries
of continuous warfare, during which borderlines were never firmly established and the authority of the central government in the frontier region
was at best nominal. The resulting no man's land attracted adventurous
free spirits from both sides who made a living from robbing each other,
justifying their action as a "defense of their faith." Even this curious way
of life required rules; what developed was a rough code of behavior and
chivalry acceptable to both sides.

Shortly after he became master of Baghdad, Tughril sent his nephew,
Alp Arslan, to secure the realm's borders. In 1071 at Manzikert (Malaz-
girt) north of Lake Van, Alp Arslan won one of the crucial battles of history, defeating the Byzantines and capturing the emperor, Romanus Di-
ogenes. Byzantium never recovered from this defeat. Eastern Anatolia
was freed from Byzantine rule, and soon several independent, mainly
Armenian, states appeared in the region. None of these states was strong,
and the instability in the region lured the *gazis* who could easily reap rich
rewards for raids. As early as 1072 Süleyman, an ambitious young relative

of Alp Arslan, was sent back to Anatolia at the head of a large army of nomadic Turkomans. He conquered most of Asia Minor and reached Nicaea by 1082. While the First Crusade was reconquering most of Anatolia, Süleyman's son Kiliç Arslan returned to Anatolia and established the state of the Seljuqs of Rum (Rome, Byzantium). From 1107 until 1307, when their state was destroyed by the Mongols, the Sultanate of Rum with its capital at Konya (Iconium) developed the features of the frontier-*gazi* state as well as certain cultural features that became the foundations of the Ottoman state.

Constantly fighting not only the Byzantines and Crusaders, but also other Turkish states—of which that of the Danishmends' was the most important—Seljuq Anatolia was in continual flux and attracted increasing numbers of Turkoman warriors. These warriors became settlers once their fighting days were over, and land was the greatest reward they could receive. Although Persian and Byzantine models existed for the creation of these military fiefs, which were known as *iqtā's*, the system was further expanded by the Seljuqs and eventually evolved into the *timar* system of the Ottomans. In its Seljuq-Ottoman form this landholding system tied to military service can be considered a very important Turkish feature transplanted into Europe. The *timar* system will be discussed in detail later, but here it should be noted that it was the institution basic to the army, agricultural production, taxation, and local law enforcement. This system, in typical Turkish fashion, was based on personal loyalty and allegiance, which, unlike in the European feudal system, was due directly to the ruler. There were no intermediary lords between the lowest fief holder and the holder of ultimate power.

The most typical, but at the same time the most complicated, development that faced the Seljuqs of Anatolia and later the Ottomans was the result not only of continuous warfare, but also of the fact that few major centers like Konya developed. The countryside continued to favor the life style of the *gazi-akritoi* frontier society. As a result the economic base for an organized state was lacking. There were several reasons for this development.

Between the Battle of Manzikert and the end of the thirteenth century, Anatolia was a constant battle ground. Except for relatively short periods when the Seljuq rulers were strong, there was no strong authority able to maintain security outside the major cities in Asia Minor. Even if the various Muslim and Christian rulers had been able to maintain order, they would have been powerless to influence the socioethnic factors that transformed Anatolia into a Turkish land during these centuries.

Most of the Turks who came into the region were Turkoman nomad warrior-herdsmen. Their migration became massive in the thirteenth century with the Mongol conquests of first Central Asia, then Persia, and finally Baghdad in 1258. These newly arrived Turks fought for various princelings and factions in a land that rapidly became overwhelmingly rural. The two major waves of Turkish conquest and migration destroyed most of the urban settlements.[5] Just as Western Europe had to find a new solution to a similar problem after the *Völkerwanderung* and the collapse of the Western Roman Empire, so Anatolia had to find a solution. A new system of production, marketing, and public order was needed.

Both the *gazis* and the *akritoi* were "fighters of the faith," but neither group was educated and sophisticated enough to understand the true meaning of the religions for which they fought. They were fanatical upholders of their beliefs, but those beliefs had little to do with what the Muslim *ulema* or the Christian theologians would have recognized as the correct understanding and interpretation of the respective religions. The religions of the frontier—with this Christian and Muslim mixture of superstitions, mysticism, traditional, and in some cases even pagan beliefs—were more similar to each other than they were to officially correct versions of the creeds. These folk-religions began to fuse and gradually became dominated by Muslim characteristics.

Just as the western medieval knight needed a code of conduct in fighting local wars of the early Middle Ages, so did the Anatolian warrior have to develop his own norms of behavior in conformity with his religious convictions. With the Turkish element dominant this code of Anatolian chivalry had to focus on the person (or family) of a leader. With military and religious considerations predominating in the frontier society, this leader could either be a religious or a military figure; ideally he should be both. When this was not possible, a close alliance between a religious leader *şeyh*, and a military leader, whose title could be sultan, *bey*, or *gazi*, was sought.

The combination of economic needs, rapid ethnic transformation, unsettled conditions, rustication, acceptable religious leadership, and the unchanged desire for a focus for personal loyalty created a new system. We still do not know how and when it developed exactly; it was a gradual process that took place during the Seljuq period and was fully developed by the time Osman began his meteoric rise to power.

The nomenclature also reflects this confusion. We have several expressions for the same phenomenon, while other terms change their meaning. A few examples will suffice. In the thirteenth and fourteenth centuries *akhi* meant either the leader or any member of a mystic fraternity, and

5. The best study of the ethnic-religious transformation is Speros Vryonis, Jr., *The Decline of Medieval Hellenism in Asia Minor and the Process of Islamization from the Eleventh through the Fifteenth Century* (Berkeley, Los Angeles, and London: University of California Press, 1971). On pp. 166-67 and 259 Vryonis lists the cities, towns, and villages that were pillaged, sacked, or destroyed, with their inhabitants either enslaved or massacred.

later it denoted the member of a trade or craft guild. *Şeyh* stood for the leader of a religious fraternity (synonymous with the early meaning of *akhi*), and also for certain tribal leaders; later it referred to the "court-chaplain" of the sultan as well as to the chief religious officer of a guild. The crucial word *futuwwa* could denote an entire mystic fraternity, but it could also stand for this association's code of ethics and chivalry. The distinction between *sufi*, a Muslim mystic, and a *derviş* is only slightly less confusing denoting at best a certain level of mystical attainment.

These difficulties aside, the final outcome can be roughly described as the establishment of fraternities on a folk-religious-mystic basis containing elements of Christianity and Islam as well as folk beliefs, but in its over-all character Muslim. These fraternities were led by their "holy man," *şeyh*, and its members (*sufis* or *dervişes*) ministered to the spiritual needs of those who selected their fraternity as the one whose code of ethics, *futuwwa*, they were willing to follow.[6]

The activity of the fraternities and the precepts of their *futuwwa*s extended beyond the religious realm to social and economic spheres. The fraternities organized or established close contacts with craftsmen, and the *futuwwa* became the regulation for all the social and economic activities of the developing guilds. The code of chivalry was also tied to these *futuwwa*s because most of the soldiers became members of the various fraternities.[7] These organizations spread, and the larger ones had *tekkes* (houses for their members) and maintained *zaviyes* (inns for the laymen) all over the country. Traveling constantly, performing not only religious duties but often also practicing the trade of the guild with which they were associated, fraternal members performed numerous duties including the very important one of disseminating news. It became crucial for rulers or for those who wished to reach the top of the social pyramid to have the closest possible relations with the fraternities, because these organizations could spread their fame, recruit warriors for them, and bring them economic advantages through the craft associations.

Osman, as we have seen, began to rise by associating with Şeyh Edebali whose *futuwwa* he accepted and whose daughter he married. He learned a trade to show that he had become a member of the fraternity, thereby setting a precedent that all his successors followed. In this manner Osman achieved the ideal position; he became both the military and spiritual leader to whom personal loyalty was due. The followers of Osman, the Ottoman Turks, therefore were not members of a tribe or clan, but simply a mixture of all kinds of Turks and turkified people of other origins who

6. These fraternities can be grouped, very broadly, into two main categories: the *akhi* organizations and the *derviş* orders. The present discussion focuses on the former, while the *dervişes* will be covered in later chapters.

7. In the period under discussion this tie existed between *akhi* organizations and *gazi* groups. In the later periods various segments of the army had close relations with various *derviş* orders.

followed Osman and later his family. The crucial traditional Turkish role of the leader and his family in society and state becomes evident from this fact because nothing held the "Ottomans" together but loyalty to the ruling family.

The fraternity system moved with the Ottoman conquest to Europe. There its religious significance declined because, unlike in Anatolia, mass conversion to Islam did not occur. There, however, its role in the craft and trading guilds and charitable institutions became very important.

Naturally, no state could recruit the learned administrators needed from among the members of the fraternities or the *gazis*, nor was folk-Islam suited to become the ideological underpinning of a major political entity. The administrators of Muslim states were always recruited from among the learned Muslims and specially trained slaves. Fortunately for the Turkish states in Anatolia, learned men moved westward along with the warriors. At the height of its power Seljuq Konya had good administrators and was an important center of Muslim learning and culture. When Konya declined and other principalities rose, including that of the Ottomans, trained, learned manpower was available. It was expanded by highly trained slaves.

Slavery had been an old, established institution all over the Near East since time immemorial and was taken over by the Muslims. Islam produced some changes. Muslims could not be enslaved, but slaves who accepted Islam remained slaves, although their manumission was encouraged. Children of Muslim slaves were free men. Because most slaves accepted the religion of their masters, there was a constant need for new slaves. This need was filled by prisoners of war and by an active slave trade. Slaves were used not only in economic endeavors, but to a limited extent also as scholars, administrators, and soldiers—in short, in all possible activities. Those in higher military and administrative posts were often extremely powerful men. In general their lot depended on the position of their master, whose prestige reflected on them. In a sense an important man's slaves can be likened to the clients of a prominent Roman patrician.

The Turks who were brought from Central Asia into the centers of Muslim power were often slaves and used mainly as soldiers. Their free Muslim descendants became powerful administrators. Those who came of their free will or were invited, as we have seen in the case of Tughril, occupied similar positions and also served a "master," the caliph. This personal service accorded well with their tradition of personal loyalty. When Turkish principalities arose this tradition survived, and slaves were used as soldiers and administrators whose functions and feelings of loyalty differed but little from the free-born servants of the same master. The important *kul* (Turkish for slave) system of the Ottomans was based on this tradition. To be a *kul* of the sultan opened the doors to the most important offices of the state, to the point where it became nearly a title of honor. Even free-born officials of the Ottoman state referred to themselves as *kuls* of the sultan. Although this type of slavery differs but slightly from the Arab-Islamic concept of slavery, it has, by its stress on personal loyalty, a certain specific Turkish flavor.

The above Islamic and Turkish characteristics will suffice to justify not only the name the Ottomans gave to their state, but also the contention of scholars that the Ottoman Empire was an Islamic-Turkish-warrior state influenced to some extent by Byzantine institutions and practices. The last-mentioned will be discussed later when they began to penetrate the Ottoman state. Whatever these were, they never did change the basic nature of the Ottoman Empire. In this short presentation only those aspects of the Islamic-Turkish tradition that will be referred to repeatedly in this volume were discussed.

2. THE FIRST OTTOMAN EMPIRE AND ITS EUROPEAN PROVINCES

Traditionally, Ottoman history has been divided into four periods. The first comprises the two-and-a-half centuries of the first ten sultans (1300-1566), culminating with the "golden age" during the reign of Süleyman I (1520-66). The second lasted roughly two hundred years, until the beginning of Selim III's reign in 1789. This was a period of decline and included an unsuccessful attempt to reverse the trend in the second half of the seventeenth century by members of the Köprülü family who held the office of the grand vezir, *Sadrazam*, the uppermost of the greatest). The third period, beginning with Selim III's rule and ending with the revolution of the Young Turks (1879-1908), was one of attempted reform. Finally, there was the period of Young Turkish rule, including the First World War, which ended with the dissolution of the empire and the establishment of modern Turkey.

Correct as this general periodization is for Ottoman specialists, it does not meet the needs of our readers. For our purposes we must differentiate four periods: the years of the first Ottoman conquest (1352-1402); those of the second conquest and consolidation of power (1413-81); the period of stability (1453-1595), which overlaps slightly with the second period; and the period of decline, instability, and even anarchy during the last two centuries covered by this volume. The origins of the Ottoman Empire and the first of our four periods will be covered in this chapter.

Assiduous research has not yet clearly established the origin of Osman's family. We know that his father, Ertuğrul, was a *gazi* warrior who held a small fief near the city of Söğüt. It was not a rich holding, so we can assume that Ertuğrul was only a moderately successful *gazi* warrior. In 1277 the Mongols, firmly established in Persia, Iraq, and eastern Anatolia, defeated the Seljuqs, who remained rulers in name only for another thirty years. During that time strong local leaders were able to carve out independent principalities. Even lesser figures were encouraged to seek their own fortune. One of these was Osman, who succeeded his father in Söğüt four years after the great Mongol victory.

A man of outstanding ability, Osman found himself in a fortunate position. With the exception of the remnants of the Greek state around Trebizond (Trapezunt, Travzon, Trabson, Trapesus) on the southeastern shores of the Black Sea, and an Armenian state in south-central Asia Minor along the Mediterranean, the only Anatolian lands in Christian hands were the Byzantine possessions along the Asiatic shore of the Marmara Sea. Their borders ran roughly from the mouth of the Sakaria (Sangarius) River on the Black Sea southward east of the important cities of Nicaea and Bursa (Prusa, Brusa), turned west about sixty miles south of the latter city, and reached the sea roughly where the Dardenelles join the Aegean near the classical town of Abydos (present-day Çanakkale). Although relatively small in size, this area was fertile, included some important cities, and was near Constantinople. For the *gazis*, who could not fight each other both for religious reasons and because of their *futuwwa* code, and who could not venture eastward where Mongol rule was strong, this Byzantine possession offered the best chances for employment, fame, and fortune. Osman's fief bordered on this territory, and he had the intelligence and the ability to take advantage of his opportunity. While other Turkish leaders were attacking the southern part of the Byzantine province, Osman moved against the larger and richer northern half, gaining his first victory, as already mentioned, in 1301 and learning on his death bed that his son Orhan had captured the great city of Bursa, which became the first Ottoman capital.

With the conquest of Byzantine lands the realm of Osman became a principality equal in importance to other principalities, but expansion into Anatolia proper was also required to make it the leading Turkish power. Here the Ottomans faced other Muslim-Turkish-*gazi* states, and military action was, therefore, difficult. The Ottomans seldom, if ever, occupied other Turkish lands outright. If attacked, they had a right to fight. In most cases, however, they gained land either by being called in to aid another principality, or by being asked to protect or serve as an ally of a relatively weak neighbor. They preferred to legitimatize claims by converting victories into alliances supported by marriages. Some former ruling families, the Cenderli (Candarli) dynasty of future grand vezirs being a good example, became leading members of the highest Ottoman ruling circles.

This practice of alliances was extended to Christians, too, once the Ottomans had crossed to the western shores of the Marmara Sea. Among Orhan's wives were Theodora, the daughter of Stefan IV Uroš, the ruler of Serbia, and Maria, the daughter of the Byzantine emperor, John VI Cantacuzene; one of Murad I's wives was the daughter of Emperor John V Paleologos, and another, Tamara, was a Bulgarian princess whose father, John Alexander II Shishman, ruled from Tŭrnovo (Tărnovo, T'rnovo). Among the wives of Bayezid I were the daughter of John Hunyadi (Maria), Lazar I of Serbia (Despina), Louis, Count of Salona (Maria), and another unnamed daughter of the emperor John V.[8] Mehmed I blamed Christian influence on policies for his father's failures and gave up marriage alliances with Christians. However, one of Murad II's wives, Mara, was a Christian princess, the daughter of George Branković of Serbia, and among Mehmed II's numerous women we find several noble Christian ladies including a Paleologos and a Comnena. These marriages would not be important if they did not denote certain policies dealing with the treatment of the European provinces throughout the first of our chronological periods and parts of the second.

When the Ottomans acquired their first foothold on the European shores of the Dardanelles at Çimpe (Tzympe) in 1352, the Byzantine Empire, torn by civil war, held an area roughly south of a line running due west from the Black Sea port of Burgas (Purgos, Burgaz) to the Struma (Strimon) River. In addition to this territory Byzantium held a small area around the city of Salonika (Thessaloníki, Selanik) as well as Euboea, Attica, and an enclave in the Morea (Peloponnesus). Most of the Morea belonged to Venice, while a Bulgarian state occupied the area to the north, which stretched to the Danube. The rest of the Balkan Peninsula belonged to the Serbs.

Three years later, in 1355, Stefan Dušan, the great Serbian ruler, died, and both his and the Bulgarian state became the scene of prolonged internal conflict. As a result the Ottomans faced the same anarchic situation in Europe that had contributed to their first conquests in Anatolia. Here, too, they could intervene at the request of one side or the other in civil wars; here, too, they could offer protection, alliances, and treaties.

What is remarkable is the statesmanship of the Ottomans. In Europe the Turks were operating in Christian territory, and they could have behaved as they had in the Anatolian provinces of the Byzantines. They did not. It would be erroneous to ascribe their moderation simply to the early Muslim policies that recommended that "people of the book" be left to their own devices if they submitted without fighting. After all, every Ottoman advance in Europe was the result of a military victory, and they could have considered the lands thus conquered justifiably theirs, in spite of the claims of the Christian princes who fought as their allies. They realized that they did not have sufficient military forces and population to permit simultaneous extension of their sway in Anatolia where they aimed to reconstruct the Seljuq Empire under their leadership, maintenance of

8. See geneological tables 22, 23, and 24 in A. D. Alderson, *The Structure of the Ottoman Dynasty* (Oxford: The Clarendon Press, 1956).

large forces in Europe, and turkification of these lands with the help of numerous settlers. Therefore, they preferred an arrangement that secured not only territorial advantages, but also additional troops through alliances or vassalage agreements with the European princes. The numerous marriages served to cement these arrangements. So long as the Ottomans did not face treachery or attempts to regain full independence on the part of their clients, they stuck to these covenants.

From the point of view of the inhabitants of these associated states, this arrangement was not too favorable. Although civil war between competing princes was curbed somewhat, the unhappy internal conditions described in detail in volume II of this series did not change. Weak princes were unable to prevent the nobles and ecclesiastic dignitaries from fighting each other, oppressing the peasantry, and engaging in religious persecution; nor could they prevent taxes—both legal and illegal—from rising constantly. Trade was disrupted, manufacture and commerce declined, and urban and rural life became more and more difficult. Discontent grew in both the Byzantine and the Serbian and Bulgarian lands.

To this the Ottomans paid little attention so long as their interests remained protected. These interests went beyond the loyalty of the allied and vassal princes and beyond tribute and tax money. The concept of *gaza* and their self-conceived duty to extend the *dar al-Islam* not only made the Ottomans consider all territories over which they had overlordship as permanently in the hands of God's people, but demanded the introduction of some Ottoman institutions. In doing so they followed not only basic religious concepts but also satisfied certain very specific needs of the state and those elements of the population on which its power rested.

The three basic social elements that were the mainstays of Ottoman power in the first period of conquest in Europe were the leading Turkish families who held most of the important state offices, the *gazis*, and the *akhi* brotherhoods. The first two groups were interested in land acquisition to enhance their wealth and social position. The leading families often received rights to land formerly owned by princes and nobles who opposed the Ottoman advance. This transfer of ownership naturally affected the people living on these lands, but in general the people regarded the change of lords as advantageous and became "loyal subjects" of the sultan.

The case of the *gazis* is more complicated. Mostly foot-loose Turkoman tribesmen, they were both a great strength and a great problem for the first sultans. They belonged to the "military class" and therefore were exempted from taxes and had the right to advancement within their class and to an income derived from landed property. For those among them who had already spent a longer period in the Turkish principalities of western Anatolia the desire to better their lot was often the main reason for their military action. Since the expansion in Anatolia occurred mainly in other Turkish principalities whose well-established military-land-owning elements simply changed allegiance when the state switched from its original masters to the Ottomans, few of these *gazis* could be compensated for their services. This increased the pressure on the sultans to gain more land in Christian-inhabited territories.

The major problem was created by those Turkomans who streamed into Ottoman lands from the east in the early fourteenth century. Fleeing from the Mongols and attracted by the growing reputation of the Ottoman state, they were far too numerous to be absorbed smoothly into the "military class." Even if such a transformation had been possible, it would have upset the balance between the military and producing elements of the state so that revenue would have lagged hopelessly behind expenditures. The aim of the Ottomans was to settle this surplus of people as the Seljuqs had done in Anatolia during the centuries following the Battle of Manzikert.

From the first Ottoman incursions into Europe to roughly the conquest of Edirne (Adrianopolis, Adrianople, Adrianopol, Odrin) in 1365 several factors, in addition to the above-mentioned population pressure, made the extensive settlement of Turks in Europe possible. The Ottomans realized the necessity to gain firm control of the Dardanelles for both military and economic reasons. They wished to secure passage from Anatolia to the Balkans and charge transit fees on goods carried through the straits. They were, therefore, anxious to create a new frontier in Europe, and the settling of this area with professional border-warriors appeared, to the government and the *gazis* alike, to be the right thing to do. Turkish raids were feared by the original inhabitants, and in these early years there were still territories and states to which they could flee. The Turkomans not only took over what the fleeing Christians left behind, but also, as will be seen shortly, established new rural and urban settlements. In this manner under Orhan (1324-60), and especially under Murad I (1360-89), the lands that roughly coincide with today's Turkish provinces in Europe became overwhelmingly Turkish. This ethnographic transformation had serious repercussions in the Christian states, which had great difficulty in absorbing the refugee population. We have no statistical data on this population transfer, but, given the fertility of eastern Thrace and its proximity to the Dardanelles and Constantinople, it was probably significant. In later periods the massive influx of Turks ceased, but it did not stop. Major military roads and strong points had to be in reliable hands, so Turks were settled around them, although in considerably smaller numbers.

Throughout, the *akhi* fraternities played an important role. The sultans supported them for political, religious, and economic reasons. Wherever the Ottomans extended their power the *akhis* followed establishing *tekkes* and *zaviyes*, which often became the centers around which Turks settled. Several new villages owed their origin to the *akhis*. Given the folk-religious character and eclecticism of those brotherhoods, they were often able to find a place in their *futuwwas* for local saints and shrines. In this way cohabitation of old and new settlers was facilitated. Furthermore, regulations were established that soon dominated the relationship of the peasantry and the landlords, and served as channels of communications and maintained customary ties.

In the cities the role of the *akhi* fraternities became even more significant because the old-established guilds had little choice but to merge with those craftsmen and traders whose economic functions were well established and protected by the Ottoman state. Although this merger protected the livelihood of the Christian city population, the administration of the urban areas soon slipped from their hands into those of the leaders of the brotherhoods. So long as the system worked properly—roughly to the end of the sixteenth century—this transformation, which began in the first period of conquest, represented an improvement over the conditions that had prevailed in the cities on the eve of the Ottoman conquest.

Income was needed to support the *tekkes* and *zaviyes*, and this too came from landholding. When a brotherhood established a new house, its *şeyh* petitioned the authorities for land. When the request was granted, the peasants acquired a new landlord in the strictest sense of the word because these grants, considered religious fundations or *vakıfs* were made in perpetuity. As will be seen when we discuss landholding, the rights of landlords were strictly regulated in the Ottoman Empire, and therefore this change of overlords usually pleased the peasantry. The granting of *vakıfs* was the best of the good works included in every Muslim's obligation to give alms. This broadly defined duty went beyond purely pious purposes to include helping fellow humans in every way possible. *Vakıfs* supported inns, baths, hospitals, fountains, bridges, and even markets where people could earn a living. The higher a person was on the social scale, the more numerous and extensive were the *vakıfs* he was supposed to establish.

These foundations were also supported mainly by the income from large rural estates. Land was set aside for them from the beginning, and this added to the change in landholding patterns and peasant obligations in the territories that came under direct Ottoman rule during the first period of conquest. Later additional sources of income were attached to these foundations. In the middle of the sixteenth century the establishment of such foundations transformed Sarajevo from a practically unknown village into a city and created the town Üzünköprü (near Edirne) in a place where there had not even been a village. Although we have no such drastic examples from the first period of conquest, in this period the establishment of *vakıfs* in Europe began to produce profound changes in the towns and villages where they were located and in those rural regions whose income was set aside to support them.

This transformation occurred in territory formerly held by the Byzantines. The conquests were significant enough to worry not only the Balkan states, but also the western European powers. While the Ottomans were crossing the Byzantine-Bulgarian border in 1366, only to be defeated at Vidin, the Pope tried to organize a crusade against them. He was not successful, but a Christian fleet was able to reconquer Gallipoli in the same year and return it to Byzantine control. Although this placed the Ottomans in a difficult situation because they still lacked a navy and the heavy artillery needed for attacking fortified places, Murad I continued his operations in the Central Balkans.

The situation in the Balkans was confused. Both the Serbian and Bulgarian states were in full dissolution. Being nearer to the Ottomans, the Bulgarians felt the new influences. The Bulgarians had lost the Macedonian lands to the strong Serbian state of Stefan Dušan first. Then, in the middle of the fourteenth century the northeast seceded and became known by the name of its second ruler, Dobrotitsa (today, the Dobrudja [Dobrogea]). In 1365 John Alexander (Ivan Alexandur) divided his realm between his two sons. After his death in 1371, the two separate kingdoms of Tŭrnovo and Vidin emerged. The same disintegration took place in Serbia after Stefan Dŭsan's death in 1355. Around the cities of Velbužd on the upper course of the Struma River, and Prilep (Perlepe) two Macedonian states appeared, and Albania began to regain her independence.

The rulers of these states were constantly fighting each other to secure boundaries and recreate greater political units. Murad I saw his chance in this disunity. When the Macedonian princes attacked him in 1371 at Chirmen (Chernomen, Chermanon), a small village on the lower Maritsa (Meriç, Ebros, Hebros) River, he defeated his attackers whose leaders were killed in battle. This opened the road for further conquests to the north and west, and the Bulgarian King of Tŭrnovo was forced to accept the status of an Ottoman vassal. The move to the north put great pressure on Byzantium, which bought peace by returning Gallipoli to the Ottomans in 1376.

For the next few years the Ottomans extended their rule in Asia Minor and interfered constantly in the dynastic squabbles of Byzantium, giving the people of the Balkans a few years of relative respite. By 1380 they had turned again to Europe and the territories of the previously defeated Macedonian states, reaching the Vardar (Axios) River and following it both north and southward. In the north they moved through the lands of the Macedonian states, and, not content, went on to conquer Sofia, which belonged to their Bulgarian vassal, and to Niš, which was in the hands of Vidin Bulgaria. Moving southward, they entered Byzantine territory again and occupied Salonika in 1387.

These campaigns frightened the Balkan princes, who put aside their squabbles and united against the common menace. Although in 1387 the Byzantine emperor and the Balkan vassals and allies fulfilled their obligations and helped the Ottomans with important military forces in defeating the Karamanids, their major rival in Anatolia, the menacing moves of their overloads forced them to change their attitude. Lazar I of Serbia, Tvrto I of Bosnia, and John Stratsimir of Vidin united against Murad I and together won a victory in 1388 at Pločnik (Plotchnik), a small village west of Niš. The sultan, however, turned around and invaded Vidin Bulgaria, forcing this state to acknowledge his overlordship. With the help of Christian vassal forces he met the last major Balkan rulers who still resisted him at the first Battle of Kosovo, on June 15, 1389, and defeated the Serbian and Bosnian forces. Although Murad was murdered by a Serb the night of this very bloody battle, immortalized in the famous Kosovo Epic, with this decisive victory he had established Ottoman rule over the Balkans, a rule that was to last for the next five hundred years.

The fact that he was the absolute master of the Balkans did not escape the attention of the next sultan, Bayezid I (1389-1402), although he could not turn to this region immediately. The death of his father had given new hope to Anatolian Turkish princes, who renounced their alliances and allegiances, and for three years Bayezid, the grandson, son, and husband of Christian princesses, had to fight them, relying on vassal Christian troops from Europe because his *gazi* forces were reluctant to fight fellow Muslims. In those years he gained complete control of Anatolia and replaced the Turkish ruling houses, who until the death of Murad I had retained their position as vassals, allies, or Ottoman governors, with governors who were his slaves and almost always of Christian origin. Although toward the end of his reign this policy cost him his throne and life, the new system of rule proved permanent and was introduced in the European provinces after these were transformed into outright Ottoman possessions.

Bayezid clearly thought of himself as a divinely appointed instrument whose duty it was to conquer the world for the greater glory of God. His ambition was to become a universal ruler. Yet he, like all Muslim princes, had to act "legally," especially since he had more enemies than friends among the Muslim Turkish aristocracy and could not simply turn around and declare a new "holy war" against those whose troops had helped him in Anatolia. His "legal" opportunity was furnished when the Hungarians and their friend and ally, the Wallachian Prince Mircea cel Bătrîn (the Old) (1386-1418), invaded the weak Bulgarian states. The Wallachian occupied the Dobrudja and the city of Silistra (Durostorum, Silistre) on the Danube, while the Hungarians tried to conquer the Vidin Kingdom. These infringements on his vassals' lands gave Bayezid authority to move.

His vassals suffered more from his "help" than did his enemies. Returning from Asia Minor to the Balkans in 1393, the sultan expelled the

Wallachians from Silistra and the Dobrudja and declared that Danubian (or Tŭrnovo) Bulgaria, unable to fend for herself, was now an Ottoman province. The last ruler, John Shishman, was accused of collaboration with the enemy and was executed at the orders of the sultan. Stefan Lazarević, the ruler of Serbia, would probably have gotten the same treatment, in spite of the fact that he quickly swore a new oath of loyalty to Bayezid, had not the sultan had more pressing problems to solve.

While the sultan had been occupied in Anatolia, the Paleologi, in an effort to save their state, made their famous promise to reunite the two Christian churches. With the help of Venice they greatly strengthened the Morea. Since the sultan was still without a navy, this was a combination he could not well face. He therefore resorted to diplomacy and called all his vassals, including the Byzantine emperor, to Serres to force them to acknowledge his overlordship. When the emperor did not come Bayezid laid siege to Constantinople and sent his forces into the Morea at the invitation of Carlo Tocco, one of the lords fighting in that region. This campaign brought the Turks important gains. With Constantinople under siege and his back secure from Byzantine-Venetian attacks, Bayezid could turn his attention to the north again.

There the Hungarian-Wallachian alliance was still in effect, and Bayezid I now moved against Mircea. Once again, many Christians, mostly Serbs, fought in his army, including Kraljević (the son of the king) Marko, the hero of another famous Epic, who died not in that battle, but in the Battle of Argeş which Bayezid fought with the Wallachians on May 17, 1395. Mircea appears to have been victorious militarily, but his forces and resources were so depleted that he had to acknowledge the loss of the Dobrudja, into which Bayezid moved Turkish garrisons. He also had to accept the status of an Ottoman vassal and pay regular tribute. This arrangement lasted until the Danubian Principalities regained their independence. Although it created problems for the Romanians, it saved them from the much harsher treatment that went with direct Ottoman rule, especially during the centuries of decline.

The situation in Constantinople and in the Morea greatly alarmed European leaders, especially King Sigismund (Zsigmond) of Luxemburg. This famous Emperor of the Holy Roman Empire and King of Hungary (1387-1437) asked for help and got it from French knights and Venice. He led his army into the Balkans only to lose the great battle at Nikopolis (Nikopol, Niyebol) on September 25, 1396. Because Vidin had opened its doors to the Christian army, Bayezid took over the Vidin Kingdom, too, transforming it into an Ottoman province. During the next few years Ottoman armies concentrated on the Byzantine possessions and the various small Greek states in the Morea where they gained land and devastated much territory.

By 1400, apart from the Dalmatian coast and some cities in the Morea, most of the Balkans were under Ottoman rule. Serbia, Bosnia, and Wallachia, were vassal states, and the Byzantine Empire was reduced to the great city and its immediate surroundings. The rest of the peninsula was divided into Ottoman provinces.

There can be little doubt that Bayezid would have completed the conquest of the Balkans had not a new Mongol attack forced him to return to Anatolia. There he lost the Battle of Ankara in 1402, was captured, and died in captivity a few years later. The victorious Timur returned the various Turkish lands to the princely families whom the Ottomans had displaced, leaving Osman's family only those he considered legitimately theirs in accordance with the provisions of the *shari'a*. There Bayezid sons fought among themselves for supremacy, giving the Balkan states a chance to re-emerge and making a second conquest necessary. The fact that not all the states took advantage of this opportunity and that European forces played an important role in settling the war between the Ottoman princes is as remarkable as is the fact that those who used this period of respite to reform their realms learned nothing from past experience and fell under Ottoman rule even faster and more easily than they had during the first conquest. These two factors contributed greatly to the establishment of the second Ottoman Empire.

3. CIVIL WAR AND THE ESTABLISHMENT OF THE SECOND OTTOMAN EMPIRE

WHEN Bayezid I's empire collapsed, Timur recognized those territories that belonged to the House of Osman on the day of Murad I's death as being legitimately Ottoman. This ruling returned some Anatolian provinces to their former masters, something Timur was able to enforce. In theory it also stripped the Ottomans of all their gains in Europe as well as the changes introduced there under Bayezid. In Europe, however, Timur was unable to enforce his rulings, and the decision was left in the hands of those, including the Christian princes, who were in a position to take advantage of the new situation. The behavior of these people during the Ottoman interregnum from 1402 to 1413 is of great interest.

Bayezid was very unpopular among several elements of Turkish society, and it is well known that he lost the Battle of Ankara because only his Christian forces remained loyal while numerous Muslim units deserted during the fight. The *gazis* resented his highhanded "illegal" treatment of fellow Muslim princes. The leading Turkish families, descendants of the first successful *gazi* leaders and of those who allied themselves with the Ottomans early and had achieved wealth and leading positions, resented the sultan's increasingly "Byzantine" tendencies: the growing centralization of power, a court that was more and more "imperial," and several new influences including slaves in the ruling and decision-making process, all of which diminished their position. Both of these groups accused Bayezid not only of abandoning the *gazi* tradition, but even of being a bad Muslim because he was too strongly under the Christian influence of his mother, wife, and European friends. Bayezid was certainly not interested in changing his faith, but his desire to become a universal ruler and his interest in the eclectic religious tendencies then fashionable made him somewhat more tolerant of other religions than was permissible under the regulations of strict High Islam. At the same time he was eager to diminish religious antagonisms. Thus, there were certain facets of his behavior that were justifiably objectionable to the *gazi*, the Turkish aristocracy, and the learned men, the major Turkish-Muslim supporters of his state.

Although two of these dissatisfied Turkish factions agreed on the need to reverse Bayezid's policies, they did not agree on what had to be restored. The *gazi* faction would have preferred a return to the days of Osman and Orhan, to continued expansion, to the great influence of the brotherhoods and folk-religion, and to the almost tribal chief role the early sultans had played. Although the leading families certainly did not object to the continuation of *gazi* wars, they wanted a polity modeled on the most glorious days of the Seljuq state when not Folk but High Islam dominated and where old Turkic traditions assured the supremacy of their class.

To these two groups must be added a third, which cannot be called Christian, but can be called European, although it had some partisans in Anatolia too. For simplicity's sake only two major elements that made up this faction will be mentioned. On the higher social level there were the important commercial interests. These persons were eager to re-establish "normal" conditions. They were not hostile to those "Byzantine" features that not only favored production and trade, but also made foreign business connections possible. For them the reunification of western Anatolia, through which numerous important trade routes led, was of prime importance, even if it involved the reabsorption of their own lands and the Turkish principalities into the Ottoman state. Small in number and without a firm religious commitment, this element needed mass support. It found such support mainly in Europe among those who were dissatisfied with centuries of religious strife and persecution and who, although they found Ottoman practices preferable to what had preceded, wanted to go further, to an elementary proto-democracy that included religious equality and freedom. This element played an important role in the civil war that restored the Ottoman Empire. The significance of this fact is enormous. The extremely elitist and hierarchial Ottoman State owed its rebirth to grass-root support. Although led by Muslim families often of European, mainly Greek, origin, this faction did not attempt to strengthen Byzantium or recreate the various Balkan states. Rather it tried to rebuild the traditional Ottoman domain.

The religious eclecticism of Bayezid I can be clearly seen in the names of his four sons who were involved in the civil war. The oldest, Süleyman, had an Old Testament name (Solomon) as had one of his brothers Musa (Moses). Isa's name is the Turkish equivalent of Jesus, while Mehmed's is the turkified form of the most favored Muslim name Muhammad.

The civil war was made possible by several circumstances. When Timur, playing the role of a Muslim legitimist, left the Ottomans some of their possessions, he appointed Isa *emir* of Bursa, and Mehmed governor of Manisa (Magnesia ad Maenderum), a position he held under his father. In this manner Timur created two strong Ottoman Anatolian bases in territories that were firm in their loyalty to the Osmanli family. Furthermore, he never came to western Anatolia himself, nor did he send his representatives to enforce his rulings. On his death in 1405 the local princes were left to settle the future political development of Asia Minor. Finally, the above-mentioned factionalism made it possible for the princes to seek followers among various groups of the population, all of whom were looking for a sultan who would represent their interests.

Süleyman, who had managed to escape from Ankara, made his way to Edirne where, with the help of the grand vezir, Ali Cenderli, he proclaimed himself sultan. He was not, however, able to force his two brothers to recognize him. When Bayezid I died in captivity, in 1403, Musa was allowed to take his father's body home to Bursa. Having accomplished this task, he left the city and joined Mehmed.

By this time the Cenderli family had important commercial interests and was allied with several other families who belonged either to the highest bureaucratic circles, to the trading community, or, like the Evrenos family of Greek origin and the Cenderlis themselves, to both. The leader of the janissary corps created by Murad I also made his way to Edirne. Consequently, Süleyman's position was very strong; the military leaders, the leading functionaries, were in his camp, and he was in the economically richest regions of the state. Mehmed, ably advised by his former tutor and competent general, Bayezid, relied mainly on the *gazis* for support, while Isa, having no clear faction to back him, was in the weakest position.

Süleyman, in accordance with the interests he represented, concluded alliances with the Bryzantine emperor, Manuel II, and with Michael Steno, the doge of Venice. To cement his major alliance Süleyman married Manuel's daughter in 1403 and returned Salonika to his father-in-law. The latter move was not well received by the *gazis* who were numerous in eastern Thrace. His relations with Serbia, Wallachia, and Albania— three states that had taken advantage of the Ottoman troubles and had regained their independence—were not satisfactory either.

Süleyman was very intelligent and well educated, according to the information that has survived, but he was also very ambitious and extremely arrogant and overbearing. He needed the support of his father's ex-vassals to force his brothers to acknowledge him as sultan, but his behavior turned them against him. Later even his close collaborators tired of him, and his disregard of the strong popular movement in his lands alienated both the Muslim and Christian lower classes.

The struggle began when Musa, now in the service of his brother Mehmed, attacked Isa in Bursa. Musa was victorious, and Isa took refuge with Süleyman. The latter now used him, just as Mehmed had used Musa, and sent him back to Anatolia to recapture Bursa. Isa failed and lost his life. In 1404 Süleyman himself crossed into Anatolia, forced Musa to flee to Constantinople and then to Wallachia, and advanced as far as Ankara by 1405. At this moment, when he had Mehmed in a precarious situation, he had to return rapidly to Europe because Musa, taking advantage of Süleyman's lack of popularity with the Balkan princes and the Byzantine habit of backing the weakest against the strongest, attacked his European possessions with the help of Mircea of Wallachia, Stefan Lazarević of Serbia, and the sons of the last two Bulgarian rulers. After suffering an initial defeat Musa regained the initiative in 1410 and defeated Süleyman whose bad habits had left him without any real supporters. As Süleyman was fleeing toward Constantinople he was killed by the discontented peasantry. Musa was now master of Europe and refused to recognize the overlordship of Mehmed any longer. Thus, the European and Asian halves of the erstwhile Ottoman Empire faced each other in preparation for a final show down.

From the point of view of the European princes, Musa is certainly the most interesting personality of the civil war. He gained his mastery of the European half of the empire with their help, yet he began his rule by moving against them. First, he attacked the Serbs whose "treachery" he blamed for his first defeat by Süleyman, resumed the siege of Constantinople, and sent raiding parties down the length of the Greek peninsula and even westward as far as Austria. He appears to have paid little attention to Mehmed and the *gazi* and to the increasingly strong bureaucratic support his brother enjoyed, and seems to have attempted to build up a new state structure on a wide popular basis. His military campaigns appear to have been directed against the leaders of the Balkan states, and he alienated the higher Turkish circles with their bureaucratic and commercial interests by constantly favoring the lower classes. Naturally, Mehmed made valiant efforts to gain the allegiance of the dissatisfied merchants, nobility, and learned men, adding their support to that of the *gazi*. Once besieged by Musa, Manuel II also shifted to an alliance with Mehmed and so did the European princes.

The best indication of Musa's revolutionary approach to what he considered to be the proper state structure was his appointment of Şeyh Bedreddin to the highest legal position in the realm. A famous *âlim* and scholar-turned-mystic, this man, who in 1416 was to lead a dangerous popular revolt against Mehmed I, was not only one of the leading spokesmen for religious peace and the union of Judaism, Christianity, and Islam into one creed, but also something of an early socialist. He was very popular among the peasant masses, and his close relationship with Musa brought this prince mass support. By about 1410 or 1411 Mehmed had become the leader of the Turkish factions including those, together with their Christian and Jewish allies, who favored commercial interests and enjoyed the backing of the various rulers in Europe. Musa had become the leader of the "populist party," whose aim was to establish a state based on social and religious egalitarianism. So far as the inhabitants of the Balkans were concerned, this division meant that the aristocratic and commercial leadership backed Mehmed, while the masses followed Musa.

Mehmed's first attempt to defeat Musa, in 1410, was a failure. For the next two years the brothers left each other alone. While Musa was feuding with the Byzantine emperor and experimenting with his new approach to government, Mehmed was occupied in Asia Minor where the *emirs* of Izmir (Smyrna) and Ankara (Angora) were contesting his rule. Only after he had defeated these dignitaries could Mehmed turn westward again, and in 1412 the final battles began. During Musa's siege of Constantinople Mehmed moved his troops south of his brother's position, entered Sofia, and pushed on to Niš where he was joined by the Serbs. He then turned around and in 1413 met Musa's forces near Sofia. Mehmed won the battle; Musa lost his life. The Ottoman Empire was finally reunited under Sultan Mehmed I (1413-21), and the reorganization of the state could begin. Thus, the first step towards the final consolidation of Ottoman rule in the Balkans had taken place.

Consolidation was difficult. Mehmed still faced challenges not only from Turkish princes in Anatolia, from Balkan rulers, and from the powerful Hungarian state, but also from a discontented population that gladly followed Şeyh Bedreddin's call to revolt. Furthermore, he had to unite the various factions under his own leadership. This Mehmed I and his successor, Murad II (1421-44), were able to accomplish. They based the new system on the state structure that Murad I had begun to develop, and while it did not reach its final form until the days of Mehmed II (1444-46; 1451-81), these two sultans virtually established what became the Ottoman social and state system for the remaining centuries of the empire's existence. For this reason the rest of this section will be devoted to a short discussion of the various, mainly military, moves of Mehmed I and Murad II in Europe, and the next chapter will deal with the "Ottoman system," stressing those aspects that became crucial for our area.

When Mehmed I became the uncontested sultan of the Ottoman state in 1413, Manuel II was still ruling in Constantinople, the capable Mircea cel Bătrîn was still Prince of Wallachia, and Stefan Lazarević ruled

Serbia. Bosnia was still independent, and Albania was in the process of becoming a unified state. Hungary, with which the Ottomans still had no common border, was a strong state ruled by Sigismund of Luxemburg and had Balkan ambitions of her own, while Venice held territories all around the shores of the Balkan Peninsula. Thus, the final outcome of the question of who would become the master of the Balkans was by no means a foregone conclusion.

Numerous possibilities of combinations and alliances existed. Mehmed realized how precarious the balance of power in Europe was and how unsettled the situation in his own lands was, and he knew that the descendants of Timur could still challenge him at any moment in Anatolia. He therefore became a man of peace after 1413, concentrating on his domestic problems. The only military campaigns he engaged in were forced on him. He had to face the Byzantine-supported challenge by his brother Mustafa who reappeared, probably from the east, after the civil war had been decided. In this war Venice destroyed his fleet near Gallipoli in 1416, but he defeated Mustafa, who sought refuge in Byzantium. In the peace that ensued the sultan promised not to attack Byzantine territory in exchange for Manuel's agreement to hold Mustafa prisoner.

Mehmed also faced the revolt of Şeyh Bedreddin, centered mainly in the Dobrudja and supported by Mircea who occupied these rich lands when the revolt was defeated. Mehmed attacked in 1419, and the only European territorial acquisition during his reign, Giurgiu (Yergögü), was the result of this war. Thus, the political situation in the Balkans was much the same when Mehmed I died, in 1421, as it had been when he reunited the empire.

The first years of Murad II's reign were difficult. The Byzantines released his uncle Mustafa who attacked him; numerous Anatolian princes moved against the sultan and backed his brother, whose name was also Mustafa. By 1423, however, the young ruler had re-established order and reigned over all the lands that were Ottoman at his father's death. While he was occupied with revolts, the Hungarians were extending their sway into the Balkans, and the Venetians, as allies of Byzantium, were gaining a strong foothold in the Morea and had received the city of Salonika from the emperor. Byzantium was really not a serious enemy, but the war with Venice continued until 1430 when the Ottomans finally reconquered Salonika.

The major menace to Murad proved to be Hungary. During the Venetian war the Hungarians and Ottomans had agreed, in 1428, to set up a buffer state and jointly recognize Djordje (George) Branković as a legitimate and independent ruler of Serbia. Obviously, this was a temporary measure. When the Venetian war ended, Murad returned to the policy of Murad I and Bayezid I, that of including all lands south of the Danube-

Sava line into his state. Hungarian influence in Bosnia, Serbia, and Walla-chia had to be eliminated; if this was not possible, at least the land al-ready in Ottoman hands had to be fully secured. Therefore, Venice had to be pushed out of its remaining Balkan strongholds. Murad constantly tried to expand his rule by raids into the Balkan states and did gain some permanent acquisitions in Greece proper, the Morea, and southern Al-bania. The various princelings turned to Hungary for protection. After 1432 Murad concentrated his energies on Hungary, conducting raids into Transylvania in that year and continuing to harass that country and its al-lies whenever he could. He intensified his efforts when Sigismund died in 1437 and attacked Transylvania again. In 1439 he occupied Serbia and made it an Ottoman province. The next year he attacked Belgrade (Beo-grad, Nándorfehérvár), Hungary's main border fortress at the time, but was not successful.

After the attack on Belgrade Murad was forced to return to Asia Minor to deal with an attack by the Karaman principality. The Hungarians, led by their most famous general János (John) Hunyadi, took advantage of the situation and attacked the Ottoman forces remaining in Europe. In 1441 and 1442 they penetrated deep into the Balkans, forcing Murad to come to an agreement. The Treaty of Edirne, in 1444, which was extended by the Treaty of Szeged during the same year, re-established Serbia as a buffer state. The Hungarians agreed to leave Bulgarian lands unmolested and not to cross the Danube. Having made peace with the Karamanids during the same year, Murad abdicated, believing that his realm was secure.

Murad's twelve-year-old son, Mehmed II, ascended to the throne, and a power struggle ensued between the grand vezir, Halil Cenederli, the tutor of the new ruler, Zaganos, and the *beylerbeyi* of the European provinces, Şihābeddīn. Taking advantage of this situation, a Hungarian-Wallachian army encouraged by the Pope and the Byzantines, and supported by various Balkan princes, of whom the Albanian Scanderbeg (George Kastriote) was the most remarkable, crossed the Danube and marched through Bulgaria toward Edirne. At the critical moment this city was destroyed by a great fire. The Venetian fleet joined the new crusade and closed the Dardanelles, making it impossible to transfer Ottoman troops from Asia Minor to Europe. Murad II came out of retirement to take com-mand of the Ottoman armies and won a great victory at Varna on No-vember 10, 1444. Varna sealed the fate of the Balkans and Constantin-ople. At this juncture the squabble of the three dignataries began to cen-ter around the question of how to handle the imperial city. The grand vezir was opposed to attacking it, the other two argued in favor of this move. In 1446 the grand vezir, backed by the janissaries, staged a *coup d'état* and forced Murad to reascend the throne and rule for another five years. The old sultan resumed his former policies and extended the

Ottoman realm in the Morea, campaigned against Scanderbeg in Albania, and reasserted his rule in Serbia. The success of his policies was assured when he defeated Hunyadi in the second battle at Kosovo in 1448.

Murad's rule represents a watershed in the history of the Ottoman Empire. Brockelmann states that "in many respects Murad's reign meant the end of the ancient culture of the Osmanlis."[9] Inalcik points out that while Murad had intended to follow his father's policies when he came to the throne, he soon realized that changes were needed, and cites the introduction of new armaments as an example of the reforms introduced by this ruler.[10] Both assertions are correct and indicate the reorganization, finished only during the second reign of Mehmed II and of equal importance to every inhabitant of the empire, was well advanced when Murad died in 1451. What emerged was the Ottoman synthesis of various Turkish, Muslim, Byzantine, and even western elements into a remarkably well-integrated state structure.

9. Carl Brockelmann, *History of the Islamic People*, trans. Joel Carmichael and Moshe Perlmann (London: Routledge and Kegan Paul, Ltd. 1949, and paperback edition New York; Capricorn Books, 1960), p. 276.

10. Halil Inalcık, *The Ottoman Empire; The Classical Age, 1300-1600*, trans. Norman Itzkowitz and Colim Imber (New York and Washington: Praeger, 1973), p. 21.

CHAPTER 2

Ottoman Social and State Structure

1. BACKGROUND

OTTOMAN social structure was bascially the result of a skillful blending of traditional Muslim sociopolitical traditions with Turkic and Byzantine elements. In Ottoman society there were two basic differentiations between individuals. The first distinguished between Muslim and non-Muslim; the second between those who in the broadest possible terms worked for the state and those who did not.

While the Muslim was obviously superior to the non-Muslim by definition, in practice during the early centuries of the empire people of different creeds were often treated almost as equals, in accordance with their profession. Muslims were not allowed to change their religion under penalty of death. Others joined the preferred religious group either by voluntary conversion or by the typically Ottoman practice of forced conversion known as the *devşirme* (child levy). Later the religious difference became crucial.

Those who worked for the state were mainly Muslims, but by no means exclusively so. The leaders of non-Muslim communities were considered state functionaries responsible for those under their jurisdiction.

The resulting social structure ressembled a pyramid-shaped grid (see diagram). The apex of this pyramid, consisting of those who worked for the state, was strictly separated from the base. The base consisted of horizontal layers intersecting confessional lines according to profession. Those working for the state have been aptly called "professional Ottomans" by modern-day scholars, who refer to the rest of the population as the *reaya* (the flock). This system was originally based on the following concepts.

Sunni Islam's theological, philosophical, scientific, and administrative structures were fully developed by the time the House of Osman began its meteoric rise. While *ijma'*, the concensus of learned men, was still required for any major decision affecting matters of faith and law, *ijtihād*, the right of interpretation, was in practice limited to the followers of the four different "legal schools." Each school recognized the others as holding equally valid principles in spite of some disagreements.[1] The Ottomans accepted the most liberal, the *hanafīte* school, but they followed a very strict and almost immutable model.

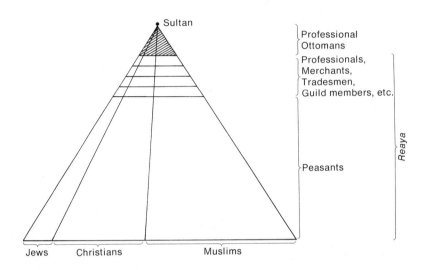

Equally well established in the Ottoman mind were certain practices introduced by the Muslim-Arab empires, and the Turkic customs that they brought with them from Central Asia. Traditions as well as strongly established principles set the limits within which the Ottomans could organize their realm. It should be stressed from the outset that the organization that they developed covered in great detail every aspect of the communal life and state activity as well as every individual from the sultan down to the lowliest subject; everybody's place, rights, and obligations in society were fixed. The various privileges and duties were not only strictly enforced, at least so long as the state had the power and authority to do so, but they also created something resembling "checks and balances," which limited even the most powerful individuals. A clear border *(hadd)* defined each individual's position in society. Not only could no one go beyond the stipulated limits, but everyone had the right—even the obligation—to resist those who violated his *hadd* by every possible means. This principle safeguarded the lowly in the social scale so long as the system

---

1. These four legal schools were: the *ḥanafite*, named after the first scholar to expound its principles, Abu-Hanifa (d. 767); the *malakite*, named after another jurist Mālik ibn-Anas (d. ca. 795); the *shafi'i* school, which got its name from Muhammad ibn-Idris al-Shāfi'i (d. 820); and the *ḥanbalites*, the followers of the legal interpretation of Aḥmad ibn-Ḥanbal (d. 855).

worked properly, and made Ottoman rule preferable to that of unprincipled nobles to the Balkan peasants.

The Ottoman Empire was "the domain of the House of Osman." So long as the ruling member of this house did not suffer from physical or mental disabilities that, according to the *shāri'a,* made him unfit to rule, and so long as he was a "good Muslim," his power was theoretically unlimited. He owned every inch of his domain and was the absolute master of everybody living on these lands. In this sense the sultan had the rights of the old Turkic tribal chiefs or the *gazi* leaders. He could appoint and dismiss anyone at will and could even order execution of the highest officials and confiscation of their property. No action could be taken without his approval. It was fortunate for the Ottomans that their first ten rulers were able men.

With absolute power went obligations, which were part of the ruler's *hadd.* He was to treat his subjects and followers kindly, justly, in accordance with established tradition. Further limitations were placed on him by Muslim law and additional customs, developed originally in Persia and the Arab caliphates.

Below the sultan Ottoman society in general was divided in two different ways. The first way, along religious lines, distinguished between Muslim and *zimmi* and meant roughly the difference between full and second-class citizen. This made a great difference in the opportunities and positions of state open to members of the two groups, and in taxation.

The second way was the distinction between those who were connected with the state and its institutions, and those who were not. The first group included members of the sultan's household, the entire military establishment, the central and provincial bureaucracy, as well as *ulema* who manned the legal system, the educational institutions, and the learned professions. From the point of view of the central government, it also included vassals and allies who were supposed to follow the sultan's orders. With the exception of the last mentioned group, whose members always tried to act as independently as possible, these people have been named the "professional Ottomans" by modern scholars. This appellation is fully justified not only because the state structure and machinery rested on their shoulders, but also because these men shared a common set of values and a basic education and considered themselves to be a social group apart from all the others. With very few exceptions, the professional Ottomans were either born or converted Muslims and could be both free men and slaves.

The second group was the rest of the population, well over 90 percent. These were *reaya* (members of the flock) whose shepherd was the sultan. These sheep, both Muslim and *zimmi,* were shorn because they were the agricultural and industrial-commercial producers whose labor supplied the goods and taxes that supported the state and the professional Ottomans including the sultan and his household. With negligible exceptions the European subjects of the sultan were all *reaya*.

This strict system, with its seemingly endless rules and regulations, had great advantages, provided it could be enforced and provided the enemies of the Ottoman Empire did not offer better economic and technological alternatives. When changes became necessary, however, it became an insurmountable obstacle. Every aspect of the system was so closely interwoven with innumerable others that even the slightest change affected and endangered the entire structure. In spite of conservatism and even a certain amount of fanaticism, changes might possibly have been made over the opposition of certain people with special interests but for two facts: the Ottomans simply had no knowledge of and could not envisage any other way of running their state, and they believed that even the slightest change would endanger the entire fabric of state and society. The Ottoman system was the empire's greatest asset from the fourteenth to the sixteenth century and became its greatest liability beginning with the seventeenth century.

The following description of the Ottoman system will touch on practically every aspect of life because the omission of a single aspect would distort the picture. However, some aspects will only be mentioned because they did not influence directly the life of the people living in the empire's European provinces, while others will simply be fitted into the over-all picture superficially at this point and elaborated in more detail subsequently due to their relevance for the people of Southeastern Europe.

2. THE PROFESSIONAL OTTOMANS

ALTHOUGH we are mainly interested in the *reaya*, a few words must be said first about the professional Ottomans who controlled their lives. We can divide this group, according to its main functions, into four major groups: the *mülkiye*, the *kalemiye*, the *seyfiye*, and the *ilmiye*. The *mülkiye* group performed a great variety of duties connected with activities that took place within the imperial palace. Its numbers were in the thousands, its influence was great. According to the rank a member had reached he could be transferred to a corresponding position outside the palace where he performed administrative and military duties. Possible transfers are clearly illustrated by a table in Inalcık's work.[2]

The *mülkiye* group broke down into two distinct subgroups; the *enderun* (inner service) and the *birun* (outer service). This distinction was based on the physical organization of the imperial palace, which was built around two large courts separated by a wall through which one could pass only by the Gate of Felicity (*Bāb-i sa'ādet*), the door that

2. Inalcık, *Ottoman Empire*, table 1, p. 82.

led to the personal presence of the sultan. Those who passed through the gate either spent their entire lives within the confines of the inner palace or were transferred out periodically to other services. The highest ranking *enderun* functionaries usually were appointed to the most important provincial positions when they left the palace. From there they could be brought back to the capital to serve in the central government, which was part of the *birun*. Those who belonged to the *enderun* were all *kapı kulus* (*kapı* being another word for gate), slaves of the Porte. After the *devşirme* system was introduced (see section 5) they came almost exclusively from the European provinces. Their education began in the palace where they moved from the school of pages to higher training centers and duties within the inner courtyard. The best reached the highest position available within the *enderun* service. When transferred, in accordance with their accomplishments in the inner palace, these men became the most important office-holders in the outer service and in the provinces.

The *birun* included a great variety of craftsmen, services, schools for these and the various governmental offices, the schools for janissaries, the *kapı kulu* military units, the offices of the central government, and the various *ağas* (officers) in charge of all these establishments. The people serving in the *birun* could be slave or freeborn, but all were considered the slaves of the sultan. The most important part of the outer service was the central government proper that functioned through the imperial council (*divan-i hümayun*). Its members, the "pillars of the realm" (*erkan-i devlet*), held the rank of vezir and served under the presidency of the grand vezir. The most important dignitaries of the empire served in the council: the *kadiaskers*, the highest judicial functionaries (originally there was one, then there were two for Asia and one for Europe); the *beylerbeyis*, the chief provincial administrators of Europe and Asia; the *defterdars*, the chiefs of the imperial treasury (originally two with a third added for Africa); the *ağa* of the janissaries; the *kapudan-i derya*, commander of the navy; and the *nişanci*, the secretary of the council who verified its decision, made certain of the sultan's approval, and attached the sultan's official seal (*tuğra*) to all documents. So long as the system functioned properly most of the council members were indeed *kapı kulus* who had been educated in the *enderun* schools.

It is important to realize that in the Ottoman Empire everybody including the members of the imperial council had a fixed place in a table of ranks. Furthermore, whenever multiple offices existed Europe (Rumeli) took precedence over Asia (Anadolu), which in turn came before Africa. Thus, it is easy to list the major dignitaries of the central government according to rank, prestige, and precedence.

Grand vezir
Kadiasker of Rumeli

Kadiasker of Anadolu
Beylerbeyi of Rumeli
Beylerbeyi of Anadolu
Defterdar of Rumeli
Defterdar of Anadolu
Defterdar of Africa
Janissary ağa
Kapudan-i derya
Nişanci

While all these dignitaries belonged to the *birun* part of the *mülkiye* class of professional Ottomans, their professions clearly placed them, simultaneously, in subgroups. The *beylerbeyi*s were both important military and provincial dignitaries; the janissary *ağa* and the *kapudan-i derya* were important members of the military establishment; and the *defterdar*s and the *nişanci* belonged to the bureaucracy proper, although the latter never left the presence of the sultan.

The two chief *defterdar*s were the main officers of the second group of professional Ottomans, the *kalemiye* (the group of scribes). They were responsible for disbursing funds from the state treasury and indirectly for collecting taxes. The provincial *defterdar*s had direct responsibility for this task until the days of Mehmed II; later they were helped by *mültezim*s (tax farmers). Thus, the provincial *defterdar*s and the *mültezim*s affected the life of the people directly, and we will deal with them when we discuss provincial administrations. While financial duties were the main function of the *kalemiye*, members of this group also manned a variety of other institutions that dealt with millions of documents ranging from simple petitions to treaties of state. They were trained in special schools and had their own hierarchy. Because of the special skills and knowledge required to perform its tasks, theirs was the first of the professional Ottoman groups to make membership in its ranks practically hereditary.

The third professional Ottoman category was the *seyfiye* group, the military men. Strictly speaking, only two types of soldiers belonged to this establishment; the free feudal warriors, the *timarlı*, and the salaried units of the sultan's slave army, the *maaşlı*. A third type, the irregulars of various kinds, will also be mentioned in subsequent chapters because of their great importance for our area. Allied armies or special troops, like sappers, are less important for this study because they had almost no effect on the lives of the people.

The *timarlı* were the members of the old "military class," the free-born warriors who originally joined a military leader voluntarily, as did their descendants. They were recruited from the *bey*s and other leading families and from those *gazi* who had distinguished themselves enough to be granted fiefs and thus enter the "regular" military establishment. This group first and foremost served as *sipahi*s (cavalrymen) in the military, but they also performed fiscal and administrative functions. The latter duties as well as the fact that they derived their income from the labor of the peasantry brought them into direct contact with the majority of the population.

Like everybody else in the Ottoman system, the *timarlıs* were hierarchically organized. Their rank, duties, and income were closely tied to past performances and the reward received for them, land. The basic land unit, called *çift*, varied in size, but had to be large enough to yield an income sufficient to maintain the holder and his family. One *çift* constituted the smallest *timar* whose holder was obliged to maintain his military equipment and horse ready for action. Holders of larger *timars* were obliged to appear in armor when the troops were mustered, and if the holding yielded amounts larger than the minimum bring retainers to the army. In Europe the smallest *timar* was supposed to yield 3,000 *akçes*,[3] an amount

3. The *akçe* (called *asper* by the Europeans) was the basic monetary unit of the Ottomans. First minted under Orhan, it was used for all official transactions until the end of the seventeenth century. From the time of Orhan until 1453, the *akçe* weighed 3.2 grams and contained 90 percent silver. Between the conquest of Constantinople and 1520 its value fell gradually (by either diminishing its weight or its silver content) to little more than half of its original value. It remained stable at this lower rate until 1575. In the next nine years its value was halved again. Its worth at this time can best be illustrated by giving the *akçe's* rate of exchange in 1684 using other currencies (both Ottoman and foreign) in circulation in the Ottoman Empire.

80 *akçe* = 1 *Kara Kuruş* (the Ottoman name for the Austrian silver *Grossus*)
100 *akçe* = 1 Austrian gold Ducat
120 *akçe* = 1 Venetian gold Ducat
120 *akçe* = 1 *Şerifi* (Ottoman gold coin minted in Istanbul on the model of the Mamluk Ashrafi based on the Venetian Ducat)

Subsequently, the *akçe* became even weaker. Its value fluctuated, but the rate fell to as low as 220 *akçe* = 1 *şerifi*. By the time of Süleyman II (1687-91), after relative stability around 150 to 1, the *akçe* was rated officially as worth 1/220th of a *Şerifi*, but in fact the value of 300 *akçes* corresponded to that of the gold coin.

With the *akçe* becoming practically worthless, new Ottoman monetary units were introduced, although the old unit was still used for bookkeeping purposes. Already in the early seventeenth century, most likely during the reign of Osman II (1618-22), the *para*, a new coin, appeared. Worth 4 *akçes* initially, it too declined in value to 3 *akçes*. Coins in multiples of these two basic monetary units also made their appearance early in the seventeenth century. Süleyman II and Ahmed II (1691-95) issued a third kind of money, the Ottoman *kuruş*. Originally of two different values, it soon became one and represented the equivalent of 160 *akçes*.

The gold coinage also had to be changed because the Egyptian and African mints began to produce debased coins. In 1696-97 Mustafa II (1695-1703) recalled the *şerifi* and replaced it with the *tuğralı* which had the same value as the original *şerifi*. His successor, Ahmed III (1703-30), kept this new coin, but in 1711 he issued a slightly heavier and finer coin called either *zincırlı* or *funduki* (about 3.3 grams), and a smaller coin (2.5 2.6 grams), the *zeri mahbub*.

From 1725 we have an official Ottoman value table listing the following gold coins and their *akçe/para* equivalents:
Zincırlı = 400 *akçe* = 133.3 *para*
Venetian ducat = 375 *akçe* = 125 *para*
Austrian ducat = 360 *akçe* = 120 *para*

Money continued to deteriorate further, and under Mahmud I (1730-54) 450 *akçes* were worth a *tuğralı* signifying a further value loss of about 16-18 percent in the silver

considered sufficient for maintaining a *sipahi*. The largest *timar* brought a revenue of 19,999 *akçes*; for every 3,000 *akçes* over the basic minimal amount, its holder was obliged to maintain a soldier who was called a *cebelü* and whose major amibition was to earn a *timar* of his own.

Holdings yielding between 20,000 and 99,999 *akçes* were called *zeamet*, and those who held them were known as *zaims*. These feudatories had more important military duties and bureaucractic obligations than the simple *timarlı*, although they had to furnish a *cebelü* only for every 5,000 *akçes* of income. Holdings yielding over 100,000 *akçes* were known as *has* and were assigned to the highest provincial officeholders, retired dignitaries, the major officers of the *mülkiye* class, members of the imperial family, and ladies of the sultan's household. Some were used for the upkeep of the imperial household.

In this manner almost every person working the land was under a landowner who belonged to the professional Ottoman group, if we remember that *vakıfs* were also supported by their labor. Those, however, who were in direct contact with them were the *sipahis*, the *mültezims*, or the agents of the *vakıfs*. The *sipahis* of each province obeyed the governor (*sancak beyi*) of the province in which they lived. He usually carried the honorific title of *paşa*, held a *has*, and was subordinated only to the *beylerbeyi*. The regimental commanders, *alay beyis* served below the *sancak beyi*. They were holders of *zeamets* as were their immediate subordinates, the *subaşis*. These last-named served as the chief police officials in the various *kazas*,[4] the subdivisions of the *sancaks*. The lowest ranking officer, a sort of military policeman, was the *çerisürücü*. He held a large *timar* and acted as the local police officer in time of peace.

The different types of agricultural holdings were supposed to follow a strictly regulated pattern of division. A "typical" *sancak*'s revenue derived from various agricultural activities was supposed to be assigned as follows:[5]

> 20 percent for *has* holding including those of the sultan (*Havas-i Hümayun*)
> 10 percent for *zeamets*
> 40 percent for *timars*
> 10 percent for the support of troops manning fortifications
> 10 percent for *vakıfs*

Part of the remaining 10 percent was reserved for the irregulars (the

---

coin. This downward trend continued for the remainder of the period covered by this volume. See H. A. R. Gibb and Harold Bowen, *Islamic Society and the West* (Oxford, London, New York, and Toronto: Oxford University Press, 1957), vol. 1, pt. 2, pp. 49-59.

4. *Kaza* was the expression used for both administrative and legal units. They were often but not always identical.

5. This breakdown is given in Gibb and Bowen, *Islamic Society*, vol. l, pt. l, p. 52, n.1.

part set aside for private property will be discussed when landholding and agriculture are covered). The oldest of these fighters were the *akıncıs*, volunteers raised in the European provinces among Turks. They performed scouting duties and were feared as raiders. They lived from booty and always had the chance to become *timarlı*, if they distinguished themselves sufficiently. The *yaya* and *piyade*, irregular infantry troops, were known only as part of the Ottoman army, but the *müsellems* lived among the Europeans. Settled Turkomans, the *müsellems* were members of the military class and performed regular military duties as cavalrymen. They had small holdings of land on which they paid no taxes and dues, and farmed their holdings themselves. Only one of every three or four served, and those staying behind farmed his plot too. They earned a strictly subsistence income.

In addition to these Muslim auxiliary forces there were some *zimmi* who performed regular military duties and had the same rights as the *müsellems*. They were known under various names—Uskok, Valachs, and Martolos among others—and were counted as members of the military class because of their occupation. Their origin is not quite clear. They might have been the descendants of Christians who fought as allies and vassals with Murad I and Bayezid I. Although they later became freebooters and bandits, they were part of the military establishment during the first 250 years of Ottoman rule in the Balkans. An article in *Islam Enciclopedisi* states that they were organized as a military force under Murad II at the beginning of his reign and mentions that of the 3,500-man garrison Süleyman I left at Buda in 1541, 1,000 were Martolos.[6] This appears quite possible, given the fact that their number was over 80,000 in 1527.[7] Some of the Christian *timarlı* probably rose to this dignity.

The *voynuks* are sometimes listed as fighting forces, and so are the Vlachs, people living in Serbia and Macedonia, who at first received certain tax exemptions in exchange for limited border duty. The Vlachs lost their status toward the beginning of the seventeenth century, although they retained their Romance dialect in the midst of their Slav neighbors until modern times. The *derbendci*, some two thousand families of Rumelia, acted as guards of mountain passes, bridges, and other strategic locations in exchange for tax relief and represent a transition from real fighters to auxiliary forces. They were not required to leave their districts in times of war, and they can be considered as something of a specialized local militia with strictly defined duties.

The *voynuks* and *doğancis* were auxiliaries in the narrowest sense of the word. The former were all Bulgarians as were the latter, with a few excep-

6. *Islam Ansiklopedisi* (Istanbul: Milli Eğitim Basimevi, 1945), 7:341-42.
7. Halil Inalcık, "L'Empire Ottoman," *Actes du Premier Congrès International des Études Balkaniques et Sud-Est Européenes*, 6 vols. (Sofia; Bulgarian Academy of Sciences, 1969), 3:90.

tions. The *voynuks* raised horses for the palace and other high dignitaries in exchange for land and tax exemptions. The *doğancis* enjoyed similar privileges, although their duty was to raise hunting falcons. Both groups were considered part of the military and derived their income from land that was left after those with higher claims were satisfied. Finally, we find *yürüks* listed as soldiers. These nomadic Turkoman tribesmen owned no land, but paid taxes for the right to use various pastures.

The *maaslı* troops were originally members of the sultan's slave army, the janissary infantry and the slave cavalry also known as *sipahis*. In later periods sappers, artillery men, etc., were also trained from the young men conscripted for janissary duty. All the *maaslı* were *kapı kulus*.

The *seyfiye* was the real military group, but all three classes of professional Ottomans listed so far belonged to what had been considered, since Turkic tribal days, as the "military class." The fourth group, the *ilmiye* and *diniye* class, was not considered military. Although families from this group might have been slave in origin, its members were most often freeborn Muslims. The double name means cultural and religious class, and the duties of this fourth group, whose members were the *ulema*, were limited to these activities. The importance of this class becomes obvious when we recall that the legal profession was part of the religious establishment.

Members of the *ilmiye* and *diniye* were trained in schools called *medreses* supported by *vakıfs*. These schools were ranked, and those established by Mehmed II and Süleyman I carried the most prestige. The rank of a given school determined the positions its teachers and graduates received when they left. Each school had only one official teacher, the *müderris*, although helpers could be appointed. What that teacher taught and believed permanently influenced his students who in turn acted in accordance with the principles they had professed or learned in the various *medreses* when they were transferred to other positions.

While only one function of the *ulema*, serving as judges, was known to the people of Southeastern Europe, it must be noted that members of this class had great influence on the central administration and were often appointed to leading positions, and that, after the decline of the state machinery, they performed duties originally assigned to members of the first-mentioned three official groups. The highest ranking of the *ulema* was originally the *kadiasker*, but he had to share his power with the *şeyhülislam* after the *müfti* of Istanbul acquired this title and gradually achieved this supreme position. In a very general way it could be stated that the *şeyhülislam* became something resembling the highest *shari'a* authority. Although he was appointed and could be dismissed almost at will, his *fetva* (written ruling) could bring about the deposition of even a sultan. The *kadiaskers* continued to oversee the court system. *Müftis*, lower ranking jurisconsults, could also issue *fetvas* concerning issues that arose in their own territories. They usually did so when a question of proper interpretation of the law was put before them by the sultan or the *kadis* of the judicial districts (*kazas*) under their jurisdiction. There were ranks within the judiciary, the highest of which being the *kadis* of Istanbul, Mecca, Medina, Cairo, Bursa, Edirne, Damascus, Jerusalem, Izmir, and Aleppo. Of greatest importance to the people of all provinces was the fact that wherever they lived there was a *kadi* and a court that administered both the *sharī'a* and the *kanuns*. Because a given *kadi* could not possibly handle all the cases of his *kaza*, the judicial districts were subdivided into *nahiyes*,[8] to which *kadis* appointed *naibs* (subjudges).

Having given an over-all picture of the four groups of professional Ottomans and their various functions, duties, and obligations, we turn now to the details of the provincial administration. Those professional Ottomans who belonged to the *seyfiye* and the *ilmiye-diniye* groups ran the provinces, but it should not be forgotten that many of them came from or returned to the *mülkiye* class. Nor were those belonging to the *kalemiye* restricted to the capital. They too had important duties in the provincial administration.

It is almost impossible to establish a clear picture of the number and exact borders of the various provincial administrations because they changed constantly. The administrations themselves were in continual flux, as can be seen from the confusing nomenclature of the top provincial officials. For example, we have seen that in the central government there were two *beylerbeyis*: one for Rumeli and one for Anadolu. By the end of the fifteenth century nearly forty officials held this title on an honorific basis, although only the two original *beylerbeyis* performed the tasks of governors general. The administrative districts of the governors general were originally called *sancaks*. Later they became known as *beylerbeyliks*, and still later as *eyalets* with subdivisions referred to as *sancaks* and later as *livas*. Furthermore, not all provinces were administered along the same lines. Those directly under the central administration in which *timars* were established were in the majority, but there were still others that managed their own affairs under traditional leaders (tribal leaders, vassal princes). The latter were known as the hereditary provinces, *hükümet sancaks*, and their only obligation, besides fealty, was the delivery of a yearly tribute (*salyane*) to the central government.

According to Inalcık, by the beginning of the fourth quarter of the sixteenth century there were four *hükümet sancaks* in Europe: Moldavia, Wallachia, Transylvania, and Dubrovnik (Ragusa). There were also six *timarlı*: Rumelia (a province around Edirne not to be confused with Rumeli), Bosnia, *Cezār-i bahr-i sefīd* (Aegean Islands), Buda, Temesvár, and

8. *Nahiye* had several meanings. It could be a small judicial district and it was also used to denote smaller administrative districts, for example, a section of a city.

Cyprus.[9] Later Nagyvárad (Varad, Oradea), Eger (Eğri), Kanizsa (Kanişa), Silistre, the Morea, Crete, and Belgrade were added, and for a short period Janów and Kamnice (Kamieniec Podolski) in Poland. Several others appeared and disappeared as the provinces were split and reunited. Of the later additions Crete, Nagyvárad, and the Morea had no *timars*. By the end of the eighteenth century the number of *eyalets*, already reduced by loss of territory, stood at 25; these were subdivided into 290 *sancaks*.

Most of the *hükümet sancaks* in Europe were either relatively small (Crete, Cyprus, Morea), or held for only short times like Nagyvárad and the two Polish provinces. Some (Moldavia, Wallachia, Transylvania, Ragusa) were independent enough to warrant separate treatment. They were in a real sense "peripheral" holdings whose obligations, besides loyalty and the payment of tribute, were limited to admitting *kadis* to the major cities, and Ottoman garrisons to the larger fortifications. Their independence also explains why the *devşirme* system affected mainly those of the Orthodox faith and did not touch Romanians and only relatively few Greeks.

The real "core" provinces were those in which *sipahis* lived on *timars*. Supreme command of each of these provinces rested with the governor. Every governor maintained smaller versions of the central government in his seats of residence and had to divide his authority and privileges with those officials who served on the provincial councils. The governors were first of all military leaders responsible for controlling the *sipahis*, fighting smaller engagements such as border skirmishes, and contributing their forces to major campaigns. Occasionally, in accordance with custom, they held court and decided a few disputes. These officials also governed directly the territory that surrounded their capitals and formed a subunit within the larger whole. The other subunits were administered by *beys*. All of these dignitaries were in charge of military officers whose major functions have already been mentioned.

While few of the provincial councils were "complete," all consisted of at least the most important officials and mirrored the division in the central administration and the already mentioned Ottoman "checks and balances." Foremost of these were the *defter eminis* (custodians of the records), who kept registrations of fiefs in order. They belonged, as did their superior the *mal defterdari* (property registrar), to the *kalemiye*. The *mal defterdari* was the province's treasurer. He received all the taxes, paid the province's expenses, and remitted the surplus to the central treasury. The *defterdars*, like the governors, were appointed by the central government. They acted independently of each other and could even check and report on each other's activities. Finally, the *kahya* of the *çavuşes* (the chief of

9. Inalcık, *Ottoman Empire*, p. 106.

the order executors) was an important functionary of the provincial assembly. It was the duty of the *çavuşe*s to execute orders, mainly those
concerning punishments, that resulted either from the governor's verdict
or from that of the various *kadis'* courts. Another functionary called the
mefkufcu served under the *mal defterdari*. Though probably not a
member of the local council, he levied the taxes on immovable property in
the province and administered those fiefs that were momentarily vacant
for the benefit of the provincial treasury.

In addition to the representatives of the *seyfiye* and *kalemiye*, those of
the *ilmiye-diniye* group were also present in each province. They consisted of the *müderrise*s and their students in the provincial *medrese*s, but
most importantly of the *müfti*s, *kadi*s, and *naib*s who manned the courts.
These courts administered both the *sharī'a* and the *kanun*s, which differed
greatly from province to province.

*Kanun*s, being based on the sultan's *urf*, were valid only for his lifetime.
Although they had to be "in conformity" with the principles of the *sharī'a*,
they consisted mainly of local laws and regulations in force before the
Ottoman conquest, which the sultan confirmed. If the sultan failed to do
so, the region had no *kanun*. Before proper authority was established in
central Hungary, for example, already appointed *kadi*s had to force *zimmi*
litigants to travel long distances to their traditional judges, their feudal
lords who had left the Ottoman occupied lands, to get rulings simply because the *kanun*s for the region were either not yet established or not yet
known to them. Each sultan promptly reconfirmed the *kanun*s of his predecessors, and the laws were repeatedly issued in complete collections for
each province, the *kanunname*s. However they were too variegated and
complicated for any jurist to handle. For this reason most judges spent
their entire professional life either in Rumeli, Anadolu, or Africa, and if
they took their duties seriously and were honest men they became real
experts in the laws of a given region. A good, experienced *kadi* was an
asset for any province and its inhabitants.

3. THE REAYA

THE *reaya*, both Muslim and *zimmi*, constituted the overwhelming majority of the population and supported the professional Ottoman establishment. So far as the Muslims were concerned, the Ottomans faced the same
dilemna that the Arabs had had to face when they extended their sway
during the first century after the *hijra:* their main duty was to spread the
true faith, but since all Muslims were supposed to be equal, if the privileges of the first Muslims were extended to all there would be no one left
to produce or pay taxes. The Ottomans inherited the Arab solution including the *haraç*, the land-use tax everybody had to pay regardless of religion. The problem, however, arose in a new form, the best example of
which being the Turkoman tribesmen. Members of the "military class,"

potential *gazi* material, they were too numerous to be absorbed among the professional Ottomans and too unproductive when considered as *reaya*. As we have seen, the situation was resolved by transforming these Muslims into *müsellems* or *yürüks*. In this manner they were not "degraded," remained members of the "military class," and became producers. The *yürüks* even paid certain taxes.

More vexing was the fact that until the conquests of Selim I (1512-20) the majority of Ottoman subjects were non-Muslims, several of whom, especially in Anatolia, showed a willingness to convert. Conversion was supposed to be the ultimate aim of a good Muslim state, yet mass conversion would have produced economic chaos and ruin. The extreme leniency, unusual even for a Muslim state, with which the first Ottoman rulers handled their *zimmi* subjects, and their great emphasis on *kanuns*—both compatible with the treatment of the "people of the book" contained in the *shari'a*—were clearly designed to keep the *reaya* satisfied with the position they occupied as producers. This also contributed to the ease with which European peasants accepted Ottoman rule and influenced the conversion pattern that will be discussed in the next section. After the conquests of Selim I, when the empire acquired a Muslim majority, the Ottomans became much less generous in their handling of the *zimmi*. By then, however, the patterns were set and the Ottomans' power was sufficient to keep the system going.

The *reaya* were grouped first informally and after 1453 formally into *millets*. Both the term and social organization according to religion had precedents. In early medieval Muslim literature the expression *millet* (*milla*) refers only to Muslims and differentiates them from the *zimmi*. There were other precedents, too, for this treatment of minorities. Religious leaders of minority groups held positions similar to the leaders of the Ottoman *millets* in Sasanid Iran, and some of Justinian's edicts concerning the Jews resemble the later Ottoman *millet* system. Curiously enough, the Ottomans used the term basically for non-Muslims, although occasionally a reference to a Muslim *millet* does appear. Officially, from the beginning—that is, since Mehmed II's relevant legislation in 1453—there were only two *millets*, the Orthodox and the Armenian. Although the Jewish *millet* was not "officially recognized" until 1839, it had a head (*millet başi*) and functioned very well from 1453 on.

Very little has to be said in this connection about the Muslims, although numerous inhabitants of the European provinces followed Islam because their relationship with the authorities depended either on their being subject to the *shari'a* regulations of their morality and private lives or on their occupations. So far as the first of these two considerations is concerned, the legal system has already been presented and a few words have been said concerning the basic religious duties of Muslims. The *shari'a* also regulated marriages, divorces, inheritances—in general all relationships within the family and community—and so long as the Muslims adhered to these and paid the required fees their lives followed a well-defined and regulated pattern.

The largest of the *millets* was the Orthodox. There can be no doubt that Mehmed II had several good reasons for creating a Christian *millet* limited to the adherents of the Eastern Rite. After he had conquered Constantinople and renamed it Istanbul, he considered himself the legitimate successor of the emperor and wanted to retain his position and prerogatives in dealing with the Orthodox church. He fully realized that the great majority of his Christian subjects were Orthodox, and that most Orthodox were opposed to the reunification of the churches to which the Emperor John VII agreed at the Council of Florence in 1439, making them potentially loyal to a ruler whose major enemies were Roman Catholics. Furthermore, he was determined to rebuild his new capital and make it once again a great trading and manufacturing center. To accomplish this goal he needed loyal Christians and he trusted only the Orthodox. He therefore wanted to give them a special organization.

Not only did he create an Orthodox *millet*, but he also picked as its first head (*millet başi*) the monk Gennadius, an outspoken enemy of the Council of Florence, and elevated him to the patriarchate. Gennadius, born George Scholarios, was a well-known theologian and qualified by his learning as much as by opposition to Roman Catholicism to become the highest ranking dignitary of a reunited Orthodox church. Because of the serious problems this reunification created in the seventeenth and especially in the eighteenth centuries, a few words must be said about it before turning to the rights of the Orthodox *millet*.

When Mehmed created the Orthodox *millet* two other sees were acting as quasi-partriarchates: Ohrid (Ochrid, Lichnida) and Peć (Ipek). A third see also existed at Tŭrnovo, until 1394 when the city was conquered by the Ottomans and its bishop recognized the Patriarch of Constantinople as his superior.[10] These sees presided over Orthodox churches whose li-

10. The first Bulgarian Patriarchate was established at Ohrid in 893 by Simeon (893-927), and St. Clement (Kliment) was the first to hold the title. Simeon, the first Bulgarian ruler to call himself tsar, followed the Byzantine model and believed that every emperor must have his own patriarch. In 1019 the Byzantines forced the Bulgarians to recognize their overlordship and, consequently, Ohrid was "demoted" to an archbishopric. From 1223 on the bishops of Ohrid began to refer to their see as the Autocephalous Archbishopric of Justiniana Prima, a title they claimed until 1767, and they considered themselves patriarchs until Mehmed II subordinated them to Istanbul in 1453. This was the major, "national" patriarchate of the Bulgarians, who had a second one briefly in 971-72 in Preslav, and a more important third patriarchate in Tŭrnovo between 1234 and 1394.

Peć (Ipek) first became an autocephalous Serbian bishropric in 1219 and was declared a patriarchate by the Serbian Tsar Stefan Dusan (1331-55) in 1346. Constantinople did not recognize this new dignity, and in 1368 the incumbent at Peć once again recognized Constantinople's supremacy. When Serbia was on the rise again under Lazar I (1371-89), Constantinople recognized Peć as a patriarchal see in 1375. Ten

turgical language was Church Slavonic, not Greek. They stood for the national identity of Bulgarians and Serbs, although theologically there were no differences between them and Constantinople. To Mehmed II, who was a good Muslim and recognized only theological differences, it made perfectly good sense to create only one Orthodox *millet* under the leadership of one partriarch who served as the *millet başi*. For the Christian communities of the Balkans this measure was to create serious problems.

Mehmed himself installed the new patriarch, following the ceremony established by the emperors. The only important innovation was that he handed Gennadius a *berat*, an imperial warrant confirming him in his new dignity. The issuance of this document was in perfect keeping with Ottoman usage, but in later years it made the sale of *berats*, and therefore the partriarchal dignity, possible.[11] With the *berat* of Mehmed II, Gennadius became patriarch, *millet başi* of the *Rum* (Orthodox) *millet*, a high ranking *paşa* entitled to three *tuğs* (horse tails) of the Ottoman Empire, undisputed master of a reunited church, and the official who was responsible for the behavior and loyalty of all the Sultan's Orthodox subjects.

Besides full ecclesiastical powers and jurisdiction, the partriarch acquired legal powers in those cases, such as marriage, divorce, and inheritance, that were regulated by canon law. Concommitant with these legal powers went certain police powers that even included a patriarchal jail in Istanbul. Naturally, the church was permitted to collect the usual ecclesiastical dues, but it was also made responsible and was often consulted in the assessing and collecting of taxes due the state. Finally, ecclesiastical courts had the right to hear and decide cases in which all litigants were Christians, provided they voluntarily submitted their cases to church courts rather than to the *kadi*.

In this manner the traditional hierarchy, from the patriarch down to the lowly parish priest, was invested with a great number of administrative and legal functions in addition to the traditional ecclesiastical ones. A bureaucracy developed that was on a lower and more limited level than the official bureaucracy, but nevertheless paralleled it. In this manner the church became the only "national" institution with which the Orthodox could identify. The fact that, unlike the Ottomans who considered them to

---

years after its subordination to Constantinople in 1453, the see was abolished. It was revived as an archbishopric in 1557 and retained this dignity until 1755, when it was again transformed into a bishopric to be abolished entirely in 1766. For the history of the various patriarchates see: N. J. Pantazopoulos, *Church and Law in the Balkan Peninsula during the Ottoman Rule* (Thessaloniki: Institute for Balkan Studies, 1967), pp. 26-34.

11. From the appointment of Gennadios to the end of the Ottoman Empire, 159 different individuals held the dignity of Patriarch, some more than once. Of these only 21 died in office and 6 were executed on the sultans' orders or by mob action. There were 105 "depositions," permitting the sale of new *berats*. Figures given in Timothy Ware, *The Orthodox Church* (Baltimore: Penguin Books, 1963), p. 99, quoting B. J. Kidd, *The Churches of Eastern Christendom* (London: The Faith Press, 1927), p. 304.

be members of one *millet*, the Orthodox Christians did not feel as members of one "nation" made the subordination of the Slavonic Rite churches to the Oecumenical Patriarch a significant move that created serious difficulties for him, the central government, and the Balkan people especially in the eighteenth century.

For all practical purposes the new powers conferred on it by Mehmed II made the church a state within a state. As time passed the hierarchy began to think of itself both as the *de facto* ruler and protector of the Christians and as the sole body to deal with the central authority. It performed these double duties with great skill, and the lives of the Balkan Christians depended as much on the efficiency of the ecclesiastical authorities as on that of the Ottomans. This explains why differences among them, which have already been referred to in connection with the Ohrid and Peć metropolitanates, were fought out to a large extent within the ecclesiastical realm. The church that survived the destruction of state had to become the institution on which a revived nation-state could be rebuilt.

Before we leave the Orthodox *millet*, a few words should be said about Cyprus, although this island was not conquered by the Ottomans until 1570-73. After conquest its inhabitants were enrolled into the Orthodox *millet*, and some Turkish garrisons placed on the island totally restructured the ethnic-ecclesiastic situation. Herein lies the origin of the modern problems of Cyprus.

Cyprus had had an autocephalous church since the Council of Ephesus in 431. This church consisted of twenty bishoprics under an archbishop. After the great schism the island was solidly Greek Orthodox. During the Third Crusade King Richard I of England captured Cyprus, in 1191, and sold the island to Guy de Lusignan whose successors ruled the island until 1475, when it became a Venetian possession. Thus, for something like four hundred years preceding the Ottoman conquest, Cyprus was ruled by Roman Catholics. During this period the archiepiscopal see became Roman Catholic as did sixteen of the twenty bishoprics. Some of the people became Catholics, but the majority remained Orthodox. When the Ottomans came, the Roman Catholic hierarchy and part of their flock left the island. Turks who had come to the island originally as occupation troops subsequently became settlers. The remaining inhabitants became members of the Orthodox *millet*, and while the number of bishoprics remained four, the archbishopric was re-established. In this manner the Turkish conquest was also, ironically if we think of the present situation, the Orthodox "reconquest" of Cyprus made possible by the *millet* system.

The *millet başis* of the other two *millets*, the *Haham başi* (chief rabbi) of Istanbul of the Jews and the Gregorian Patriarch of Istanbul, had the same rights, privileges, and duties that the Orthodox patriarch enjoyed. Therefore, only those aspects of their offices and subordinate organizations will be mentioned that differ significantly from that of the *Rum millet.*

Although, as already mentioned, the Jewish (*Yahudi millet*) was not officially recognized until the nineteenth century, Mehmed II appointed the first *Haham başi*, Moses Kapsali, in 1453. At the same time he declared that Jews were permitted to settle in Istanbul. Kapsali was given protocolar precedence over the partriarch, and beginning with the rule of Süleyman I, the Jewish community was the first to be given the privilege of appointing an agent (*kahya*) to represent it before the central government. While the *Haham başi* needed the sultan's *berat* to assume his office, all of Moses Kapsali's successors were freely elected by their coreligionists.

There were several reasons for the preferential treatment given to the Jews. While Mehmed II looked at the Orthodox as *potentially* the most loyal of his Christian subjects, he was *certain* of the fidelity of the Jews. No other state in fifteenth century Europe had treated them better than had the Ottoman. Since the days of Murad II they had served the sultans well, mainly as court physicians. Furthermore, they possessed several valuable skills including the knowledge of languages (besides Turkish, Arabic, and Persian) that were occasionally needed. Moreover, the Jews were the original "people of the book."

In the eyes of the Ottoman government, the Jews, like the Orthodox, were one *millet.* The Jews did indeed present a united front toward Muslims and "gentiles," but they were anything but united within their own community. First, there was a marked difference between those Jews who had been living in the land at the time of Ottoman conquest and the emigrants who, persecuted elsewhere and learning about the tolerance of the Ottomans, came in great numbers in the fifteenth and sixteenth centuries. Furthermore, both of these groups were further divided into two subgroups. The "original" Ottoman Jews belonged either to those who followed the Talmud (the rabbinical Jews), or to those who did not (the Karaites). The latter group formed during the rule of the 'Abbasids in Baghdad, first appeared in Palestine and then spread all over the lands of the caliphs. Only a few of the Karaites reached those parts of Europe under Byzantine rule. There, Greek-speaking Talmudic Jews known as Romanios or Gregos were in the majority.

The emigrants were either Sephardic or Ashkenazi Jews, depending on their land of origin and their mother tongue. Of these two groups the Sephardic Jews are the more important for two reasons. First, they were the most numerous Jewish settlers in Istanbul and the Balkans; second, they became the most influential group and dominated communal life and the election of the *Haham başi* for centuries. Besides Istanbul, where they became the best known armament makers and performed the already mentioned functions for the central government, Salonika, Edirne, Nikopolis, and to a slightly lesser degree Sofia and Sarajevo became important

Sephardic centers in the Balkans where important Jewish cultural developments occurred during Ottoman rule.

While some of the Ashkenazi emigrants settled in the European lands of the Ottomans and in Istanbul, most moved to Palestine. They came from Germany, Austria, Hungary and the Romanian Principalities. In the Holy Land they soon mingled with rabbinical Jews and became the traditional Jewish population of Palestine.

The Jews were almost never involved in agricultural pursuits, but their tax loads and obligations were no lighter than those of the other *reaya* because taxes were attached to their professions. In order to insure the unity of this *millet*, Selim I abolished the office of *nagid*, the highest ranking Jewish office in the Near East, when he conquered Cairo in 1517. Because religion and "nationality" coincided for the Jews in the early modern period, the *millet* system suited them perfectly. Under that system they were able to live for centuries better than anywhere else.

If the Jewish *millet* was a case of theory coinciding with practice, the Armenian *millet*, which lacked both ethnic and religious homogeneity, was a prime example of theory diverging from practice. Although some Armenians maintained a connection with Rome, the great majority belonged to a monophysite church, which had been established some time in the third century by Gregory the Illuminator. Once a strong church spreading beyond the borders of Armenian-inhabited territories, it had lost some of its influence by the time the Ottomans appeared. Its strongholds were outside the realm of Mehmed II in Greater and Lesser Armenia, and the seat of its head, the Catholicos, was also outside Ottoman territory, in Erivan (Echmiadsin). Yet there were several people in the Ottoman Empire who did not fit into any of Mehmed II's *millets*, and these not only included Armenians but also an Armenian bishop who resided in Bursa. He was clearly the highest ranking religious dignitary who could not be fitted into either of the two other *millets* in the lands ruled by the Ottomans. This bishop, called Horaghim, was appointed Armenian Patriarch of Istanbul by the sultan, and his *millet* was recognized in 1461.

This *millet* is so special because its head, who had all the rights, honors, privileges, and duties of the other *millet başi*, officially presided over those subjects of the sultan who could not be subordinated to the leaders of the other two *millet* groups. While he was not responsible for the few Roman Catholics, who were considered members of the Orthodox *millet*, he was in charge of the splinter sects and heretics living in the Ottoman Empire. In Europe the most important of these were the Paulicians and Bogomils, although by the time of Mehmed II their numbers and importance were declining. Only a small group, the *Pavliniki*, survived into modern times near Sofia. It was from these European heretical groups that the first major groups converted.

4. THE PROBLEM OF CONVERSION[12]

IT was, of course, strictly forbidden under penalty of death for a Muslim to leave his faith. The Ottomans did not pay any attention if *zimmis* converted to a religion other than Islam because this did not affect their status in the Ottoman Empire. What was at issue was conversion to Islam. When the Ottomans first established a permanent foothold in Europe in the middle of the fourteenth century, there was a small Muslim colony in Constantinople and a few small settlements scattered throughout the Balkans proper. By the beginning of the 1970s there were almost seven million Muslims living either in European Turkey or in those parts of Southeastern Europe that had once been under Ottoman rule. Of these about 2.5 million lived in Turkey, the same number in Yugoslavia, an estimated 1.2 million (no official figures are available) in Albania, 0.5 million in Bulgaria, and the remainder either in Greece or Romania.

Ethnically, the Muslim population of the Balkans is either Turkish or Slav, Greek, Albanian, etc. The Turks came as settlers, and the others were converted. This early and important transformation in the ethnic and religious composition of the Balkan population deserves a few words.

The problem of the Turkomans and the attempt of the Ottoman authorities to settle them has already been mentioned. Their influx into Ottoman lands was especially strong in the fourteenth and early fifteenth centuries, but, like the emigrants who came to the United States, most of these nomads settled in the eastern provinces of the empire. In the fourteenth century the Ottomans moved some of them to Europe, particularly into the lands of today's European Turkey, where they were either settled as *müsellems* or remained nomadic for a longer period as the already mentioned *yürüks*. As we know, after this first massive settlement of Turks most of those who were brought over from Asia Minor were settled along major military roads, at fortified points, or in the major cities. The only Muslims in the countryside were the *sipahis* and a few officials, the descendants of whom can still be found in these strongly Christian regions.

In 1478 the Ottomans conducted a census in Istanbul, and in 1520-30 for the provinces. They counted taxable hearths (households), not individuals. The Muslim and *zimmi* hearths paid different taxes so they were counted separately. These figures were analyzed and published by the excellent Turkish historian, Ömer Lutfi Barkan. His findings confirm in detail the general picture. In Europe 18.8 percent (194,958) of the hearths

12. This entire section follows closely the exposition of Speros Vryonis, Jr., "Religious Changes and Patterns in the Balkans, 14th-16th Centuries," in Henrik Birnbaum and Speros Vryonis, Jr., eds., *Aspects of the Balkans; Continuity and Change* (The Hague-Paris: Mouton, 1972) and a work on which Vryonis also relied heavily, Ömer Lutfi Barkan, "Essai sur les donnés statistiques des régistres de recensement dans l'empire ottoman aux XVe siècle," *Journal of the Economic and Social History of the Orient* 1 (1958): 7-36.

were Muslim, 80.7 percent (832,707) were Christian, and .5 percent (4,134) were Jewish. Of the Muslim hearths 85 percent—the great majority —were concentrated in ten of the then twenty-eight European *kazas*. In only four of these *kazas*, those of Vize (in today's European Turkey), Silistra and Chirmen (both in Bulgaria today), and Gallipoli, were the Muslims in the majority. Outside of the eastern Balkans there were also significant Muslim settlements in Macedonia, Bosnia-Hercegovina, and Thessaly, regions that present a special problem.

Equally important is the fact that even in those regions where the Muslims were numerous they were heavily concentrated in the major cities. The figures given by Barkan and analyzed further by Vryonis for twelve major cities are highly relevant. The urban nature of the Muslim population is well demonstrated by the figures given in table 1 and is quite understandable. The settlement of nomads and the granting of fiefs occurred in the countryside, but the major centers of provincial administration, and most importantly the points of interest to the trade guild-connected *akhis*, were the cities, which also controlled major roads that the Ottomans wanted in safe hands.

TABLE 1

RELIGIOUS BREAKDOWN OF POPULATION IN
MAJOR EUROPEAN CITIES
(Based on 1520-30 Census)

City	Muslims (in percentages)	Christians (in percentages)	Jews (in percentages)	Percentage of Muslims in *kaza* where city was located (if available)
Istanbul (1478)	58.2	31.6	10.2	—
Edirne	82.1	12.8	5.1	26
Salonika	25.2	20.2	54.3	—
Sarajevo	100.0	—	—	46
Larissa	90.2	9.8	—	17.5
Serres	61.3	32.8	5.9	—
Monastir	75.0	20.2	4.8	10.5
Skopje	74.8	23.7	1.5	10.5
Sofia	66.4	33.6	—	6
Athens	.5	99.5	—	—
Nikopolis	37.7	62.3	—	—
Trikala	36.3	41.5	22.2	17.5

Of the Muslim hearths listed only 19 percent were nomadic, the rest being families settled either in the cities or in the countryside. Vryonis argues convincingly that about 30 percent of the additional Muslim hearths listed in the 1520-30 census can be attributed to Turkish immigration, leaving about 96,500 hearths that were Muslim as the result of conversion.[13] Several examples of forced conversion exist dating from the pe-

13. Speros Vryonis, Jr., "Religious Changes," pp. 165-66.

riod when the empire became more conservative than it was in the earlier
centuries, less tolerant and even fanatical. The best known example is the
conversion drive in the Rhodope Mountain region beginning around 1666.
In the period predating the census on which these figures are based, however, only the *devşirme* can be considered forced conversion. Yet, because
those taken under this system were removed from their native land, this
form of forced conversion did not influence the religious composition of
the Balkans revealed in these figures. The conversion of the Albanians is
also a seventeenth century phenomenon; earlier even the majority of the
timarlı were Christians. Thus, these earlier conversions must have been
"voluntary."

Vryonis lists as the major reasons for earlier conversions: economic and
legal advantages, the influences of the *medrese*s and other Muslim institutions, fear, and the adaptability of folk religion. He is right, but I and
other scholars believe that the fourth reason is the most important. Folk-
Islam and the role of the *akhi*s has been mentioned already in the first
chapter. The role of Şeyh Bedreddin both under Musa and later as the
leader of a popular revolt of 1416 indicate that similar beliefs must have
existed among the majority of his followers, the Balkan Christians. According to anthropological and sociological studies among both the Greek and
Slav Orthodox in the Balkans a phenomenon paralleling that discussed in
connection with Islam existed. Here, too, lack of thorough religious training, the resulting misunderstanding of basic dogmas, the survival of pagan
rites connected with fertility, health, etc., in an environment that did not
change with the acceptance of Christianity, the willingness of the clergy
to accommodate their flocks, the great division between higher and lower
clergy, and the discontent with authorities who were closely identified
with the "established" church led to the inclusion of enough pagan rites,
customs, superstitions, and beliefs to create a folk culture and religion
whose remnants are still observable in the folk customs of today's Balkan
people.

Many of these rites and beliefs were universal. People everywhere were
interested in rain at the right time of the year, in fertility, and in other factors basic to primitive rural life, and were continually seeking to ensure
that everything would go right by creating spirits, demons, etc., who if
handled properly would behave in a manner favorable to those who depended on their good will. If one keeps in mind that the customs connected with these basic beliefs, fears, and habits were only in part Turkish
or Islamic, and remembers that part was learned from the Greek inhabitants of Asia Minor during the long centuries of frontier life, the similarities between certain aspects of folk religion as practiced by the Muslims
and Christians will not come as a surprise.

The Christians, of course, had certain rituals and beliefs that the Muslims did not—or rather were not supposed to—have. Among these the be-

lief in saints, the use of icons, and baptism were the most important. As we know, the *akhis* were able to accommodate everybody on the frontier with ease. By the time that the Ottomans began to make serious gains in Europe, the *akhis* had become pretty much "urbanized," almost a part of the "establishment," and were basically nothing more than guild organizations with broad, folk-religious codes that permitted them to settle in the towns of Europe, organize and lead the various guilds, and dominate town administrations. Together with the *medreses* and other religious-charitable institutions they probably account for conversions, possible mainly on a family basis, that occurred in the cities.

The role that the *akhis* once played in the Anatolian countryside now devolved to the *derviş* orders which were responsible for the important conversions that occurred prior to the 1520-30 census in Macedonia and Bosnia, and for the later ones in Albania. Although some of these *derviş* orders followed the "road" of the *akhis*—and became urban and well established—the most important of these were the *Bektaşi* and the *Mevlevi*—most of them remained basically rural and retained their folk character. It is not quite clear how many different *derviş* "orders" and "suborders" existed at any given time and how many operated in the European provinces where the two groups just mentioned made a lasting early impact. We do know that their numbers were considerable.

Like the *akhi*, the *dervişes* had their *tekkes*, and their code or path (*tarikat*) describing the proper life leading to a mystic understanding of Allah. And like the *akhi*, the *dervişes* built on the long tradition of *sufism* and independent search for the right life. Yet, there were marked differences. Soon after his death the founder of a given *derviş* order, around whose home or tomb the central *tekke* was usually located, became venerated much as a Christian saint and was often credited with miraculous powers. These "saints" were known as the friends (*evliyas*) of God and could be dead or living. The ease with which the patron saint of a European village could be established as one of the *evliya* recognized by a given *derviş* order requires little explanation.

In order for this identification to occur, the *dervişes* had to move around and reach the various localities of the Ottoman Empire. Unlike the *akhi*, the *dervişes* wandered almost constantly, preaching and practicing their *tarikat* and numerous related ceremonies. They were the *babas*, a sort of combination of holy man, miracle worker, medicine man, etc., and were often regarded as living saints. Their eclecticism and pragmatism knew practically no bounds. Given the numerous similarities between folk-Christianity and folk-Islam, they had little difficulty in fitting local customs into their *tarikats*. Furthermore, what they preached had certain advantages. The old formulae that ensured "good fortune" were broadened by the addition of customs that they had brought with them, and by the not negligible circumstance that those who followed them passed from the *zimmi* to the Muslim group. What emerged was a curious variety of European, or rather Balkan, "folk-Islam," which included icons, baptism to prevent mental illness, and many other basically non-Muslim features.

It was not difficult for Christians whose faith was of the superstitious folk variety to pass over to a similar but more secure folk version of Islam. I believe that this explanation of the early mass conversion, advanced by several scholars, is more believable than the equally popular interpretation that attributes such conversion either to the wish of the population to retain its landed possessions or to the desire of previously persecuted heretics (mostly Paulicians and Bogomils) to become the master of their oppressors.

There were people like the Christian *timarli* in Albania elsewhere in the Balkans, too, in the early period. Furthermore, a Christian family could retain a basic *çift*, although it could neither increase its size nor subdivide it. To these considerations can be added the example of Bosnia, where in the rural regions Bogomils were numerous at the time of the Ottoman conquest.

Table 1 shows that by 1520-30 Sarajevo was 100 percent Muslim. While this city had been built by the Ottomans on the site of a small village, the ratio of Muslims in other towns and cities was equally impressive. The same table indicates that the *kaza* of Bosnia as a whole was 46 percent Muslim by this time. For this *kaza* there is also data from a census taken about thirty years earlier, in 1489, indicating that at that time the Muslims made up only 18.4 percent of the district's population. Obviously, a mass conversion occurred during that thirty-year period and was strongest in the urban centers where the Bogomils were the weakest. This problem has not yet been resolved, nor have similar cases elsewhere been fully explored. It might be perfectly true that with time the great majority of the Bogomils, Paulicians, and other "heretics" turned to Islam, but it appears unlikely that they were the spearheads of conversion.

One final argument supports the theory that conversion was really only an easy transition from one folk level to another. Religious social movements, which took newer forms with time, not only remained a constant phenomenon leading to several serious disturbances to be discussed later, but were also so strong that they even affected the Jewish *millet*. There are many reasons why conversion to Islam was much less extensive in the European than in the Anatolian provinces of the Ottoman Empire, but it is not necessary to investigate them in the context of this study. What appears to be important is that while numerous socioeconomic factors did exist that would have made conversion appear desirable, the Ottoman's rapid regulation of the situation in the various European provinces made those factors less impelling than they were in constantly troubled Anatolia. In Europe conversion was limited pretty much to certain elements who had really never understood or practiced their faith correctly and for whom, therefore, apostasy was less a question of belief than of convenience.

5. THE DEVIŞIRME SYSTEM

IF voluntary conversions were convenient for those who changed their faith, the *devşirme* system, the best known form of forced conversion, was convenient for the sultans. In this system were contained all of the issues discussed in this chapter: the professional Ottomans and their institutions, the *reaya*, and conversion.

The verb *devşirmek* can be translated to mean either to collect or to enroll. From the point of view of those whose children were periodically taken, the *devşirme* certainly was a collection of a very special due or levy. For the Ottomans it represented an enrollment of new recruits into their well-established institutions. It is important to realize that the slave institutions of the sultans, including the janissary corp (*yeni çeri*), antedate the establishment of the *devşirme*. It has already been mentioned that not only was slavery a long-established institution in the Muslim world by the time the family of Osman became important, but attention has also been directed to the nature of Muslim slavery and to the slave body guards, mostly Turkish, of the 'Abbasid caliphs in Baghdad.

The Muslim ruler, like every other person with sufficient means, could buy slaves, but he had also been entitled since the earliest Muslim days to what the Turks called *pencik*, the possession of one-fifth of all prisoners of war who could be enslaved because they resisted. It is traditionally accepted and probably true that Murad I (1360-89) organized the first janissary units from the slaves he owned. When the *devşirme* system began and when it turned into the major source for recruits is not certain, although tradition credits Murad with this innovation as well. Our earliest written reference comes from a Christian sermon of 1395. That slaves were used early not only as cannon fodder is attested by the fact that when Bayezid I, at the beginning of his rule, subdued various Turkish principalities in Anatolia, he appointed slaves as their governors. Thus, by the early 1390s a slave system was attached to the Ottoman court. The *devşirme* recruits also served this double function. Despite the uncertainty it appears likely that the *devşirme* was introduced sometime during the last quarter of the fourteenth century.[14]

Equally uncertain are the frequency of the levy, the number of youths enrolled, and the date of abolition of the *devşirme*. It appears most likely that there was no fixed time interval between the levies, nor was there a specified number of recruits to be furnished. The levies were probably ordered when recruits were needed, first infrequently, then frequently,

14. Gibb and Bowen argue that the *devşirme* system was introduced between 1421 and 1438 (*Islamic Society*, vol. 1, part 1, p. 59, n. 8). Unless they are referring to its reintroduction after the interregnum, the date they give is certainly too late.

and finally again rarely, and in each case the authorities fixed the number of youths according to their needs. I am one who believes that the total of young Christians taken "officially" from their homes by the *devşirme* amounted to approximately two hundred thousand during the roughly two-hundred-year period when it was practiced. Traditionally, Ahmed II (1691-95) has been credited with the final abolition of the system. This is not certain, but as a regular measure it ceased toward the end of Murad IV's reign (1623-40), and continued on an occasional basis until sometime toward the end of the seventeenth century.

Even when it was the major source for the recruitment of *kapı kulus*, the *devşirme* was by no means applied to all *zimmi* living in the Ottoman Empire. Once again, numerous details remain without satisfactory explanation. The acquisition of slaves by the sultan was certainly not only permissible but clearly "legal" according to the *sharîʿa* under circumstances defined by the *pencik* or by purchase. The *devşirme* affecting "protected people," however, appears to have been "illegal," although Paul Wittek argues that according to the *shāfiʿi* legal school only those who were "people of the book" prior to 622 were entitled to *zimmi* status.[15] This might have explained why relatively few Greeks and Armenians were drafted had the Ottomans followed *shāfiʿi* doctrines; they did not. Whatever the explanation, in practice the *devşirme* exempted youths residing in cities, married young men, *voynuks*, *doğancis*, and people in other special occupations such as mining and in villages responsible for repairing passes and roads. There were other temporary exemptions, and in practice a large number of those subject to the child levy were Slavs from the Orthodox *millet*. Yet, there are too many exceptions to allow any clear pattern to emerge.

From the point of view of the sultans the *kapı kulu* system made excellent sense. It followed the established tradition of slave body guards, put the various slaves to good use, and created a group of men entirely dependent on the ruler. Bayezid I's appointment of slaves as governors was not without precedent in the Muslim world. What was new, besides the *devşirme*, was the ever broadening use to which slaves were put. When eight months after the conquest of Istanbul Mehmed II appointed a *kapı kulu*, Mahmud Adeni, grand vezir, the displacement of free-born Turks in the administration was completed, although occasionally a few of them achieved high office even before the *kapı kulu* system disintegrated some two centuries later. The reasons for this switch to slaves should be obvious from even the few facts of Ottoman history that have already been presented.

The various princes of allied Turkish states were always trying to regain independence, and even after they became leading families of the

---

15. Paul Wittek, "Devshirme and Shāriʿa," *Bulletin of the School of Oriental and African Studies* 7 (1955): 271-78.

Ottoman upper class, they stuck to the *bey* tradition and remained a force that could challenge the power of the ruler. The most remarkable example of this behavior presented thus far was the deposition of Mehmed II and the re-enthronement of Murad II engineered by Halil Cenderli in 1446. No wonder, then, that it was Mehmed II who completed the steadily growing tendency of the rulers to rely only on their slaves and that it was he who gave the slave training schools their final form.

The reason for establishing a slave-ruled administration does not explain the innovation of the *devşirme* system. There are no facts but there are three rather good arguments for the introduction of the *devşirme*. The first is simple and obvious: while the purchase of slaves was expensive, the recruitment of *devşirme* youths was free, although certain slaves continued to be purchased in the Crimea and the Caucasus. Furthermore, if the last decades of the fourteenth century are accepted as the time when the *devşirme* was introduced, this innovation coincides with a period in which slaves were not only very expensive, but in very short supply. In Europe the conquered lands were, as a rule, attached as vassal states to the Ottoman Empire and could not supply *pencik* manpower in sufficient quantity. In Central Asia, Persia, and Iraq, the rising Mongol Empire was cutting off the slave trade routes and reserving slaves for itself, while in Anatolia even direct conquests could not supply enough slaves because most of the conquered were Muslim Turks. It was at this time of slave shortages that Murad I and Bayezid I, who had great difficulties with the *beys*, extended more and more the use of slaves in the administration and military of the Ottoman Empire increasing the demand for slaves. The coinciding of these factors might possibly explain the introduction of the *devşirme* way of acquiring *kuls*.

The reason for extending the imperial slave system by collecting *devşirme* recruits served not only to recruit cannon fodder as janissaries, *sipahis* of the Porte, and later as sappers, artillery men, and other special troops. While the soldier-slaves were in the majority and were assigned to the leading men or the *acemı oğlani* (foreign sons) training establishments of the *birun* services, the most promising among them went to the various *enderun* schools as *içoğlanis* (inside sons-pages), and, as previously indicated, became the masters of the state on graduation.

The fact that most of the masters of the state for two-hundred years were of Balkan-Slav-Christian origin raises the last set of problems to be discussed before this section, and with it the introductory part of this volume, can come to a close. What did the *devşirme* mean to those whose children were affected by it? Did they profit from friends and relatives in high places, or was the experience entirely negative?

Quite apart from the inhuman features of a system that separated children forever from their parents, the negative aspects of the *devşirme* are obvious, if we remember that the recruiting ground was relatively narrow (mainly the Slav Orthodox), that the ablest youngsters were taken, and that the number of those removed was greater than the previously offered estimate of "official" *devşirme* recruits because the *yaya-başis* (janissary officer in charge of selecting young people), in cahoots with the local *kadis* and *sipahis*, made a profit by illegally gathering and selling extra boys as slaves. The ethnological and economic damage resulting from this practice has never been accurately measured or scientifically estimated, but it must have been considerable. Although these people were forced to convert to Islam and were often fanatical upholders of the Ottoman system and their new faith, it is very unlikely that they completely forgot their origin and native language. Some of the fairly good relations certain provincial officials had with their charges and the rapidly developing *modus vivendi* between some *sipahis* and the peasantry living on their fiefs can probably be explained by these memories.

There is better proof that the Ottoman officials of *devşirme* origin did indeed remember their childhood. Ibrahim *paşa* of Greek origin, who held the office of grand vezir under Süleyman I for thirteen years prior to his execution in 1536, was accused of many wrongdoings while in office, including the charge that he feathered his relatives' nests. Mehmed Sokollu, grand vezir from 1564 to 1579, not only established contact with his family, but also helped all the Serbs by successfully arguing for the re-establishment of the Metropolitanate of Peć in 1557 with his brother as archbishop even before he had achieved the highest dignity of the state. While the deeds of the most famous are the best known, it is more than likely that lesser grandees acted in a similar manner. If this had not been the case why were the *yaya-başis* frequently bribed not only to overlook one's children, but to pick them even if they did not meet the standards of recruitment? Finally, a striking example exists in the case of the Bosnian Muslims who insisted that their children be taken to Istanbul. [16] As early as 1515, at the request of the Muslim community, one thousand young Bosnians were enrolled in the schools of the *enderun* without the customary selection process that divided the *acemi* from the *icoğlanis*, and the process was repeated several times later in the sixteenth century. Both those Christian parents who paid bribes to have their sons enrolled as well as the Muslims in Bosnia and elsewhere who tried to extend the *devşirme* to their children must have expected certain advantages not only for the youngsters but for themselves as well. Otherwise their behavior would make no sense at all.

In spite of these possible advantages, the disadvantages in human, ethnological, and economic terms were overwhelming and, on balance, far more important than the beneficial aspects of the *devşirme* system. To-

16. A short presentation of Bosnian *devşirme* together with references to the pertinent documents can be found in V. L. Menage, "Devshirme," *The Encyclopaedia of Islam; New Edition* (Leiden: E. J. Brill; London: Luzac & Co., 1965-), 2:211.

gether with a use of slaves that was far more extensive than in earlier Islamic states, the *devşirme* that made this slave system possible was a unique Ottoman innovation. It is also the most prevalent example of forced conversion in the years predating the seventeenth century.

Part Two

LIFE IN THE EUROPEAN "CORE" PROVINCES
OF THE OTTOMAN EMPIRE, 1413-1574

CHAPTER 3

The Final Establishment
of Ottoman Rule, 1451-1566

1. INTRODUCTORY REMARKS

PART II of this volume deals only with the "core" provinces following the re-establishment of the empire under Mehmed I, covering the time during which the Ottoman state was strong and its various institutions functioned well. The expression "core" provinces needs some explanation.

While the Ottoman Empire was a highly centralized state with strictly defined hierarchies of classes and professions and of individuals within each social and professional group, it was also amazingly variegated. Two reasons for this diversity have already been mentioned. There was, obviously, a great difference between life in the Ottoman provinces proper and in Moldavia, Wallachia, Transylvania, and Ragusa-Dubrovnik which were vassals or allies of Istanbul. While the *kanuns* had to "conform" to the principles of the *sharī'a*, they represented basically the Ottomans' acceptance of the statutory law and even folk organization of each newly conquered region and, consequently, produced important differences among the territories ruled directly by the Ottomans, the "core" provinces. On pages 41-42 those *sancaks* have been listed that would qualify under this definition as "core" provinces. Although later they were reorganized repeatedly to finally form sub-divisions of larger *eyalets* around the middle of the seventeenth century, until the empire lost them, these were the European lands that were directly under Ottoman rule.[1] Not

1. The administrative changes were considerable. According to the 1668-69 census the *eyalet* of Rumelia (most of the Balkan peninsula) consisted of 25 *sancaks* divided into 228 *kazas*, 4 independent *vakıf* districts, and 1 *nahiye*. These figures do not include the *sancak* of Semendria (basically Serbia) and its 19 *kazas*. That *sancak* was usually part of the *eyalet* of Rumeli, but when this census was taken it was attached to the *eyalet* of Buda. Besides Buda and Rumelia, the European mainland *eyalets* were Bosnia and Temesvár prior to the seventeenth century. Shortly after 1600 the *eyalet* of Kanizsa was added, and for a period of about twenty-five years after 1660 Várad became an *eyalet* too.

only the *kanuns* produced great differences, but so did the daily behavior of political-military and legal officials, based on common sense. Clearly local problems in the *sancak* comprising the Aegean Islands (*Cezār-i bahr-i sefīd*) differed markedly from those of the *sancak* of Temesvár.

Finally, it should be remembered that the Ottoman state began its rise as a frontier society. Just as in the United States or Russia this frontier moved with the growth of the state. Although the number of *gazis* who could move with it dwindled to practically nothing, the rulers continued to treat the frontier as a special region. Large areas of the *eyalet* of Buda as well as the northern districts of the Bosnian province were handled as "frontiers," although both belonged to "core" provinces.[2] Frontier institutions were developed on the other side of the border too, and, thus, while no revival of a *gazi-akritoi* confrontation and symbiosis occurred, peculiar institutions and behavior patterns developed, which were clearly understood on both sides of the border. Border fortifications, border captains, border guards, and undeclared border wars in these regions created a new "frontier" that had very little in common with the life of the interior. These differences must be kept in mind.

A few words must be said about the time-span covered in Part II. Prior to the reign of Bayezid I most European lands were tied to the Ottoman Empire by vassalage or by alliances. Bayezid began to transform the lands of his clients into outright Ottoman provinces, but his work collapsed in 1402. It was only with the beginning of the rule of Mehmed I (1413) that the lands of Southeastern Europe became permanent Ottoman provinces. For this reason it was not difficult to pick the initial date.

The terminal date requires more explanation. Historians have picked the end of Süleyman I's reign in 1566 as the end of the "golden age" because trouble signs were already clearly visible. From the Ottoman point of view this judgment is correct. Selim II, whose reign ended with the date picked, 1574, is considered a very weak ruler. Under him the power and organization of the state were declining rapidly. There can be no doubt that already under the great reign of his father, Süleyman I, the signs of trouble were clearly visible.

From the point of view of the provincial population, however, the reign of Selim II can still be included in the "golden age" because the provinces hardly felt the troubles that were beginning to beset the central administration. Mehmed Sokollu, who remained grand vezir until 1579, was able

2. Hazim Šabanović studied this phenomenon in his numerous works dealing with Bosnia. Of these the most relevant for the problem are: *Krajište Isa-bega Ishakovića. Zbirni katastarski popis iz 1455 godine* [The military marches of Isa beğ Išaković. Survey of the landed properties in 1455], *Monumenta Turcica* (Sarajevo; Institute for Oriental Studies, 1964), vol. 2, "Bosansko krajište" [The Bosnian Military March], *Godišnjak* (Sarajevo) 9 (1957): 177-220, and especially 'Vojno uredjenje Bosne od 1463 do kraja XVI stoljeća" [The military organization of Bosnia from 1463 to the end of the sixteenth century], *Godišnjak* 11 (1960): 173-224.

to keep the machinery of state working fairly smoothly. Military expansion continued both in Hungary and elsewhere. Although the *akçe* was sinking in value, the devaluation was very gradual and did not affect the economic life of the provinces too drastically. It was during the reign of Murad III (1574-95) that economic problems became uncontrollable; inflation became rampant, and the corruption of the central administration began to spread to and seriously affect the provincial administrative machinery. Life in the provinces began to deteriorate markedly. By the end of Murad III's rule even military events had begun to turn somewhat to the disadvantage of the Ottomans. All these factors indicate that it was roughly in the 1574-95 period that the provinces began to feel the results of a weakened and corrupt central government.

The military expansions under Selim II fall at the end of the period to which this section of this volume is devoted. Between those of Murad II and those of Selim II very important territorial changes occurred. The conquests of Selim I (1512-20) interest us only indirectly because they took place mainly in Eastern Anatolia and the Arab countries, but they are of importance. Selim's was the first Ottoman state with a majority of Muslims in the population. Under the influence of the newly acquired lands and their religious leaders, secure in the Islamic nature of their state, the sultans became more orthodox and even reactionary in religious matters. The same trend existed among the *ulema* and also led first to a stricter differentiation between the Muslim and Christian *reaya*, and finally, in the seventeenth century, to the attempts at forced conversion mentioned above.

It was the conquests of Mehmed II, Bayezid II, and Süleyman I that rounded out the lands that were to become the European "core" provinces of the Ottoman Empire. For this reason they will be surveyed next.

2. EXPANSION IN EUROPE, 1451-1566

THERE are several reasons given in the literature for why the Ottoman Empire could not live in peace. Those most often mentioned are the need for booty, which was a major source of revenue for the treasury, the need for more land to establish *timars* and keep the military class satisified, the need to keep a large military establishment occupied to avoid unrest at home, the need to extend the *dar ul-Islam*, and, by the time of Mehmed II, an "imperialist mentality" of conquest for its own sake. Each of these explanations contains some truth, but they are by no means exhaustive.

While Mehmed II's conquest of Constantinople served all the above purposes, it was also a political and strategic necessity. The existence of a Christian cidatel—not only for the Christian subjects but also for all of Europe—in the middle of the sultan's lands in a very strategic position was a threat to both the internal and external security of the empire. So long as there was a Christian Emperor and a Patriarch independent of Ottoman power, the sultan's Christian subjects, who at that time constituted the majority of the population, had to be considered as potentially revolutionary elements. The threat of renewed crusades, especially after the Council of Florence, could be diminished if not fully eliminated by the conquest of the great city. The city had also become a source of intrigue, which reached into the Ottoman upper class supposedly as high as the grand vezir Halil Cenderli, whom Mehmed II executed for treason after the fall of Constantinople. Mehmed II had no choice but to lay seige to Constantinople, which fell on May 29, 1453.

There are several other explanations for the military actions taken by Mehmed II and his successors in Europe after they became masters of their new capital, Istanbul. In this discussion problems in Asia Minor, Persia, and Iraq will be disregarded, and only those related to Europe will be considered. Serbian, Bosnian, and Albanian states still existed in the Balkans, and the Duchy of Athens and several parts of the Morea were still independent. Venice had several positions on the Dalmatian coast and in the Morea, and north of the Danube-Sava line two Romanian principalities were always ready to come "to the aid" of the remaining Christian states in the Balkans, especially in alliance with the then powerful Hungarian state.

Mehmed II was more interested in conquest *per se* than in containing any challengers. Returning to the policy of Murad II, he sought to eliminate the independent states and then push the Venetians and Genoese from the coastal regions and islands. By the time of his death in 1481, he had nearly realized his first goal and had even begun to move further, attacking not only Hungary but also Italy where his troops landed, at Otranto, in 1480. The principality of Wallachia was tied to him by agreements of vassalage and tribute.

Events in Hungary, the only state that in those years could have organized a dangerous coalition against Mehmed, made his task easier and in part explain the submission of the Romanian states. After John Hunyadi died in 1452 the great feudal nobles took advantage of the minority of the thirteen-year-old king, László (Ladislas) V, to get involved in the partisan struggles and did not pay much attention to events in the Balkans. Between 1458 and 1490 Hungary had a very strong kind in Matthias, the son of John Hunyadi. Although Matthias organized a permanent army on his southern borders and was able to defeat the attacking Turkish armies, he did not pay sufficient attention to the events in the Balkans. His interests lay to the north where he first tried to gain the throne of Bohemia and then conquer Vienna in the hope of becoming Emperor of Germany. Thus, Mehmed was relatively little troubled by the potentially most dangerous of his enemies.

Instead, the sultan's greatest adversary turned out to be the Albanian hero Scanderbeg (George Kastriote). Scanderbeg and his friends formed, in 1444, the League of Lezhë (Leş, Alessio), the basis for an Albanian state. As a result of several previous Albanian insurrections, the future commander of the league's armies had to spend some time in Edirne as a hostage. As the son of a vassal chieftain, he had to fight with the Ottoman armies and proved his ability to the point where the sultan gave him the honorific title of *sancak beyi.* In 1436 the sultan sent him to govern the Albanian region of Dibra. From here he took three hundred horsemen to the sultan's army that was massing to meet an attack of Hunyadi in 1443, but he used this chance to begin his own operation, which finally led to an Albanian uprising of great size and to the establishment of the league. He fought until 1460 when he signed an armistice with Mehmed II. For a short period hostilities revived in 1462, but his final campaign began when Mehmed's forces attacked in 1464. The war was still undecided when Scanderbeg died in January, 1468. Even after his death resistance continued, and it was not until 1479 that Albania was fully subjected to Ottoman rule.

Bayezid II, a man of basically peaceful nature, did little more than finish what Mehmed II had almost brought to a successful conclusion. He withdrew his troops from Otranto, but continued to round out the Ottoman conquests in the western Balkans and succeeded in expelling the Venetians from the Morea. He secured the crucial area of the Dobrudja and forced Moldavia into a vassalage agreement with the empire. Important as these moves were, they can be considered either as mopping-up operations after the great victories of Mehmed II, or as the rounding-out of the state south of the Danube-Sava line, which was a good natural border in those days and guaranteed the relative security of the Ottoman possessions in Europe.

The actions of Süleyman I are much harder to evaluate. He was known in Europe as Suleiman the Magnificent; it was during his reign that the Ottoman Empire reached its zenith. Despite the fact that the Ottomans considered his legal work the most remarkable of his various achievements and gave him the agnomen of *kanuni,* the lawgiver, he was clearly a warrior sultan who led an army almost every year of his forty-six on the throne. Many experts blame his practically continuous absence from Istanbul for the rise of cliques in the central government, for the excessive power wielded by his grand vezirs, especially Ibrahim, and for the emergence of the inner palace, the ladies and eunuchs, as a political force leading to the rapid deterioration and corruption of the central ruling institutions.

Süleyman's conquests in Asia and in Europe were extensive and significant. According to most students of Ottoman history they were so far-reaching that they stretched the northern east-west axis of the Ottoman state to its utmost limits, running from the doors of Vienna to Iran and the Persian Gulf. Further permanent conquest would have been impossible because of the length of the campaign season and the need of the *sipahi* to return yearly to their holdings to collect their dues. The campaign season began late in the spring because of poor road conditions, and ended with the return of bad weather. Furthermore, the *sipahis* had to return to their holdings soon after harvest time in order to take care of their households and fulfill their nonmilitary local duties. These circumstances supposedly account for the troubles with the military and more importantly for the decline of the *timar* system during the following reigns.

True though these observations may be, they do not sufficiently explain the great sultan's actions, even if it is assumed that Süleyman, like several of his forefathers, took his duty to expand the realm of Islam seriously and thought of himself as the potential master of the world. His well-known alliance with Francis I of France (1515-47) and especially his Hungarian policy do not fit exactly the image of a would-be world conqueror. His reign coincided with that of the greatest of all Habsburgs, Charles V (1519-56), who came much closer to world domination than Süleyman ever did. Notwithstanding Germany's internal problems created by the beginning of the Reformation, Charles V represented a serious danger not only to Francis I but also to Süleyman. This explains the alliance of these two rulers. It also explains the contacts between the supreme lord of the great Ottoman-Muslim state, and the Protestant princes of Germany.[3] The Habsburg problem touched Hungary as well. In order to understand the possible nonimperialistic explanation of Süleyman's European expansion, it is necessary to examine the affairs of Hungary, especially as they concern the rapid expansion of Habsburg power.

The first Habsburg to be crowned King of Hungary was Albert, who became King of Hungary in 1437, King of Bohemia in 1438, and Emperor Albert II in the same year. When he died young in 1440, the Hungarian magnates, who did not want to be tied to a strong ruling house, elected Władysław III Jagiełło, King of Poland, as their ruler and crowned him Ulászló I (1440-44). The Habsburgs did not give up their claim to the Hungarian throne and turned to Albert's son, the child king László V. When Hunyadi's son King Matthias died, the Hungarian nobles, once again looking for a weak ruler, turned to another Jagiełło who was King of Bohemia, and he, Ulászló II (1490-1516), was followed on the throne by his son Lajos (Louis) II (1516-26).

During this time the Habsburgs were building their own party among the numerous magnate factions in Hungary. They made certain that they had a strong claim to Hungary's throne by a clever double marriage. Charles V's sister, Maria, became the wife of Lajos II of Hungary, while his brother, Ferdinand, the future Emperor of Germany, married Anna,

3. Stephen Fischer-Galati, *Ottoman Imperialism and German Protestantism, 1521-55* (Cambridge, Mass.: Harvard University Press, 1959).

the sister of the Hungarian ruler. Thus, unless Lajos II had sons the Habsburgs' claim to the throne was secure.

Because legitimate claims to thrones were extremely important, two others affecting the history of Southeastern Europe must be mentioned. Two daughters of King Sigismund I of Poland (1506-48) married Hungarians. Isabella married one of the richest and most powerful Hungarian magnates, the governor of Transylvania, John (János) Zápolyai, and Anna wed another great lord of the same province, Steven (István) Báthory. Both these marriages are important not only for Polish and Hungarian, but also for Ottoman history. With these dynastic considerations in mind the policy of Süleyman I can be studied further.

Süleyman's first moves were to capture Belgrade in 1521 and Rhodes and Orşova in 1522. These actions can still be explained by the need for rounding-out possessions to their "natural" borders and by reasons of security. Situated on the southern side of the Danube, Belgrade was the last major fortress in non-Ottoman hands in the Balkans. Orşova controls the Iron Gate, all-important for navigation on the Danube. Rhodes was a serious danger not only to Ottoman naval operations, but also to trade and commerce.

Süleyman's crucial move came in 1526 when he crossed the Danube, attacked Hungary, and won the decisive Battle of Mohács on August 29. At this moment Hungary represented no threat to the Ottomans, nor was it yet in Habsburg hands. The country was still suffering the effects of the great peasant revolt of 1514, was rent by factions, and had a young king quite capable of producing children. Süleyman's attack could, therefore, be interpreted as an aggressive step aimed at further conquest, but it could also be seen as a move to take advantage of the troubled situation in the country and deal a blow that would render the country powerless for many years. A weak Hungary would allow the Ottomans to concentrate on their Persian frontier where, indeed, they had great difficulties. We will never know what Süleyman had in mind when he moved into Hungary, but the policy he pursued after his victory, whose magnitude must have surprised even him, indicates that he had no permanent conquests in mind.

Ferdinand of Habsburg, twice brother-in-law of King Lajos II who lost his life at Mohács, had a better claim to the throne than did his opponent. The majority of the nobility, however, especially the lower ranking and more numerous segments, were opposed to him. Their candidate was John Zápolyai, whose army was intact. Zápolyai was the richest man in the country and was also related to the last king by marriage. He was elected King of Hungary in November, and his forces occupied most of the country evacuated by the Ottomans. The other noble faction elected Ferdinand a month later, and the two kings engaged in a civil war that lasted until 1538. At this time an agreement was reached assuring Ferdinand the throne after the death of King John, who was still childless.

The details of the civil war and the negotiations are outside the scope of this study, but Süleyman's action is not. Understandably he favored the non-Habsburg Zápolyai king, especially after John, who was very ineffective during the first years of the civil war, turned to him for help and recognized him as overlord. Nothing is better proof of Süleyman's aims than this kind of arrangement which had characterized the first European conquest of the Ottomans but had been given up in 1413 in favor of forming Ottoman provinces from conquered territories. Süleyman's numerous Hungarian campaigns between 1528 and the death of King John in 1540 had two aims: to keep Hungary out of Habsburg hands and to transform her into a vassal-buffer state. A few months before he died, John Zápolyai and his Polish wife, Isabella, had a son, John Sigismund (János Zsigmond). John promptly renounced his agreement with the Habsburgs. When he died his wife could not hold the throne for her infant son and keep the Habsburgs out. No other forces being available in the country to block Habsburg power effectively, Süleyman returned to Hungary in 1540, established the *eyalet* of Buda, and recognized the child as his vassal and king of Hungary. He assigned to him, with Isabella as regent, the eastern provinces of the country. This decision divided Hungary into three parts. The west was held by Ferdinand, the center was a Turkish *eyalet*, and the east rapidly developed into a new Ottoman vassal state, the Principality of Transylvania. When Ferdinand, who was more interested in German than in Hungarian affairs, recognized the Turkish conquests in 1547 and agreed to pay a yearly tribute to Süleyman—something that in the eyes of the Ottomans meant the acceptance of vassal status—the sultan considered all of Hungary rightfully his, consisting of one Turkish and two vassal provinces. After that date his moves resemble those of his predecessors who campaigned against any Balkan and Romanian ruler who did not act as vassals.

Even from the developments just described it appears obvious that Süleyman would have preferred, after his astounding victory at Mohács, to transform all of Hungary into a vassal state on the model of Moldavia and Wallachia, and that he viewed the final solution, the tripartite division of Hungary, as a less than desirable solution. After all, if outright conquest had been his aim he could easily have taken over the eastern lands instead of assigning them to Isabella and her son. In choosing the latter solution it appears that he realized that the lands north of the Danube-Sava line were too distant to hold without difficulty, and, more importantly, that he did not have the manpower to transform these lands into Ottoman provinces by settling Turks, assigning numerous *timars*, and taking the other measures that had transformed the Balkans.

The *eyalet* of Buda had its Muslim masters, officials, *timarlı*, etc., but hardly any of these were Turks; most were recently converted Bosnian lords. Nor was their number ever really significant. In Buda the same population exodus occurred that has been described in connection with the early Ottoman conquests in the Balkans, but there Serbs moving north from the Balkans and not ex-nomads, *akhi*, and *timarlı* replaced the departing population.

The disaffection of the tribal groups in Eastern Anatolia created numerous problems for Bayezid II, Selim I, and Süleyman I. Their ruthless extermination by Selim I and the subsequent shift of their loyalties to the rising Safavid state of Persia, which now both received and had to fight against new Turkish migrants from Central Asia, together with a decline in the Muslim birthrate as a result of continued wars, finally deprived the Ottomans of a source of manpower that had made not only previous conquests, but also the establishment of "Turkish" provinces in Europe possible. Süleyman was forced to turn to the older Ottoman practice of vassal states even in a region, Hungary, where a strong bastion had to be erected against his main European enemies, the Habsburgs.

Under these circumstances the creation of the *eyalet* of Buda was a solution forced on him by necessity and by the weakness of his Zápolyai vassals. While Buda was to become, for the next 150 years, second in importance only to Rumelia as an Ottoman "core" province, these circumstances explain why the histories of these two most important *eyalet*s differed so markedly from each other.

With the establishment of the Buda *eyalet* the creation of Ottoman provinces in Europe came to an end. The short-lived existence of the Ottoman provinces on Polish territory in the last quarter of the seventeenth century can be discounted because no real Ottoman province was established there except on paper. Nor were campaigns under the rule of Selim II important because they only changed the borders of the Buda *eyalet* and did not introduce important modifications. With Süleyman's successes the "core" provinces became established.

CHAPTER 4

City Organization and Administration

1. OTTOMAN ATTITUDES TOWARD TRADE; THE TRADE ROUTES

CITIES cannot flourish if the government does not promote those activities on which their very existence rests. Of all these activities those concerning trade are the most essential. The Ottomans have often been accused of not understanding the importance of commerce and of failing to support it. The very fact that cities developed and prospered in the Ottoman Empire contradicts this assertion. To show that there was a basis for city life and that it rested to a considerable extent on the central government's understanding of the importance of trade, it is necessary to examine trade policy before life in the cities can be discussed.

Until quite recently scholars dealing with the later Middle Ages and the early modern period have usually blamed the decline of Byzantium and the rise of the Ottoman Empire for the disruption of the Mediterranean trade that occurred in those periods. Recent scholarship has shown that this view was erroneous, but the image of the Turks as savage horsemen destroying and looting still prevails. The great interest that the Ottomans had in trade and production, while known to the experts, still awaits a specialized monograph. Nevertheless, enough is already known to be able to state that the Ottomans regarded economic pursuits, including manfacture and trade, as essential to the well-being and financial stability of their state and favored such pursuits, although they regulated and taxed the producers and traders heavily.

Their approach is not surprising; it follows logically from both the Ottomans' experience and their view of the state. Although weakened considerably by the time the Ottomans entered on the stage of history, Byzantium still had the financial resources to buy off enemies or to subsidize allies, including the early Ottomans. The few manufactured goods needed by the western Anatolians were supplied, to a considerable degree, by merchants in touch with the imperial city, and the various caravan

72

routes and ships laden with merchandise going to Byzantium passed near and later through Ottoman-held territory. It was not difficult to connect this lively commercial activity with the seemingly inexhaustible supply of money the Byzantines appeared to have. If the Ottomans were willing to fight for booty, as to some extent they were, how much more tempting must the easier, Byzantine way have been.

Nor should it be forgotten that the Ottoman Empire was the domain of the House of Osman and that its official name included the adjective "well flourishing." Almost by definition Allah's domain had to flourish, but under the Ottomans it was also considered the duty of the subjects to add to the power and prosperity of the ruling house. Productive work was, therefore, considered not only a religious and civic duty, but also a pledge of loyalty to the ruler. On the other hand, it was part of the sultans' *hadd* to create circumstances that contributed to the well-being of their subjects. In this manner experience, basic philosophy, and the duties of both ruler and ruled combined with the growing needs of an expanding state, court, and bureaucracy to create a climate favorable to economic pursuits.

Beginning with their capture of Bursa in 1326, the Ottomans not only confirmed the privileges of artisans and traders in each city that they conquered, but also tried very hard to build up flourishing centers of manufacture and trade. These cities were connected by roads, and those among the *zimmi* who were exempt from various taxes to maintain them in good repair worked not only on major military, but also on other roads whose significance was mainly commercial. The privileges accorded to those who served in the merchant marine fall into the same category of special treatments accorded to the road crews.

The major roads in the European provinces, both military and commercial, were often the old Roman *iters* and had been in use since the days of the Roman Empire. The major road started out from Istanbul, the terminal point of numerous roads coming from Asia, Asia Minor, and the Arab lands, and led to Edirne. There it split and moved on in four directions. The northern line passed through the Dobrudja to the mouth of the Danube and followed the Prut to the northern border of Moldavia, where it entered Polish territory. The southern side road leading to Gallipoli was short but very important strategically. The major, central road moved from Edirne to Plovdiv, Sofia, Niš, Belgrade, and Buda. Very important commercially, this was also the major military highway. The fourth main line ran south of the major military highway to Serres, Salonika, Monastir, and Ohrid, reaching the Adriatic at Durrës (Dıraç, Drač, Durazzo), and was primarily of commercial importance. The main military highway was of economic importance not only because it connected Istanbul-Edirne and Niš-Belgrade-Buda, but also because it served as the first half of an extremely important trade route, the fifth major artery, that forked off near Sofia at Pazardzhik (Tatarpazarcik) and passed through Skopje (Üsküb,

Üsküp, Skoplje, Skopije, Shkupi), Priština (Priştina), Sarajevo, and Mostar before reaching Dubrovnik (Ragusa) on the sea. Secondary roads branched off from these main roads. Another major commercial "highway" was, of course, the Danube, and the rivers feeding it or leading to the Aegean Sea were also important trade routes.[1]

The most important cities were located along these major and minor roads and waterways. Several, as indicated earlier, were Ottoman foundations, but the great majority owed their existence to their geographic locations and had been urban centers since Roman or Byzantine times. A few had been established by the Slavs.[2] Although these cities housed only a minority of the population, they became the economic heart of the Ottoman Empire. During the period presently under discussion the population of most of them increased, thanks in part to the arrival of Turkish settlers, in part to the influx of people from the countryside who sought refuge in times of war, and in part to the opportunities city life offered. These cities supported the state not only by their production and trade, but also by the considerable tax revenue these activities produced. By analyzing them from different angles it is possible to explain much about life in Southeastern Europe during the best years of the Ottoman Empire. The task is made easier by the fact that most cities in the "core" eyalets of Rumelia and Bosnia were organized along similar lines. Differences existed, depending on location, major economic activity, and other circumstances, but the basic organization and life patterns were nearly identical. Cities in Hungary and the Aegean region offer significantly divergent patterns and warrant separate description.

2. THE LAYOUT OF CITIES IN THE "CORE" PROVINCES

PRACTICALLY every city in the world has a business district, good and bad residential neighborhoods, industrial districts or suburbs, parks and recreational centers, "ghettos," and several other similar sections. The combination of these areas determines the unique nature of each city. In older European cities, whose histories go back to antiquity or medieval times, it is still possible to point to the old part of the city built around some fortification or royal or noble residence and separated from the new districts by a belt of major avenues or boulevards that follow the lines of the protective walls of the old city.

Cities in Southeastern Europe follow this familiar pattern almost without exception. They grew up around the acropoleis of the old Greek cities

1. Of the easily accessible works Inalcık, *Ottoman Empire*, pp. 122-23 has the best map of Ottoman roads.

2. An excellent short historical survey of the Balkan cities is Traian Stoianovich, "Model and Mirror of the Premodern Balkan City," in Nikolai Todorov, ed., *La Ville Balkanique, XVe-XIXe siècles*, vol. 3 of *Studia Balcanica* (Sofia: Bulgarian Academy of Sciences, 1970), pp. 83-110. The entire volume deserves close attention.

or around important geographical features like the castle hill in Buda, the Kalimegdan in Belgrade, the small peninsula between the Golden Horn and the Sea of Marmara in Constantinople, or the various bays along the sea coast and the Danube that offered the best port facilities. The Ottomans did not disturb the pattern in the cities that they took over, although they did alter the character of the focal points by making them Turkish or Islamic and by adding new ones such as schools and markets. In the cities that they established or that grew spontaneously around Ottoman focal points the same pattern was copied.

What differentiates any given city under Ottoman rule from what it had been prior to conquest was that the divisions existing between districts were institutionalized and made more strict and explicit. The repeatedly mentioned Ottoman custom of arranging everything in a strict hierarchical order and producing regulations for everything was reflected in their cities also. In a sense the European cities of the empire took on a Near Eastern character. Not only were the inhabitants and professions, as will be discussed later in this chapter, ranked in strict order, but so were their places of business and habitation.

The city was really nothing more than a conglomeration of more or less self-contained boroughs grouped around a common core. Each borough was separated from the others either by natural obstacles such as ravines or by walls. These walls were often the windowless backs of houses with doors that were closed at night. On the basis of data covering several cities Stoianovich has calculated that the "average" borough (*mahalle*) contained between twenty-five and fifty houses; those of really large centers like Istanbul, Edirne, and Athens were considerably larger.[3] This author's estimates based on his own research confirm Stoianovich's findings. In *sancaks* where habitations were taxed by the number of doors opening on a street, the *mahalles* were further subdivided by additional walls surrounding large courtyards which enclosed several habitations but had only one door opening on the street. Not only did Muslims, Christians, and Jews live in different *mahalles*, but the practitioners of the various trades belonging to the three *millets* lived in one or several separate boroughs, depending on their number in a given city. The distance of the *mahalles* from the center of the city depended on the religion and profession of those who lived in them.

Each *mahalle* had its own night watchmen and was administered by its own headman, who was usually called *muhtar* but sometimes *şeyh*. If it was large enough, it had its own place of worship and clergymen, coffee house, public bath, and small local market. The walls are now gone, but the names of the districts remain in today's Balkan cities to remind us even now of the old *mahalles*.

3. Stoianovich, "Model and Mirror," p. 96.

A bird's eye view of any city disclosed to the observer the plan of the city. Its center was clearly distinguishable by the major mosques, large buildings housing the chief markets, a fortress if any, and even a large open square. The size and height of structures in a given *mahalles* indicated clearly to which *millet* its inhabitants belonged. Not only were public buildings more substantially constructed than were the private homes, but their shapes were also indicative of their functions. Thus, while Christian churches could not be high or have towers, their manner of construction and shape differentiated them from the occasional synagogue and indicated whether a given *mahalle* was inhabited by Christians or Jews. Not only did the lack of minarets indicate the location of a non-Muslim *mahalle*, but so did the height of houses. Each city had its own regulations, but Muslim houses were by law always higher than the homes of *zimmi* while shops and locales of manufacture outside the central market area were limited to even less footage vertically. The numerous building regulations and zoning laws were strictly enforced, giving the Ottoman city its specific look and characteristic. For the most part residences were very small and consisted of one room that served all purposes, including food preparation, although every city also had large buildings of several stories and rooms.[4] In spite of these rather limited quarters built along narrow and winding streets, the cities were clean, as noted by all Europeans who traveled through the European provinces of Turkey.

The great majority of the people living in the *mahalles* worked in the center of the city. The configuration of this area differed depending on the origin of the city, on its exact location within city limits, and on its major buildings. Whatever its exact lay-out and location, it almost always included the major mosque of the city and the great market, and depending on the type of pious endowments bestowed on it by various dignitaries a number of fountains, *medreses*, public baths, inns of various types, at least one major square, and on its fringes the most elegant homes of the dignitaries and richest merchants. The larger the city, the greater were the number of mosques and other public buildings and the greater the likelihood of a fortress or garrison.

Various religious, commercial, and public service buildings, including in some cases hospitals, were always added by the Ottomans to those already in existence at their arrival. They usually formed part of a smaller or larger *imaret*, another old Muslim institution adopted by the Ottomans that had roots in one of the "Five Pillars of Faith," almsgiving. The donor set aside income-producing property, most often tracts of agricultural

4. For a detailed calculation of the percentages of houses of various sizes in the major Bulgarian cities under Ottoman rule see Nikolai Todorov, "La differenciation de la population urbaine aux XVIIIe siècle d'après des registres des cadis de Vidin, Sofia et Ruse," *La Ville Balcanique*, pp. 45-62.

land which were frequently large enough to become a separate administrative entity (see Chapter 3, note 1), or revenues produced by tolls, rents, etc., to support a specified "good cause." He drew up a document of donation (*vakfiye*), and after it was properly registered by the competent *kadi* and confirmed by the sultan, the income-producing property became a *vakıf*, the unalienable property of God. The income could be used only for the originally specified purpose. The buildings that were erected for the Glory of God were of stone or brick and were to last for eternity. They dominated the cities' skylines. The *tekkes* and *zaviyes* of the *akhi* and *dervişes* as well as a few large warehouses of the richest merchants complete the picture of the center of each town and city.

While schools, baths, fountains, inns, and other public buildings served the people's daily needs, the mosques served their spiritual needs, and the hospitals took care of their health problems, the market (*çarşi*) determined their livelihood and the prosperity of the city. The heart of the market was the *bedestan*, called bazaar by the European travelers. Often the most impressive building in the city, apart from the great mosques, the *bedestan* was a strong structure, a virtual fortress of the economy, with thick walls, heavy gates, and its own force of watchmen. It contained stores dealing in the most expensive goods, as well as the safe deposit vault where the merchants kept their money and the rich of the city their cash and other valuables. The stores and even workshops of the lesser crafts ranged along narrow streets around these impressive, covered buildings and were often covered by mats to keep out the rain and sun. Within both the *bedestan* and the *çarşi* surrounding it the various artisans and craftsmen, traders, and merchants were assigned stalls in accordance with their position in the official hierarchy of economic endeavors. Proximity to the center of the *bedestan* marked the importance of the stall to the economy of the city. The practitioners of a given profession always worked in a specific location irrespective of their religion. Thus, the carpet vendors worked on the street of carpet vendors, tailors on the street of tailors, and so on. When a city was large enough to require several markets, each was organized along the same pattern around smaller *bedestans* or the most important public building in a given part of the city.

3. THE GUILD SYSTEM AND THE CITY GOVERNMENT

ALL *reaya* of the Ottoman Empire belonged to officially listed classes ranked according to importance. At the very bottom of the social scale were Gypsies and other people with no visible permanent professional affiliation. Together with the nomads these people did not fit neatly into the Ottoman social pyramid, and pressure was often brought on them to move away or to settle into "useful" occupations. The other social classes were all considered useful, and therefore their membership had to be protected for the good of the state. That meant that in theory social lines were frozen, although people were encouraged to better their position within their own class.

The lowest ranking of these useful classes were the peasants and the animal husbandsmen. Next in importance came the members of a group called *esnaf*, the small merchants and tradesmen who served local markets and needs. Above the *esnaf* came the craftsmen, and at the very top were the large merchants, *tüccars* or *bazirgans*, who handled empire-wide or export-import trade. All but the peasantry lived and worked in the cities. The top three classes worked in and around the *bedestans* of the cities, and, with the addition of the drifters, civil, military, and religious officials, and the soldiers of the garrison, if any, formed the population. While the ratio between Muslims and *zimmis* varied from town to town, and while the Muslims enjoyed certain tax advantages and received better living quarters, the daily lives and activities of all these peope followed a similar pattern. Their activities were regulated by guilds, and the various officers of these guilds, together with the numerous government officials appointed to supervise, constituted "city government." There was no formal municipal government with officers of its own. The members of the *esnaf* group and all the craftsmen were organized in guilds and very strictly regulated, while the top group of *tüccars* was practically free to run its affairs as it pleased acquiring, as a result, great import beyond the limits of their own professions.

By dealing with the guilds and their activities not only can life in the city be presented, but, by mentioning the various state-appointed officials that controlled these activities or with whom the guild masters had to negotiate, most of the city government can also be described. To make this presentation intelligible, it is necessary to examine the principles that regulated both internal, voluntary and external, state-imposed regulations concerning the guilds.

Although there were numerous guilds in the cities before the Ottoman conquest, the *akhi* organizations that followed the armies of the sultan quickly absorbed them. They brought their organizations and *futuwwas* with them, but were broad-minded enough to incorporate the existing regulations and often even religious practices. Regardless of the *millet* to which they belonged, people usually became members of the same guild, produced or sold their goods on the same street of the *çarşi*, and followed the same rules and regulations, although they lived in different *mahalles*. Most of them were involved in economic activities that had only a rather narrowly limited scope, the utilizations of locally produced or imported raw materials for the manufacture and subsequent sale of articles needed by the city and the countryside. As will be seen, these limitations together with guild regulations set bounds to activities and to the number of individuals that any given guild could accommodate. Admission to the various guilds involved a mystic religious ceremony, which varied ac-

cording to the religion of the entrants. Their number was strictly regulated, as were their activities in accordance with the just mentioned two
factors unless the guild produced goods for the empire-wide internal or
the export trade.

The guilds had a social-moral function besides an economic one. They
acted as a benevolent society, taking care of those among them in need,
especially widows and orphans. The moral, religious, and beneficial activities of each guild were supervised by the old head of the fraternity, the
şeyh, who was considered the highest ranking member, but economic
power rested with the *kethüda*[5] whom the masters elected from their own
ranks. The latter ran the business side of the guild, negotiated with other
guilds and with government officials, and represented his fellows when
decisions had to be made affecting the whole city. Thus, he became a
member of the "city government." When business that concerned all
guilds came up, another official, who had the same title, became important. The second *kethüda* was the city's agent and not a guild official. He
took matters to the capital when the inhabitants wished to have grievances redressed. In order for a guild to be established, the two chief officials had to be selected first. They then went to the *kadi* and registered
the association and its rules, provided no opposition was raised by existing guilds.

When new officials were elected, they too had to be registered by the
kadi who, in these cases, acted as a cross between a notary public and a
keeper of city records. In addition to the *şeyh* and the *kethüda*, the following also had to be registered: the *yeğitbaşı* and his deputy, and the
two officials called *ehl-i hibre*. Both were selected from among the *usta*
(masters) by their colleagues. The *veğitbaşı* acted as a buying agent for the
guild and procured raw materials for all masters. He was also responsible
for picking up and delivering the finished goods, depending on their nature, to other guilds, to shops in the *çarşi*, or to other buyers. The *ehl-i
hibre* were involved in quality and price control and settled any disputes
about workers.

The *usta* were the full members of the guilds. In large shops *kalfas*
worked under the master. Full members of the guilds, both had earned
their mastership, but the *kalfas* were unable, for various reasons, to open
their own establishments because there could only be a certain number in
a given city. They were the real master craftsmen. Lower in the scale
came the *gediks*, journeymen, and the *çiraks*, apprentices. Although

5. *Kethüda* is one of those Ottoman terms that can only be understood in context. It
has a vague basic meaning that approximates "agent." The *kethüda* of the guilds was
their agent in dealing with the authorities, but most of his duties were performed within
the guilds of which he was chief officer. All major officials, the *beylerbeyis*, *defterdars*,
etc., had officials under them bearing this title, but these were either "seconds in command," or officials with very important functions of their own. The *kethüda* also denoted a city official to be discussed later in this chapter.

Muslims and *zimmis* were treated equally in the guilds in this first, well-regulated period, the existence of *kalfas* indicates that while the guilds were producers and distributors, they were also an economically repressive force.

In many ways the activities of Ottoman guilds paralleled those of the guilds of medieval Europe. Like their western counterparts, their aim was two-fold: to produce enough to cover local needs and to assure a decent living to their members, and to prevent any "outsider" from infringing on their monopoly. Both the western guilds and those in the Ottoman Empire achieved these goals by strictly regulating production, quality, prices, and membership. Yet, there was a great difference. In major western urban centers the guilds responded to economic stimuli and grew as trade, production, and urbanization expanded, until they reached a limit beyond which they could not go. This led to their decline and final dissolution. In the Ottoman Empire, where everything was strictly regulated supposedly for eternity, once the number of masters of a given guild had been fixed in a given location, it was kept constant. This arrangement protected the interest of the guild members, but it hampered the growth of the various production sectors and, therefore, the growth of the city and the economy. This led to numerous problems including disregard of regulations in spite of repeated imperial edicts, and the creation of new guilds and even illegal associations. The least harmful of these developments was the first because it corresponded to real economic needs; however, by its very illegality it tended to lead to bribes and other corrupt practices. The creation of new guilds presented greater difficulties. During this early period it produced such degrees of specialization that prices steadily increased and new monopolies were created. A good example of this tendency is the production of woolen cloth after the settlement of Sephardic Jews in Salonika. Their guild rapidly achieved a monopolistic position preventing the new skill from spreading and necessitating continued large-scale importation of woolen goods. The restrictive practices of the guilds created the most problems, but this occurred in the later period when it will be analyzed.

Restrictive practices also operated within the guilds and stifled both innovation and incentive. Laws that conformed with a section of the sacred law, the *hisba*, regulated prices, weights, and quality and punished cheaters of all kinds. Each workshop received enough raw material and skilled labor to assure its owner and his family and employees of a living. *Hisba* legislation was based on the old Islamic *ihtisab*, i.e., part of the ruler's duties that enjoined him to make certain that his subjects were treated fairly, and its aim was to secure just that for both producer and consumer.

Unfortunately, however, quality control was so strict that it virtually prevented the introduction of new and better methods and ideas, and, coupled with the Muslim belief that earthly life is only a preparation for paradise and that, therefore, ostentatious good living was not only unnecessary but practically sinful, these controls also regulated profits very strictly without regard to needs and changing market conditions. Most professions were limited to a 10 percent profit.

If regulations had achieved the Muslim ideal of an egalitarian society, they could be defended. The law, however, favored the middle man at the expense of the producer, because it did not cover the *tüccar* class, which conducted business according to the principles of supply and demand and made tremendous profits. Furthermore, it did not prevent amazing inequalities from developing within the ranks of each guild. It could not prevent *tüccars* from establishing a sort of putting-out system and thus degrading some masters, nor did it stop them and other capitalists who made a lot of money from large *timars* from using their influence to have some regulations waived in favor of those guild masters in whose enterprises they had become silent partners. Todorov gives good examples of this inequality in a study of the value of workshops that were registered by the *kadis* as inheritances. Theoretically, each of these should have belonged to a master. In fact, he found the following distribution:[6]

	8 individuals owned	more than 10 workshops
a minimum of 1,759 workshops	53 " " " " 5 "
	65 " " either 3 or 4 "
	126 " " " " 2 "
	834 " " " " 1 "

These figures indicate that of the 925 workshops listed in the first four lines, only 252 were legally owned if the guild regulations serve as the norm of legality. His study also reveals that these multishop owners were not artisans. One of those who owned 5 shops, Elhac Musa, also owned 8½ mills, 1¼ inns, and considerable other valuables.[7] Clearly a man like the tailor Farvan, who left no shop to his heirs and whose tools were valued at only 1.5 *kuruş*, worked for somebody like Elhac Musa. On the other hand, Lazar, who was in the same profession and left behind tools, raw materials, and finished goods valued at 1,171 *kuruş*, was clearly a well-established *usta* in his own right.[8]

While Todorov's data come from the eighteenth century and are based on the study of three cities only, there can be no doubt that the development that led to these disparities was not limited to his localities and must

6. Todorov, "Population urbaine," p. 57. The 65 owners' holdings listed as 3 or 4 were calculated as 65 times 3.5 = 228. All others were calculated at the minimum given for their group.
7. *Ibid.*, p. 60
8. *Ibid.*

have begun in the previous centuries. Clearly, the strict guild regulations and *hisba*-based laws, while serving certain goals satisfactorily, did not prevent abuse and were detrimental to economic development. This might explain in part why the cities of the "core" provinces that grew in population and prospered at the beginning of the Ottoman period shrank in size in the later centuries.

The different professions not only produced goods, but also added considerably to the revenue of the state. All members paid taxes on their homes and workshops, additional fees for every document they needed, dues for permission to get married and to inherit, a tax on remaining unmarried after a certain age—in short on almost every possible activity of their personal lives. If they were *zimmi* they also paid the *cizye*, and all of them paid numerous fines to the *kadi* for an incredible number of "misdemeanors," like talking unkindly to a fellow citizen. To these can be added the extraordinary taxes like the present due to the sultan on his accession and special war contributions. They also contributed handsomely through their professions. Taxes had to be paid on raw material brought into the town. During transport there were numerous tolls at river crossings and other strategic locations on the road. When the materials finally reached the city they were inspected by one of the city officials, the *muhtesib*, who established their fair value and levied a tax before, again under his supervision, they could be sold by the assigned broker to the guilds for distribution to the various workshops. This same official was in charge of markets, weights, and quality control, independently of the guild officials and the collector of the various market dues. With the help of the *kadi* and the guild officers he fixed prices. In short he was the state-appointed economic master of the city, and one of his main duties was the collection of numerous taxes and fees. The magnitude of the amounts collected becomes evident from the figures available for 1553, when the empire was at its military and economic zenith. The income of the state treasury that year amounted to about 12,750,000 gold ducats. Of this sum the *cizye* constituted 1,000,000, the land tax 800,000, and trade and custom related revenues 1,200,000 ducats.[9]

The mentioned *kethüda* and the various *kethüda*s of the guilds, the *muhtesib*, the all-important *kadi*, or in smaller localities his *naib*, and on the *mahalle* level the *muhtars*, all constituted something resembling "city government." The last-mentioned officials were paired with a third form of *kethüda*, the city-appointed supervisor of the *mahalle*. With the exception of the judicial-religious-public notary functionary, the *kadi*, all the functionaries worked in pairs. Each of these pairs had an "elected" and an appointed member: guild *kethüda*s-city *kethüda*; *muhtesib-ehl-i hibre*;

9. Afet Inan, *Aperçu general sur l'histoire économique de l'Empire Turc-Ottoman* (Istanbul: Maarif Matbaasi, 1941), p. 28.

muhtar-mahalle kethüda, with the appointed offical carrying more authority. In addition, everywhere there was a tax collector, although his
rank and personality differed greatly; for example, he could be an appointed official, a local dignitary, or a tax farmer. Equally omnipresent
were the "police" officials who could be *subaşis, çavus başis* commanding
forces usually called *çavuşes* whose main duty was to carry out the decisions and punishment decided on by the various authorities. Although
these officials were not considered members of the city's administration, in
those places that were seats of *sancaks* or *kazas* the entire component of
Ottoman provincial officials was present and carried great weight, especially if the city was either part of a given *bey's sancak,* or of an imperial
or other type of *has.* Other informal participants in the local decision-
making process were the officers of *vakıf*-supported establishments (public
baths, inns, etc.) because the institutions under their supervision played
an important role in the city's life, and because they frequently disposed
of considerable sums of money. If the *vakıf* establishment happened to be
a *medrese* the role of the teacher and his students in the life of the city was
far from negligible. Even less official, but often important was the role of
the Christian and Jewish clergy and teachers, especially in those cities in
which members belonging to their *millets* constituted important segments of the most essential guilds.

One last group, the city notables, influenced the life of each place.
These men always carried great weight and participated in the discus-
sions leading to decisions that either affected the entire city or brought it
in touch with authorities on a higher than local level. In this category
belonged the *tüccars* and people who became with time known as *âyans.*
The former will be discussed shortly. The latter were rich and distinguished people, either wealthy *timarlı* who lived in the city nearest to
their fiefs or retired officials and their descendants who brought their
prestige and often their wealth to their places of retirement. From behind
the scenes they often controlled much of the city's economy, had great
prestige due to their social position, and often enjoyed good connections
in the capital. They were consulted on most issues of importance.

What developed was not a city government in the formal, accepted
sense of the word, but rather a "city government" consisting of a group of
people who were "elected" by their peers, appointed, or enjoyed local
presitge, and constituting something like a city oligarchy. That "government" was responsible for carrying out the various laws and regulations,
but it also kept the city's interests in mind, consulted others, made decisions, and in numerous cases formulated petitions or lists of grievances
that either the city *kethüda* or one of the influential *âyans* took to the *beylerbeyi,* the *sancak beyi,* and in some cases even to the central government.

The *âyans* did not belong to the *reaya* class, although they lived among them, participated in their activities, and belonged to the small "upper class" of each city; it was the *tüccars* who were members of the "flock." Whether Muslim or *zimmi*, their position differed markedly from all professional Ottomans and *reayas* discussed so far, and indicates the importance the government attached to large-scale economic activity. Without them the Ottoman economy could hardly have functioned. As already indicated, they were the people who were involved in long-distance internal commerce and in the export-import trades. In the European provinces of the empire there were Turks, Greeks, Serbs, Jews, and occasionally some Armenians in their ranks. This group was initially free from regulations, unlike everyone else in Ottoman society. Although its activities, including relationships of its members with each other, were controlled, the various rules and regulations applying to them can properly be compared to commercial and business law in the western sense without which any regular trading activity would be difficult to organize. Furthermore, while the *tüccars*, too, were guild-merchants, the Muslim disdain for those who accumulated wealth did not apply to them; on the contrary, they were supposed to accumulate wealth (*mal*), and for these reasons *hisba* regulations did not apply to them.

Like the lower ranking merchants and the artisans who contributed to the welfare of the state both by their labor and the taxes and dues paid, the *tüccars* performed many other functions. The most important of these was the distribution of raw material, food, and finished goods throughout the empire. Next in importance came their activities in the export-import trade, and, finally, from the viewpoint of the central government, their large contributions in customs and tolls. All these were large-scale activities in most cases or, in the case of luxury goods, high in value. Few were those *tüccars* who had enough capital to handle these activities, and all needed associates. These circumstances resulted in a variety of partnerships and contracts, and the establishment of chains of agencies regulated by law. Whatever the composition of a given business complex, a single individual or a few men in partnership were in command of the entire operation and made the largest profits. While these *tüccars* concentrated in major trade centers, in Istanbul, Edirne, Athens, Salonika, Sarajevo, Belgrade, and a few others, smaller trade centers, including the major port cities on the Danube or along the Aegean coast, also served as the homes of some very important commercial entrepreneurs. Even the smallest city harbored at least a few agents of the big enterprises. These men, who were in touch with others all over the state, were the main sources of domestic and foreign news.

Naturally, it was *tüccars* who took advantage of the state's encouragement and accumulated considerable liquid wealth; only rarely did they acquire real estate, apart from their own homes and summer houses. With the help of this accumulation they started a sort of putting-out system when there was a demand for some merchandise that was not produced in sufficient quantity by the guilds. This system not only undercut the autonomy of the guilds, but even extended into the countryside in the form of cottage industries. Unlike in the West, however, it never developed into the beginning of a true industrial establishment.

There were probably two main reasons for the *tüccars'* reluctance to go beyond the putting-out system. First, they were organized as trading associations. The putting-out system could be justified as a source for trade in those goods they were supposed to sell, but industrial enterprises would have taken these capitalists into activities for which they were not licensed, and this would have been too risky. Second, the few industries that did exist, mainly those connected with the military establishment, were state-owned and worked by slave labor. They presented a model that the *tüccars* could not duplicate.

While the *tüccars* were among the most important and influential inhabitants of every city, they were also among the least popular. Given the profession and the understanding of the market economy of these people, it is not amazing that they always aimed to maximize their profits involving speculative ventures of the simplest kind like buying cheap and selling high. Because this speculative activity included food and raw materials, the *tüccars* were blamed for all shortages that occurred occasionally. Their standing sank even lower in the later period when their wealth permitted them to go into such professions as tax farming, which was certainly very unpopular with the population at large. This last-mentioned activity, together with the loans they were able to extend to the central government, made these men the only *reaya*, except for a few translators, clerks, and occasional professionals like doctors, who managed to become part of the administrative-political establishment of the Ottoman Empire even while it was still functioning well.

The *tüccars'* only serious competition came from other merchants who performed the same duties and lived in the same cities but enjoyed extraterritorial status because they were not subjects of the sultan. Not only did these merchants contribute to the economic life of the "core" provinces' cities and to that of the empire as a whole, but they were also Southeast Europeans. Most of them were citizens of the city republic of Ragusa, but some came from other Dalmatian cities. Their *mahalles* were cities within cities because they were not subject to the local authorities and had the privileges of organizing and running their own communities in accordance with the laws of their native cities. Like the *tüccars*, they belonged to large and often very complicated business establishments, but their home offices, banks, and other sources of credit lay outside the sultan's realm. It is astounding to find Ragusan colonies in practically every important city of the European provinces of the Ottoman Empire. One gains the impression that at least half of the city republic's citizens lived outside its borders.

These Dalmatian colonies are important for the history of Southeast European people not only from the commercial, but also from the religious and cultural point of view. Life in Dalmatian towns was closely tied to that of Italy and therefore mirrored, as will be seen in Part Three, the various cultural, political, and other changes that occurred there. The colonists who came from these cities to those of the Balkan interior brought this western culture with them. Although they lived in isolated, self-contained settlements in each city, both by choice and in accordance with Ottoman regulations, they could not avoid all contact with their neighbors. If nothing else, their architecture, clothing, and the organization of their community was something the local inhabitants could not avoid observing. It should also be remembered that these people were Roman Catholics. By bringing their priests with them, they offered an alternative to the Orthodox *millet*, although they were strictly forbidden to engage in missionary activities. Nevertheless, their very presence contributed to the appearance of Roman Catholics as far east as Bulgaria where they were severely persecuted in the seventeenth century. Not only were the Dalmatians as prosperous as the *tüccar*s were, and the *Kulturträger* of the Balkans during the long centuries of Ottoman rule among the Slavs, but, unlike their Greek and Slav fellow merchants, they represented the only example of a different way of life for the inhabitants of the European Ottoman provinces. Their influence, at least on the cities, cannot be overvalued.

Each city had an additional group of inhabitants who belonged to the lowest social order, the "drifters" and Gypsies. These "undesirables," were needed to carry loads and perform some of the most demeaning labor. Since they were outside the "pale" very little is known about them except in those cases where the *kadis*' records show punitive actions taken against them individually or as a group, or where the records speak of attempts to get rid of them altogether. All that can be said for certain is that they were not considered a part of the city population and had no real *mahalle*s of their own. Each night they returned to whatever type of housing they were able to erect beyond the city limits. They represent the urban equivalent of the nomads and *yürük*s.

Generalized as this image of the "core" province's city is, it represents a fairly accurate description that, with slight modification, can be applied to most Ottoman cities. Istanbul is one of the great exceptions, although it too had its guilds, *mahalle*s, and the various functionaries mentioned. The imperial capital had to have features that no other city had, but because it does not truly fall within the scope of this survey, and also because numerous excellent works deal with this city and its special institutions it will not be covered. There are, nevertheless, a few other peculiar city situations that deserve special mention.

4. THE "ATYPICAL" CITY OF THE "CORE" PROVINCES

SEVERAL types of settlements in the "core" provinces do not conform fully to the description of cities presented so far in this chapter. Only the most important of these can be discussed, because if all were treated a special study would have to be written. One of the major groups, the border settlements, was more of a rural than an urban phenomenon and belongs, therefore, in the next chapter. Such settlements were located mainly in those lands bordering on Habsburg possessions.

Geographically nearest to these border settlements were the towns of Hungary, Slavonia, Eastern Croatia, and northern Bosnia. Prior to the Ottoman conquest all these regions were either Hungarian or alternately Hungarian, Serbian, or Bosnian, and so they were neither typically Balkan nor truly western cities although in Hungary "royal free cities" began to develop paralleling developments in the West. Most of the Slav cities developed along the lines already described, but some acquired interesting privileges. Most notable is the case of the almost purely Muslim town of Sarajevo, which was really "self-governing" to the point where troops were not permitted to enter the place.

Ottoman occupation in the Balkans usually did not entail large-scale permanent destruction, although life along the major military roads was not secure until Ottoman rule was firmly established, and occasional campaigns produced major damage. These devastations were, as a rule, rapidly made good. The *timarlı* needed peasants to work the land, and when the original population did not return the Ottomans settled Turks and/or transplanted other people forcibly to the areas where they were needed. The importance the Ottomans placed on trade, commerce, and crafts has been mentioned and their settling in towns and cities that, during the first period of their rule, prospered was also discussed.

Once the Ottomans crossed the Danube-Sava line the situation changed. The most important variations occurred on the Hungarian-Slav border and in Hungary proper. Here two phenomena deserve special attention, especially in view of modern historical developments. First, as indicated, the Ottomans attempted to create vassal states, and later, when they established their own *eyalets* in these lands, they lacked settlers. Even if such people had been available, it is unlikely that the government would have sponsored large settlements.

When the Ottomans moved into Croatia-Slavonia-Hungary the situation resembled very much that which followed the first permanent Ottoman crossing of the Dardanelles. There were Christian states nearby —Habsburg Hungary and Transylvania—to which the population could flee. Their flight in this case was encouraged by the nobility, which itself had fled and urged its dependents to follow. The Ottomans did not have the manpower that they had had in the fourteenth century to fill this void. Furthermore, the settlement of nomads would not have worked in these regions because of the nature of the land.

The large plain between the Danube and Tisza (Theiss) rivers, the Great Hungarian Plain, is basically poor land. Prior to the arrival of the Ottomans it had supported a relatively large population (estimates run from three to five million) and produced a great variety of grains. Steady deforestation, however, had reached the point where it threatened the water supply for crop production. The cultivators had to know exactly how to operate under these special conditions. When they ran away the land apidly deteriorated; spring floods of unregulated rivers, sand dunes, and alkali flats produced a wasteland of marshes. Newly settled nomads working basic small *çifts* could not have survived under these conditions. The original damage caused by Süleyman I's first campaigns could possibly have been repaired had not the civil war between the two kings, Süleyman's numerous interventions, and finally the fact that the Habsburg-Ottoman wars, which lasted almost continuously until 1699, made these lands into a permanent frontier battlefield creating an erosion that can be observed even today.

The permanent battlefield situation coupled with soil erosion and the flight of the population made it very difficult for cities and their burghers to make a living. Many Magyars and most Germans followed the example of the nobility and peasantry and moved away. The major Ottoman administrative centers, including Buda, Pest, Pécs (Fünfkirchen), and Szeged (Szegedin), attracted the necessary administrators, garrisons, and artisans and tradesmen as in the Balkans. Yet here, unlike in the Balkans, there was no indigenous population with which to cooperate and coexist; consequently, these places became truly Muslim towns. Buda had about five thousand inhabitants around 1500 and they were, naturally, all Christians. By 1547 the number of Christians in Buda was around one thousand, and eighty years later it had fallen to about seventy.[10] The other cities showed the same decline in number of original inhabitants, but those in the south of Hungary gained a few Christian inhabitants, Serbs, and Romanians. They moved into the Bácska (Bačka), Baranya, Banat, and what is today the Vojvodina, as well as into Slavonia where there were already a considerable number. This ethnographic change had lasting historical consequences.

These movements can be fairly easily explained. Most of the "Turkish" officials in Hungary were Bosnians who naturally spoke Serbian and had

10. József Perényi, "Villes hongroises sous la domination Ottomane aux XVIe-XVIIe siècles. Les Chefs-lieux de l'administration Ottomane," in *La Ville Balkanique*, p. 25-31.

had contact with Serbian merchants and artisans for centuries. Although religion separated them, these two groups had enough in common to facilitate cooperation not only in the cities but also in the countryside, west of the Danube and north of the Drava, where Serbian peasants had replaced the fleeing Magyars. East of the Tisza, roughly in today's Romanian province Crişana, the same phenomenon occurred. The Magyars fled either to the north or into Transylvania. It was only natural for the Romanians, who were both the most numerous and the worst off of the people in Transylvania proper, to move into these empty lands. Although they did not enjoy more freedom under the Ottoman masters of Temesvár and later Nagyvárad than they had been granted in Transylvania, they could settle and become agriculturalists, something that was impossible in Transylvania where the sparse good land was already fully populated. In this manner the nature of the cities changed ethnographically not only west of the Danube, but also east of the Tisza.

The most interesting development occurred in the devastated central plain, which was not suitable for *timars* and remained part of the sultan's personal property. During the second half of the fifteenth century the Hungarian peasantry had been slowly rising from its totally servile status. On the great plains several villages had grown into agricultural towns, which also served as market centers. They were not free cities but holdings of various lords. Yet their inhabitants were not considered serfs, had certain rights, and were clearly on their way to total emancipation—at least to the degree to which "free towns" were free.

Legally, these towns (in Latin *oppida* and in Hungarian *mezővárosok* [prairie towns]) lost most of their rights and privileges when the Hungarian Diets passed massive anti-peasantry laws and regulations following the great peasant uprising of 1514. Despite the laws these towns were still clinging to their way of life when the Ottomans arrived only twelve years later following the Battle of Mohács. Situated as the region was between the two rivers, in the center of the first Turkish attacks, it was not easy for the inhabitants to run away. Furthermore, being at odds with the nobility, the peasantry was not tempted to follow it. Thus, around these curious towns a new life developed. Of the dozen or so prairie towns, Nagykőrös, Kecskemét, and Cegléd became the most important and are among the leading Hungarian cities today.

There occurred in these prairie towns a unique development, made possible by the Ottoman occupation of Central Hungary. On the one hand, these towns tried to survive and to revive and even to extend their privileges. On the other hand, the Ottomans needed some way to make this large deserted plain useful; the only way, given the deterioration of the land, was through pastural-type animal husbandry, which was well suited to the vast expanse of newly created desert. When the Ottomans arrived

Nagykőrős, the most important of the three largest *oppida*, held legal title to about 92,500 acres, mostly in pastures.[11] By the middle of the seventeenth century the town had increased its holdings to about 466,000 acres by acquiring the lands of the deserted villages around it. It is important to realize that these lands were considered *miri*, that is, state-owned, by the Ottoman government. They were assigned either to the various *havas-i hümayun* or to the *hases* of the *beylerbeyi* of Buda, but were identified with these cities and considered part of them.

These towns naturally paid a land tax, *haraç*, the *cizye*, and the tithe on the product they raised, animals. The last-mentioned tax amounted to about eight to ten thousand head of cattle each year for all cities together. Considering that the custom station of Vácz alone saw as many as two thousand head pass from Ottoman-held to Habsburg territory each month and that the total export from Hungary westward amounted to as much as a hundred thousand head per year, this was a real tithe.[12] These custom stations as well as fords and bridges across the Danube were leased and produced considerable revenue for the Ottoman government. For example, the customs and ferry station on Csepel Island (just south of Buda) paid a lease of six hundred thousand *akçes* for the three-year period between 1543 and 1546. The large sums also indicate the importance of animal raising and trade of the *mezőváros*.[13] The *oppida* prospered. The sample city of Nagykőrős had about 1,500-2,000 inhabitants before the Turkish occupation and about the same number some 150 years later. To get the true picture of the economic life of these towns, their increased landholding and large cattle business must be compared with their obligations. In 1631 Nagykőrős had four types of cash or delivery duties that amounted to:

Haraç —	46,000 *akçes* approximately
Cizye —	24,000 *akçes* approximately
"Beef Tax" —	48,000 *akçes* approximately
Value of 200 carts —	17,000 *akçes* approximately
of wood for the	
Buda *beylerbeyi*	
Total —	135,000 *akçes* approximately

What is important to realize is that "in comparison with figures we have from the sixteenth century and considering also the devaluation of the

11. The economic data concerning the *oppida* come from József Perényi, "Trois villes hongroises sous la domination Ottomane au XVIIe siècle," *Actes du Premier Congrès International des Études Balkaniques et Sud-Est Européenes*, IV (Sofia; Bulgarian Academy of Sciences, 1969), 3:581-91 unless otherwise mentioned.

12. Bálint Hóman and Gyula Szekfű, *Magyar Történet* (History of Hungary), 5 vols. (Budapest; Királyi Magyar Egyetemi Nyomda, 1939), 3:415.

13. Hóman and Szefű, 3:434.

akçe, the tax load of the city increased only slightly."[14] Clearly the city lived well when its obligations remained the same and its income increased.

The prairie towns had other irregular features, too. There were no Muslim settlers and, therefore, no Ottoman *akhi* or functionaries. These towns ruled themselves; the representatives of the authorities appeared only to collect taxes. They had no *kadis* and only limited jurisdictional rights; certain litigants were forced to travel long distances to reach their "legal superiors," their old feudal lords, to get rulings.

This and the fact that taxes were calculated in Austrian currency indicate another peculiarity that affected not only these towns but some border villages too: double suzerainty. The Hungarian nobility did not give up its legal rights to territories under Ottoman rule and even claimed the right to travel and temporarily reside unmolested and tax free on "their" Ottoman-held lands. They also laid claim to income and taxes. The Ottomans made counterclaims and taxed localities that were officially on the other side of the frontier but within easy reach of their border guards. These claims and counterclaims figured in every negotiation between the Ottomans and Habsburgs on a state-to-state basis, and in those of local frontier authorities. The result was, in several cases, *de facto* double taxation, although those who wanted to collect in lands held by the other side usually got but a token. If this curious system had affected only the real "frontier" where the military could raid and "collect" anyhow, it would not have been too remarkable. However, when it touched on localities far from the border, such as the *mezővaros* (although these towns usually ignored their nominal absentee lords), it represents a unique situation in the Ottoman "core" provinces.

The case of the *oppida* developed out of the dual circumstances of economic interest and proximity to the enemy. In a sense the same situation applied to the Aegean islands, the best examples being Khíos and Rhodes. Most of them acquired Ottoman governors after they were conquered, but retained their institutions, governed themselves, and in general managed their own affairs. They were not subjected to the standard Ottoman taxes, but were assessed fixed dues to be delivered annually. These were not light. The Island of Khíos contributed the same amount during the time of Süleyman I (ten thousand ducats) that Ragusa, which was much richer, and Wallachia and Transylvania, both of which were richer and larger, paid as tribute.[15] In general the islands suffered from the endemic Ottoman-Venetian wars and from the "revenge" of the victorious, but in time

14. Perényi, "Trois villes," p. 588. The tax figures given are approximations because Perényi calculated in Florins which flunctuated in value between 60 and 70 *akçes.* The figures given were calculated on a 1 to 65 ratio.

15. Inan, *Aperçu general,* p. 28.

of peace their cities and villages were left much to their own devices and were better off than were the Greek settlements on the mainland.

On the Greek mainland a few "self-governing" regions also existed. Where geography and special local circumstances made direct rule too costly, the Ottomans settled for taxes, a few other fringe benefits, and recognition of their suzerainty. This situation created few problems in the glorious first period of Ottoman power, but it became a dangerous precedent that created great difficulties in the later centuries. The Greek mainland had several of these virtually self-governing regions of which the best known were in the Soulíou Mountains in western Epirus centered around the town of Ioannina (Janina, Yanya), in the Maínalon Mountains, north and east of today's city of Trípolis in the central Morea where the Mavromikhalis family practically "reigned," and in the central massives of the Pindus Mountains. Some of these local potentates became so closely connected with the "establishment" that they were allowed to bypass the local, provincial authorities and send their own representatives (*vekils*) to Istanbul to negotiate directly with the central administration. In Albania and Crna Gora several small regions enjoyed similar "freedoms." Only those who were able to establish local power enjoyed such privileges. The peasantry was probably worse off than were those subject to direct Ottoman rule.

It is clear from the above discussion of selected cases that there was enough flexibility in the strictly centralized and regulated Ottoman Empire to make these variations in the cities of the "core" provinces possible. This very flexibility, in turn, made it easier to keep order in a large region whose inhabitants had different customs and needs.

CHAPTER 5

The Countryside

1. THE LANDHOLDING SYSTEM

ANY discussion of rural life must begin with a short look at the land-holding system, because both in theory and practice it affected the lives of almost everybody living outside the cities' limits. The Ottomans recognized three basic types of land tenure: *mırı*, *mülk*, and *vakıf*. In theory in lands conquered by the Ottomans all landed property was *mırı*, state property, provided that the sultan did not confirm the existing property rights. All *timars* were *mırı* land; the *timarlı* had no property rights but only usufruct contingent on satisfactory service. Beginning with the various arrangements in Asia Minor, when the fortunes of the Ottomans began to rise and where many of those whose lands came under Ottoman rule were fellow Turkish Muslims, the sultans either confirmed existing ownership patterns or bestowed gifts of land on their major supporters. These lands, owned by individuals whose descendants could inherit them, were *mülk* properties. The third type of property, that set aside to support "pious foundations," the *vakıfs*, belonged to God in theory and were, therefore, unalienable. Originally, these lands had been either *mırı* or *mülk* and were transformed into *vakıf* lands either by the state, that is by the sultan, or by individual owners.

The relative importance of all three types of holdings in Europe was calculated by Ömer Lutfi Barkan for 1527. During that year total income from European provinces amounted to 198 million *akçe* or roughly 37 percent of all revenues of the state. Of this amount 42.3 percent was made up of *cizye* payments; the rest came from customs and other duties connected with trade, mining, and agricultural pursuits. Of the total amount collected in Rumelia 48 percent went into the central treasury and 46 percent represented the income of the *timarlı*. Only 6 percent belonged to the *vakıfs* and to the owners of *mülk* property, showing how relatively small these holdings were.[1] With the help of data supplied by Inalcik and Inan, and indirectly by Barkan, an attempt can be made to break down the total given by Inalcik to show the exact source of the revenues and their distribution according to urban and rural origins. The first of these calculations gives the following results:

21.2%	of income was generated by mining, customs, commerce	41,976,000	akçes
42.3%	of income was derived from *cizye*	83,754,000	akçes
24.8%	of income was contributed by taxes on *has* peasants	49,104,000	akçes
11.7%	of income was contributed by taxes on other peasants	23,166,000	akçes
100.0%		198,000,000	akçes

The second breakdown shows the following divisions of income:

36.5 %	of income was generated by taxes of all peasants	72,270,000	akçes
90.0 %	of *cizye* revenue of 83,754,000 *akçes*	75,378,600	akçes
74.56%	of total revenue was generated in rural areas	147,648,600	akçes
21.2 %	of income derived from mining, customs, commerce	41,976,000	akçes
10.0 %	of *cizye* revenue of 83,754,000 *akçes*	8,375,400	akçes
25.44%	of total revenue was generated in urban areas	50,351,400	akçes

These figures[2] reflect the relative importance of both the towns and the villages. The urban population did not exceed 10 percent of the total population, and yet urban-generated contributions, a quarter of the total,

1. Halil Inalcık, "L'Empire Ottoman," *Actes du Premier Congres*, 3:75-103. The figures cited as well as those used in the calculation in n. 2 are based on the works of Ömer Lütfi Barkan and can be found on pp. 89-91.
2. These calculations are based on data given by Inalcık, *ibid.*, and by Inan, *Aperçu general*, pp. 27-28. While the data furnished are for different years—Inalcık's for 1527 and Inan's for 1553—they can be used without difficulty because Inalcık indicates that taxes rose sharply after 1527, but the proportions of sources of income and expenditures remained about the same until about 1584. Inan estimates the total income of the state treasury in 1553 to be between 10.5 and 15 million ducats, but gives specific figures only for revenues generated by mines, customs, and levies on trade. Taking these figures and applying them to 12.75 million, the average of the grand total given, it is possible to put revenues generated by these three sources at 21.2 percent of the total. I

amounted to 47.1 percent of the amount retained by the treasury. Not only did the rural areas furnish the heavy *cizye* contribution, without which the treasury would have been half-empty, but they also supported the *timar* system, so important for military and administrative purposes. How important this last-mentioned consideration was becomes clear when it is realized that the already mentioned 46 percent of Rumelia's revenue that went to the *timarlı* was shared in 1527 by 17,288 individuals, providing them with an average income of 5,268 *akçes*.

Landholding of any kind was tied to duties. The military obligations of the *timarlı* as well as their local functions as policemen and tax collectors have already been repeatedly mentioned. Equally stringent were the requirements for *vakıfs*. They could be established only with the special permission of the sultan to serve a specific purpose. Not only was the founding of a *vakıf* strictly regulated, but the *kadi* of the district in which the establishment was located had to control regularly its functioning and, should misuses be discovered, could either recommend the dismissal of the *vakıf*'s administrators or, in cases where the entire function of the pious establishment was either totally neglected or not needed, suggest that the property revert to the state. Both Mehmed II and Süleyman I dissolved numerous *vakıfs*, but the real difficulties with them appeared in the seventeenth and eighteenth centuries when the sultans were not strong enough to take effective measures. The label *vakıf* included not only Muslim, but also Christian pious foundations. The latter too were supported quite often by land specifically set aside for that purpose. Although much church-owned land was indeed confiscated after the Ottoman conquest, monasteries and some bishops retained their lands. These were subject to the same controls as were the Muslim *vakıfs*. From the viewpoint of the cultivator, working *vakıf* or imperial *has* lands became very advantageous as time passed because these two types of properties were unalienable.

---

accepted this percentage although it appeared somewhat high for Rumelia in 1527, and split Inalcık's total 46 percent of all revenues coming from Inan's three sources and from *has*-generated income accordingly into 21.2 percent coming from mines, customs, and trade, and 24.8 percent from the *has* holdings. Finally, I assigned the 11.7 percent that was not accounted for by Inalcık when he listed the sources of income to peasants working lands other than *has* because most other possible sources had been covered and because peasants working *timar* lands also paid taxes to the state. These are the figures used in my first calculation.

In breaking down the *cizye* figures I considered the size of the cities in 1527. The largest city, Istanbul, did not figure in the income of Rumelia; Edirne was relatively large, but of the other cities only two, Salonika and Athens, had more than 2,000 taxable families. In that year Rumelia had 1,111,799 taxable units (counted by hearths or houses), so at least 90 percent of these had to be outright rural dwellings (villages) or towns of such small size that their main occupations had to be agriculture. While errors are possible, the figures resulting from these assumptions based on exact figures appear to be fairly accurate in accordance with our general knowledge of Rumelia at the beginning of the sixteenth century.

Therefore, they escaped first the abuses of some ambitious feudatories and later those stemming from the breakdown of the entire system.

It is important to realize that Christian *vakıfs* and *timars* existed side-by-side with comparable Muslim holdings, although in much smaller numbers. If to these are added the holdings of the Christian "military" and auxiliaries as well as the small *çift* holdings that individual *reaya* families could retain, it becomes clear that the old and often repeated statement that Christians lost all their land when the Ottomans arrived is erroneous. These basic landholding patterns together with the situation of the Hungarian *mezőváros* and the special *salyane*-type regimes in different parts of European Turkey amounted to non-Muslim landholding of considerable proportions.

Regardless of the landholding pattern in force in a given region, the cultivator or husbandsman produced basically cereals, vegetables, fruits, or animal products and was obligated to pay a great variety of taxes. Unfortunately, the countryside has not been as thoroughly studied as the cities, and there are still no reliable data specifying the kinds and quantities of agricultural products. Nevertheless, it can be stated that with the exception of such items as wool, hides, and similar by-products few, if any, "industrial crops" were produced.

The enterprising landowner who began to emerge elsewhere in the sixteenth century and who had his eye on the market did not exist in the Ottoman Empire. The *vakıf* administrators were not agricultural experts but managers of institutions of various kinds; they were satisfied if the income they received supported the establishment they managed. *Mülk* holdings were too few and too small to permit experimentation. The *timarlı* and the managers of imperial *has* lands were not landowners; they were merely temporary beneficiaries of certain incomes or bailiffs.

The other side of this coin, which benefited the cultivator, was the elimination of an authority that owned the land he worked and controlled every aspect of his life. There was no serfdom in the Ottoman Empire. Every person was the direct subject of the sultan and dependent on his laws and his administrators. Consequently, the types, if not the magnitude, of taxes and other obligations of the peasantry varied relatively little from place to place and from one type of landholding to another. The peasantry's obligations to the beneficiary of the land's income could differ depending on where the land was situated and what was produced. Basically, the peasantry paid tithes of various kinds, while the taxes owed to the state were rather uniformly fixed in theory and remained so even in practice so long as the Ottoman system functioned properly. This well-regulated system explains why so many Southeastern Europeans helped Ottomans during their conquests and why living under direct Ottoman rule was preferable to living under a local lord. Although taxes, which are usually described as having been lighter under the Ottomans than under previous masters, might in fact not have been lighter, at least they were regulated and fixed. At regular intervals census takers appeared everywhere and counted the number of taxable inhabitants (heads of households), surveyed the economy, and established the tax load for each individual, which remained in force until the next census, usually ten years later. Consequently, each peasant knew what he owed to his "lord" and to the state and could plan accordingly. This was very important because the Ottoman tax system placed much greater emphasis on taxes to be paid in cash than had the previous regimes, a fact that could have made their system more onerous than the preceding ones had not the people taxed known exactly what was expected from them.

There were many reasons for the Ottomans' insistence on cash taxes. While there were numerous slaves in the empire, and class differentiations were strictly drawn along professional and confessional lines, the Ottomans were reluctant to sanction labor services by one nonslave for another. This reluctance stems from their centralizing tendency and from the basic legal tenet that all land and people belong to the sultan. Labor services tended to make one man subject to someone other than the sultan, and this was not acceptable to Ottoman legal minds. In addition to this theoretical—if one wishes, constitutional—reason there was also an economic consideration of great importance. The expenses of the state-maintained imperial establishment, the *birun* and *enderun*, in Istanbul has been calculated to amount to 3.5 million *akçes* in 1527.[3] Besides this amount the state needed money to pay for the *maaşlı* military, the naval forces, and certain imports used by the state-owned factories. With the economy of its trading partners in Italy and France developing rapidly into a money economy, the state needed a steady cash income in addition to supplies for markets in the cities, towns, and villages. Consequently, taxes in kind and in cash were equally important. Those in kind belonged chiefly to the feudatory beneficiaries and *vakıf* administrators, while those in cash went mainly to the state treasury.

The peasantry paid the required taxes to the beneficiaries who had claims on the fruits of their labor. The beneficiaries retained what they themselves needed and sold the surplus, keeping what money was left after paying their cash taxes. It was this reserve that the state tapped by legal fines and, when extra income was needed, by the promulgation of extraordinary taxes (*avariz*).

In conformity with the Ottoman state's desire to control and regulate everything and to make certain that the system did not break down, not only were subjects supposed to stick to their classes and professions, but measures were also taken to make certain that they were not forced out of

3. Ömer Lütfi Barkan, "H. 933-934 (M. 1527-28) Mali yilina âit bütçe örneği" (the budget pattern for the fiscal year H. 933-934 [A.D. 1527-28]), *Istanbul Üniversitesi Iktisat Fakultesi Mecmuasi* 15 (1953-54): 251-329.

them against their wills. Naturally, every *timar* holder, every owner of *mülk* property, and every *vakıf* had documentary proof of possession of or right to enjoy the revenues of certain properties. These documents were periodically reviewed, and when abuses were detected they were rectified so long as the state had the power to enforce its demands.

Right to property or its use were basic rights and could hardly be questioned in the case of *vakıfs*, unless they were established illegally or did not serve a "useful" function, or in that of *mülk* holdings. Their regulation, however, was crucial not only in the case of the *timarlı*, but especially in that of the peasantry. It was in regard to property rights that the principle of *urf* and that of imperial legislation expressed in the *kanuns* became so important. The *kanuns* permitted the Ottomans to enforce certain rights to property that were not in accordance with the sacred law and even contradicted it. A good example would be subdivision of landed property at the death of the owner. According to the *sharī'a* such land should be divided among the heirs, but this was forbidden in the Ottoman Empire, whose masters understood that this practice would harm production.

The *timars*, originally granted by the governor but soon on their recommendation by the central government, were fundamental economic units and the mainstay of the feudal component of the army. Each fiefholder was entitled to his benefices so long as he performed strictly regulated duties. What is important from the point of view of property rights is that although the *timars* were *mırı* lands and had to revert to the state on the death of the *sipahi*, certain provisions were made that recognized something like hereditary claims, if not to the land itself then at least to the enjoyment of its income. This was done to ensure the stability of both the military establishment and the economic system.

Within each *timar* there was a certain section called the *has çift*, the special land, which the *timarlı* cultivated directly or through a special tenant who represented him. Its size, just as that of the entire *timar*, depended on the fertility of the soil, but as a rule it was between fourteen and thirty-five acres.[4] This basic holding was also known as a *kılıç* and was almost always granted to the dead *sipahi's* oldest son, assuring him a "basic living" (*dirlik*). If the *timars* were large enough, any younger sons also had certain rights to the remaining parts of the *timar*, but only to the extent of a basic *dirlik*. If there were no sons, the most distinguished *cebelü* of the departed *timarlı* took his *kılıç*. Additional lands had to be earned on the battlefield. These regulations, which were more or less unified for the entire state by the law codes (*Kanunname*) of Mehmed II and Süleyman I, did not conform to the *sharī'a*, or to the basic principle on which the entire *timar* system rested, but they did achieve some very important ends. They kept members of the "military class" in their class;

4. In Turkish measures this equals 60 to 150 *dönüms*. One *dönüm* equals 1,124.24 square yards.

they prevented the appearance of "soldiers" without an income who could have become a real danger for the state; and they assured legal continuity of property rights, the continuity of the *timarlıs'* nonmilitary functions, and the uninterrupted pattern of agrarian production. The relationship between the *sipahi*, who knew the region and its customs, and peasantry was also assured.

It has already been mentioned that at the time of the conquest, the Ottomans prepared census books (*tahrirs*) for a given province and usually confirmed most of the laws prevalent in the region, at least until further notice. It has also been mentioned that at this time peasant households could retain up to one *çift* of land as their own property when their legal rights and their behavior toward the Ottomans warranted it. When several families who recognized relationships among themselves in the form of the widest possible interpretation of blood ties acquired *çifts*, they were able to continue to live in accordance with their traditions. This explains the survival of the *zadrugas* in the Serbian lands. Peasants owning *mülk* property in this manner were not numerous. Most of them appear in the *tahrirs* as belonging to a *timar* of any given size or name, a *vakıf*, or an imperial *has*. The *hadd* of these peasants had to be protected from arbitrary actions on the part of the members of the "military class."

Each peasant owned some private property and was entitled to the use of different types of lands in accordance with an arrangement that resembled tenancy in the western states. His rights to his own property and tenancy, called *tasarruf*, which he should not have had according to the *shaī'a*, were recognized by the *kanuns*. If the peasant cultivated his fields and paid his taxes, his oldest son inherited this *tasarruf* automatically without paying any inheritance taxes. If he died without a son, his daughter had the right to inherit; her husband in fact became the owner of the *tasarruf*. If he died childless the claim devolved first on his brother and then on his sister (in fact her husband); his father and mother were also able to inherit. In all these cases a group of "objective" Muslims were called in and asked to evaluate the *tasarruf*. On the basis of this valuation a tax (*tapu*) was established which the inheritor had to pay before the *tasarruf* could be registered in his or her name. If the *tasarruf* became available at the death of a woman, only her son had a right to inherit it by paying the *tapu*. If there were no legal heirs, the *mefkufcu* (see p. 43) administered the holding until somebody was found who was willing to take it over. Whoever was responsible—the *timarlı*, the *mütevelli* (bailiff of *vakıf* property), or the *has* administrator—had to offer the holding first to the peasants of the departed owner's village. If he found no takers there he could then turn to outsiders.

In this manner the peasants' rights were safeguarded. Peasants could not be driven off the land they worked, and their tenure was more secure than in most western states. On the other hand, they could not leave the land either unless they found somebody to take over their *tasarruf* who was acceptable to both their fellow villagers and whoever profited from his labor. All this conformed strictly to the Ottoman belief that people should stick to their class and profession to maintain the social equilibrium of the state, but it also made the growth of cities difficult and prevented technological progress in the countryside. So long as the peasant could make a living and those who profited from his efforts were satisfied there was no incentive to change the system.

2. RURAL TAXES

THE obligations discussed in the preceding section stemmed either from taxes levied on land and its products or on individuals, the heads of households, because personal taxes, with the exception of a few to be specified below, were levied on "houses" (*hans*). The following breakdown shows all the taxable property or land whose fruits were liable to payments and also indicates which of these were *mülk* and which were *mıri/vakıf*.

Taxable property	Type of ownership	
	mülk	*mıri/vakıf*
1) Agricultural lands		
a) Arable lands		X
b) Pastures		X
2) Forest lands		X
3) Orchard and Vineyards		
a) Land		X
b) Trees and Vines	X	
4) Homes and farm buildings (incl. plot)	X	
5) Garden plot of ½ *dönüm* (562 sq. yards)	X	
6) Communal Hay Field of village	X	
7) Other Hay Fields		X

All these properties and their produce were subject to taxes, with two exceptions: the hay from the community hay field and the produce from the garden plot if used by the peasant and not marketed. The *timarlıs* collected all taxes from those working on lands assigned to them, the *mütevellis* collected on *vakıf* lands, and imperial tax collectors (*mültezims*) on the imperial estates.

Besides the *yürüks* (see p. 40), who numbered thirty-seven thousand families in Rumelia at the end of the first quarter of the sixteenth century, there were other groups called *yerli* (their number is not known) who were traditionally herdsmen and animal raisers in the European provinces of the Ottoman Empire. These people paid pasturage fees (*otlak resmi*), both on winter and summer pastures. While it is not clear whether these fees were paid in kind or cash, the value was fixed according to the size of the herd and ranged from a low of ten to a maximum of twenty-five *akçes*. Both these nomads and the sedentary husbandsmen paid a wintering fee (*ağıl resmi*). The only indication I found in the records spoke of the minimum due for the smallest herds consisting of one sheep and fifty *akçes*. All who raised animals, both nomads and settlers, paid a sheep due (*adeti ağnam*). The lowest rate I found, from the year 1550, exempted the first hundred animals from the tax and amounted to half an *akçe* for every additional animal. Seventy years later the rate was one *akçe* for every animal including the first hundred. While this was a "sheep" tax, it applied equally to other small four-legged animals like goats and pigs. I found no taxes on cattle and horses and none on poultry, although these animals are mentioned in inheritance cases, forced deliveries to *sipahi*, and other legal cases recorded by the *kadis*. In the case of the *oppida* of central Hungary the tithe due for these animals, as we know, amounted to exactly 10 percent on cattle, and there are also indications that the seller paid a sales tax on them as well as on horses. It is not clear, however, whether these were regular or extraordinary taxes, or simply impositions that the husbandsmen could not resist. These people also paid some personal taxes.

There is much more information available about the payments made by the agricultural sector. Here the basic tax was the tithe (*âşar*). It was assessed each year just before harvest time, but the peasant was obliged to harvest and thresh the tithe part of his harvest and to deliver it either to a warehouse or to a stipulated market. The *âşar* differed from locality to locality, and could be as low as a one-tenth and as high as one-half of the produce, depending on the region, on the crop, and on custom. It had to be paid on all cereal crops and on hay, straw, fruits, vegetables, and a grape jelly called *pekmez*. While the amount varied greatly, according to the records a special tax on must appeared to be uniformly 15 percent. This tax was called *salariye*. The same name also applied to another tax that was levied, besides the basic *âşar*, on barley, millet, oats, and rye and amounted to as much as 25 percent of the harvest. This second *salariye* was fodder money to keep the *sipahi*'s war horse in good shape. Finally, a tax called *resmi kovan* covered beehives. It could be paid either in kind at the rate of one hive out of ten, or in cash at a rate varying from one-half to two *akçes* for one hive. All these tithes could be transformed into cash payments, *rusum*, and this was done in the cases of most vineyards and orchards.

Cash payments were levied on all buildings and on the use of mills, smithies, and other facilities. Again, the amount differed greatly from locality to locality and from time to time. Until a detailed study is made it is practically impossible to give any meaningful indications of the amounts that the inhabitants of the European provinces paid. Nevertheless, it is fair to assume th.at these dues also rose, as did some of those for which amounts were given, as a result of inflation and the treasury's growing need for tax money.

Turning to taxes levied on persons, it is necessary to differentiate between those paid by Muslims and those paid by *zimmi*. The main tax paid by the Muslims, the *raiyyet rusmu*, was made up of two of the three personal taxes. The most important one was the *çift resmi*, which replaced the old feudal services. Mehmed II fixed it at twenty-two *akçes* corresponding to the following valuation:[5]

> 3 *akçes* for 3 days corvée
> 7 *akçes* for 1 cartload of hay
> 7 *akçes* for ½ cartload of straw
> 3 *akçes* for 1 cartload of wood
> 2 *akçes* for the use of the cart

This amount remained virtually unchanged. By the middle of the seventeenth century it totaled thirty *akçes* for a whole *çift* and fifteen *akçes* for smaller units of land. Married men paid an additional twelve *akçes* as *benak*, while bachelors paid half this amount as *mücerred*. A household with more than one male over twelve years of age paid one *çift resmi*, one *benak* and as many *mücerreds* as there were unmarried males living in the household. In place of the *raiyyet rusmu* the *zimmi* paid, irrespective of marital status, a fee called *ispence*, whose amount varied in accordance with the value of the land worked. Even landless *zimmi* were subject to this tax, but in their case it was fixed at twenty-five *akçes*.

All non-Muslim males over the age of twelve, irrespective of occupation, economic condition, or marital status, paid the *cizye*. One of the oldest Muslim taxes, it is usually translated as poll-tax or head-tax, which in fact it was. Those who imposed it, however, regarded it as the protection-money paid for the privileges of living in the "well-protected" state whose defenses fell on the shoulders of others. The amount of the *cizye* theoretically depended on the wealth of the man who paid it, and there were to be three categories: high, medium, and low. In the earlier Muslim states theory was put into practice, and the Ottomans also started with this concept. Later the amounts collected at different times differed, and there were considerable deviations from the basic theory.

It is easy to calculate the amount paid by household if we return to the income figures presented at the beginning of this chapter. Taking as *cizye* the amount collected in the European provinces in 1527, 83,754,000 *akçes*, and realizing that this total was collected from 916, 841 *zimmi* households, we arrive at the approximate sum of 91.5 *akçes* per household. Assuming

5. Inalcık, "L'Empire Ottoman," *Actes du Premier Congres*, 3:82.

that most of the households were "medium" rate payers and had two males each, a medium rate of 45-46 *akçes* per male becomes the "medium" *cizye* figure. This would place the 70-*akçe* rate mentioned in the protocols of the Sofia *kadi* in 1550, before the great inflation, in the high category.[6] Yet the same *kadi*'s records show that this tax rose much more steeply than the rate of inflation, to 200 *akçes*, and that the order he received from Istanbul in which this figure is mentioned also states that "this amount should be collected from everybody." Apparently, by 1610 the distinction between the three payment steps had disappeared.[7] Nor is this the only irregularity. During the same year the Sofia *kadi* received another *berat* (imperial order) asking him to help an individual assigned to collecting the *cizye* from the Gypsies. These people were not among the very rich, but their contribution was fixed at 250 *akçes*, with the exception of Muslim Gypsies who had to pay only 180.[8] While these amounts are totals and include other small taxes besides the *cizye*, they indicate that Muslims also paid *cizye* simply because they were Gypsies. The only other possible explanation for this irregular procedure, that the differences of 70 *akçes* signifies that Muslims did not pay this tax, has to be rejected in light of the fact that in 1610 in the *sancak* of Sofia "everybody" had to pay 200 *akçe* of *cizye* from which the despised Gypsies were certainly not exempted. All that these figures could mean is that while the Gypsies were considered such low people that even Muslims could be taxed illegally, their religion was still worth a 70 *akçe* tax discount.

These examples come from only one *sancak*, but it is not very likely that the sharp increase in this tax, the elimination of categories, and the taxing of Gypsy Muslims were occurrences reserved for this one district. What is more likely is that irregularities occurred in each *sancak*, although not necessarily the same, as a result of a large deficit in the central treasury.

One more personal tax was "regular" but applied to both Muslim and *zimmi*, the marriage tax (*aruş resmi*). When the bride was a Muslim this fee amounted to sixty *akçes*, but when she was a widow or divorcée it was only forty. In the case of marriage to *zimmi* women half of these amounts · was charged, and if anybody married a slave girl there was no fee at all. So far as I know, this is the only case where Muslims paid more for something than did the *zimmi*. The father of the bride paid, according to his means, another tax of nine, six, or three *akçes*; if he was a *yürük* he paid five *akçes*. What this tax had to do with weddings and how it became instituted is not clear, and its name, smoking or tobacco use tax (*resmi duhan*), explains nothing.[9]

6. Gălăb D. Gălăbov and Herbert W. Duda, *Die Protokollarbücher des Kadiamtes Sofia*, vol. 55 of *Südosteuropäische Arbeiten* (München: Oldenbourg, 1960), doc. no. 211, p. 56.
7. *Ibid.*, doc. no. 487, p. 120.
8. *Ibid.*, doc. no. 506, p. 127.
9. Joseph von Hammer, *Staatsverfassung und Staatsverwaltung des Osmanischen*

All these taxes added up to considerable amounts. The city people also paid crier and marriage fees, but the rest of their taxes and dues were connected with their profession and could be included in the cost of their

product on which they were assured a minimum of 10 percent profit. The rural population, on the other hand, paid *âşar* on what it produced, and its profits depended on weather, market conditions, and other variables. When everything is added up they were obviously paying a much heavier amount, either in kind or in cash or both, on what they produced than were the city dwellers. There were only three reasons why they might have felt that their lot was easier than it had been prior to the Ottomans' arrival: (1) instead of a capricious and uncontrolled nobility that often took much more from the peasantry than it was entitled to take, they had "lords" who acted in accordance with the law or could be sued success-fully if they did not; (2) at least between censuses they knew exactly what they owed on what and to whom; (3) the constant wars that ruined their crops and fields ceased.

Heavy as the rural taxes were, they could have been borne by the culti-vators and husbandsmen if these regular taxes had represented all their obligations. Such was not the case. Both the rural and urban population also had to pay extraordinary taxes on either festive occasions like the enthronement of a new sultan, or in emergencies like a long and costly war. When these taxes were levied only occasionally even they could be tolerated, but already by the end of the sixteenth century several had be-come "regular" taxes called *bedels*. When a great number of additional extraordinary taxes were added to the *bedels* the load became too heavy, and when coupled with the state's inability to keep the "lords" honest in the next two centuries the rural order broke down. Part Four will deal with this situation. While there were occasional signs of unrest even prior to the end of the sixteenth century, they appear to have had been caused by factors other than economic oppression.

3. THE FRONTIER

SERBO-CROATIAN, Turkish, and Hungarian share the word *palanka* (*pa-lánka*). It has various meanings, but one of them in all three languages is palisade. This is not surprising because the people who spoke these three languages manned the palisades along hundreds of miles of ill-de-fined border which at its longest started in northern Bosnia, moved north-eastward crossing the Sava just east of Zagreb, ran straight north slightly to the east of today's border between Austria and Hungary, to the Danube. From here the line followed the Danube for a while leaving the

---

Reiches, 2 vols. (1815; reprint ed., Hildesheim: Georg Olms, 1963), 1:206. Hammer indicates that this tax was taken over from the Byzantines, but this must be wrong be-cause they did not know tobacco. His remark only indicates that this curious tax was not an innovation of the later period.

various islands in this region in Habsburg-held territory, then crossed the river, moved a bit north until it reached the southern slopes of the Carpathian Mountains. It followed this mountain line, in today's Czechoslovakia, to the Tisza River, along which it continued until it reached the mountain ranges that under various names form a north-south line separating today's Transylvania proper from the Crişana, until it reached the point where this chain joins the Transylvanian Alps that formed the Ottoman-Transylvanian border. This line was not always that extensive because the lands held by the Ottomans expanded and contracted repeatedly during the long years of constant wars with the Habsburgs and was never clearly defined. In fact, it is hard to speak of a border in the modern sense of the word. What existed was a frontier region, something like a no-man's land, although peace treaties and armistices always defined borders.

Just as several centuries earlier the steadily moving band of land that separated Muslim from Byzantine in Asia Minor attracted a typical frontier society, so did this frontier region. Those living along the new frontier were not called *akritoi* and *gazi*, and in many ways they differed from the earlier frontier warriors, but there were also numerous similarities. Fortifications stood at key points on both sides of the "border" and were usually located in towns or smaller cities that were, on the Ottoman side, seats of *sancak beyi*s or lower ranking officials responsible for a *kaza*, or simply garrison commanders. Numerous small strong points, the *palankas*, were placed between these fortified points and inhabited by small military units. On both sides of the border each *palanka* had a special core, *végvár*, whose exact translation, castle at the end, describes its function and meaning better than does the literary translation, border fortress. Seen from both sides, these strong points stood at the end of the world. On both sides these castles were supposed to be part of an organized military system subject to an over-all commander, but in fact the local officers acted pretty much on their own and had little or no control over the armed bands inhabiting the *palankas*.

The frontier society living in this *palanka* world resembled the old *gazi* and *akritoi* society in that it was composed for the most part of foot-loose warriors and not of regular military units. A relatively large number of converts who had deserted from the Christian armies or regions lived on the Ottoman side, but there was no true symbiosis such as had existed in Anatolia. Nevertheless, a certain "frontier code" of behavior was worked out. It was based not only on the *gazi* tradition but also on a more recent local one. During the long confrontation between the Hungarians and Ottomans that preceded Süleyman I's conclusive victory, something like a border-guard mentality developed among Bosnians, Serbs, Hungarians, Romanians, and Croats living along the Danube-Sava line. King Matthias' famous "black army," which won several victories against the Ottomans, was the result of an attempt to organize and utilize these frontier warriors

the Banat, and lasted until 1881.[10] The effective "black army" disintegrated after Matthias' death, and the Austrian institution did not really
become fully established and effective until the end of the seventeenth
century.

In the meantime the frontiersmen lived their own life and followed
their own rules. Most of the "soldiers" inhabiting the *palankas* were
mainly interested in making a living and, if possible, in distinguishing
themselves enough to be transferred to the regular military establishment.
If armies moved across those districts in which they resided, they participated in the major campaigns, but they constantly disregarded any official
"peace" between the Ottoman government and European powers. They
could not do otherwise. For the most part they were living in badly devastated areas whose sparse population could barely produce enough to support itself, let alone the resident military which seldom, if ever, received
pay. Raids became a necessity to keep body and soul together. The *beylerbeyi* of Buda and the commander of the Habsburg military border
complained to each other regularly about border violations, as attested by
thousands of extant letters. Even the Habsburg and Ottoman governments
corresponded on the issue, but most interesting are the exchanges between border fortress and even *palanka* commanders who were facing
each other.[11] It is from these exchanges that the picture of frontier life
emerges.

The soldiery was clearly not so much interested in destroying the
enemy as in gathering booty and prisoners, although atrocities did indeed
occur. It valued the basic items needed for daily life, and anything or
anyone, including prisoners, that could be transformed into cash. A dead
peasant could not produce, a dead soldier could not be ransomed, a totally destroyed field could not be worked for years. Life, therefore, became somewhat more valuable on the frontier than it was when regular
armies clashed, and this respect for life, together with a certain economic
value attached to it as well as to movable goods of all kinds, produced a
frontier code that both sides respected.

Ransom became the major source of income and livelihood on the fron-

10. See the two volumes of Gunther E. Rothenberg, *The Austrian Military Border in
Croatia, 1522-1747* (Urbana: University of Illinois Press, 1960) and *The Military
Border in Croatia, 1740-1881* (Chicago-London: University of Chicago Press, 1966).

11. An excellent collection dealing with the exchanges that were conducted in Hungarian is Gustav Bayerle, *Ottoman Diplomacy in Hungary* (Bloomington: Indiana University Press, 1972). The material is very well organized in the Hungarian National
Archives in Budapest where most of the material relating to the borders is included in
the family archives of the Batthyány, Festetich, and Esterházy families whose members
were border commanders for most of the period.

tier. The prisoners were used for labor and in they were ransomed, but kept in fairly good shape to make it worth the other sales made to buy their freedom. Naturally, the price demanded depended on the prisoner's importance, on whether he was a soldier or peasant, but the documents describing the various negotiations clearly show that a value system developed indicating what goods were or were not in demand. By the end of the sixteenth century even "ransom-brokers," whom this author describes elsewhere as "professional prisoners," made their appearance. Their negotiations and agreements with the commanders who held prisoners give the best information about the earthly possessions of the peasantry living in the region and the economy of and the life in the frontier regions.[12]

The ransom for peasants, especially Serbs in the southern Hungarian regions to which they migrated in the years under consideration, was often higher than that for a border warrior. The sparseness of the agricultural population explains this curious set of values and also the fact that some peasants continued to live and even to migrate into the border regions. They were valued and treated accordingly. Prisoners had only ransom value because the *devşirme* system and the availability of the old slave markets after the campaigns of Selim I made it uneconomical to transport slaves from the farthest border regions to the centers of the slave trade, and the frontier warrior did not have the organization needed for this trade. Those who wound up as slaves, and many did, were captured by the regular army during the wars fought between Ottoman and Habsburg forces.

Although dominated by the military, frontier life was rural life. The frontier consisted mainly of an occasional village whose inhabitants were involved in both agricultural and pastural pursuits and were both protected and endangered by the latter-day border warriors concentrated in their little forts and even smaller *palanka*s. Not too many people were involved in this curious type of rural existence, yet it was important. With the exception of Bosnia and certain regions of Albania, it was only on the frontier that Muslim and non-Muslim developed a certain understanding of each other's habits and way of life and an otherwise harsh existence for both was eased. Furthermore, without this understanding and mutually observed behavior pattern devastation of human life and natural resources would have been even greater than it was, making recovery, which was very difficult and took centuries, practically impossible. Finally, it was in this border zone that enemies were able to develop a certain respect for each other and where traces, even if only the slightest, of humanitarian action could occasionally be observed.

12. Peter F. Sugar, "The Ottoman 'Professional Prisoner' on the Western Borders of the Empire in the Sixteenth and Seventeenth Centuries," *Études Balkaniques*, vol. 7, no. 2 (1971), pp. 82-91.

4. CONCLUDING EVALUATION

A few concluding observations must be made about life in the "core" provinces prior to 1574. This "golden age" of the Ottoman Empire was by no means uniformly pleasant either in the city or in the countryside. It is true that the Jews, who came to the Ottoman Empire during this period, lived better than anywhere else in Europe. There were those among them, however, the Sephardim, who had forgotten the difficult times in Spain and remembered only the "good old days." They must certainly have resented being relegated to "second class" subjects. It is true that the Christians enjoyed peace and "law and order." Although they were far from being nationally conscious, more and more they found their identity around their churches. These churches retained some properties and even gained the power to regulate the life of their flocks, but they were rent by internal dissention and suffered from a decline in erudition. The clergy lacked security of tenure, especially in higher ecclesiastic offices, and resented the restrictions such as no towers or bells placed on their churches, the inability to build new ones, and the great difficulties they had even in repairing those in use. There was discrimination and this was resented. Even if the *zimmi* had been inclined to forget their lowly status, they were reminded daily of their places. They were fined for not wearing prescribed clothing, for riding horses, for not showing enough respect to Muslims, and for an almost endless number of other "breaches of etiquette."

While people were fairly secure from marching armies or bandits, they were not free from the old health problems of malaria and contagious diseases such as the plague which ravaged all of Europe in the sixteenth century. It is remarkable that in spite of the severe toll taken by the plague the population of Rumelia increased very rapidly until the middle of the sixteenth century. The number of people in the *eyalets* of Buda and Temesvár, on the other hand, decreased very rapidly, especially in the second half of the century. The great Hungarian plain with its numerous new marshes and semideserts produced a great variety of disease-carrying insects which made the land between the Danube and the Tisza probably the least sanitary region of Europe at the time. In the numerous wars that the Habsburgs fought with the Ottomans between 1526 and 1699, they lost more men to various epidemics than to warfare. In Germany, whence most of their troops came, people began to speak of the "Hungarian disease," and as late as 1866 Bismarck cited the health conditions on the plain when he tried to convince Moltke that peace had to be concluded after the Battle of Königgrätz before the enemy troops retreated to Hungary.

Life was rather monotonous. People performed their duties, returned to their small homes, and locked up for the evening. The old pastimes of hunting, fishing, racing, religious processions, and other festivities were forbidden or reserved to Muslims. Chances of getting out of one's rut were minimal, if that, and with the exception of successful *ustas* or *tüccars* the people enjoyed little comfort or luxury.

The Ottomans were not bothered by the drabness and shabbiness of life. They moved around freely, even if only as soldiers, and hunted, rode, and most importantly ruled a state that functioned exactly as they hoped it would. So long as this situation lasted and the *zimmi* kept their place, they were not interested in them. The subject people profited from the fountains, baths, inns, and other public structures that the Ottomans built, but there was no social, let alone welfare, policy that would have helped to make these people not simply superficially obedient, but in fact satisfied with their rulers. As a matter of fact the Pax Ottomanica permitted the masters to pay the least possible attention to the ruled, and, thus, the gulf between these two elements of society was wider at the end than it had been at the beginning of the "golden age," when Mehmed II ascended the throne of his forefathers for the second time.

It was this gulf that made communications almost impossible between the Muslims and *zimmis*, the professional Ottomans, and the *reaya*, and excluded any possibility of cooperation between them when the state began to face serious difficulties and needed the understanding and good will of everybody to solve its problems. Instead, those in power tried even harder than they had before to keep the old order going by increasing unpopular measures like the various extraordinary taxes, and at the same time breaking the rules of proper behavior and conduct. The breach widened into a chasm, and suddenly the Ottomans discovered that they ruled millions of discontented enemies.

The people of Southeastern Europe were not responsible for this rift, but curiously neither were the Ottomans. The idea of nation-building was just beginning to assert itself in vague forms in the most advanced western states at the time of the Ottoman "golden age," and this concept was totally alien to a ruling elite that did not even consider itself part of an ethnic group and used the expression "Turk" as a pejorative for the Anatolian peasantry. The only distinctions they knew were those of religion and position. So far as they were concerned, they were preordained by God to dominate the world. There was nothing in their beliefs and institutions to induce them to use the years of internal peace and financial prosperity for anything but the continuation of a policy that had proved so successful since Osman won his first great victory in 1301.

Thus, at its zenith the Ottoman Empire was a highly centralized, bureaucratic, even legalistic state, but its masters were totally unaware of what a true state really was: a legal, geographic, traditional, and cultural entity whose identity could be upheld by its rulers, even in times of trouble, because it rested on the will and desire, even if unexpressed, of the majority of its inhabitants whose common background had created the entity in the first place. The Ottoman Empire was a golden shell bristling with weapons, whose cover became thinner and thinner as it grew and the supply of men to increase the military classes began to dry up. Like any shell, once its thin wall was pierced it could not be saved. It lacked the one essential element that any state needs to be saved, a population that identified with the state.

It was during the Ottoman "golden age" that the population of South-eastern Europe, which was originally certainly not hostile to its new masters, slowly changed its attitude, first to indifference and then to latent hostility. The main reasons for the change lay in the attitude of the rulers, the hopeless drabness of life without a chance of change, and, in my opinion, first and foremost the very quality most admired in the Ottomans, their administrative ability. The descendants of Osman overadministered and overregulated life to the point where even the illiterate, modest, and not very ambitious Balkan peasant felt that he had to make a move before the last vestiges of his personality were completely eradicated. Given the overbureaucratization of the state, any move he could possibly make was "illegal" and, therefore, entailed fines and more serious punishments. Such measures alienated the sullen peasants or city dwellers, the more so since these people saw that those who punished them were themselves acting in an increasingly illegal manner. When lawbreakers are themselves the rulers and punish others for misdemeanors, the punished will seek revenge.

I believe that fewer laws, fewer regulations, and fewer rules and special prescriptions would not only have made cohabitation of ruler and ruled easier, but could also have avoided both the stifling atmosphere and the mutual incomprehension among the social classes that in the end created most of the internal difficulties of the seventeenth and eighteenth centuries. These numerous regulations were created and enforced by an efficient bureaucracy during the "golden age." In this fact I see the least glorious facet of the great centuries and disagree with most of those who saw the Ottoman genius in its ability to rule effectively and efficiently millions of people with whom the rulers had nothing in common. The empire's greatest asset was fundamentally its greatest weakness.

Part Three

THE VASSAL AND
TRIBUTE-PAYING STATES

CHAPTER 6

Moldavia and Wallachia

1. THE PERIOD OF NATIVE PRINCES

THE Ottomans considered as their vassals all states whose rulers agreed to pay tribute. Even the Habsburgs fell into this cateogry after Ferdinand I (1526-64) agreed to buy peace from the Ottomans in 1533. In fact the Habsburgs were vassals in name only, as was Ragusa. Transylvania depended much more on the good will of the Ottomans than did those ruling in either Vienna or Ragusa, and the so-called Danubian Principalities, Moldavia and Wallachia, were indeed vassal states in the strictest legal sense of the term. They too, however, had enough freedom to develop independently of the Ottomans to a very considerable degree.

Obviously, within the one chapter devoted to each of these regions, it is impossible to present even a schematic history of any of these dependent states. All that will be att npted, besides showing their ties with the Ottomans, is to give a few references to the most important individuals and developments. The Danubian Principalities were tied to the Ottomans for a longer period than was Transylvania and more closely than Ragusa, and for that reason will be discussed first.

Both principalities are inhabited by Romanians whose origin goes back to the Dacians known both from archeological finds and from Roman records dealing with their Dacian province. Hardly any traces have survived of the Dacian language, but the Romanians speak a Latin language that may or may not have its origin in the days of Roman Dacia. Whatever the reasons for the adoption of the Latin language, by the time of the first princes of the two Danubian Principalities, Basarab in Wallachia (ca. 1310) and Dragoş in Moldavia (ca. 1352), the forefathers of the present-day Romanians spoke this language. The capital of the northern state was located in several cities and was finally transferred from Suceava to Iaşi in 1466. Wallachia's capital moved from Argeş to Tirgovişte, and in 1659 to Bucureşti.

113

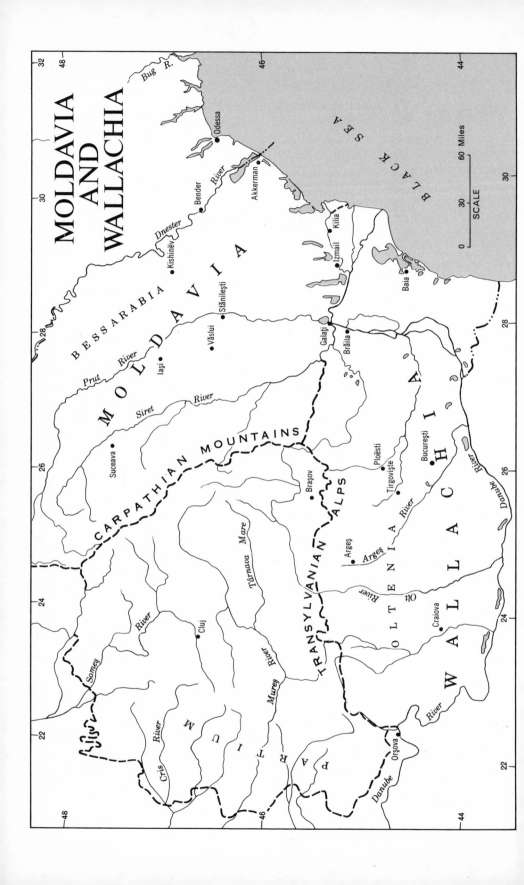

MOLDAVIA AND WALLACHIA

BLACK SEA

SCALE

0   30   60 Miles

Bug R.

Odessa

Bender

Dnester River

Kishinёv

Akkerman

BESSARABIA

Kilia

Izmail

Baia

Stănileşti

Văslui

Galaţi

Brăila

Prut River

Iaşi

Siret River

M O L D A V I A

Suceava

Ploёsti

Bucureşti

Tirgovişte

CARPATHIAN MOUNTAINS

Braşov

W A L L A C H I A

Argeş

Argeş River

OLTENIA

Craiova

Danube River

Ott River

TRANSYLVANIAN ALPS

Târnava Mare

Cluj

Mureş River

Someş River

M U N T E N I A

P A R T I U M

Criş River

Orşova

Danube River

Mircea cel Bătrîn was the first Romanian ruler to agree, in 1391, to pay tribute to the Ottomans, but two years later he was fighting the Ottomans once more. The defeat of Bayezid I in 1402 at Ankara temporarily removed Ottoman pressure, but by 1417 Mircea was again forced to recognize Ottoman overlordship and pay three thousand ducats in tribute yearly. This arrangement was not permanent, and several Wallachian rulers were able to resist the Ottomans. Vassalage became firmly established, however, after the death of Vlad Tepeş in 1476. Moldavia, located farther away from the Balkans, maintained its full independence longer and did not become a tributary state until 1512. For almost exactly two hundred years, until the Ottomans unilaterally altered the agreement with the principalities and took away the right to elect their own rulers in 1714, this vassalage system remained unchanged. It was followed by the so-called Phanariot period, which lasted from 1714 to about 1830, when for all practical purposes the tie to the Ottomans was severed and the history of independent Romania begins.

Until 1512 several Romanian princes, from Mircea cel Bătrîn to Ştefan cel Mare (the Great) of Moldavia, took every opportunity to act independently of their suzerain and regain independence. Included among these princes was Vlad Tepeş, who earned his historic "fame" as the legendary Dracula by the unparalleled magnitude of his cruelties. Yet, as an ally of both John Hunyadi and King Matthias, he fought the Ottomans repeatedly, although rather unsuccessfully.

A much more impressive figure was Ştefan the Great, who earned the epithet. He became ruler of Moldavia in 1457 under difficult circumstances. Constantinople had fallen, and Mehmed II was rapidly transforming the Balkans into Ottoman provinces. Matthias of Hungary was westward oriented, and the eyes of Casimir IV of Poland (1447-92) were turned to the north. Vlad Tepeş helped Ştefan to gain the throne, but was anything but a reliable friend. After Vlad had fled before Mehmed's army to Hungary in 1462, where he remained for fourteen years, his weak successors offered little help to the Moldavian ruler who found himself practically isolated.

Ştefan began his rule by organizing an army. Opposed at first by the landed aristocracy, the boyars, he managed to raise an army of free peasants whose freedom was tied to military service. We do not know the exact size of this force, but it was considerable, probably between forty-five and seventy-five thousand men. It was very badly equipped and could ill afford to fight a pitched battle against a well-organized force like that of the Ottomans. Its only chance for success lay with a first-rate general. In Ştefan the Moldavians had such a military leader; he knew exactly what his forces could and could not do. He first proved his ability in 1467 when the Hungarians, who wanted to transform Moldavia into a vassal state, attacked him. Ştefan retreated before the superior Hungarian army

until it reached Baia, some thirty-five miles south of Suceava where, not
having encountered any resistance, it encamped. In the middle of the
night of December 14, Ştefan's peasant army infiltrated the Hungarian
camp in modern-day guerilla fashion and won a decisive victory.

The real threat to Ştefan was posed by the Turks and not by Matthias,
whose venture had merely been a deviation from his westward oriented
policy. Radu cel Frumos (the Fair), who had ruled Wallachia since Vlad
Tepeş' flight in 1462, was totally submissive to the Ottomans and allowed
their armies free passage through his lands. Ştefan, feeling the need of a
more reliable man on his southern border, invaded Wallachia in 1471 and
replaced Radu with Basarab-Laiotă, a willing collaborator. Under Ştefan's
leadership the two princes' armies were able to push back the Ottomans in
1473. Mehmed answered with an ultimatum the next year, demanding the
submission of Moldavia. Before replying Ştefan conceived a scorched-
earth policy of defense and secured the agreement of both boyars and
peasants. After he refused Mehmed's demands an Ottoman force led by
the grand vezir was sent against him. Ştefan put his plan into execution
and withdrew, leaving no means of subsistence for the invaders. Winter
also contributed to the enemy's discomfort, and it was a hungry and dis-
pirited Ottoman force that Ştefan finally attacked on January 10, 1475,
about forty-five miles south of Iaşi, near Văslui. The same plan that had
worked a few years earlier against the Hungarians worked here, too.

In spite of his victories Ştefan was still in dire straits because he was isolated. His calls for help brought nothing but complimentary letters from
the Pope. Thus, he faced a new Turkish attack alone when Mehmed led
an army against him in 1476. This time the Ottomans were victorious, and
Ştefan had to retreat to the extreme north of his country. He was saved by
an outbreak of cholera in the Ottoman camp and by the timely arrival of a
Transylvanian force. The sultan was forced to withdraw. No more Turkish
attacks came until 1484, when Bayezid II's forces occupied Kilia (Kili, Ki-
liya) and Akerman (Bielgorod, Cetatea Alba, Moncastro), cutting Moldavia off from the Black Sea. The Ottoman forces advanced further and
conquered the capital, Suceava, only to be defeated by Ştefan's great generalship in 1486. They then withdrew from all Moldavian lands, except
the two fortress cities on the Danube. For the remaining eight years of his
reign Ştefan had to defend himself against Poland, which was trying to
extend her suzerainty over Moldavia. Although successful, he was thoroughly and justifiably disgusted with the policy of his Christian neighbors
and suggested that his son and successor submit to the Ottomans in pref-
erence to the Hungarians and Poles should the terms be decent. This was
the advice his successor followed.

Ştefan was not only a soldier, but also a builder of churches and monasteries and an extremely capable and just administrator. He balanced the
various forces within his country well and had the support of clergy, boy-

ars, and peasants. It was unfortunate for him and his people that his powerful neighbors did not understand the Turkish danger properly and did not give him the support he deserved.

The internal situation under this remarkable ruler was stable and still based on the old customs of both Danubian Principalities. In theory the princes were absolute rulers, although they were "officially" elected by an assembly of nobles and clergy whose decision was then accepted by the masses who were surrounding the place in which the elections were held. The princes ruled with the assent of an advisory council made up of the highest dignitaries of the land who were always selected from among the leading noble families. Admission into the ranks of the nobility was reserved to the princes alone, and only they could grant land to the ever greedy boyars and church. Only a few very strong rulers were able to maintain themselves for longer periods on the throne (see Appendix IV), because succession to the thrones was never well regulated, and palace revolts and depositions were numerous. Anyone who wanted power had to "buy" friends. Consequently, the number of free peasants (*călăraşi*) declined steadily and that of the peasants working on estates owned by lords or the church, called *dorobanţi*, increased. The latter cannot really be called serfs because they retained some right to property and could even change their place of domicile.

The major income of both the state and nobility was the tithe, and the lot of the peasantry became harder and harder as time passed. It became really difficult only after the decline of Ottoman fortunes brought about an increased demand for deliveries and payments from vassals who, in turn, raised the dues of the peasantry. These groupings below the prince, clergy, nobility, and two kinds of peasantry, to which a merchant class was later added, survived into the period of Turkish influence, and some of the major offices as well as the prince's council even became known under Turkish names.

Although the institutions remained basically unchanged, the last century before the appearance of the Phanariots was almost wholly dominated by the boyars because there were no strong rulers after Ştefan the Great's death, with one or two exceptions. Princely elections, which continued to follow no firm rule, had to be confirmed by the sultan in exchange for an appropriate gift, and there were chances for intrigue thanks to the need for collaboration with Turkish laic and Greek ecclesiastic authorities. The boyars contributed to the growing misery of the population at large at least as much as did Ottoman corruption and the rapacity of the clergy, although they maintained Romanian institutions intact and even contributed to some salutary new developments. Their power was rooted in their ability to influence the selection of princes and in their steadily growing fortunes.

Before this later period can be surveyed, however, this narrative must be continued from Ştefan the Great's death and deal with two more princes who deserve mention: Petru Rareş of Moldavia (1527-46) and Mihai Viteazul (the Brave) of Wallachia (1593-1601). These two men were very different personalities and have received equally different treatment from Romania's historians. Mihai was the nobler character and had military abilities of significant scope, but it is doubtful that he would have become the great hero of his nation but for the fact that for a short time he united the two Danubian Principalities and Transylvania under one rule, becoming the forefather of modern Romania.

Both men were masters of intrigue, a prerequisite for a successful Romanian prince in the sixteenth century. Their lands were tied to the Ottoman Empire by agreements of vassalage, a fact that did not deter the Habsburgs or the Jagiełło and later Vasa rulers of Poland, all of whom were empire builders. Thus, the Romanian princes not only had to satisfy their masters in Istanbul, but they also had to maneuver between the ambitions of their strong Christian neighbors, including even the princes of Transylvania. Rising Moscowy, the strong Crimean Tatars, and occasionally even the Cossacks had to be included in this very difficult game of warding off claims, interventions, pretenders backed by one or the other of these foreign powers, and outright military attacks.

This situation had a few advantages. The Romanian princes controlled "foreign relations," which were more often dangerous than helpful, and still very much regulated trade with their neighbors. Most important, cultural contacts, especially with Poland, were not cut off, and the principalities were able to participate more fully in the European cultural movements than were the "core provinces." The Romanians paid heavily, however, for these advantages. While the Ottomans protected their own provinces, they seldom lifted a finger to defend their vassals whom they often attacked and "punished" for having relations with the "enemy," not realizing that under the circumstances this was unavoidable.

Petru Rareş, who saw Zápolyai losing the civil war with Ferdinand, naturally wanted to secure his western borders and in 1529 and 1530 occupied parts of Transylvania. The next year as an ally of Moscowy he attacked Poland, but was defeated. For the next seven years he maneuvered between Ferdinand, Zápolyai, the Poles, Moscowy, and his Ottoman overlord, who finally lost all confidence in him. In 1538 Süleyman I led a large army against him and conquered all of Moldavia, replacing Rareş with his son on the Moldavian throne. It was at this time that the Ottomans constructed the fort of Bender (Tighin, Bender'i), completing a line of strong points on the lower Danube and Dnester in which they continued to keep garrisons to the very end of their rule. When Zápolyai died Rareş, who was his prisoner, escaped and went to Istanbul; by 1541 he was back on the throne. The price was heavy. He had to accept a janissary guard at his court and agree that the tribute figure be raised to twelve thousand ducats. He died in 1546 and was followed by several princes who were distinguished only by the great variety of vices they displayed. Thus, the sixteenth century closed on a sad note in Moldavia.

Mihai Viteazul, Prince of Wallachia, ends this century. His international position resembled that of Rareş in that he too had to maneuver and double-cross and was, in the end, fatally double-crossed by the Habsburg general Georg Basta. His position, however, was even more precarious than Rareş' had been. Istanbul was steadily sinking into a morass of corruption. The princes of Moldavia were weak and usually under the influence of the first Vasa king of Poland, Sigismund III (1587-1632), a very ambitious man. Having passed through its first period of strength, Transylvania was ruled by two very weak princes, Sigismund and Andrew Báthory, who could not prevent the Habsburgs from sending armies into their land. Sigismund Báthory even went so far as to cede his land to Emperor Rudolf.

Under these circumstances Mihai had no choice but to institute countermoves before his little principality was hopelessly surrounded by giants. He had a strong but limited army based mainly on a new force in the Danubian Principalities, the rural gentry. The interests of this group coincided with the prince's so far as maintaining the internal independence of Wallachia was concerned, but the gentry was instrumental in the rapid deterioration of the peasantry's situation. Mihai mounted two brilliant military campaigns: the first in 1595 against the Ottomans, who resented his overly independent diplomatic moves, and the second in 1599 against Andrew Báthory. The following year he became master of Moldavia.

The weakness of Mihai's position at this moment lay in the fact that in Transylvania, too, he had to rely on the nobility, the only force that could recognize him as ruler and furnish the necessary military forces. Yet, this nobility was Hungarian, and while a segment of it supported the Wallachian, another resented his nationality and a third continued to scheme with the envoys of Rudolf. As a result of complicated intrigues the Habsburgs sent an army into Transylvania to help their faction. Led by the able general Basta, they defeated Mihai in September of 1600 and forced him to recross the Carpathians. Encouraged, the Poles moved into Moldavia and put their own candidate on the throne. Maintaining his composure, Mihai came to an agreement with Rudolf and was back in Transylvania as Basta's ally the next year. These two able generals had no difficulty crushing all opposing forces, but Basta, who realized that his and his ally's aims were not identical, double-crossed Mihai and had him murdered. With his death the last Romanian prince capable of making independent policy disappeared from the scene, and power fell more and more into the hands of the boyars.

The dominant position of boyars was threatened only during the roughly two decades when Matei Basarab (1632-58) was ruler of Wallachia and Vasile Lupu (1634-53) was prince of Moldavia. Their unusually long reigns indicate that these were men of exceptional ability, but they were unable to reverse the trend for several reasons. First, by the time Matei and Vasile had become rulers most princely lands had already been granted to boyars or to the church by previous princes. Thus, the only way the two rulers could reward the support of their respective nobilities was by permitting their nobles to acquire more and more power over the peasantry. Second, Vasile Lupu was a very ambitious man who was not satisfied with being prince of Moldavia and coveted the richer Wallachian throne. Third, the Ottomans, who were in a very unfavorable position before the appearance of the Köprülü grand vezirs and probably were in no position to resist united Romanian pressure for concessions, favored Lupu's adventurous plans. Consequently, instead of joint action by two relatively strong princes the two principalities fought each other three times, in 1637, 1639, and 1652, to the delight of the Ottomans. Each time Vasile Lupu was the aggressor.

Although it might not have been possible to wring serious concessions from the Ottomans even by joint action, it might indeed have been possible to stabilize the internal situation in the two principalities under the relatively long rule of strong princes in spite of the steadily growing power of the nobility if both men had concentrated on internal affairs. Given Lupu's character, reinforced by Ottoman encouragement, this last chance of curbing the growing influence of the nobility was not utilized.

It is worth noting, before other issues are discussed, that it was during the reigns of these two princes that Phanariot families acquired their first footholds in the principalities with the help of the Ottomans and the Orthodox Patriarch (see section 4 of this chapter). The Phanariots used their geographic and financial position to influence ecclesiastic appointments. Most importantly, they became involved in the various payments that the principalities had to make to Istanbul and in the growing trade between this city and Moldavia and Wallachia. The next section will deal with these questions.

Both the rule of an occasional strong prince in the sixteenth century and the domination of the boyars in the seventeenth were made possible by the Ottoman attitude towards the Danubian Principalities. So long as these lands did not get involved in foreign affairs to the point of endangering Ottoman policy, and so long as dues and taxes were delivered and the key fortifications kept securely in Ottoman hands, Istanbul paid relatively little attention to what went on in Moldavia and Wallachia. The above mentioned obligations became much more onerous in the seventeenth than they had been in the sixteenth century, and this fact contributed considerably to the rapid deterioration of the Romanian peasantry's position and to the speedy rise of the lower boyars. Therefore, before their century is reviewed the demands the Ottomans placed on their Romanian vassals must be examined.

2. OTTOMAN RELATIONS WITH MOLDAVIA AND WALLACHIA

THE vassalage agreement that Ştefan cel Mare's son, Bogdan III, concluded with the Ottomans early during his rule was similar to that between the Ottomans and the Wallachians. The Ottomans were to receive a yearly tribute; certain "exports," mainly food stuffs, of the principalities had to be directed toward Istanbul; and the princes, once elected in the traditional manner, could not assume power until they were confirmed by their overlord, the sultan, In exchange all internal matters were to be left to the princes and to the "local ruling institutions"; elections for princely dignities were to be conducted as before; no Muslims were to settle in Moldavia and Wallachia; no mosques were to be constructed in the principalities; and no Ottoman garrisons were to be stationed there. These provisions were not strictly kept. Kilia and Akerman were occupied, Bender was constructed, Rareş had to accept the janissaries as his "body guard"—these were only foretastes of similar later moves, including the settling of Muslims in the Dobrudja. On the whole, however, the illegal moves were not of such magnitude that they left a permanent imprint on the development of Romania. There were small borrowings like calling the council of the princes *divan* and a few pieces of clothing or furniture, but on the whole the Turkish influence in the principalities was not too important.

Much more important were the "official" relations and economic problems created by the vassalage ties, whose first permanent feature was the yearly tribute that both principalities had to deliver to Istanbul. From the few data supplied by Romanian historians it is possible to construct a rather revealing table indicating the yearly fluctuations of tribute payments (see table 2). Richer Wallachia always paid more than Moldavia.[1]

While the rise in the tribute amounts can be explained by inflation and the central treasury's growing need for money, not all the fluctuations make good sense. For example, the great inflation that occurred during the years immediately following 1584 affected the *akçe* and not the ducat. The sudden rise in tribute money can only be explained indirectly by the inflation. With most of the income coming in from the "core" provinces in depreciated *akçes*, in order to meet its obligations the central government doubled the tribute of those who continued to pay in good money. The highest figures for both provinces, in 1593, are also explainable if it is assumed that they represent basic tribute payments as well as *avariz* in the midst of a very costly and protracted war with the Habs-

1. Tribute figures given in P. Constantinescu-Iaşi, Em. Condurachi, C. Daicoviciu, et al., eds., *Istoria Romîniei*, 4 vols. (Bucureşti, Editura Academiei Republicii Populare Romîne, 1960-62), 2:779-80 and 3:14-16.

TABLE 2
TRIBUTE PAID BY THE DANUBIAN PRINCIPALITIES

Wallachia		Moldavia	
Year	Tribute in Ducats	Year	Tribute in Ducats
1417	3,000	1456	2,000
1503	8,000	1465	3,000
1541	12,000	1481	6,000
1542	24,000	1503	10,000
1545-59	50,000	1552-61	30,000
1567	65,000 prox.	1568-72	35,000
1584	125,000	1593	65,000
1593	155,000	1620	38,000
1601	32,000	1634-53	25,000
1632	130,000	1685-93	26,000
(The figures remain fairly unchanged until the beginning of Phanariot rule.)		(The amount rose to 42,000 just before the Phanariot period began.)	

burgs. The low 1601 figure in the case of Wallachia probably reflects Mihai Viteazul's ability to drive a hard bargain. The rather even amounts collected after the middle of the seventeenth century coincide with the re-establishment of fairly regular administrative practices by the Köprülü grand vezirs.

In addition to this regular contractual tribute payment the Danubian Principalities paid contributions called *peşcheşurile* by the Romanians. This was clearly a Romanian version of the Turkish *peşkeşler*, meaning literally gifts, and was in practice an accession gift paid to the sultans when they mounted the throne. In the case of the principalities, however, these gifts were paid whenever a new prince assumed his dignity in the principalities. The first indication of a payment of this kind is the gift of twelve thousand ducats together with various deliveries in kind made by Petru Rareş when he became Prince of Moldavia.[2] Rareş' gift went to the sultan, but as corruption grew after Mehmed Sokollu's death, more and more officials of both the *birun* and *enderun* had to be satisfied with gifts. When one considers how frequently the princes in Moldavia and Walla-chia changed, it is no wonder that the Romanians began to look at the *peşcheşurile* as a regular tax. In fact it was a much heavier imposition than the basic tribute payment. For example, these "gifts" averaged 650,000 ducats yearly between 1581 and 1590.[3] In later years the averages were not so fantastic but the practice continued.

The records do not include under the heading "payments" additional amounts that were spent rather freely on "gifts" in Istanbul. The two *kapı kahyas*, representatives officially assigned to the central government to watch over the interests of the masters, paid substantial amounts, as did the unofficial agents of those ambitious persons who tried to gain the

2. *Ibid.*, 2:780.
3. *Ibid.*, 2:782.

princely office. Monies paid by these people should also be included when payments to Istanbul are calculated. Thinking of these various cash payments and other deliveries in kind, one cannot but be amazed by the wealth of the Danubian Principalities and even more so by the labor of the peasantry that not only supported the local princes, boyars, and churches, but was able to produce these "exportable surpluses."

Various figures are available for deliveries in kind, a form of fixed tax independent of the "exports" that were directed toward Istanbul. One example, however, will have to suffice. Around the middle of the seventeenth century Wallachia delivered yearly 42,000 pounds of honey and 25,000 pounds of cereals, while Moldavia contributed 28,000 pounds each of honey and cereals, 600 ox hides, 600 "weights" of tallow, 500-600 "pieces" of cloth for the uniforms of galley slaves, and an additional 2,800-3,300 pounds of cereals to feed the workers in the arsenals.[4] Naturally, the principalities also had to supply the garrisons stationed on their own soil. Obviously, the fixed obligations of the principalities, including the various "gifts," amounted to large sums and represented a serious economic drain. Although officially the princes were responsible for collecting and delivering the cash and goods that went to Istanbul, they relied heavily on the nobles, or at least on those whom they either controlled or who backed them, to collect what was required from the peasantry. The steady growth of the boyars' power could be attributed to this fact alone, but it was made much easier by the weakness and rapid succession of rulers.

The famous Romanian historian A. D. Xenopol calculated that early in the the seventeenth century the two principalities were able to produce a yearly revenue of 600,000-800,000 ducats, of which about two-thirds went to Istanbul and 100,000 was spent by the princes on their courts and mercenary troops. That left about 100,000 ducats for the princes' own cash boxes.[5] If Professor Xenopol's figures are correct, one wonders why so many men constantly intrigued and spent large amounts on being placed on the thrones and what were the sources of the monies they spent on these pursuits. Clearly, few could afford these expenses. The only explanation must be found in the existence of boyar cliques that wished to get the most lucrative positions once their candidate became prince, hoping against all odds that his rule would last long enough to permit them to make a profit on their investment. Such an explanation would also shed light on the rising power of the nobles and steady degradation of the peasantry. It is, therefore, not surprising that many Romanian historians con-

4. *Ibid.*, 3:21-22.
5. Alexandru Dimitrie Xenopol, *Histoire des Roumaines de la Dacie trajane*, 2 vols. (Paris: E. Leroux, 1896), 1:531, quoted by R. W. Seton-Watson, *A History of the Roumanians* (1934; reprinted, Hamden, Conn.: Archon Books, 1963), p. 73.

sider the period between the death of Mihai Viteazul and the beginning of the Phanariot period the century of the boyars.

At the end of the first section of this chapter, reference was made to the beginnings of financial involvements of the Phanariots in Romanian affairs. These had to do not only with the tribute and *peşcheşurile* payments, but also with a third kind of Ottoman demand that affected local lords, merchants, Greeks, and several other people: Istanbul had to be supplied with food and raw materials for the city's industries.

During the last days of its independent, city-state existence Constantinople's population was probably as low as forty thousand, but by 1520 the forcible resettlement policies of Mehmed II and his successors had increased the number of inhabitants by about 700 percent according to the census of that year. Toward the end of the sixteenth century slightly more than a half-million people lived in Istanbul. To this number must be added the population of several substantial suburbs. While the sultans forcibly repopulated villages both in Europe and Asia near their new capital, these could not supply the needs of a true metropolitan area. Not only did the usual needs have to be satisfied, but occasional food shortages led to riots which threatened the stability of the state. In order to solve this problem, the exports of certain European and Asian provinces and at times even those of Egypt were reserved for the capital.

The Ottoman rulers faced a dilemma. On the one hand, they had to make certain that Istanbul received the necessary supplies at a reasonable price; on the other hand, they had to make sure that the agriculture and trade of the donor regions were not ruined. The major problem was the fact that the "market price" in the provinces was often higher than what the government believed could be borne by Istanbul's markets, given the large number of relatively poor people living in the city. *Fermans* of numerous sultans deal with this problem. In essence these imperial edicts specified the kinds of supplies, the quantities to be delivered, and the price to be paid. At the same time, in order to keep the provincial economy going the government remitted certain taxes for those whose products were involved, trying to equalize costs and incomes. The purchases were entrusted to a special kind of buyer, who was sometimes sent from Istanbul with specific orders, but more often resided in the provinces. Although the appointment of these agents was not limited to the principalities, discussion of these businessman-city dwellers was left for this part of the volume because their operation in the principalities was "illegal" according to the vassalage treaties. Therefore, it is of greater interest to survey their activities in the Romanian context. Nevertheless, it should be remembered that they operated in all European *eyalets*, particularly in Rumelia where they were especially active in the Bulgarian, Thracian, and Macedonian *sancaks*.

The forced purchase of food, mainly of cereals, sheep, and cattle, was known under different names (*iştira, mubaya, mukayese*). The people who were charged, often against their will, with buying a fixed quantity for a fixed price were known as *celeps* (dealers).[6] If they were also forced to raise some of the livestock they were supposed to deliver they were known as *celepkeşans*. Usually people with some means were picked for this task, including members of the professions and guilds, irrespective of religion. The earliest evidence of this system dates from 1586; by the middle of the next century it was used throughout the provinces. The assignment was not popular, and those who could avoided it. Although deliveries were freed from tolls, taxes, etc., en route and from pasturage fees during the raising and delivery stages, the *celeps* usually had great difficulty making ends meet without cheating. Those who did became small capitalists and took advantage of their position in the eighteenth century. The majority of these people appear to have been *zimmi*. In the principalities most of them came either from the craftsmen and traders in the cities, or from the rising rural gentry.

The magnitude of deliveries cannot be presented in tables for lack of data, but a few figures are available. Cvetkova indicates that during the last decades of the sixteenth century lands about the size of today's Bulgaria supplied over 440,000 sheep yearly.[7] Information concerning the principalities is less exact, but the few data at hand are impressive. *Fermans* of Süleyman I for the years 1558, 1559, 1560, and 1566 specify that for the imperial stables alone the principalities had to deliver 80,000 to 100,000 kile of barley at a price of 6 to 10 *akçes* per kile.[8] In 1566 Süleyman fixed the delivery of Moldavia at 1,000 oxen per year, and for 1591 the same province had to supply 141,000 sheep.[9] One interesting example from Moldavia illustrates the financial difficulties of the princes, the importance of these deliveries, and the growing importance of those involved in this monopolistic trade. In 1589 a butcher named Pervana, clearly acting as a *celep* or *celepkeşan*, forced the son of the ruling prince to deliver 9,000 sheep against a debt of 420,000 *akçes*.[10] He probably made a good deal because by 1585 the price of an *oka* of mutton in Istanbul was 3 *akçes*.[11] If it is remembered that around this time about

---

6. The best short study in a western language dealing with the problem of forced purchases is Bistra Cvetkova, "Le Service des 'Celep' et le ravitaillement en bétail dans l'Empire Ottoman (XVe-XVIIIes.)," *Études Historiques* (Sofia; Bulgarian Academy of Sciences), 3 (1966): 145-72.

7. *Ibid.*, p. 158.

8. Maria Alexandrescu-Dersca, "Quelques données sur le ravitaillement de Constantinople aux XVIe siècle," *Actes du Premier Congres*, 3:666. One Istanbul *kile* (there were various *kiles* in the empire) equals about 88 pounds.

9. *Ibid.*, pp. 669-670.

10. *Ibid.*, p. 670.

11. *Ibid.*, p. 671. There were one hundred *okas* in each Istanbul *kile*.

180 *akçes* were equal to a Venetian ducat, it becomes obvious that the butcher was very rich and the prince deeply in debt.[12]

This trade, which for all practical purposes constituted a monopoly, was made even more stringent by a special forced purchase that was considered a tax, *sürsat zehiresi*, a similar forced sale in favor of the armed forces during times of war. This "tax" amounted to fixed deliveries at fixed prices, which were collected in the same manner as the *iştira* deliveries. It is difficult to find any significant figures, but given the frequency of wars and the size of armies, these "sales" must have been considerable.

By creating a class of fairly well off individuals numbering in the thousands in both the core *eyalets* and the principalities, the Ottomans created a new socioeconomic force that played an increasingly significant role in the histories of these lands. Although the Ottomans might have had the right to establish monopolies in their own provinces, they were certainly not entitled to do so in the principalities. The fact that they did indicates quite clearly the extent to which the princes were incapable of defending the rights of their lands. There can be little doubt that Ottoman actions and exactions not stipulated by the vassalage agreements had greater influence in Moldavia and Wallachia than did the provisions included in these contracts, although the sultan's right to confirm princes, combined with the unregulated method of succession and the ambitions of the many who wanted the throne, cannot be underestimated.

3. THE CENTURY OF THE BOYARS

THE seventeenth century was dominated almost entirely, with the exception of the reigns of Matei Basarab and Vasile Lupu, by the boyars. A detailed description of this groups' rise to power and its rule is already available.[13] When the entire development is surveyed, the story that emerges is familiar to everybody who has studied periods of noble supremacy in any European state. Petru Şchiopul, who ruled intermittently in Moldavia between 1574 and 1591, spoke of a boyar republic in describing his domain. As the nobility grew in number it first made itself masters of princely lands and then transformed most of the free peasants into dependent ones. As the power of this group increased so did its various demands for deliveries and services, and the peasantry was pushed down almost to the level of serfdom. In a sense the nobles produced the various deliveries that had to be made to the Turks for the "market," but also for other ex-

12. *Ibid.* Assuming small sheep yielding about 50 *okas* of meat each (about 45 pounds), 8,000 animals would have represented the market value of 1,200,000 *akçes*. This takes into account 1,000 animals lost in transit. Adding about 50 percent to the buying price for expenses and bribes, the total expenses amount to 630,000 *akçes* leaving this "butcher" a very handsome profit. Most *celeps* handled much smaller quantities and often had serious problems in meeting their obligations.
13. *Istoria Romîniei*, 2:850-56, 861-67, 921-25, and 3:76-77, 128-54 especially, with indications on several other pages.

ports that were still being shipped out of the Ottoman Empire in the seventeenth century.[14] As the nobility did everywhere and especially in Eastern Europe, the boyars became market-oriented without knowledge of modern agricultural or marketing techniques. They achieved maximum profits by steadily increasing the duties of the peasantry. In this endeavor to get rich at the peasantry's expense they had good partners in the monasteries, which owned large estates and proved to be just as unrelenting as the boyars were. As will be seen, a somewhat similar development occurred during the same period in the "core" provinces of the Ottoman Empire. There, however, this development was illegal and proves the weakness of the central authorities. In the principalities the weakness of the central authorities was also a factor, but it made the development entirely legal.

An equally familiar development in the history of nobilities occurred: stratification appeared with the very rich magnates, who had no titles in the Romanian case, above the lesser nobility. Some of the great families (Movilă, Strioci, Ureche, and others) became more powerful than the princes were, and several members even attained the throne. These great families monopolized the important offices and became the real political masters of the principalities; their less powerful fellow nobles occupied lower positions. Naturally, the nobility as well as the clergy managed to get rid of all its obligations to pay taxes and render other services by shifting them to the shoulders of the peasantry, thereby creating a situation that plagued their lands until the end of the second World War.

The above developments are not specific to Romania, but the influence of the boyars in the cities is certainly a unique phenomenon. The end of the Middle Ages and the beginning of the modern period in Western Europe saw the steady liberation of cities from the old feudal restraints. It has been mentioned that this trend existed even in Hungary, where the nobility was able to reverse it by moving against the *oppida*, using the peasant revolt of 1514 as a pretext. In the Danubian Principalities the nobility was strong enough, especially toward the end of the seventeenth and at the beginning of the eighteenth century, to force the princes to make donations touching on lands held by towns and cities and later even the soil on which these urban centers stood. Toward the end of the eighteenth century both laic and ecclesiastic lords received permission to establish towns that were entirely their domains.[15] In some cases even the

---

14. A good study in English of the export trade giving much information on that of the Principalities is Paul Cernovodeanu, *England's Trade Policy in the Levant, 1660-1714*, vol. 41, no. 2 of *Bibliotheca Historica Romaniae* (Bucharest: Academy of Sciences Publication House, 1972). Most of the trade was directed towards Transylvania, Poland, and even the Habsburg domains.

15. The best article in a western language on the Romanian towns is Valentin Georgescu, "Le régime de la propriété dans les Villes Roumaines et leur organisation admin-

revenue of a town was assigned to a lord. In certain instances monasteries and nobles went so far as to consider towns their own on the same basis as their land and to try to exact the same dues and services that they received from the peasants. In spite of these pressures the cities developed and retained some of their rights and privileges. The influence of the lords, however, was felt well into the nineteenth century.

The seventeenth was an unhappy century for the Danubian Principalities, especially for the peasantry, but developments and several personalities merit more detailed treatment than the generalizations offered so far. Two factors, the growth of the influence of Greeks and the Greek language, and cultural developments in Moldavia and Wallachia, were somewhat interconnected and served as the foundation of developments in the eighteenth century.

In Istanbul the influence of the Greeks was growing. Concentrated around the Orthodox Patriarchate in the Phanar district, the Phanariot families were acquiring more power through their control of the ecclesiastic establishments, through their interests in shipping and commerce in general, and through acting as bankers for everybody including the Romanian princes. They really became influential and powerful, however, when their knowledge of foreign languages and their familiarity in general with the West and its culture became indispensible to the Ottomans, who had to rely increasingly on diplomacy in dealing with the Habsburgs, the Poles, and the rising power of Russia.

In 1669 the office of grand translator was created, and the holder of this position became, for all intents and purposes, the foreign minister of the Ottoman Empire. The first holder of this office was a Greek, but not a Phanariot, a man called Panagiotis Nikousios from the island of Khíos. In 1673 he was succeeded by Alexander Mavrocordatos, a young Phanariot in his late thirties who held this office, with two relatively short interruptions, until his death in 1709. Mavrocordatos was a remarkable individual who had studied both law and medicine in Western Europe, where he had published several scientific works. Beginning with his tenure as translator, the Phanariots became junior partners in the Ottoman administration. Several, including members of the Mavrocordatos family, became *hospodars*, princes of the two principalities. Their influence became paramount in political and other domains of the two Danubian lands during the last three decades of the seventeenth century.

Among the Phanariot families that later ruled in Romanian lands were the Ducas, Ghicas, and Rosettis, who in time became romanianized. The first of these families to establish itself north of the Danube was the old Byzantine ruling family of the Cantacuzene, who moved to the principalities in the early 1600s. In 1679 the first member of this partially romanian-

---

istrative aux XVIIe-XVIIIe siècles—Valachie et Moldavie," *La Ville Balkanique*, pp. 63-81.

ized family, Şerban (1678-88), became Prince of Wallachia. Thanks to romanianization a small but extremely important addition was made to the boyar class. People with means and culture began to give a new tone to the life of the richest and most influential segment of this dominant social group.

Less prestigous persons came, too. Greek merchants were attracted by the large-scale export trade of the Danubian Principalities, and more importantly Greek clerics flooded the lands. The growing influence of the church in landowning, even in the cities, was the result of a long process, familiar from the history of all European countries, dating back to the habits of the earliest rulers, of establishing churches and monasteries and endowing them with land and prvileges. During the reigns of Vasile Lupu and Matei Basarab donations of this nature, both by the princes and leading nobles, were made increasingly in favor of monasteries outside the Romanian lands in famous Orthodox centers such as Mt. Athos. This action placed large domains under the Greek clergy, and by the middle of the seventeenth century Greek practically supplanted Church Slavonic as the ecclesiastic language of the principalities.

At the same time Protestantism was gaining large numbers of followers among both the German and Hungarian populations of Transylvania, and these Lutherans and Calvinists began to translate the Scriptures into their own languages and into Romanian. Because Greek was as poor as Church Slavonic as a vehicle to counter this missionary effort, Romanian had to be used. Matei Basarab established the first printing press in 1634, and the first volume printed in Romanian in the principalities was published in 1640, a collection of canon laws. By 1688 the first printed Bible in Romanian (*Biblia lui Şerban*), commissioned by Prince Şerban Cantacuzino, was published. Its supposed translator, Nicolae Milescu, could match an Alexander Mavrocordatos in training, erudition, and European-wide travel, proving that culture was not the exclusive monopoly of the Greeks. By the time the Phanariot period began, 457 works had been printed in Romanian.[16]

Given the instability of the period, the growing influence of Greek, and the selfish behavior of the boyars and clergy, the cultural life of the seventeenth century is remarkable. In the cultural domain the otherwise sad behavior of the masters of the principalities followed a more constructive line because this development had the support of the wealthy and powerful. Works published included translations and original compositions of legal and religious tracts, a few examples of belles lettres, an occasional philosophical treatise, and an an amazingly large number of historical studies. Moldavian historians Grigore Ureche (1590-1674), Miron Constantin (1633-91), and Ion Noculce (1672-1745) wrote during this period.

16. *Istoria Romîniei*, 3:258. Pages 256-94 of this volume give an excellent picture of the cultural history of the seventeenth century.

Of their works Ureche's *Letopiseţul Ţării Moldovii*, ending in 1594, is the most valuable. The most interesting figure among these writers was Dimitriu Cantemir (1673-1723), the last non-Phanariot Prince of Moldavia. A very well-educated individual who understood something of true history and the need for documentation and proof, Cantemir rates as the first historian and not just a chronicler of the Ottoman state with his *Istoria Imperiului Ottomanu*, which was written in exile in Russia between 1714 and 1716. In 1716 he also finished his history of Moldavia (*Descriptio Moldaviae*). He became one of the founders of the St. Petersburg Academy and was elected a member of the Prussian Academy. Although much of this remarkable cultural work was done by Romanians in their native language, there can be little doubt that the example and often the inspiration for their work, if not the themes, were the result of the growing Greek influence in Moldavia and Wallachia. This influence was fundamental in revitalizing the training of the clergy and in changing the cultural habits and values of the upper layer of rich boyars. Just as the Greek influence laid the basis for Phanariot rule, so did it help cultural developments by infusing new elements into them. It should, nevertheless, be remembered that these new elements did not represent the bringing of "western" ideas into a "turkified oriental cultural milieu," because the contacts with Transylvania, Hungary, and especially Poland never permitted the total orientalization of Romanian cultural life and western ideas were never excluded from the principalities. It was only during most of the Phanariot period that the principalities were cut off from the West and had to rely on the Greeks and their culture. It is in the cultural realm that the sad century of boyar supremacy made important contributions to the history and development of the Romanian people.

The fact that Cantemir had to write most of his works in exile is a good indication of the insecurity of the times in which he lived. Not only did boyar pressure on princes, who were for the most part worthless, increase steadily, but so did the demands and interference of the Ottomans, coupled with that of the Phanariots. A good example of Ottoman pressure would be the steady increase in the *peşcheşurile* payments, which reached 650,000 *akçes* when Şerban Cantacuzene assumed his rule.

Additional exactions were levied in the case of princes who ruled "too long." The Wallachian Constantine Brîncoveanu was such a prince; he ended his life watching the execution of his family before he himself was beheaded in Istanbul. His is the best example of a long reign and the real difficulties involved in the position of seventeenth century Romanian rulers. His rule covered the years from 1688 to 1714, which saw the steady retreat of the Ottomans from Hungary following their second attack on Vienna in 1683, ending with the famous Peace of Karlowitz (Karlovci, Karlócza). This Habsburg advance entailed the disappearance of the independent principality of Transylvania, thus making a world power the neighbor of Moldavia and Wallachia. The growth of Habsburg power and the decline of Ottoman might have presented a diplomatic and often military dilemma for the principalities. The fact that in spite of their steadily increasing weakness the Poles continued to claim the right to interfere in Moldavia, whose weak princes were of no help to Brîncovea-nu as he tried to maintain a neutral position in the long Austrian-Ottoman war, presented additional difficulties. When the Ottomans ceded the eastern Ukraine to Russia at the Peace of Radzyń in 1681, a new force appeared on the scene.

By the end of the century the boyars were clearly split into three parties: those who favored the continuation of ties with the Ottomans, the Russophiles, and the partisans of Austria. In Moldavia there was still a pro-Polish faction. Brîncoveanu, therefore, not only had to maneuver among four powers without any help from Moldavia, but also among several boyar factions. That under these circumstances he was able to maintain himself on the throne for twenty-six years is the best proof of his extraordinary diplomatic ability.

Often forced to engage in wars he did not want to fight, Brîncoveanu always made certain that those whom he fought understood that he acted under duress. Although this tactic saved Wallachia from the fate of Moldavia, which was repeatedly overrun by Tatar forces moving to the aid of the Ottoman armies, by Polish raiders, and occasionally even by imperial troops, it earned him the reputation of an unreliable double-dealer. Several times he was put into perilous situations when one side or the other came into possession of correspondence between him and whoever was supposed to be the enemy. So far as the Ottomans were concerned, he could usually slip out of such situations with the help of monumental bribes, but in so doing he placed a very heavy load on the peasantry and helped to alienate even that boyar faction that was backing his policy of the moment. In the end, when he was arrested in his own palace by an envoy from Istanbul, no one raised a hand in his defense. Yet, Brîncoveanu saved his country from even greater difficulties than those into which he was forced to place it repeatedly with his dangerous game, a game that illustrates not so much his "devious" character and ambitions as the impossible situation in which the Danubian Principalities found themselves once the Turkish attack on Vienna failed in 1683.

Dimitriu Cantemir understood the situation correctly. When the Ottomans gave him the throne of Moldavia with the expressed order to eliminate Brîncoveanu, he came to the conclusion that the best policy to pursue in 1710 was collaboration with Russia. Brîncoveanu arrived at the same conclusion at the same time, and, therefore, a rare moment occurred when two able Romanian princes could and did work together. Yet, while Cantemir pursued a policy with determination once he believed that it was right, Brîncoveanu, after many years of trying to keep alternatives open, acted with less vigor. When the Ottomans declared war on Russia, Cantemir was the wholehearted ally of Peter. In April of 1711 he concluded a secret agreement that covered his future whether he won or lost, and later made it possible for him to live "in style" in St. Petersburg. Brîncoveanu was also supposed to help the Russians, who depended heavily on the aid he was to supply. Yet, the Wallachian prince, accustomed to looking for ways out and much closer to the center of Ottoman power, did not make a move after Peter crossed the Prut in July, 1711. Thus, he contributed significantly to the Ottomans' victory over Peter on July 11 at the Battle of Stanileşti.

Cantemir, who with the leaders of the pro-Russian boyar party of Moldavia fled to Russia, was replaced on the Moldavian throne by the son of the great and recently deceased imperial translator, Nicolae Mavrocordatos, whose assumption of the Moldavian throne marks the beginning of the Phanariot period. Brîncoveanu had an enemy in Nicolae, who coveted the Wallachian throne. The good connections the Mavrocordatos had in Istanbul, the growing French influence in this city which was also hostile to the Wallachian prince, and the discovery of fresh correspondence between him and Vienna together with some domestic problems finally put the old prince into the totally isolated position that made his arrest and subsequent execution possible. After his downfall Nicolae Mavrocordatos was placed on the Wallachian throne, and the Phanariot rule began in the second of the two principalities.

4. THE PHANARIOT PERIOD

Much more material is available for the eighteenth than for the previous centuries, and consequently much more has been written about it. Even in western languages monographic studies and articles of great interest have appeared.[17] This makes my work easier, but also requires even broader generalizations than have been presented so far. Moreover it should be noted that this section does not cover the entire Phanariot period. Depending on one's view, that period ended either with the Treaty of Edirne in 1829 or with the Organic Statutes, a quasi-constitution issued in 1831 by the Russian general Count Paul Kiseleff while Russia was occupying the principalities. Clearly, even earlier the French Revolution and the

17. Numerous relevant articles have been published in *Bulletin de l'Association Internationale d'Études du Sud-Est Européen,* and in *Revue Roumaine d'Histoire,* as well as in other journals. There are several monographic studies available, but two will suffice to show the scope of publications: V. Mihordea, *Maîtres du sol et paysans dans les Principautés Roumaines au XVIIIᵉ siècle,* vol. 36 of *Bibliotheca Historica Romaniae* (Bucharest: Academy of the Romanian Socialist Republic, 1971), and Vlad Georgescu, *Mémoires et Projets de réforme dans les Principautés Roumaines, 1769-1830* (Bucharest: A.I.E.S.E.E., 1970.) Vlad Georgescu can also serve as an example of several authors who published good articles in western journals. See his "The Romanian Boyars in the Eighteenth Century: Their Political Ideology," *East European Quarterly,* vol. 7, no. 1 (Spring, 1973), pp. 31-40.

great changes that occurred in the Ottoman Empire at the same time influenced Moldavia and Wallachia, altering the nature of the Phanariot regime somewhat from what will be described in these pages. Nevertheless, the story can be carried up to this European and Ottoman watershed.

The first question that has to be answered is: who were the Phanariots? Their origin in the Istanbul Greek community, the Phanar districts, has led most authors, until quite recently, to state that the Phanariots were members of families recruited, connected with, or descended from that special group of people. Not only has this view been modified of late, but it has also been a patent impossibility all along because, if true, it would have meant that the Phanar district was the most densely populated area on earth and everybody in it an influential millionaire. There can be no doubt that in identifying the Phanariots one must begin with the members of the most important Istanbul-Greek families, whose entire careers were tied to the Ottoman administration and whose fortunes were made in trade, various services, and numerous political and economic functions that they slowly erected into a monopoly thanks to their influence in the center of power. To these leading families must be added hundreds of others, by no means all of which were Greek, who made up their retenue and clientele in Istanbul and throughout the empire. Together these families constituted a smaller empire within the empire, which could not exist without the latter. While there can be no doubt that the larger empire dominated the smaller to the point where even the most powerful Phanariot was a plaything in the hands of an ambitious grand vezir of other important members of the Muslim ruling circles, by the beginning of the eighteenth century a sort of partnership had developed between the two to the point that one could hardly exist without the other. In this respect the numerous references in the historical literature of the Slavs and Romanians to the double Turkish-Greek rule is well taken.

In the case of Romania another element, the local nobility, enters into the picture. Already in the seventeenth century numerous Phanariot businessmen and members of the clergy had found their way into the Danubian Principalities together with their retenues. They had to adjust to local conditions, and numerous intermarriages between them and the local boyars took place. As we know, in the process several originally Phanariot families became romanianized—the Cantacuzene being the most important early example—while several boyar families acquired Phanariot attitudes, habits, customs, and even the Greek language. This process became much more important and involved many more people in the eighteenth century when each newly appointed prince brought several hundred of his followers whom he placed into the most important positions, and, using his princely powers, enrolled them in the ranks of the Romanian nobility. While the fates of the most important of these imported dignitaries were closely tied to those of their masters, the great majority survived the changes of rulers and formed the "new" nobility of Moldavia and Wallachia. In order to protect their interests from the next prince's numerous hangers-on, many of the newcomers made common cause with the "old" nobility.

Consequently, Phanariot, especially in the Romanian context, does not mean Greek. Rather it stands for a group of people who indeed spoke Greek, but could be of any origin and nationality, including Romanian. These people identified themselves and their fortunes with the smaller empire and thus with the larger one by implication. When speaking of Moldavia and Wallachia, the label Phanariot applies to most, but by no means all, of the princes who ruled in the eighteenth century and to the segment of the nobility that formed the pro-princely and, in a larger context, the pro-Ottoman faction. All other persons, even if they belonged to leading Phanariot families residing in the principalities, cannot be considered Phanariots but must be regarded as members of the opposition.

This definition of Phanariots points both to the main influence and to the greatest difficulties of these people. The most drastic change that their appearance represented was a total subservience to Istanbul. Because this was taken for granted they finally were used by the Ottomans in new capacities, including first and foremost the position they acquired in Moldavia and Wallachia. The old rulers, whose long line ended with Brîncoveanu and Cantemir, were "elected" locally and considered by their subjects rulers, *domn* or *voievod*, but the new type of master, who was appointed not elected, was considered only a governor, *hospodar*. This distinction, which the Romanians made as early as the eighteenth century, is a good one and indicates exactly why Istanbul suddenly turned to a new system in selecting its Romanian vassals. The *domns* were too independent; the *hospodars* were, indeed, governors who could be appointed and removed like a *beylerbeyi* and whose main duty was to execute the wishes of the central government. This change was far-reaching and was correctly summarized by Vlad Georgescu, who wrote:

> The army was dissolved. The political, economic and cultural orientation toward East-Central Europe, so predominant throughout the 17th century, was replaced by one patterned on and inspired by the Oriental world of Constantinople. The frequent ties entertained in the 17th century by intellectuals with Europe became uncommon in the eighteenth since the Ottomans, as well as the Phanariots, were afraid of the impact of Europe upon the Romanians (and when we think of Europe we are thinking of it in terms of Europe stretching from St. Petersburg to Paris). For more than a century the Principalities had to accept that which all the political leaders and thinkers had tried to avoid during the previous centuries: integration, albeit limited, into a system dominated by Ottoman and Phanariot values.[18]

The above is an excellent description of what the change to Phanariot rule meant for the Romanian lands. Without an army there could be no

18. Georgescu, "Boyars in the Eighteenth Century," p. 32.

independent foreign policy, even to the limited extent to which, for example, a Brîncoveanu tried to act independently of Istanbul during the wars
of the late seventeenth and early eighteenth centuries. Consequently,
Moldavia and Wallachia became Ottoman provinces to a larger extent
than they had ever been before. When the leading intellectual figures of
the late seventeenth century died or emigrated, restrictions on travel and
trade made it difficult for a new generation to acquire the necessary
training and experience. Not only intellectual life, but even basic education declined rapidly. Only church-supported institutions retained their
ability to perform, but these were entirely in Phanariot hands in the eighteenth century. Thus, the change from ruler to governor brought about not
only a political downgrading, which the difference between these titles
clearly indicates, but also a cultural retrogression.

Among the nobility and rich traders this cultural void was filled by the
acceptance of Greek values. Unfortunately, Greek values did not mean
classical Greek learning, or the major contributions of the giants of the
Orthodox church, or the slow revival of Greek learning and culture; rather
they reflected a curious type of life style that the Phanariots had developed in Istanbul in imitation of the "professional Ottomans." By the end of
the eighteenth century the homes, clothing, and even dietary habits of the
Romanian nobility could hardly be distinguished from those of a well-to-
do Phanariot or even Ottoman living in or around Istanbul. This gradual
change was inevitable and significant.

There were several reasons for this inevitability, the first of which being
the difficulties created for the Phanariots by the fact that they belonged to
this special category of people. They were either Ottoman officials for all
practical purposes or clients of these officials during a century when Ottoman administrative practices were descending to an all-time low in efficiency and corruption was rising to its acme. Although corruption helped
to preserve life, it made tenure in office very uncertain. Appendix IV indicates that twenty-five members of only eleven families ruled in both Moldavia and Wallachia from the beginning of the Phanariot period to 1804,
many of them repeatedly, giving us a total of sixty-two "reigns." Once
ousted, no *hospodar* could be certain of reappointment; several of these
twenty-five men ruled only once and for a short period. The procurement
of appointments involved huge outlays of cash in Istanbul, of which the
future "prince" paid the lion's share. His followers supplied the rest; they
had to be reimbursed and make a profit as rapidly as possible. From this
first fact stemmed the second.

In order to make their "rules" pay, the *hospodar*s had to fill all the important positions quickly with those people who had helped them collect
on their investments. At the same time, the *hospodar*s also had to make
rapid gains for themselves. With all the important positions in the hands
of Phanariots whose homes and life style mirrored that of the *hospodar*,

the local boyars were soon forced to imitate the same life style unless they wanted to be considered backward country cousins. This trend was reinforced by the creation of the "new" nobility mentioned above, which retained its way of life even after its members had become Romanian boyars or in spite of their intermarriages with the "old nobility." This amalgamation of the Phanariot and non-Phanariot nobility was the third factor that led to the introduction of a foreign life style into the upper classes of Romanian society. It should, nevertheless, be remembered that this new way of life did not necessarily mean total identification with Phanariot values. Opposition did exist and grew stronger as the eighteenth century progressed, although in outward appearances its members could not be distinguished from those it tried to displace.

Not only did the outward trappings of the nobility's life change, but its position in the state underwent significant alterations as well. This explains, to a large extent, the opposition of many boyars. In the principalities, as anywhere else, nobility was something an individual acquired by birth unless it was conferred by a ruler. Originally, a noble was a warrior who in exchange for his services, which later included office-holding, was given tax exemptions and feudal rights over the peasantry with landholding providing the basis of his prestige and power. Constantin Mavrocordatos changed this system while ruling over Wallachia in 1739 and introduced his new laws into Moldavia when he became *hospodar* there two years later. He transformed the hereditary nobility into a "service nobility," a concept well known to students of Russian history. Old prerogatives were eliminated, and status within the noble class together with the corresponding privileges and tax exemptions was tied to positions. Descendants of those who held various positions enjoyed the same rights as their ancestors. This reform really completed the transition from the old Romanian to the Phanariot system because it placed princely appointees, Phanariots, and "new" nobles at the top of the official and nobilitary class pyramid. The resulting realignment of rank completely changed the position of those families that were used to power and could become the center of a serious resistance movement.

Constantin Mavrocordatos' reforms extended beyond the nobility and included the monasteries, fiscal matters, and even the position of peasantry. For these reasons he was the most important Phanariot prince of the first half of the eighteenth century.[19] *Hospodar* of Moldavia four times for a total of seven years and of Wallachia five times for a total of fifteen years, he understood the principalities' problems much better than did any of the other early Phanariots. He appears to have understood the difficulty presented by the fact that the Phanariot regime's financial and "trade" obligations toward Istanbul were totally unregulated because the old taxes and exactions were replaced by large-scale bribery whenever

19. See the section devoted to his reforms in *Istoria Rominiei*, 3:435-46.

the throne was assigned to anyone, when princes tried to keep it, or when they tried to replace a rival, and by an unpredictable but steadily growing demand for deliveries and trade being directed to Istanbul. Coupled with the need of the Phanariots to make good their investments and that of all the boyars to make a living, these demands put heavier and heavier pressure on the peasantry. The situation was made worse by the tendency, dating from the previous century, of monasteries, nobles, and princes to exact ever greater feudal deliveries from anybody they could force into submission, including cities. The peasants reacted by slowing down, by hiding produce, and by emigrating in great numbers. It became increasingly difficult for boyar, Phanariot, and even Istanbul to get what they wanted. Between 1741 and 1746 Wallachia alone lost 77,000 peasant families out of a total of 147,000 through emigration, mainly to the region south of the Danube.[20]

In order to alleviate this situation and stem the degradation of the peasantry into serfdom, Constantin Mavocordatos issued reform decrees in Wallachia in 1746 and in Moldavia in 1749. Three taxes (for which the boyars were responsible but which the peasants paid) on cattle, wine presses, and vineyards were abolished, and peasants were permitted to buy their freedom for ten *akçes*. Furthermore, peasants were classified according to the number of oxen they owned; on the basis of these numbers some of their old rights to pastures, wood gathering, and a corresponding amount of land to cultivate were returned. The decrees fixed the tithe the peasants were obligated to pay as well as their *corvée* duties, limiting them to from eight to ten days' labor yearly. Garden plots and orchards were exempted from tithe, but "a peasant who has his own land, which he has inherited [has] no right to abandon the soil."[21] Although these reforms were minimal, they were the maximum Constantin Mavrocordatos could secure from the nobility and the clergy. Serious flaws in the reforms themselves made the peasantry's small gains illusory. Besides tying the peasant to his land for the first time, the labor services were not only defined in days, but also in the amount of work to be accomplished. The amount was set so high that it doubled or even tripled the number of days the peasant had to work if his obligations were measured in terms of labor, which they were. The supervising agents appointed by the prince to enforce his decrees were generally members of the gentry, and so they interpreted the regulations in favor of the landowners. This flaw opened the door to the final enserfment of the peasantry in the second half of the century.

The reasons for this steady worsening of the peasants' lot are basically the following. The increase in deliveries of agricultural goods at fixed

20. David Mitrany, *The Land and the Peasant in Rumania* (1930; reprint ed., New York: Greenwood Press 1968), p. 16.
21. *Ibid*, p. 21.

prices to Istanbul simply meant more money for the boyars, in spite of low prices, because they could sell goods produced for them by the peasants in the form of tithe or other obligations so long as they could increase these deliveries at the expense of the peasantry. The luxurious living patterns introduced by the Phanariots also demanded more income, and this the boyars could get only by exploiting the peasants more than before. Finally, the introduction of distilleries using potatoes and other agricultural products represented another source of income and also made the landlords eager to get more deliveries than ever before from those who worked their lands.

The peasants of Moldavia suffered more than those of Wallachia. In 1766 the boyars forced Grigore III Ghica (1764-67) to issue a new edict that not only raised the peasants' *corvée* to twelve days, but also set the work-per-day demand so high that what the peasant really was forced to do amounted to between thirty-five and forty days of labor each year. Nor were the boyars satisfied with this gain. In 1775 they forced Grigore II Ghica (prince for the fifth time, 1774-77) to add another five days to the peasants' labor obligations, together with additional work duties to repair dams, irrigation works, and other water-connected duties. These new duties amounted roughly to what the ecclesiastic and lay landlords demanded at the time, a tithe on the peasants' labor to equal their obligations of deliveries in kind. All this additional free labor represented a force that could be put to work on previously uncultivated land. Thus the lord's income was increased considerably, but at the same time the degradation of the once-free peasant into a serf was completed.

In Wallachia Alexandru Ipsilanti (1774-82) did increase the labor obligation of the peasantry to twelve days in 1776, but this obligation could be transmuted to fixed cash payments. Furthermore, only the number of days was stipulated; the amount of labor required was not. Thus, it was impossible for the lords to transform twelve days of *corvée* into three times that many. By the end of the century the peasants of Wallachia seldom worked even the required twelve days. I have not found any satisfactory explanation for this marked difference between the two provinces, although several explanations have been offered. In both provinces further restrictions and obligations were put on the peasantry in the nineteenth century, and not even the famous Organic Statutes of 1831 significantly alleviated the peasantry's plight.

While the boyars used most of the new wealth for conspicuous consumption, many were active in formulating political and legal reform programs. During the last quarter of the century, they were influenced by the Enlightenment and by the works of the enlightened despots, especially the legislation of Joseph II and Catherine the Great. In the main, however, their views were based on the works of Romanian thinkers of the previous century,[22] which fact indicates that the promising cultural beginnings of the seventeenth century were not developed significantly during the eighteenth. For this sad state several developments were responsible, all of which have already been mentioned: "foreign" rule, increasing corruption, the severing of ties with Poland and Transylvania, and the growing influence of the Greek language and the Phanariot value system. They also explain the growing interest in political and legal reform of those boyars who had more than just their own personal advantage in mind.[23] At first the formulators of these plans aiming at reform and "independence" had simply had the re-establishment of native rule in mind; later they developed plans for real independence in the true sense of the word, and even for the unification of the two principalities. For this development foreign affairs were as responsible as were domestic developments.

Between the beginning of the Phanariot period and 1792, when the interests of the great powers became focused on the events originating in France, the Ottoman Empire fought three wars with Russia (1710-11, 1768-74, 1789-92), one with Austria (1716-18), and one with both great neighbors (1736-39). Austria also joined briefly the last of the wars with Russia (1788-91). During these wars the armies of Austria and Russia occupied the territories of the Danubian Principalities four times for periods lasting from a few months in 1711 to five-year periods in 1769-74 and 1787-92. That these occupations left their marks on the thinking of the Romanians is obvious. More importantly it made them realize that their strategically located lands had become the bone of contention between their overlords, who were less and less able to protect them, and two great powers who made it increasingly clear that they considered Moldavia and Wallachia territories potentially destined to become parts of their own realms.

While during the eighteenth century only the Bukovina was lost (*de facto* in the fall of 1774 and *de jure* in the spring of the following year when the Ottomans legally handed the province over to the Austrians), the realization that much more than northwestern Moldavia could pass from Ottoman into Austrian and Russian hands influenced the thinking and action of *hospodars* and boyars alike. The division between factions favoring one of the three contending parties deepened, but those who favored annexation by either Russia or Austria or permanent inclusion into the Ottoman realm were few. Most of the factions were agreed on one

22. See the works of Vlad Georgescu cited in n. 17.
23. For a good western language summary of legal reform attempts see Valentine Al. Georgescu, "Initiative et échec: deux structure phanariotes en matière de droit (1711-21). Leur insertion dans le contexte des réalités roumaines," *Bulletin d'Association Internationale d'Études du Sud-Est Européen,* vol. 10, no. 1 (1972), pp. 15-37.

point: first power had to be returned to the Romanian nobility, and then "autonomy" broadened as far as possible. They disagreed on the means to achieve these goals. Naturally, the three great powers had no intention of being used for Romanian ends. Their partisans were pushed into more and more extreme positions. This further complicated the domestic political scene. The moves and countermoves were too numerous to be related in detail within the framework of this volume. Suffice it to say that policies affecting domestic affairs and foreign commitments, most of them made in foreign capitals without the participation of Romanians who could only react, became completely intertwined. The resulting growing danger for the principalities' future independence increased the search for political solutions at the expense of most other activities.

The famous Treaty of Küçük Kaynarca, signed on July 21, 1774, is a good example of commitments made without Romanian participation. The principalities had been under Russian occupation for five years prior to the signing of this treaty. It was entirely in Russian hands to decide what the two Danubian lands would gain from the war and the long Russian occupation. While the treaty is best known for Articles 7 and 14, which gave the Russians "the right" to protect the "Christian religion" in the Ottoman Empire, and Article 3, which made the Crimean Tatar lands an "independent state," it also contained several clauses that affected the principalities and their inhabitants. Article 1 assured all those who opposed the Ottomans, including the inhabitants of Moldavia and Wallachia, of general pardon for helping the enemy, including the restoration of honors and properties. Article 9 gave Russia the right to establish consulates wherever she desired. Article 16 restored the principalities to Ottoman rule, but they were freed from paying any "tribute" for two years, after which time the amount was to be fixed and no deviation was to be tolerated. Russia reserved the right to make representations in Istanbul on behalf of the principalities. This last stipulation and the establishment of Russian consulates in Iaşi and Bucharest were designed to keep both Russian influence and possible further intervention in the principalities alive.

What Russia really had in mind became clear after the first partition of Poland, when Catherine the Great once again returned to her southern expansionist plans in the form of her famous "Greek Project." This brought on the last of the wars in which Austria, Russia, and the Ottomans were engaged before the events set in motion by the French Revolution temporarily interrupted the rapid development of what was to be known in history as the Eastern Question. At least the peace treaties (Sistova with Austria in 1791 and Iaşi with Russia in 1792) did not demand further sacrifices on the part of the Danubian Principalities. Documents prove that by this time the ruling classes of the principalities were not satisfied with having their countries returned to the Ottomans. They were right. Given the preoccupation of Austria and Russia elsewhere, the Ottomans violated all provisions of Küçük Kaynarca. They played musical chairs once again with the *hospodar*ships and exacted large bribes, but they were unable to protect Wallachia from the raids of the formidable *paşa* of Vidin, Pasvanoğlu, who created havoc in the regions north of the Danube. At the close of the century this unfortunate province saw the worst of all princes, Constantine Hangerli (1797-99). Fortunately, he was murdered on the sultan's orders before he could ruin Wallachia's economy completely.

By this time, in response to Napoleon's invasion of Egypt, the Ottomans had formed an alliance with Great Britain and Russia. The last-named took advantage of the situation to strengthen her position in the Danubian Principalities. In 1802 she forced the Ottomans to agree to revoke all illegal taxes imposed since Küçük Kaynarca, to appoint *hospodars* for seven years, and not to remove them without Russia's consent before their tenures expired. Under these circumstances it is not surprising that the last *hospodars* who ruled before the Serbian revolt of 1804, Constantine Ipsilanti (1802-6) in Wallachia and Alexandru Moruzi (1802-6) in Moldavia, were strongly pro-Russian in their sympathies, and that their lands appeared to drift once again into the Russian orbit.

Yet, by the turn of the century the Phanariot period was nearing its end, and enough western ideas had penetrated the Danubian lands to make their history in the nineteenth century quite different from what the observers who wrote about them during the Napoleonic period had predicted. These lands were taking the first small steps toward independence and unification, using every possible chance to extricate themselves from the Ottoman overlordship. Ipsilanti tried to help the Serbian uprising and urged Russian intervention, starting a chain of events that led to war between the Ottomans and Russia in 1806. With this war begins, in my opinion, the "modern history" of Romania.

CHAPTER 7

Transylvania

1. HISTORICAL BACKGROUND

TRANSYLVANIA proper is a triangular-shaped land enclosed on the east by the Carpathian Mountains from the source of the Tisza River to their southernmost extension, roughly where the city of Braşov (Brassó, Kronstadt) is located and where they merge with another range, extending westward, known either as the Southern Carpathians or the Transylvanian Alps. This second range is the southern border of the triangle of Transylvania whose third side is made up of a chain of lower mountains— the Semenic (Szemenek), Poiana Ruscăi (Pojána Ruszka), Munţii Metaliferi (Érchegység), Munţii Bihorului (Bihar hegység), Munţii Meseşului (Meszes hegység), and the Culmea Codrului (Bükk hegység). Several times while Transylvania was an independent principality under Ottoman protection, parts of the flat land between the last-listed chain of mountains and the Tisza (the Crişana region of modern Romania) and eastern Slovakia as well as the Sub-Carpathian Ukraine (Ruthenia) were part of this state.

Transylvania first appears in written history under the name of Dacia, which the Romans attacked toward the end of the first century A.D. and which they ruled from 105 to 258. The Dacians left numerous archeological remains and are considered by the Romanians as their forefathers. During the Roman rule they accepted the language of the conquerors from which the modern Romanian language developed. This claim of latinization in Roman times has been disputed by the Hungarians, who agree that Dacians indeed lived in Transylvania while the Romans ruled it and are even willing to admit that they might have learned the language of their masters. The Hungarians claim, however, that they either left when the Romans moved south of the Danube or disappeared during the long centuries between the end of the Roman rule and the appearance of the Hungarians at the end of the ninth century, unable to resist Goths,

TRANSYLVANIA

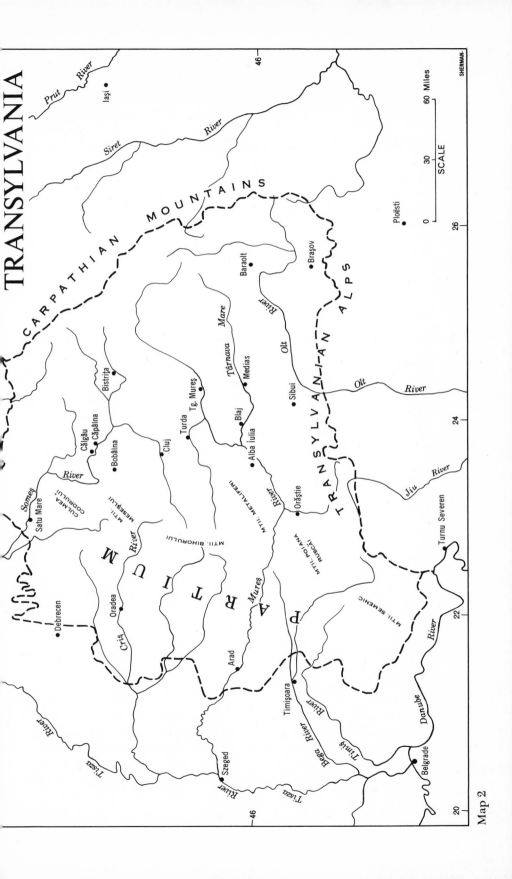

Map 2

Huns, Gepids, Avars, and Bulgarians who ruled Transylvania in the intervening period. The Hungarians claim that the Romanians returned from south of the Danube in the twelfth and especially the thirteenth century.

Much ink has been spilled and a good deal of bad feeling engendered by these conflicting claims. There can be no doubt that the Dacians lived in Transylvania when the Romans conquered this land, and it is perfectly possible that they learned the language of the more civilized conquerors during the 150 years under Roman rule. It makes equally good sense to assume that those who were most adjusted to Roman values left with the legions and even that many of those who remained perished during the turbulent six centuries that followed. This does not mean, however, that there were no Daco-Romanians left in Transylvania by the end of the ninth century. On the contrary, there probably were some, but their number had to be much smaller than it had been when the Romans arrived. Their presence would explain the undoubted re-emigration from south of the Danube of additional Romanians during centuries when life there was much less secure than it was north of the river and when Romanians living there would have looked for safer places among people who were their relatives. In other words, I believe that the Romanians are right in claiming continued residence in Transylvania, while the Hungarians are right when they point out that the number of Romanians living there increased sharply in the twelfth and thirteenth centuries. Whatever the truth may be, there can be no doubt that by the time Transylvania became an independent principality the Romanians made up at least half of her population.

The accepted date for the Hungarians' conquest of Hungary is 896. It is less certain when they turned eastward from the Hungarian plain and passed the western mountain border into Transylvania. There were several moves lasting roughly a hundred years, with the final conquest coming in 1003. At that time the old Roman Apulum, today's Alba Iulia, became the residence, Gyulafehérvár, of a Hungarian comes (*ispán*) appointed governor by St. Steven to rule Transylvania. Beginning with this appointment Transylvania's history paralleled that of Hungary, including the growth of the rule by the nobility over the rest of the population and the country's division into various counties, each ruled by a comes appointed by the king. As time passed the Hungarian counties developed into administrative districts dominated by the nobility. The Transylvanian development was different.

The Hungarians were not the last people to push westward from the Eurasian steppe; Transylvania became the eastern defense zone of the Hungarian Kingdom. It was placed under the jurisdiction of a special royal officer, the *vajda* (*voievod*), who acquired practically independent vice-regal powers and as early as 1263 had the right to appoint the comes for the seven Transylvanian counties. He was the only official of the king, besides the *bán* (banus) of Croatia, who practically ran a small kingdom within the kingdom and could even hold assemblies of those under his jurisdiction—although only with royal consent. This not only gave the Transylvanian Hungarian nobility a special status, but made them the members of the first of the three "nations" of Transylvania. "Nation" (natio) did not mean anything like a modern nation. It simply denoted a group of people—in this case the Hungarian nobility—with full political and legal rights. By the end of the fourteenth century this first nation included among its members several families whose ethnic origin was not Hungarian. The famous Hunyadis are the best example of a family of Romanian origin that became a member of the Hungarian "nation."

The example of the Hunyadis indicates the problem the Romanians faced. There was no reason for the conquering Hungarians, whose values were not national in our sense of the word but feudal once St. Steven had accepted the prevalent western values together with Christianity, to look at the inhabitants of Transylvania, whatever their ethnic affinity, in any way but according to feudal class lines. When this system was accepted by the Hungarians the old leadership element acquired the status of nobility automatically, but there was no such element at the time among the Romanians. When Romanians rose—and especially in the early centuries of Hungarian rule this was not too difficult for anybody—from the lower to the higher strata of society, they automatically became members of the class into which they were elevated, leaving the rest of their nationals behind without the possibility of developing into a "natio" in the medieval sense. In time religious and other problems were added to this original difficulty, until the Romanians were the only people without a "natio." Moreover, they were considered unfit to become one by all those who had achieved this status by the time Transylvania acquired its independence.

In addition to the Hungarians the so-called Saxons (German settlers who came from as far as Flanders) and the Székelys (secui, szekler) had nations. Of these two peoples the latter are hard to define ethnically. According to tradition they were the remnants left behind when the Huns retreated from Europe. Although they spoke Hungarian by the time they first appeared in documents and were clearly related ethnically and linguistically to the Hungarians, they were not part of the people who had moved from the Eurasian steppe to Hungary in the ninth century. Living in their own communities, later counties, in southeastern Transylvania and enjoying complete autonomy in exchange for border guard duties, they were considered nobles to a man and elected their own comes. Their lives, if not tribal then at least nomadic in origin, were organized along communal lines. Thus, it was very difficult for any one of them to become a big lord or the owner of large properties. They lived their own lives as a distinct community that followed its own traditional customs and rules. Being considered nobles from the very beginning of Hungarian feudal rule, they automatically became the second nation of Transylvania which had to obey the king and the *vajda* who communicated with them through their own comes. They paid no taxes and yearly elected their local officials in each district from among themselves. Just before Transylvania became an independent principality they became a bone of contention (see below).

The first German settlers were invited to Transylvania during the reign of King Géza II (1141-62), were used, once again, to guard border passes, and were assigned land in the region of Sibiu (Nagyszeben, Hermann-stadt). Some of the later settlers established themselves in the region around Bistriţa (Beszterce, Bistritz), but most of them moved into the region of their original settlement, which they called the *alte lande* and expanded mainly to the east along the northern slopes of the Transylvanian Alps and also to the north into the lands situated between the Olt and Târnava Mare (Nagy Küküllő, Grosse Kokel) rivers. Because they were invited for reasons that the kings of Hungary considered important (border defense, colonization, trade), the settlers received privileges from the beginning. In 1224 these were codified and extended when King Andrew II (1205-35) issued a charter, the *Andreanum,* assigning them, as a united "natio," the region situated between Orăştie (Szászváros, Broos) and Baraolt (Barót). Nobody but Saxons could be settled in this territory. The Saxons were given the right to elect their own comes who was responsible only to the *vajda* and to the king; they received immunity from fiscal dues in exchange for the payment of 500 "marks" in the value and weight used in the days of King Béla III (1172-96); and their military obligations were fixed at five hundred men for service within the country, one hundred beyond the borders provided the king led his own army, and fifty if somebody else was commander. Furthermore, they had the right to elect their own priests and judges and could be brought before a royal court only if their judges were unable to settle disputes. They also had the right to hold their own fairs and to travel and make deals at other fairs anywhere in the country free from taxes and dues. The *Andreanum* elevated the Saxons to the status of the third full Transylvanian "natio."

All three "nations" had their own political and ecclesiastic organizations, and self-government in their own affairs. The Hungarians and Székelys had their own nobility from the beginning, and soon the Saxons too developed an equivalent group of privileged individuals, the *gräves.* With the rapid development of the Saxon towns, the leading members of the bourgeoisie were the really important element in that "natio."

The last of the Árpád kings died in 1301, and after two short insignificant reigns the Hungarians turned to the Anjous of Naples and elected Charles Robert as their king. Led by the *vajda,* the Transylvanian Hungarians refused to acknowledge his election, and it was only sixteen years after he became king that the forces of Charles Robert broke the Transylvanian opposition, in 1324. The king reorganized the political and administrative structure of the seven counties, placing them for all practical purposes in the hands of his supporters, the petty nobility and the gentry. From the days of the first Anjou dates the struggle between the leading aristocratic families and the much more numerous petty nobility for power in the Hungarian state. In Transylvania the Székelys counted among the latter and suffered grievously from the resurgence of the magnates after the death of King Matthias I in 1490. Out of this struggle grew the power of the Zápolyai family. Before this important event is presented, however, another occurrence of far-reaching import must be discussed: the great peasant revolt of 1437-38, which finally fixed the rule of the three "nations" firmly, excluding the Romanians from all possible participation in the political life of Transylvania.[1]

There were two major reasons for the peasant revolt: the changes in the situation of the peasantry in Transylvania, and the growing Turkish danger. Louis the Great, the son of Charles Robert, was interested in protecting the serfs from the growing demands of the landlords. In 1351 he issued a law fixing their obligations at a tenth of their produce for the church and a tenth for the lord. This law was not strictly enforced in Transylvania where the established custom prevailed. The beginning of the Turkish wars coincided with the growth of towns which resulted in a decrease in the number of Hungarian and Saxon peasants either from losses suffered on the battlefield or from migration into the cities. In order to replace them the ecclesiastic and lay lords forced the Romanians to settle on their lands and become serfs. This produced a significant loss of revenue for the church because the new serfs, being Orthodox, did not pay the tithe at a time when its military obligations as a landowner were growing. In order to make it possible for the ecclesiastic lords to furnish the required number of soldiers, the Romanian peasants were finally forced to pay the ecclesiastic tithe increasing their obligations and discontent considerably. Once new serfs were settled on the land the laws of deliveries and services were strictly enforced. The old serfs also suffered. With their military obligations increasing the nobles began to collect the tithe to which they were entitled according to the law of Louis the Great; at the same time they continued to collect the "traditional dues."

While these internal developments were occurring, the growing Turkish danger forced the king, Sigismund of Luxemburg (1387-1437), to debase the currency and to institute new taxes. He finally issued new military regulations for Transylvania, which demanded, among other things, that one serf out of every thirty-three serve in the armed forces. The three "nations" felt that this did not give them enough men, and the Transyl-

1. The best description of the events of 1437-38 in a western language is Ştefan Pascu, *Der Transsilvanische Volkaufstand, 1437-38*, vol. 7 of *Bibliotheca Historica Romaniae* (Bucharest: Romanian Academy of Sciences, 1964).

vanian assembly voted that one serf out of every ten had to join the forces.

These double demands, economic and military, brought increasing unrest beginning with 1429. The authorities did not try to understand the disquiet; they only tried to supress it. The peasants responded by refusing to pay taxes and by hiding from the recruiting officers. The bishop of Alba Iulia, George Léper, answered by excommunicating those who refused to honor their obligations, making the situation even worse. He went even further and in 1436 accused the recalcitrant peasants of Hussitism, invited the Inquisition into Transylvania, and not only started the usual activities of this institution but used it for the forced conversion of Romanian serfs to Roman Catholicism as well. Finally, he also demanded the payment of all dues that had not been delivered in the past in a new currency that put an increased burden on the peasants. They had no choice but to revolt and did so regardless of ethnic origin in the spring of 1437. Several members of the lower nobility, which supplied most of the military leaders, and even members of the bourgeoisie joined the peasants, showing their own growing discontent with the arbitrary rule of the high clergy and aristocracy.

In a great battle toward the end of June, 1438, in which the peasantry used tactics learned from the Taborites, the peasants defeated the *vajda's* armies near the small town of Bobâlna. Their victory was followed by a settlement in which the nobility agreed to restore the rights of the peasantry, freeing them from serfdom. Bishop Léper gave up his claims to uncollected dues and to the tithe of the Orthdox, while the nobles gave up their right to all new taxes and impositions. Furthermore, the right of the peasants to free migration was not only recognized anew, but a new right of armed assembly once a year to judge and punish those lords who usurped their power was added as well. Out of these basic rights there could have grown either a fourth "natio," which, given the great number of Romanian peasants, would have been Romanian, or another development that would have given the peasants in Transylvania more liberty than anywhere else in Europe. Naturally, these possible developments were what the nobility did not want; what finally happened was just the opposite, a formal reorganization of the three "nations" into a Union of the Three Nations. The new union was formally established on September 16, 1437, at a meeting of the leaders of the three nations in the village of Căpâlna near the present-day town of Călgâu in northern Transylvania. Directed against all "enemies" of the three united nations, in the short run it led to renewed hostilities and in the long run to the ossification of the structure that it established. All rights were reserved to its members, and it was impossible for a new element, first and foremost the Romanian, to gain any rights in Transylvania.

After several further defeats the union, with some help from the king, finally defeated the peasants, took bloody revenge on the leaders and prisoners, and for a while deprived the city of Kolozsvár (Cluj, Klausenburg) of its privileges for having backed the peasants to the end. Meeting for the first time as the Union of Three Nations in 1438, the new ruling coalition deprived the peasants of all their rights except migration in limited form, and, naturally, reimposed all the dues and obligations that they had agreed to abolish less than a year earlier. This revolt and the union that resulted from it gave Transylvania her sociopolitical institutions and organization during her existence as an independent principality.

Returning now to the revolt of the Székelys, which helped to bring the Zápolyai family into prominence, we find that the Székelys, limited as they were to their jointly owned districts, soon ran out of land. Many were unable to support themselves on an economic level that permitted them military service on which their privileges were based. Taking advantage of this situation, the well-to-do among them tried to acquire most of the land and transform the rest of the population into serfs. Fortunately for the would-be serfs, these were the days of King Matthias I (1458-90), who distrusted the magnates and tried to build up the lower aristocracy. On the king's orders John Szentgyörgyi, who was both *vajda* and comes of the Székelys, confirmed this people's privileges in 1466, forbidding their enserfment. Yet, the economic and related military problems remained the same, and the king was forced to issue new regulations in 1473. The new ruling differentiated between those who could join the army with three men on horseback, those who were able to appear similarly equipped but only in person, and those who could appear only as light infantrymen. All were recognized as free nobles, and only the small segment that could not even serve as infantrymen could be enserfed. Although this ruling preserved Székely liberties, it did not change the economic problems of their lands. When in 1491, after Matthias' death, Steven (István) Báthory became both *vajda* and comes of the Székelys, he treated them as his own subjects, if not serfs, in total disregard for the law. Fortunately, Báthory had important enemies and on their request was dismissed by Ulászló II (1490-1516) in 1493. The king reconfirmed the Székelys privileges in 1499.

The dismissal of Báthory was part of the struggle between the magnates and lower nobility, which had gained much influence under Matthias I. The rich and influential Zápolyai family took advantage of this split and took the part of the lower nobility, hoping to reach the throne with their help as Matthias had. The Székelys, belonging to this group, took part in this struggle and held several meetings without either royal consent or the *vajda's* permission. They backed Zápolyai, who in 1510 at the age of twenty-four forced the king to name him *vajda* of Transylvania. Once he had gained a solid base for his plans, John (János) Zápolyai wanted this area quiet and submissive, and in 1519 he crushed the Székelys, confiscating much of their property. Having played the role of the "savior" five years earlier during the Dózsa revolt (see Chapter 3), he became the "national" candidate for the throne after his victory over the Székelys, when King Louis (Lajos) (1516-26), who was only thirteen years old, made him the strongest man in the country with a unified and apparently "pacified" Transylvania serving as his power base. Outside his own province he still acted as the spokesman of the lower nobility, which elected him king in 1526, while the magnates turned to the Habsburg Ferdinand. The result was civil war, the final intervention in Hungarian affairs by Süleyman I in favor of Zápolyai's infant son in 1541, and, as discussed in Chapter 3, the tripartite division of the country and the establishment during that year of an independent principality of Transylvania as an Ottoman vassal state under the rule of Zápolyai's widow, Isabella. Although the attempts of her chief minister, Cardinal Martinuzzi, who wanted to reunite Hungary to fight the Turks, succeeded in having Habsburg rule established in Transylvania between 1556 and 1559, Süleyman I's intervention placed Isabella back on her throne, and the new principality began its century and a half of independent existence.

2. THE LEGAL FOUNDATIONS OF THE TRANSYLVANIAN PRINCIPALITY

IN many ways the development of Translvania into a principality was well underway by 1526. The *vajda* had tremendous powers and for about a century had also held the title of comes of the Székelys. The three "nations," while represented in the diets of Hungary and bound by that country's laws, had had, since the fourteenth century, a diet of their own. This independence was reinforced by the formal Union of the Three Nations and by the actions of strong *vajdas* of whom Zápolyai was the last. The three "nations" continued to be the "political" nations of Transylvania, and the social stratifications remaining unchanged. What resulted was an unique political arrangement that lasted throughout Transylvania's existence as an independent political entity. This unique situation developed during the reign of Isabella (1541-59) and her son John-Sigismund Zápolyai (1559-71) and is therefore best presented by dealing with the events of their rules. But first a few words must be said about the dual legislation and dual law codes mentioned above.

After many years of work at the behest of the king, Steven (István) Werböczy submitted his codification of Hungarian law to the assembly, at the same diet that took the drastic measures against the *oppida* and the peasantry in 1574. It became known as the *Codex Tripartitum* because it had three major sections and was accepted by the king and by the diet but was never officially promulgated because of the opposition of some strong magnates. However, after Werböczy published it three years later in Vienna, it became the basic law of the kingdom. Its influence was very great, and for centuries it served as "the law." The diets did little more than produce interpretations and regulations in conformity with it. To some extent the relationship resembled the connection between the *shari'a* and the *kanuns* in the Ottoman Empire, although the *Triparititum* certainly never had any religious significance.

Transylvania was still a part of Hungary when this new code became the basic legal document of that kingdom, and the code was accepted there, too. Not only did it remain the basic code of the principality after separation from Hungary, but the Transylvanian diet restricted itself even more scrupulously than did the Hungarian to the role of mere interpreter of the law. Thus, Transylvania followed the same laws that royal Hungary, a country that she fought repeatedly, did.

While the *Tripartitum* and events in the Habsburg dominion influenced the position of the king and his administration in Hungary, the princes of Transylvania, the heirs to the position of the *vajda*, retained much of the near absolute power of this former official without the threat of removal from office. This power, coupled with the diet's tendency to limit its function to legal interpretations, made the princes virtually absolute rulers. The princely council of twelve was hardly the instrument to curb their power because its members were appointed and could be removed at will by the princes.

Yet, these nearly all-powerful rulers were vassals not of one, but of two strong monarchs: the king of Hungary and the sultan of the Ottoman Empire. This double vassalage was a unique phenomenon in the sixteenth and seventeenth centuries, but the Transylvanians never took it seriously. They pursued their own policies, and repeatedly fought both of their overlords. For all practical purposes the dependence on the Ottomans dates from the double royal election of 1526 and John Zápolyai's reliance on Ottoman help during the long civil war. Isabella depended even more on the sultan's good will. It must be remembered (see Chapter 3) that originally Süleyman I was not interested in establishing an outright Ottoman province in Hungary; rather he had great interest in having a weak, dependent ruler there. After John Zápolyai's death he had to change his policy, but it was certainly to his advantage to keep the Habsburgs out of eastern Hungary and Transylvania.

After her return to the throne Isabella was fearful that she might be dethroned again. She trusted nobody and fought a hard battle with her nobles not only for absolute power, but also against their attempts to influence her son's education. Yet, she needed the nobility to help her retain not only Transylvania and her royal title, but also those lands of eastern Hungary, which were called for short *Partium*, that lay between the western borders of Transylvania proper and the Tisza River and were under her jurisdiction. By 1556 King Ferdinand I was willing to recognize the existence of Transylvania, but claimed the *Partium* lands. This issue was still unresolved when Isabella died.

Her nineteen-year-old son, who assumed the throne with the title of Elective King of Hungary, was a pleasant, highly educated, and learned individual, but his health and will were weak. For the duration of his rule he retained his mother's friends as chief advisors, including the able diplomat Gáspár Békés, the court physician George Blandrata, and the three young Báthory brothers.

Recognizing the weakness of John-Sigismund Zápolyai, Ferdinand attacked him in 1561. The discontents, including the Székelys, made common cause with the enemy, and the situation became so desperate that John-Sigismund was ready to surrender. His young general Steven Báthory talked him out of doing this, repressed the revolts, and with Ottoman help was able to produce a military stalemate that led to an armistice in 1563. When Ferdinand died the next year, Báthory went over to the attack, but was defeated. In 1565 the Peace of Szatmár (Satu Mare, Sathmar) gave the Habsburgs all of the *Partium* except for the city of Nagyvárad (Oradea, Grosswardein, Varad). More importantly, John-Sigismund was forced to renounce his royal title, accept that of prince of Transylvania, and agree that his land was part of Hungary by swearing an oath of fidelity to the new king, Maximillian (Miksa) I (1564-76). Furthermore, he married Maximillian's sister and recognized the Habsburgs' right to the Transylvanian throne should he die intestate. The first formal dependency was established.

Naturally Süleyman I did not like this arrangement. The army that he sent to a grateful John-Sigismund brought an imperial *ferman* asserting that Transylvania was a vassal state of the Ottoman Empire and obliged to pay a yearly tribute of ten thousand ducats. At the same time this principality was given the same rights that Moldavia and Wallachia had, namely that of electing her princes. John-Sigismund and the anti-Habsburg faction accepted this arrangement and, in so doing, the second formal dependency was established.

The next year, 1566, saw Süleyman I lead an army against the Habsburgs; he was met by John-Sigismund at Belgrade. The war that Süleyman I had begun and in which he lost his life continued between John-Sigismund and Maximillian until 1570, when the Peace of Speier returned most of the *Partium* to Transylvania in exchange for John-Sigismund's reaffirmation of vassalage and the repeated assurance that Transylvania was part of Hungary. Maximillian could accept this arrangement; he knew that John-Sigismund was a sick man who would never have children. Shortly afterwards, in the spring of 1571, John-Sigismund died. The Habsburgs now had a valid claim to Transylvania, but the nobility of that land took advantage of Süleyman I's *ferman* and elected Steven Báthory their prince.

Before we leave the Zápolyai years, one more event must be discussed that gave Transylvania its final and unique structure: the addition of the "four accepted religions" to the "Union of the Three Nations," which completed an arrangement that Baron Miklós Wesselényi called, in the nineteenth century, the "seven deadly sins of Transylvania." The very concept of four accepted religions indicates that this development was the result of the Reformation.[2]

The history of the Reformation in Hungary parallels that of the movement in Central Europe in general. Interestingly enough, its earliest protector was a Habsburg, Queen Mary, the wife of Louis II. Her unpopularity among the Hungarians made the diffusion of Luther's teachings difficult at the beginning and limited to the German settlers in Slovakia and Transylvania. In the latter province it was Johann Honterus of Braşov who became the great apostle of Lutheranism, gaining first the city and soon after most of the Saxon population. The Reformation spread from the Saxons to the Hungarians. This development was facilitated first by the fact that John Zápolyai, although remaining a Roman Catholic, showed great impartiality in religious matters because he had been excommunicated for being an ally of the Ottomans. By the time Queen Isabella returned to Transylvania the majority of the non-Romanian population was Lutheran, although most of the magnates and their families remained Roman Catholics.

By 1556 Calvinism had made its appearance not only in Hungary, where its center had become the city of Debrecen and its main spokesman Martin (Márton) Kálmáncsehi, but also in Transylvania. That year Kálmáncsehi organized the first religious discussion in Kolozsvár, but he gained no adherents. Three years later his successor, Péter Méliusz-Juhász, converted the clergy of that city to Calvinsim. By 1564 most Hungarians were Calvinists, while the Saxons held to their Lutheran beliefs and established their own separate church.

In 1564 the Transylvanian Diet passed a new law giving the "Religion of Kolozsvár" and that of "Szeben (the Lutheran)" equal rights with the Roman Catholics; each locality was to select its own creed, but those who followed another creed were assured the right of remaining in their towns and cities and practicing their religions freely. This remarkable edict of toleration did not extend to the Orthodox, the Jews, or the few Armenians. What the edict of 1564 created was in fact "three accepted religions" following the model of the "three nations." All other creeds were merely tolerated, but they had no rights and their clergy no privileges. This remarkable development was made possible by the sympathies of the ruler John-Sigismund, whose major interest was theology. He was also strongly

2. There are a number of good works dealing with the Reformation and Counter-Reformation in Transylvania, but very few in western languages. Of these, three deserve mention. János György Bauhofer, *History of the Protestant Church in Hungary from the Beginning of the Reformation to 1850 with Special Reference to Transylvania*, trans. J. Craig (New York: J. C. Derby, 1854); John Foisel, *Saxons through Seventeen Centuries; A History of the Transylvanian Saxons* (Cleveland: The Central Alliance of Transylvanian Saxons, 1936); Earl Morse Wilbur, *A History of Unitarianism in Transylvania, England and America*, 2 vols. (Cambridge, Mass.: Harvard University Press, 1945-52).

influenced by the Protestant leanings of his chief advisor, Michael Csáki, and his personal physician, the Italian George Blandrata.

Blandrata had had to quit his native Italy because of his antitrinitarian beliefs, which he carried to Poland, whence he followed Isabella to Hungary and Transylvania. He influenced not only the prince, but also Francis Dávid, Calvinist bishop of Kolozsvár, who in 1564 became what was later called a Unitarian. Thus, in the very year that three religions were "accepted" a fourth made its appearance.[3] Numerous debates followed, and the Diet that met at Torda (Turda) in 1568, under pressure from the prince, gave partial recognition to "the creed of Francis Dávid" and placed it half-way between the accepted and tolerated religions. The next year John-Sigismund embraced the new religion, and finally, in 1571, the Diet of Marosvásárhely (Tîrgu Mureş) officially raised the number of accepted creeds to four. Acceptance came none too soon for the Unitarians, who would otherwise have suffered the same fate that they had met in Italy and Poland. By 1571 Steven Báthory, a strong Roman Catholic, was prince; he called in the Jesuits and started the Counter Reformation. While Báthory's efforts proved successful among the Hungarians, he upheld the law and did not force the Protestant churches into submission. He did preclude further religious development by declaring that the Marosvásárhely decision fixed forever the "accepted" and "tolerated" creeds, and that no others were ever to be permitted to exist in Transylvania. Thus, the province's "deadly sins" were kept to the biblical number of seven.

After Báthory nations and religions began to coincide. The Saxons were Lutherans, the Székelys Unitarians, and the Hungarians Calvinists and Roman Catholics. This not only made the division between the "nations" clearer than it ever had been; it also put a double barrier on the road that could have led to the improvement of the lot of the Romanians. In 1572 Báthory did recognize the old, established Orthodox bishopric at Alba Iulia. Its existence, however, was only tolerated, and the Counter Reformation made its functioning very difficult. It was practically impossible for this see to take the lead in improving the position of those who followed the Orthdox faith.

In conclusion, by the time John-Sigismund died the basic legal system of Transylvania was established. She had a prince who was twice vassal but virtually unhampered in his rule by his council or diet; she had a double set of laws, the *Codex Tripartitum* and those passed by her own legislature or prince; and, finally, she had a unique system defining social and political rights based on belonging to one of the three nations and to one of the four accepted religions. There is a vague resemblance here to

3. The first document using the label Unitarian dates from 1600 (the procedings of the Diet of Léczfalva), and the church to which it was applied began to call itself Unitarian as late as 1638.

early Switzerland with its oligarchic rule, Lutheran Germans, Catholic Italians, and Calvinists in Geneva well protected by mountain chains. But there is also a great difference: unlike the case of early Switzerland where everybody fit somewhere into the picture, in Transylvania at least half of the population, the Orthodox Romanians, was left outside the political, social, and religious structure of the state.

3. THE BÁTHORY PERIOD, 1571-1613

AFTER the death of John-Sigismund Zápolyai the list of Transylvanian princes is dominated by the names Báthory, Rákoczi, and Bethlen. With the exception of the last mentioned they were all relatives of both the Zápolyais and the Polish Jagiełłos. This explains why the Báthorys and Rákoczis were always involved in Polish affairs. The partial family tree given in figure 1 illustrates these relationships.[4]

The Báthorys, using their family connections with the Jagiełłos and Zápolyais, were destined to become a dynasty. That their claim was accepted is proven by the fact that the two princes who were not Báthorys

FIGURE I

THE BÁTHORY FAMILY TREE

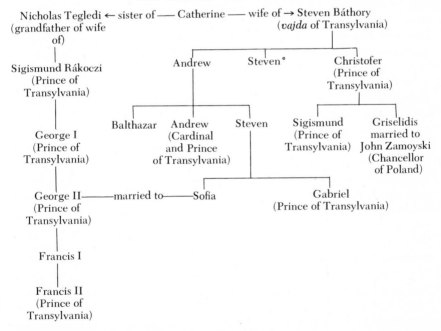

* Husband of Anna Jagiełło, brother-in-law of Isabella Zápolyai, Prince of Transylvania, King of Poland.

4. Based on complete family tree in Ladislas Makkai, *Histoire de Transylvanie* (Paris: Les Presses Universitaires de France, 1946), between pp. 184-85.

prior to the death of Gabriel were Sigismund Rákoczi, shown on the preceding family tree, and Steven Bocskai, who was Christofer's brother-in-law. Unfortunately for the Báthorys, Gabriel, who died in 1613, was the last male of the family.

The Báthory period started very auspiciously. Steven Báthory was a man of great learning and had outstanding diplomatic and military abilities. He was, however, a very hard and even tyrannical ruler. The most glorious years of his life were spent in Poland where he ranks among the country's greatest kings. It was probably unfortunate for Poland, Hungary, and Transylvania that he died childless. Although his place in history is assured by what he did in Poland, he was also able to restore order rapidly in Transylvania once he became prince. While he ruled the principality first personally and then through his brother Christofer after he moved to Poland in 1576 and finally through his nephew Sigismund, everybody regarded him as the Prince. His prestige produced a period of tranquility and prosperity that would only be matched once in the course of Transylvania's independent history.

Hungarian historians see in Steven Báthory a great patriot who understood that Transylvania's independence was needed for the "future greatness of Hungary," and who recognized that the Habsburg and Ottoman dangers were of equal magnitude, with that of the Habsburgs more pressing. This explains to their satisfaction why Báthory's policy of neutrality tipped slightly in the Ottomans' favor. It is clear that Báthory did indeed maneuver very ably between the two great powers, keeping peace with the Ottomans on the one hand and constantly locking horns with the Habsburgs on the other, but his involvement in Polish affairs practically from the day he became ruler of Transylvania makes it difficult to accept this interpretation of his policy. Admittedly, any Hungarian patriot, even one without personal ambitions, would have opposed the Habsburg's attempt to gain the throne of Poland, and it will never be possible to determine what motivated Báthory who could hardly have acted any other way under the circumstances. His moves, however, resemble too much those of a clever and ambitious man who tried to establish himself, and hopefully his family, on the thrones of Poland and a reunited Hungary-Transylvania, creating a new power structure of prime importance in European affairs.

At the death of John-Sigismund Zápolyai Báthory's great rival for the Transylvanian throne was Gáspár Békés, the deceased prince's chancellor. When Báthory was elected, Békés fomented a revolt among the still discontented Székelys and moved unsuccessfully against Báthory. Immediately after this revolt was suppressed the last Jagiełło died, in early 1572. Maximillian wanted the Polish throne for one of his sons, claiming it on the basis of family ties. Báthory, who had taken an oath of allegiance to Maximillian when he had become ruler of Transylvania, had similar ties and became the only logical rival of the Habsburgs. For this reason Maximillian took Békés' side, and war between the two candidates appeared inevitable when the Poles elected Henri de Valois as their king. Békés left for Vienna, but because the Habsburgs had no further use for him he moved to Istanbul, where he hoped for Ottoman backing of his claim to the throne of Transylvania. He was disappointed. The Ottomans used his presence only to raise the yearly tribute of Transylvania to fifteen thousand ducats. Báthory was secure in Transylvania, but the calm did not last long.

In 1574 Henri returned to France, and Maximillian and Báthory once again became the logical candidates for the Polish throne. The Habsburgs called Békés to Vienna and sent him to Transylvania where, backed by the Székelys, he started another revolt. Báthory was again victorious and took bloody revenge on the leaders of the revolt, except for Békés who escaped. He punished the Székelys by revoking their liberties and thus started a feud that lasted until the last Báthory, Gabriel, died. During the next year the same thing happened in Poland that had happened in Hungary in 1526. The lower nobility elected Báthory king on December 15, 1574, and two days later the magnates offered the throne to Maximillian. War was prevented by Maximillian's death early in 1576, and the Polish throne was secured for Báthory.

Although Steven Báthory moved to Kraców and was never to return to Transylvania, his prestige was all his brother Christofer needed to "rule in his place." Christofer, who had excellent relations with Steven, was a decent man and popular with all segments of the population except for the Székelys. Transylvanians participated in Báthory's wars against Russia, and in general the two countries worked together closely. Unfortunately, Christofer died in 1581, and his son Sigismund took his place.

Sigismund was ambitious, jealous of everything and everybody, and probably insane or, at best, highly unstable. Strongly influenced by the Jesuits, he regarded the Ottomans as his enemies and was interested in joining a Christian crusade against them. In this desire he was strongly opposed by those who believed that his great uncle's policy was correct and also by the Protestant nobles, who were afraid that a close collaboration with the Habsburgs might endanger their religious freedom. The opposition rallied behind the new prince's cousin, Balthazar, and in 1588 succeeded in having the Jesuits expelled from Transylvania. Although most members of the order left, those who agreed to become secular priests were allowed to remain. One who remained and became the major influence in the prince's life was Alphonse Carillo of Spanish birth, Sigismund's chaplain and father confessor. Steven Bocskai, an able general and the uncle of Prince Sigismund, also belonged to the war party.

Although the antiwar party led by Balthazar was in the majority in Transylvania, its position became difficult when, in 1593, the Ottomans launched a new campaign in Hungary marking the beginning of the so-called "long war" that lasted until the Peace of Zsitvatorok in 1606. The Pope preached, unsuccessfully, a crusade; the Poles advised that Steven Báthory's policy should be followed, but Sigismund, encouraged by the first defeats of the Ottomans, sent Carillo to Prague to negotiate an alliance with the Habsburgs. His plans to attack were only frustrated by the need to send his army to the north against the Tatar forces that were approaching to help the Ottomans. With his generals and chief advisor gone Sigismund threw a tantrum and suddenly abdicated in favor of his main adversary, Balthazar. Just as quickly he changed his mind, remounted the throne with the help of Bocskai, and executed his enemies, including Balthazar.

The road to war was open. This time Bocskai went to Prague, concluded an alliance, and found an archduchess as wife for his prince. The Danubian Principalities joined Báthory, and both in Wallachia, where the able Mihai Viteazul was prince, and in Hungary the campaign went well at first. Nevertheless, the situation was critical. Sigismund's instability was revealed in his desire to dissolve his marriage and in his dreams of becoming a cardinal, while the Poles, who opposed any Habsburg connections, attacked his allies the Moldavians. Their approach encouraged the Székelys to revolt again, forcing the Transylvanian army to return home. Gaining a respite, the Ottomans attacked again. This time they succeeded in occupying several fortresses in Hungary. Finally, in late 1596 at Mezőkeresztes they dealt the joint Habsburg-Transylvanian forces a decisive defeat. Sigismund again lost his composure, and after a year of negotiation abdicated at the end of 1597 in favor of the Emperor Rudolf. The peace party now had a chance, but Bocskai intervened and managed to bring Sigismund back. When the emperor refused to recognize him as prince of Transylvania, in 1599, he abdicated a third time in favor of his cousin, Cardinal Andrew Báthory.

By now the situation was desperate. In an attempt to get support for a peace with the Ottomans, Andrew negotiated with the Poles for aid. Bocskai retreated to his estates in the Bihar region where he tried to raise a new army among the landless professional mercenaries (hajdu). The Habsburgs decided to settle the Transylvanian problem once and for all and sent an army under George Basta to occupy the country. At this moment, under pressure from the Poles to the north and the Ottomans to the south, Mihai Viteazul moved into Transylvania to prevent a Habsburg occupation. His forces were joined by those of the Székelys, and the cardinal had no choice but to flee toward Poland, only to be captured en route and beheaded by the Székelys.

During the next five years Transylvania became a battlefield for Polish, Turkish, Wallachian, and Habsburg forces. In the midst of this confusion Sigismund returned with Polish help, and once again, in 1601, mounted the throne for a few weeks. After Basta disposed of Mihai Viteazul, Sigismund remained in the country as cocommissioner with Basta for the Habsburgs, until he finally left the country for good in 1603. The land that he had left sadly devastated was now under the rule of General Basta who was attacked and defeated by Moses Székely with the help of the Turks. Székely was elected prince by his followers, but was unable to get the "three nations" behind him. With the aid of the Prince of Wallachia, Basta defeated him at the end of 1603; in the battle Székely lost his life. By the following year Basta was the absolute but very unpopular master of Transylvania.

4. THE LAST PRINCES

THE leadership of the resistance was now in the hands of a young twenty-three-year-old who was in hiding in Ottoman territory, Gabriel Bethlen. Bethlen knew that he did not have the means to act and thought of Bocskai as a possible leader. Having realized that the pro-Habsburg line had proved sterile, the general was willing to change his policies but hesitated while corresponding with Bethlen. One of the letters fell into Habsburg hands, but before Bocskai could be arrested he turned to the *hajdu*, promising them land in the event of victory. In October of 1604 his troops defeated the royal army sent against him. On Bethlen's advice the Ottomans offered Bocskai the throne of Transylvania. His troops not only managed to keep the Habsburg armies at bay, but moved as far west as Bratislava (Pozsony, Pressburg). In April of 1605 he was elected to the kingship of Hungary, but he declined and instead initiated peace negotiations.

Peace was concluded in Vienna in the early summer of 1606. The Habsburgs recognized Bocskai as prince of Transylvania, which now included, at least for his lifetime, the Sub-Carpathian Ukraine and eastern Slovakia. Rudolf also promised religious freedom for Hungary and obliged himself to fill the kingdom's offices with Hungarians. These two commitments secured Bocskai a place of honor in Hungarian history. He kept his promise to the *hajdu* and settled them on the plain around the city of Debrecen. When peace with the Ottomans followed soon thereafter, in November, the situation appeared stabilized, although the Ottomans claimed two fortresses in Transylvanian hands. Unfortunately, Bocskai died unexpectedly in December, 1606.

Before his death Bocskai recommended a Slovakian noble as his successor, but the Transylvanians elected Sigismund Rákoczi. The main goal of Rákoczi's election was to block the claims of seventeen-year-old Gabriel Báthory. The situation was again critical because the royal Hungarian government asked for and got the return of the lands left to Transylvania only for the lifetime of Bocskai. The Hungarians handled the *hajdu* badly. The *hajdu*, in turn, revolted and contacted the Báthory party. In order to secure peace Sigismund Rákoczi resigned, in 1608, in favor of Gabriel.

The last Báthory's reign started well. He was popular, settled the *hajdu* and Székely problems, and concluded a treaty with the Habsburgs that made clear his land was not obligated to fight Turks. Unfortunately, Gabriel Báthory was a playboy and ladies' man. He was also very unstable and subject to violent tempers, a second Sigismund Báthory, and lacked any political know-how. He did not realize the magnitude and especially the aggressiveness of the Counter Reformation in Hungary and was totally unprepared for a plot among the Hungarian Catholics, the Catholic nobility of Transylvania, and Radu Şerban of Wallachia until they made an unsuccessful attempt on his life. He confiscated the holdings of all Catholic nobles and expelled the last Jesuits in 1610, thereby provoking the Hungarians and Poles. To make matters worse, he turned against the Saxons, whom he accused of Habsburg sympathies, occupied Sibiu, suspended their privileges, and confiscated their holdings. Having "accomplished" that much, he sent the *hajdu* forces into Moldavia, thereby provoking a Turkish attack on their lands forcing them to retreat. He was suddenly surrounded by enemies and soon reduced to defending himself in hostile Saxon Sibiu. Now the Turks, for reasons quite apart from the Transylvanian situation, changed sides and Báthory was saved.

The Saxons, led by Michael Weiss of Braşov, were organizing a revolt. Some Székelys joined in the movement, which was finally led by the prince's closest friend, a useless and totally corrupt individual, Anthony (Antal) Ghyczy. Báthory defeated the revolt, in which Weiss lost his life, but his instability now manifested itself at its worse. He executed the leader of the *hajdu* and replaced the only able man around him, Gabriel Bethlen, with the traitor Ghyczy. He now had to reinstate the Saxons' rights, but it was too late. With the help of a Turkish force Bethlen marched against him. Seeing the writing on the wall, Ghyczy changed sides again and had Báthory assassinated in October, 1613. The first step that the new prince Gabriel Bethlen took was to order the execution of Ghyczy.

With the accession of Gabriel Bethlen the second "golden age" of Transylvania began; it lasted until the death of his successor, George I Rákoczi, in 1648. Both were able men, good soldiers and administrators; both became important figures in European history, fighting on the Protestant side in the Thirty Years War. Their abilities and importance cannot be denied. Nor is it unreasonable to accept the claim of Hungarian historians that their actions saved Hungarian Protestantism and even the special position of Hungary in the steadily growing realm of the Habsburgs. Nevertheless, the motives of these two men are suspect for two reasons: their religious conviction and Hungarian patriotism. Both had great plans and envisioned themselves on the thrones of Hungary and Poland and even of Moldavia and Wallachia. Like the great Báthory, Steven, they were dreaming of a great Central European empire. Many of their moves cannot be explained in any other way. Given the general European situation and their own ability, they were fairly successful, although they never achieved everything they wanted. Bethlen was elected king of Hungary, but he was a good enough diplomat not to allow himself to be crowned, and he used his advantage to get great concessions from the Habsburgs at the Peace of Nikolsbourg in 1621. Both princes had great influence in the Danubian Principalities, with whose rulers they made common cause. The Ottomans were unable to take effective measures to prevent this power play on the part of their "vassals."

The two Transylvanians followed the example Gabriel Báthory set by confiscating estates, and in this manner they became rich and totally independent of the estates and the diet and were able to run the affairs of their country as they saw fit. Most of their soldiers were mercenaries paid out of the income of their growing estates and were thus immune from the Transylvanian authorities. This at least had the advantage of saving the population from military duties. Both, especially Bethlen, were interested in culture, and under them mercantilism made its appearance in Transylvania, considerably increasing state revenues and trade with the Danubian Principalities. At the death of George I Rákoczi Transylvania was a prosperous land. Recognized as independent by everybody, she was a power with which all European courts counted.

Everything suddenly changed in 1648. The Peace of Westphalia freed the hands of the Habsburgs, at least momentarily; George I died and was succeeded by his son, who was a religious fanatic; the Ottoman Empire was slowly recovering and had become once again a power factor. The events that changed Transylvania's fortune began with the revolt of the Cossacks, under Bogdan Hmelniczki, who made common cause with Vasile Lupu against Matei Basarab, nominally George II Rákoczi's vassal. The Cossack problem occupied Rákoczi's attention until 1565, when Charles Gustave of Sweden attacked Poland. The Poles asked for Rákoczi's help, but as a good Protestant he offered it to the Swedes and in January of the next year led his troops into Poland in hopes of gaining that country's throne. By this time the Ottoman Empire was headed by the first and greatest of the Köprülü grand vezirs, Mehmed, who ordered Rákoczi to return home. Ignoring Mehmed, George II continued to fight in Poland, where he was suddenly without allies when the Swedes broke off the hostilities, just when his country had come under Turkish attack. He finally retreated, but his army was destroyed by Poles and Crimean Tatars. The country was hostile to George when an order arrived from Istanbul deposing him. He was replaced by the aged Francis Rhédei in the hope that he would soon die, giving the Turks time to forget their anger and permitting Rákoczi to retake the throne. George could not wait; in 1658 he returned to Transylvania from his lands in Slovakia, Mehmed now led a large Ottoman army against him, calling on the Crimean Tatars to back his attack from the north. These two forces occupied the principality bringing its ecomomic prosperity to a rapid end. The leading political figure of Transylvania, Ákos Barcsai, started negotiations with Köprülü, agreed to payment of a war indemnity and a tribute of forty thousand ducats yearly, and was placed on the throne by the grand vezir. In 1659 George tried once again to regain his throne, but his attempt only brought about a new Ottoman attack, further devastation, and his own death on the battlefield in 1660.

His successor, John Kemény, tried to fight the Turks and was defeated. The Turks now put Michael I Apafi on the throne. Apafi's was a long and very unhappy reign in a devastated country constantly at war and split by factionalism and intrigues. The prince himself vacillated between pro-Turkish and pro-Habsburg policies. He turned pro-Turkish again at the worst possible moment, in 1683, and when the great victories of Charles of Lorraine delivered Hungary from Turkish rule, he had no choice but to sign the Treaty of Blaj (Balázsfalva, Blasendorf) on October 27, 1686. That treaty permitted him to keep his throne and the "nations" to retain their privileges, but it forced the Transylvanians to accept the "protection" of Leopold I (1657-1705). This new dependency involved the admission of Habsburg garrisons into Transylvanian fortifications and the payment of a yearly tribute that was much higher than that demanded by the Ottomans, a hundred thousand ducats. The Transylvanian Diet ratified this agreement and proclaimed the return of Transylvania to Hungary.

Leopold sent General Anton Caraffa to Transylvania as imperial commissioner. Apafi, his council, and the diet lost all power, and Transylvania lived the life of an occupied country. When Apafi died in 1690 the Ottomans appointed Imre Tököli as prince of Transylvania, while the Diet elected Michael II Apafi. The former was able to enter the principality and maintained himself there for one month before the imperial troops forced him to flee. Apafi's election was never sanctioned by Leopold I, and he was at best a nominal prince living as a semiprisoner in Vienna until his death in 1713. Nevertheless, Tököli's invasion was not without results. The war between the Ottomans and the Habsburgs was still going on, and there was always the possibility of an unexpected Turkish victory coupled with a change in the Transylvanian situation. For these reasons Leopold I was open to the argument of Nicholas (Miklós) Bethlen, whom the Transylvanian Diet had sent as its representative. On December 4, 1691, he issued the *Diploma Leopoldinum*, an attempt to secure the lasting loyalty of the Transylvanians. This step was in accordance not only with what Bethlen and his friends had in mind, but also with Leopold I's policy. In 1690 and 1691 the emperor had issued similar diplomas to the Serbs, who at his invitation were entering southern Hungary in great numbers.

Although the Ottomans did not give up their claim to overlordship in Transylvania until the Peace of Karlovci in 1699, the *Diploma Leopold-*

inum in fact ended the independence of Transylvania and created a political framework for its existence within the Habsburg realm that remained unchanged until 1848. The diploma reaffirmed the "seven deadly
sins," the privileges of the "three nations," and the special position of the
"four accepted religions" within the framework of an independent principality that was not reunited with Hungary. It recognized the titles and
functions of office-holders and limited the role of "outside forces" to the
stationing of imperial military cadre in Transylvania. It also reaffirmed
the annual payment of a hundred thousand ducats to the imperial treasury, only now in the form of taxes. Leopold continued to reject the election of Michael II Apafi as prince of Transylvania, and in his place
appointed a governor, George Bánffy, to rule in his name. When his successor, Joseph I (1705-11), assumed the title of Prince of Transylvania, the
role of governor became somewhat analogous to that of the *vajda* prior to
1526. The governors, however, never achieved the independence and
power that the *vajdas* had had. Although the Diet did use its right to elect
a prince once more in 1705, electing Francis (Ferenc) II Rákoczi who was
at the time leading a revolt against the Habsburgs, this fact did not
change the situation established by the 1691 diploma.

5. CONCLUSIONS

THE history of Transylvania as an independent principality is the story of
sadly missed political opportunities. The Ottoman overlordship was in-
comparably lighter there than in the Danubian Principalities. The tribute
never exceeded forty thousand ducats and only reached that sum in 1658.
Compared to the amounts paid by Moldavia and Wallachia (see figures on
p. 122) this imposition was insignificant. Furthermore, Transylvania was
not saddled with special taxes and did not have to bribe Istanbul constantly as did the lands east of her, nor was she obliged to "direct her exports" in fixed amounts and at set prices towards the Ottoman Empire.
Consequently, when properly governed under Steven Báthory, Gabriel
Bethlen, and George I Rákoczi, Transylvania prospered economically.
Finally, once again in contrast to Moldavia and Wallachia, Ottoman interference in Transylvanian affairs occurred only when her princes, especially Sigismund Báthory and George II Rákoczi, embarked on adventures that truly endangered the interests of the Ottoman Empire. The
principality had a chance to mold its own fate to a much larger extent
than did the other two vassal lands of the Ottomans and often used Ottoman overlordship very cleverly in its contacts with the Habsburgs.

Habsburg intervention, both in the form of imperial expansion and the
Counter Reformation, was much more of a danger than was Ottoman
meddling in Transylvanian affairs. Yet, even here the full weight of Habsburg power was never directed against Transylvania because the many
other interests of the imperial family and the split among various parties

in royal Hungary always prevented the Habsburgs from concentrating their forces against Transylvania. Properly handled, even this danger could have been countered more successfully than it was.

On the economic level not only did Transylvania have its own natural resources, as had Moldavia and Wallachia, but her cities and more importantly her bourgeoisie also enjoyed much more freedom of action than did their counterparts in Moldavia and Wallachia. Counted among the city dwellers were the Saxons, whose economic ability and sophistication were unmatched in Eastern Europe in the sixteenth and seventeenth centuries. Their lands, originally assigned to them for reasons of defense, became ideally located economically when the Ottoman occupation of central Hungary forced Transylvania's trade in an eastward direction. The trade with the Danubian Principalities, which was carried mainly through the Saxon cities by Saxon and by Romanian and other Balkan traders, increased enormously, thus tying these lands closer together and permitting Gabriel Bethlen to institute his very successful mercantilist policies.

As has been seen, the relations with the Danubian Principalities were much broader than simply commercial. Given their geographic location and common problems, political and military cooperation between the three principalities was inevitable, although it was never properly exploited either by the Transylvanian or by the Moldavian and Wallachian princes. While the instability of the situation in the Danubian lands accounts in large part for this lack of significant political cooperation, the more stable Transylvanians also failed to take the necessary energetic leadership. The fact that Moldavia and Wallachia were ruled by Romanians and Transylvania by Hungarians should not be blamed for this lack of cooperation. Nationalism was not a force in the centuries under discussion, and although it is true that the Transylvanian ruling circles looked down at their Romanian serfs, there was no "national hatred" on either side that would have prevented cooperation on the political and military level.

Several East European princes looked at their lands as possible nuclei for the creation of a strong, non-Habsburg Christian state. If any of them had a chance to play this role it was indeed the Transylvanians. The opportunity was missed. The question that must be asked, "Why it was missed?" has no easy answer.

Although Transylvania already had three of her seven "deadly sins" when her independent existence began, it was by no means inevitable that these had to be increased to seven instead of being transformed into lesser evils. After all, feudalism had been less firmly entrenched in Transylvania than in Hungary in 1526, and the very existence of the "three nations" with their different interests and privileges pointed toward a pluralistic social structure at that time. This direction was followed up to the time when Steven Báthory fixed the number of accepted religions at four and reversed the trend toward pluralism. It was then and only then that feudalism in its worst forms became firmly established in Transylvania. Yet, even in this form it faded into the background when the princes using traditional prefeudal rights began to assert their power and to amass fortunes at the expense of the "three nations," relegating them and the Diet to impuissance.

The above short summary points to two basic flaws in the internal sociopolitical structure of Transylvania. The first is the ease with which the princes could play off the "three nations" against each other. In Moldavia, Wallachia, Poland, and royal Hungary the rulers faced only one force, the nobility. Although the nobility was often split into factions, these groups always agreed on one thing: the safeguarding of their position within the state structure, including the continuation of their privileges and the resulting limitation of the rulers' power. In Transylvania there was little love lost among the "three nations," and the princes could always count on the backing of one or two of them when moving against the others. In a sense Transylvania was both a prefeudal and a feudal society. The fact that there was no truly united upper class prohibited the proper functioning of either system. This lack of unity gave her enemies, especially the Habsburgs, the chance to find rebellious followers, thereby weakening the ability of Transylvania to direct all her energies in any given direction.

The second flaw is the total exclusion of the Romanian population from the "political nation." While the explanation of "national" feelings must be rejected, discrimination along ethnic lines certainly did develop, especially after religious differences were added to the political and even more importantly the economic ones. Everywhere a serf was regarded as an inferior being, but when he spoke another language and went to a different church than his master the gulf became too wide to be bridged. Except for the economic exploitation that was the fate of the serf everywhere, Transylvania paid no attention to her Romanian population and, consequently, operated with the backing of only half of her people. Only under George I Rákoczi did something like the vague stirring of princely interest in the Romanians begin, but by then it was too late.

Even George was more interested in foreign affairs than in domestic problems. It is in this overwhelming interest of absolute princes in foreign affairs that one finds the major reason for the missed opportunity inherent in Transylvania's independent existence. All her princes fought wars, and while those of John Zápolyai were basically defensive, to maintain himself on the throne, the wars of his successors were primarily aggressive. In this respect incompetents like Sigismund and Gabriel Báthory and George II Rákoczi did not differ from the ablest, Steven Báthory, Gabriel Bethlen, and George I Rákoczi.

Historians, mainly the Hungarians, have advanced several reasons for these constant aggressive wars. They have pointed out that being situated between the Ottomans, Habsburgs, and Poles but in a better position than Moldavia and Wallachia, the Transylvanian princes understood that it was their destiny and duty to lead the struggle of the people of Southeastern Europe. They have stressed religious reasons in explaining the wars of the Transylvanians, and have repeatedly referred to the Hungarian patriotism of these princes and underscored the fact that these wars prevented the total religious and political subjugation and absorption of royal Hungary by the Habsburg superstate. Undoubtedly there is much truth in these arguments. One should never forget that the Bethlen and Rákoczi families were not Transylvanians, and that their original holdings lay in the *Partium* so they were deeply interested in events that transpired in royal Hungary.

Valid as these arguments are, however, they do not explain the behavior of the Transylvanian princes to this author's satisfaction. Just as these princes aimed to gain and successfully achieved total power at the expense of the "three nations" at home, they strove to achieve a similarly absolute goal in foreign affairs that went beyond those required by religious or even Transylvanian ends. This goal was almost constantly the eventual creation of a great state including Hungary, Poland, Moldavia, and Wallachia in addition to Transylvania. Going beyond the objectively achievable or the religiously and even politically desirable, this imperialistic policy steadily weakened the princes' power base, Transylvania, making it less and less likely that this land could indeed serve as the nucleus for the revival of independent states in Southeastern Europe.

Although personal ambition and the desire to establish a dynasty certainly played an important role in this grandiose policy of Transylvania's princes, one must not forget that these princes also started with "legacies" that they could not forget. Zápolyai, whom they succeeded and to whom the first of his successors were related, had been elected King of Hungary, and thus the Báthorys had a vague claim to the Hungarian throne. After Steven Báthory became king of Poland his family and that of the related Rákoczis also believed that they had a right to that kingdom, too. No prince in modern European history has ever voluntarily given up any claim to land, and the Transylvanians were no exception. Their ambitions had so-called legal justifications, and in the years of the religious wars these could be advanced with relative ease by princes whose homeland practiced more religious toleration than any other. By adding these circumstances and the personal ambitions of the princes to the explanations furnished by the historians, it is possible to understand the behavior of the Báthorys, Bethlen, and Rákoczis a little better.

One basic flaw, however, remains. Even the able princes were too blinded by their goals to realize that they had insufficient forces and that their actions weakened their power base making it less and less likely that Transylvania could serve the desired function. It was this miscalculation and desire for strength that destroyed the power of the "three nations" and weakened any cohesive Transylvanian feeling on the part of the population. It was this miscalculation that undermined the economic situation of the province, which became apparent when the first serious defeat, that of George II Rákoczi, left Transylvania without any recuperative ability and led to the rapid end of her independent existence. The rulers of Transylvania based their policy on a vision, not on reality. This was the basic flaw in their polity.

Given the attitude of the Ottomans towards Transylvania, the inability of the Habsburgs to concentrate enough force to subdue her, and the basic economic wealth of the land, the principality was, indeed, the potential Piedmont of Southeastern Europe in the sixteenth and seventeenth centuries. The policy of her princes left this potential unrealized and bequeathed to future centuries an impoverished and sadly divided land. Although royal Hungary gained from this policy, the question remains of whether these gains satisfied the Transylvanian Hungarians, let alone the other people of the land, sufficiently to justify the sacrifices made. Using hindsight, the answer must be negative, especially when one considers the chances that were not properly utilized but neglected in favor of those that resulted in advantages for the population of royal Hungary at the expense of those living in Transylvania.

CHAPTER 8

Dubrovnik (Ragusa)

1. HISTORICAL BACKGROUND

SEVENTY years ago an Italian scholar, Luigi Villari, wrote a history of Dubrovnik that is still useful. Villari described the state in which he was interested in the subtitle of his work, "An Episode of the Turkish Conquest." In doing so he placed too much emphasis on the relationship between Dubrovnik and the Ottomans because by 1458, when the first agreement between the two was signed, the Dalmatian city-state had fully developed and was the greatest economic force in the Balkans.[1] Dubrovnik was one of several Dalmatian port cities including Split (Spalato), Zadar (Zara), Šibenik (Sebenico), Kotor (Cáttaro), and Trogir (Trau) that for centuries had maintained close ties with Western Europe, mainly Italy. These cities lived from navigation, trade, and manufacture and served as the doors through which western cultural influence entered the Balkans during Ottoman rule. Culturally and economically, Dubrovnik was the most important of these cities. It was also the only one to remain independent of the Venetian state in 1420 and thus the only possible outlet for Balkan trade (apart from the much less important Durrës) for the "core provinces" of the Ottoman Empire. The unique position explains the importance the Ottomans attached to Dubrovnik; the city profited greatly from her connection with the land of the sultans. It is in this connection that Villari's is an exaggerated subtitle.

As has been indicated in Chapter 3, between 1459 and 1499 the Ottomans eliminated the last remnants of independence in the Balkans. The one exception was Dubrovnik, which remained the only independent Balkan state until 1806, when it was occupied by Napoleon's troops. Dubrovnik's most important feature, her trade, will be discussed in this

---

1. Luigi Villari, *The Republic of Ragusa, An Episode of the Turkish Conquest* (London: J. M. Dent, 1904).

DUBROVNIK

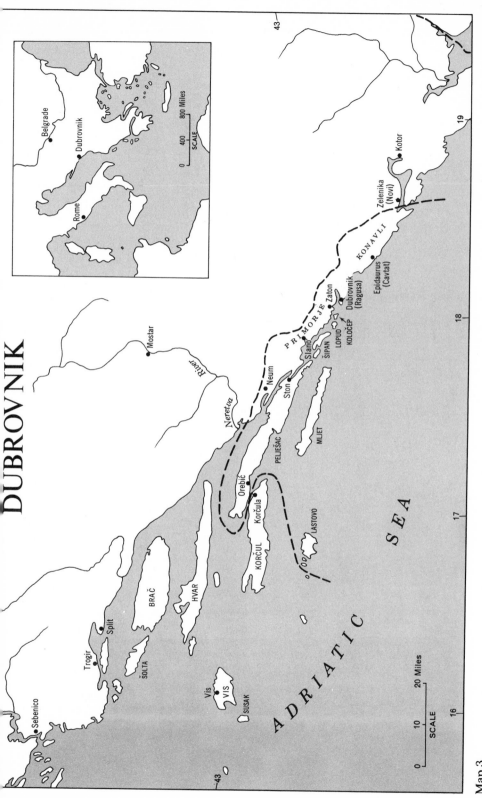

Map 3

chapter only when necessary,[2] as will the general history of the city-state. We will concentrate instead on two aspects of Dubrovnik's history only: the city's connection with the Ottoman Empire, and the significance of her existence for the historical development of the Southern Slavs.

According to Constantine Porphyrogenetus, in the seventh century Avar raiders destroyed the city of Epidaurus. The survivors moved about fifteen miles north to a more protected location and founded a new city, Ragusium.[3] The immediate neighborhood of the new settlement was practically all barren rock, and from the beginning the inhabitants had to pay tribute to the chiefs of the neighboring Slav regions, called *mogoriš*, for the right to cultivate land to support themselves. Even when the territory of Ragusa was extended from the Astarea on the mainland and the three small islands of Koločep, Lopud, and Šipan to its final size in 1426, it was never able to produce sufficient food to support itself.[4] By the middle of the fifteenth century the city itself had about five to six thousand inhabitants, and the total territory of the state was something between twenty-five and thirty thousand people. Considering that between 1348 and 1691 the plague visited Dubrovnik eighteen times, and that the city was devastated by an earthquake in 1667, it is safe to assume that its citizens never numbered much more than thirty thousand, although higher figures are mentioned by some authors.[5]

The early relations with the Slav countries continued throughout the centuries, and to these were added those with the neighboring powers: Venice, the Serbian and Bosnian states, Croatia, Hungary, and Naples. Being a port city, Dubrovnik was naturally interested in building up her maritime trade, but from the beginning she was also interested in overland trade connections with the Balkans. In 1191 the Byzantine Emperor, Isaac II Angelus (1185-95) granted the merchants of the city the right to trade freely in his lands. A few years prior to this grant Dubrovnik had gained similar privileges from Serbia (1186) and from Bosnia (1189).

---

2. Those interested in this trade as well as in a good history of Dubrovnik can turn to the excellent study of Francis W. Carter, *Dubrovnik (Ragusa); A Classic City-state* (London and New York: Seminar Press, 1972.).

3. Section 1 of this chapter follows closely the short history of early Dubrovnik presented in the first and second chapters of Barisa Krekić, *Dubrovnik in the 14th and 15th Centuries: A City between East and West* (Norman: University of Oklahoma Press, 1972).

4. The Island of Lastovo was added to the original territory in the middle of the thirteenth century. This was followed, in 1333, by the purchase of the Pelješac Peninsula from Serbia, which was united with the original territory when Dubrovnik acquired the land separating the two, called the Primorje in 1399. Between these two acquisitions the Island of Mljet was annexed, and between 1419 and 1426 Dubrovnik added the Konavli region south of Astarea, including the city of Cavtat built on the ruins of Epidaurus. Together with the small island of Lokrum, practically at the entrance of the city's harbor and considered part of it, all these possessions added up to only 421.5 square miles.

5. Carter, *Dubrovnik*, p. 16.

These three treaties opened up the peninsula for Dubrovnik's merchants. The Bosnian treaty contained, for the first time, the Slav name for Ragusa, Dubrovnik, although the official name was still the Latin Communitas Ragusii. By this time the city had been an archbishopric for more than one hundred years, and its populace had become bilingual. By the end of the thirteenth century the Slav element had become the majority. Soon after these trade advantages were gained Dubrovnik had to submit to Venice, in 1205, and remained under the overlordship of that city until 1358, when Louis the Great of Hungary (1342-92) defeated Venice and stripped her of her Dalmatian holdings. Louis concluded a treaty with Dubrovnik, making her fully independent under his nominal overlordship.

It was under Venetian rule that Dubrovnik acquired the final form of her political and social organizations. A Venetian comes stood at the head of the city. His place was taken by a locally elected rector (*knez*) after the Venetian rule terminated. The comes was an important man, but he had to rule in agreement with the local nobles; his successor, the rector, was nothing more than a figurehead and served only for a month at a time. Both the comes and the rector were assisted by a Minor Council (Consilium Minus, Malo vijeće) of eleven nobles and judges who acted as the Supreme Court and performed police and market-regulating duties. The Major Council (Consilium Maius, Veliko vijeće) of about three hundred nobles elected the members of the other political bodies. It had legislative powers and the final say on all decisions of major importance, although its acts did not become law until they were countersigned by the archbishop. The most important of the political bodies was the Senate (Consilium Rogatorum, Vijeće umoljenih) with a membership of forth-five including the rector and members of the Minor Council. This body was the exclusive domain of the oligarchical patriciate. The members of the Senate were always from the same small group of families and were appointed for life. It was this body that prepared the legislative bills for the Major Council, discussed war and peace, ratified treaties, and handled the all-important diplomatic problems of the city-state.

Although the patricians dominated the political and economic life of Dubrovnik and owned most of the land outside the city as well as much of the city itself, they did not monopolize either its political or economic life. They cooperated with the merchants, traders, sea captains, and guild members, who retained much of their right to regulate their own affairs. The interests of all these groups were, after all, the same; the patricians, however, dominated because of their claim to nobility and their wealth, which made them the bankers and creditors of the rest of the population. Dubrovnik served not only as a trade center but also as a manufacturing center. Craftsmen were grouped into guilds and fraternities, but the importance of their activities did not become significant until the fifteenth century.

When slavery was outlawed in 1416 by the Major Council the peasantry became the bottom of the social pyramid. While very few peasants, who constituted the majority of the population, owned land, they resisted the patricians and the church who tried to enserf them and remained free men. Their obligations were fixed by contracts. Legally, they were subject to the laws of the state; they could not be judged by their lords and retained the right to free migration. The booming city's growing need for people accounts for this treatment of the peasantry. The peasants always gravitated to the city; their place was taken by incoming Slavs, Albanians, and other inhabitants of neighboring lands.

To these developments, which did not begin with Venetian rule but reached (with the exception of the abolition of slavery) their final form under that rule, must be added a few others. The most important Venetian contribution was the help she gave in maintaining Dubrovnik's independence from the rising Slav states. It was also during the Venetian period that Dubrovnik concluded trade agreements with the Greek and Bulgarian states, thereby extending her economic network further into the Balkans. Toward the end of Venetian rule good relations with Bosnia and Serbia were re-established. These ties were extremely important because it was in the thirteenth century that Dubrovnik's trade pattern took its final shape and mining began to be a serious enterprise in Serbia. From the beginning the people of Dubrovnik were deeply interested in mining, and by the time Venetian rule ended they were not only trading in silver, copper, lead, and iron, but even managing and owning Serbian mines. They acquired a similar position in the Bosnian mining industry as well. Given the privileges they enjoyed in the Balkan lands, including freedom from taxation and unhampered right to trade as well as the right of settlement under their own laws and judges, their importance increased steadily. Throughout the Slav lands of the Balkans, with the exception of Bulgaria, there were Ragusan colonies in all major trading centers by the middle of the fourteenth century. It should also be remembered that Ottoman *kanuns* confirmed pre-existing arrangements and, therefore, the privileges that the Ragusans enjoyed in the future Ottoman lands were highly significant.

The end of Venetian rule removed the maritime restrictions that city had placed on Dubrovnik, permitting her to extend her sea-going trade, carried by as many as 180 of her ships, to match her mainland connections. The trade pattern, which had remained unchanged under Ottoman rule of the Balkans, also took final shape in the second half of the fourteenth century. Dubrovnik exported minerals, a great variety of animal products, and even some food items from the peninsula and supplied it with salt, western manufactured goods, mainly textiles, and luxury items. Dubrovnik's trade grew rapidly, extending to Spain, Syria, Egypt, and in general to the entire Mediterranean world. Beginning with 1373 the merchants of Dubrovnik repeatedly obtained from the popes permission to trade with the Muslims. This made their early contacts with the Ottomans relatively easy.

Dubrovnik's first contact with the Ottomans occurred in 1392, while the Ottomans were conquering the surrounding lands. By 1397 Dubrovnik had obtained from the Ottoman government permission, basically the reaffirmation of existing rights, to trade and settle freely in the Balkans. This agreement was renewed in 1447 and was followed in 1458 by a final treaty that placed Dubrovnik under Ottoman protection in exchange for a yearly payment of 1,500 ducats. The amount grew to 12,500 ducats in 1481, when it was fixed for the entire duration of Dubrovnik's relations with the Ottomans. Although Scanderbeg (1403?-68), Matthias Corvinus (1458-90), and even the popes repeatedly called on Dubrovnik to cut her Turkish ties, the city realized the advantages of this connection and never did so.

By 1481 Dubrovnik had worked out her internal organization and her trading patterns and had established the merchant colonies throughout the Balkans that she was to extend further while the Ottomans were masters of the peninsula. Early in that century she had also changed her official name from Communitas to Republic. All the Ottomans had to do was to recognize what already existed, provided they were interested in permitting Dubrovnik to retain her independent existence and to continue with her trading activities in the Balkans. We know how important trade was to the Ottomans. The trade of their newly conquered European provinces along the traditional routes had to be kept out of the hands of their enemies, the Venetians. The Republic of St. Mark recovered rapidly from the defeats inflicted on them by the Anjou rulers of Hungary and once again controlled, after the first quarter of the fifteenth century, all important ports in Dalmatia with the exception of Dubrovnik. Therefore, the Ottomans, as long as they were interested in securing a trade outlet on the Adriatic for the Balkans, had little choice but to secure, either by conquest or treaty, the port and trading facilities of this city. It was due to the diplomatic ability of the Dubrovnik Senate that the Ottomans chose negotiation.

2. DUBROVNIK'S RELATIONS WITH THE OTTOMANS

THE diplomats of the Republic of Dubrovnik did not have an easy task. When they concluded their first agreement with the Ottomans, Hungary, the nominal overlord of their state, was still capable of aggressive action. The statesmen of Europe, especially the pope, were still thinking in terms of an anti-Ottoman crusade and looked askance on any Christian government that maintained good diplomatic and trade relations with the "infidels." It took great foresight, in 1397, to realize that the Ottomans had already become the major power in the Balkans and to stick to this evaluation after the great Ottoman defeat at Ankara in 1402. It also took great skill, at least prior to the Battle of Varna, in 1444, to remain aloof from anti-Ottoman alliances without incurring the hostility of those who were fighting the sultans. The diplomats of Dubrovnik even managed to obtain papal permission (1432) to trade with the enemy. After Varna it again took great skill to maintain Dubrovnik-Ottoman relations practically unaltered throughout the centuries, despite the many changes that took place in the Ottoman Empire. The fact that these relations were mutually advantageous helped the diplomats of Dubrovnik, but in no way diminishes the magnitude of their accomplishment.

The relationship between the little city-state and the large empire is extremely interesting and *sui generis*.[6] Dubrovnik was the only vassal state of the Ottoman Empire whose territory was never invaded during its long vassalage, in whose internal affairs the Ottomans did not once interfere, and whose status was ambiguous from the point of view of Muslim-Ottoman jurisprudence. There can be no doubt that Dubrovnik was less hampered by her ties with the Ottomans than were Moldavia, Wallachia, and Transylvania, and that her citizens received special considerations from the "overlords."

The treaty relations established in 1397 had lapsed after 1402. They were resumed in 1442, renegotiated in 1458, and received their final form in 1481. While the Ottomans repeatedly changed the basic, 1481, agreement unilaterally in their own favor, Dubrovnik always opposed these breaches, and its diplomats were always able to get them reversed after short periods, re-establishing the basic stipulations that remained practically unchanged until the arrival of Napoleon's army in Dalmatia. These documents or treaties were *Ahdnames*, the same type of Muslim legal documents that tied the other vassal states to the Ottomans. They did not fit clearly into the neat division of the universe into two parts, *dar al-Islam* and *dar al-Harb*, nor did they fit into the precepts of the dominant legal school of the Ottoman Empire, that of the *hanafītes,* because they created a third world. The Ottomans solved this legal problem by considering every land that paid them anything as part of the *dar al-Islam*, and they underlined this interpretation of their agreements with other rulers by calling whatever was paid *haraç*, the tax paid in exchange for the permission to enjoy the usufruct of land. In the case of those, including Molda-

---

6. The literature covering the history of Dubrovnik is both rich and very impressive, but there have been relatively few studies on the city's dealings with the Ottomans. Of those published three deserve special attention and were used extensively in writing the following pages: Ivan Božić, *Dubrovnik i Turska u XIV i XV veku* [Dubrovnik and Turkey in the fourtheenth and fifteenth centuries] (Beograd: Srpska Akademia Nauka, 1952); Vuk Vinaver, *Dubrovnik i Turska u XVIII veku* [Dubrovnik and Turkey in the eighteenth century] (Beograd: Srpska Akedemia Nauka, 1960); and Nicolaas H. Biegman, *The Turco-Ragusan Relationship according to the Firmans of Murad III (1575-95) extant in the State Archives of Dubovnik* (The Hague-Paris: Mouton, 1967).

via, Wallachia, and Transylvania, whose relationship was not only vassalage by legal sophistry but in fact, the inhabitants were always referred to as *zimmi* and were treated accordingly whenever they entered other parts of the empire. The already often discussed intervention in their affairs was, consequently, fully justified.

Although on paper Dubrovnik's relationship with Istanbul was the same as were those of the other vassal states, in fact it was not. Biegman coined a felicitous phrase when he called Dubrovnik the "autonomous part of the Ottoman Empire."[7] The city-republic not only governed itself as it saw fit, but was able to perform the basic duty of any sovereign state, the protection of its citizens at home and abroad, even when facing its nominal "master." Although most Ottoman documents refer to the Ragusans as *zimmi*, several describe them as *frengi* (an expression used for the Christian inhabitants of the *dar al-Harb*), and Biegman even found one document using the expression Latins to identify the inhabitants of Dubrovnik. Obviously, the precise status and position of the city and its inhabitants were not quite clear in the minds of the Ottomans. The ability to maintain this vague status for centuries was certainly the major accomplishment of Dubrovnik diplomacy and explains, to a large extent, their ability to maintain full independence for all practical purposes.

In addition to the common interests of Istanbul and Dubrovnik and the skill of the latter's diplomats, a significant factor in the special status of the Dalmatian city was its form of government. The Ottomans always dealt with individuals— kings, princes, emirs, Mamlūk sultans—in their foreign relations, and even when they had to make concessions within their own state and gave local strong men certain privileges, these were always the result of an individual's or family's ability to acquire and maintain a position of power. Consequently, in accordance with the Ottoman view of their own state, the "prince" was the key figure in all their calculations. He was their vassal, he owed loyalty to them and was responsible for the behavior of his subjects, the payment of taxes, and the conduct of a policy acceptable to the Ottomans. The right to confirm or appoint him, as well as the ability to remove him and to insure his reliability by surrounding him with "advisors" or "bodyguards," settled, so far as the Ottomans were concerned, all the political problems arising out of a vassal-master relationship. They had neither the experience nor the theoretical concepts needed for dealing with an oligarchic republic. So long as they tolerated Dubrovnik, they had to accept the republic and deal with her senate, a corporate body. There was no leading personality through whom the Ottomans could control city affairs as they did elsewhere. The very fact that all Ottoman communications addressed to Dubrovnik were sent to the *beys* (senators) of that city indicates the Ottomans inability to deal with

7. Biegman, *The Turco-Ragusan Relationship*, p. 26.

the concept of a corporate ruling body, and is also a clue to the standing of Dubrovnik in the Turks' hierarchical sense of values. A *bey* was a high ranking, important personality in Ottoman society. The nobles of Transylvania or the boyars of the Danubian Principalities were never, so far as I know, considered *bey*s in Istanbul, but the senators of Dubrovnik were.

Another significant difference between the position of Dubrovnik and that of the other vassals was the place accorded her citizens who lived in the Ottoman Empire proper. Once again, the situation does not fit the established legal structure of the Turkish state. If Dubrovnik had been considered by the Ottomans as an independent state its denisens should have been considered foreigners and permitted to reside in the empire as visitors for a year, provided they received the required permission. By staying longer than a year they should have lost this special status, automatically becoming *zimmi* subjects of the sultan. If their city had been considered an integral part of the empire, they should have had *zimmi* status with all the restrictions and obligations attached to it. Obviously, under neither of these alternatives could Dubrovnik have carried out the commercial activities that made her cooperation with the Ottomans so advantageous for both parties, and in fact her citizens enjoyed special status.

Dubrovnik had established settlements with special rights in all the important trading centers of Bosnia and Serbia. These settlements had extensive trading and tax-exemption privileges, lived according to the laws of their city, and were practically self-governing. After the Ottoman conquest the major trading centers in Bulgarian territory, and even Buda and Pest, also acquired smaller or larger settlements of Dubrovnik merchants. My rough calculations place the number of those who, as citizens of Dubrovnik, had the right to special status in the Ottoman Empire at from two to three thousand, or about 10 percent of the republic's population. Dubrovnik's trade could not have existed without these people. Their special status made this possible.

The inhabitants of the Ragusan settlements retained their Dubrovnik "citizenship" irrespective of the length of their residence in Ottoman territory. They were free of all personal taxes levied on *zimmi*s and did not have to pay the transit and market fees the *zimmi*s and Muslims who were engaged in business had to pay. After the Ottoman conquest the number of places where Dubrovnik was permitted to maintain resident consuls did diminish sharply, but those Ragusans who lived abroad were still tried by their own authorities according to their own laws. Their property was guaranteed; there were no inheritance fees or taxes on the estates of the deceased, even if the inheritors lived in Dubrovnik and not in the settlements where the deceased had his fortune. These important concessions made Ottoman-Dubrovnik cooperation both possible and profitable.

Another unique feature in the relations between Dubrovnik and the Ottoman Empire was the consuls. Not only was Dubrovnik the only vassal that had consuls in a few Ottoman cities, but it also maintained contacts with the central government practically in the same manner as independent states did. Instead of *kapı kahya*, resident agent, handling her problems in Istanbul, every year Dubrovnik sent special envoys with specific instruction to the imperial capital. These envoys were charged with discussing and settling all issues and questions of common interest. Naturally, settlements frequently involved bribes, but the bribes were strictly limited by the instructions the envoys received from the Dubrovnik Senate. Thus, Dubrovnik, unlike Moldavia and Wallachia, did not carry the heavy burden that these bribes became as corruption deepened in Istanbul.

If, in addition to the above special features we consider Dubrovnik's right to maintain consuls in foreign states, conclude treaties with them, and sail her ships under her own flag, we are left with the impression that Dubrovnik was an independent state in all but strictest legal form. Besides recognizing an overlord, the only function of an independent state that Dubrovnik did not—and indeed could not—perform was national defense. Although her position was never seriously endangered after 1420, the very fact that everybody knew that the Ottoman army was protecting her was a serious deterrent to would-be aggressors. In the case of pirates Dubrovnik repeatedly turned for help to Istanbul and usually got the needed intervention.

The Ottomans granted this special status to Dubrovnik in exchange for economic services. They gained an outlet to the Adriatic Sea, and a reliable source for needed imports and luxury goods. Besides the commercial advantages, Dubrovnik also served as the Ottomans' "window towards the west," and much needed information and even intelligence reached Istanbul through the republic.

To make this flow of goods and information possible, the Ottomans gave Dubrovnik "most-favored-nation status," in the strictest sense of the word. On goods exported from Ottoman territory a trader from Dubrovnik paid a 2 percent duty as did every other trader, whether he be an Ottoman subject or a foreign merchant. The "most favored" status was reflected in the import duties. These amounted to 5 percent on goods imported by foreign merchants, 4 percent on those handled by *zimmi* traders, and 3 percent on merchandise imported by Muslim businessmen. Dubrovnik merchants paid 5 percent on those goods they sold in Istanbul, Edirne, and Bursa, but only 2 percent on goods they took to the other markets in the empire. The 5 percent duty was collected in the mentioned three cities when the goods were sold. Here responsible Ottoman officials supervised the collection, and there usually was a Dubrovnik envoy nearby, in Istanbul, to defend the rights of his countrymen when difficulties occurred. Such was not the case in all other places, and for that reason the diplomats of Dubrovnik managed to get from the Ottomans an arrangement that transformed the 2 percent duties into a yearly payment of a hundred thousand *akçes* to be remitted in two installments every six months. Furthermore, this amount, which was considered by the Ottomans as a "tax-farm," had to be collected and delivered to Istanbul by a *mültezim* (tax farmer) appointed from among its own citizens by the Senate of Dubrovnik for a three-year period. This important stipulation made it impossible for local authorities, outside the three cities of Istanbul, Edirne, and Bursa, to create difficulties for the merchants of Dubrovnik, and it also prevented the abuses connected with tax farming that plagued all other Ottoman territories increasingly from the late sixteenth century onward.

Besides the export and import duties, the goods imported, the profit on goods that the merchants of Dubrovnik exported, and the relatively low amounts Ottoman officials received as bribes, the only financial advantage the Ottoman Empire gained from her relationship with Dubrovnik was the tribute of 12,500 ducats the city paid every year. The entire agreement made sense from Istanbul's point of view because without Dubrovnik the empire would not have had a single first-rate trading outlet on the Adriatic capable of handling a surprisingly large amount of trade of a great variety of goods keeping the economy of the Balkans going.[8]

This short summary of Dubrovnik's position as a vassal of Istanbul for over three hundred years not only presents the third variety of this form of dependency that the Ottomans established, but also indicates why Dubrovnik was able to play the cultural role in the history of the Balkan people to which the beginning of the chapter referred and to which its third section will be devoted. Only such a small, virtually independent state situated in the Balkans themselves, with free and frequent contacts with the West and sufficiently prosperous to be able to pay for the work of artists and writers, could have acted as the "cultural Piedmont" of the Southern Slavs.

In her important cultural role, Dubrovnik was also aided by her entire history. The city-state, first founded by Roman colonists of Dalmatia, became the copy of the Italian city-state on the eastern shores of the Adriatic. Her political organization, her reason for being, trade, and the position and self-image of her citizens mirrored those of the Italian city-states. Dubrovnik never ceased to be "Roman," and later "Italian," in her world view and mentality, but, unlike the Italian models with which she can be compared, Dubrovnik lived in two worlds, the Italian and the Balkan. While her people cherished western values, they were Balkan Slavs who understood perfectly the milieu from which they had come and in which their conationals continued to live. To some extent the people of Dalmatia

8. Carter, *Dubrovnik* contains excellent information on trade, prices, changes in monetary values, and importance of various commodities in the total trade between Dubrovnik and the Balkans. Those interested in these aspects of Ottoman-Dubrovnik relations are referred to this volume.

can be included in these generalizations, but independent Dubrovnik was ideally placed to serve not only as a "window to the west" for the empire in general, but also for the Balkan people in particular.

3. THE CULTURAL CONTRIBUTIONS OF DUBROVNIK

GIVEN the geographic location, form of government, commercial interests, and especially the trilingual (Latin, Italian, and Slavic) training of its leading classes, Dubrovnik's cultural life was modeled on the trends prevalent in Italy, but included local elements and was often expressed in the Slavic vernacular of Dalmatia. Like the Italian city-states, whence many of her learned men and artists came and to which she sent numerous sons for study and work, Dubrovnik was the home of important architects, painters, carvers, gold- and silversmiths, and even scientists. These men served the well-educated patrician and merchant classes as well as the church. Some of the buildings that they erected and some of the paintings they produced have survived to the present, attesting to the ability of their creators and clearly showing the place occupied by Dubrovnik in the major cultural trends of Europe—and especially Italy—throughout the ages.

Among these buildings and paintings are several masterpieces, but these never influenced the Slavs under Ottoman rule, who were unable to see and understand them. Nor did the two most famous sons of Dubrovnik, the scientists Marin Getaldić (1568-1626) and Rudjer Bošković (1711-87), both of whom were well known all over Europe in their life time and are important figures in the history of science. Today the Yugoslavs are justifiably proud of their accomplishments.

The great contribution of Dalmatia, and of Dubrovnik in particular, to the growth of the cultural history of these people came through literature. Folk poetry, especially the *Kosovo Epic*, predates the greatest contributions of Dubrovnik to the common literary treasures of the present-day Yugoslavs, but most of the great poets who lived and worked after the intellectual awakening dating from Dositej Obradović (1739-1811) and Vuk Karadžić (1787-1864) built on the works created along the Adriatic coast during the previous centuries. Dubrovnik's literature is of the greatest importance to the cultural history of all Serbo-Croatian speakers and deserves a short summary.[9] Although the writers of Dubrovnik wrote in

9. No volume in any western language is devoted specifically to the literature of Dubrovnik. Josip Torbarina, *Italian Influences on the Poets of the Ragusan Republic* (London: Williams & Norgate, 1931) contains information on most writers of Dubrovnik. Dragoljub Pavlović, *Iz Knjizevne i kulturne istorije Dubrovnika; Studije i članci* [On the literary and cultural history of Dubrovnik; studies and articles] (Sarajevo: Svjetlost, 1955) is interesting for the subject under discussion. More detailed is the Dubrovnik section in Mihail Kombol, *Povijest hrvatske književnosti do narodnog preporoda* [The history of Croatian literature up to the National Revival], 2nd. ed. (Zagreb: Matica Hrvatska, 1961). In English the best book in which to find relevant information is Antun Barać, *A History of Yugoslav Literature*, trans. Petar Mijušković

three languages, those who wrote in Slavic are the ones who became the forefathers of Yugoslav literature and are, therefore, of interest for this study.

None of the writers made a living from writing. They were clergymen, teachers, merchants, and diplomats, among others. Most came from patrician or rich merchant families, although occasionally a son of the lower classes also turned to literary pursuits. These authors, as well as their readers, had to be educated to utilize and understand not only the classical and later Renaissance imagery and references in their works, but also to be able to judge their quality by comparing them to the Roman and Italian "originals" as far as style and versification were concerned. A basic education, including the ability to read and write at least in Italian and Slavic, and some mathematics was necessary for everybody involved in manufacture, shipping, and especially trade, and for this reason Dubrovnik maintained several "elementary schools" in which these subjects were taught. Those who needed or wanted and could afford it went on to more advanced studies in Italian universities. In 1433 the city-republic established a higher school to make advanced education available to more people at a lower cost. Teachers were imported from Italy. One of the first was Philippus de Diversis de Quartigianis, who taught in Dubrovnik from 1434 to 1440 and whose book, *Situs aedificiorum, politiae et laudabilium consuetudinum inclytae civitatis Ragusii* (Building sites, policies, and praiseworthy habits of the distinguished city of Dubrovnik), published in 1440, is one of the best descriptions of Dubrovnik dating from the fifteenth century.

People who received this type of education were naturally interested in many phases of public life, but also in literary works and many of them collected books. One of these individuals, Ivan Gazul (1400-65), an astronomer who worked in various parts of Europe, left his books to the Cathedral church of the city with the proviso that they be kept together and accessible to all, and thus became the founder of Dubrovnik's public library. Just as the first books available were either in Latin or Italian, so were the first poems and plays written by Dubrovnik authors.

The first two authors of any significance to write in Slavic were Šiško Menčetić (1457-1527) and Djorje Držić (1461-1501). Their writings are copies of contemporary Italian works with occasional inclusions of folk poetry motifs. They started writing Slavic poetry in the Latin alphabet. The best works contain local themes cleverly mixed with Italian models like the plays of Marin Držić (1508-67), and are still performed in Yugo-

---

(Beograd: Center for the Rehabilitation of Disabled War Veterans, 1955), reprinted as no. 1 of The Joint Committee on Eastern Europe Publications Series (Ann Arbor: A.C.L.S., 1973). Short summaries can be found in most books dealing with Dubrovnik including the Krekić and Carter volumes mentioned in n. 2 and 3. There is an interesting chronological table in Carter, *Dubrovnik*, pp. 511-13.

slavia today. Many of the works of these early Slavic writers survived in the original in the collection *Zbornika Nikša Ranjina* (The N. Ranjina Collection), prepared in 1507.[10] Unfortunately, the collection was destroyed during World War II. Another playwright of note was Nikola Vetranić-Čavčié (1482-1576), in whose works folk poetry elements were important. All these writers came from patrician or rich merchants' families. It is certainly no accident that the writer most admired by literary critics for his ability to handle the Slavic idiom, Andrija Čubranović (d. ca 1550), belonged to the lower classes.

Several other names could be mentioned, but nobody became more important for Yugoslav literature than did Ivan Gundulić (1589?-1638). Gundulić belonged to one of the oldest and greatest patrician families. He spent his life in public and diplomatic service, serving on the very important Minor Council and in the Senate. He took as his stylistic model Tasso's poetry, believing that it was more suitable for Slavic than were the previously used verse forms. His contribution to literature in general is his great epic poem, *Osman*. Although the central figure is the tragic sultan Osman II (1618-22), Romanian, Polish, and other Slavic heroes and heroines play important roles in this wide-ranging story about the European provinces of the Ottoman Empire. There are numerous references to earlier heroes like Stefan Dušan in the work, Dubrovnik receives repeated praise, and the future of the Southern Slavs is predicted in happy terms. The historical scope, style, composition, and story line of *Osman* rank it among the really great epics in world literature, and together with the *Kosovo Epic* and Petar II Njegoš' *Gorski Vijenac* (Mountain Garland), published in 1847, it makes up the great trilogy in Yugoslav epic poetry. Poets continued to write after Gundulić. Although none produced works of literary value, they did keep a tradition alive.

The prose writers of Dubrovnik are not notable for their contributions to the *belles-lettres*. A few of them, like Benko Kotruljević (1400?-69), are worth remembering as pioneers in their field, while others are of importance as historians. Kotruljević was a merchant who finally settled in Naples in 1451. There he became Dubrovnik's consul and a high-ranking official in the court of the Neapolitan kings. He is noted for a book he published in Italian, in 1458, *On Commerce and the Perfect Merchant*. According to one scholar, "This was the first attempt ever made to deal in a scholarly way with the origins of commerce, its nature, and its many aspects and techniques . . . it emphasizes the views of the emerging modern citizenry on nature, education, religion and social problems." [11]

None of the historians wrote in Slavic. For this reason they do not have the cultural value the poets have, but serve only as transmitters of information not contained in the documents in the Dubrovnik Archives. Be-

10. Carter, *Dubrovnik*, p. 503.
11. Krekić, *Dubrovnik*, p. 125.

sides the work of de Diversis the most interesting is a collection of annals by unknown authors, the first of whom wrote toward the end of the fifteenth century. This collective effort covers the years from the earliest known details about Dubrovnik to about the end of the seventeenth century.

Of particular value to those interested in Southeastern Europe is the work of Ludovik Tuberon Crijević (1459-1527). Crijević returned to Dubrovnik from Paris where he had studied philosophy, theology, and mathematics, and turned to history late in life. His eleven-volume *Commentarii suorum temporum* dealing with the years 1490-1522 concentrates mainly on Ottoman and Hungarian affairs. Even a hundred years later it was so highly regarded that it was printed in Frankfurt in 1603. By far the best history is the *Ragusan Chronicle* written at the end of the eighteenth century by the classical scholar and Dubrovnik politician Džono Rastić (1755-1815). It tells Dubrovnik's story to 1451.

In addition to these original works numerous translations of literary and scientific classics from Latin, Greek, and Italian into Slavic were prepared in Dubrovnik. Making these classics available to the Slavic reader was as significant as was the creation of original works when judged from the point of view of cultural development and history.

Dubrovnik's contribution to the history of the Southern Slavs cannot be equaled by any other city or region prior to the establishment of the Metropolitanate at Karlovci at the end of the seventeenth century. After that date an Orthodox cultural center grew up that matched that of Catholic Dubrovnik. Around this center there emerged men of Obradović's stature and importance. Without the Dalmatian and particularly the Dubrovnik tradition, all these later cultural centers would have had a much more difficult time in beginning their work.

4. SUMMARY

DUBROVNIK has a long and well-documented history.[12] It has already been stressed that no other vassal of the Ottoman Empire was able to maintain the independence from Istanbul that Dubrovnik enjoyed. Naturally "self-governing" regions within the empire proper, including various districts in Greece, Crna Gora, and Albania, were even more dependent on the moods of the Ottoman central government than were the vassal states. If any of these vassals and local lords was able to secure special privileges of great importance, the relative dirth of information in the records makes it impossible for the historian to learn much about them. Consequently, Dubrovnik remains our only example of a relationship that was advantageous to both the Ottomans and to one of their "clients." The cultural con-

12. Systematic preservation of records began in Dubrovnik in 1278. A full description of the archival holdings of the city can be found in Carter, *Dubrovnik*, Appendix 3, pp. 601-61.

tributions of Dubrovnik to the history of the Yugoslav people were also shortly mentioned. There remains only one last feature of Dubrovnik's contribution to these people that must be noticed.

With the exception of the major Greek merchants, the Ragusans were the only traders, merchants, or entrepreneurs who kept up with the development in their professions in the west. They used modern banking and credit facilities, were familiar with insurance practices, and understood the operation of the European-wide market. Unlike the Greeks, they spoke the language of those with whom they did business in the Balkans. Furthermore, once again unlike the Greeks, they were not considered *zimmi*. Thus, it was easier for them to operate in the Ottoman provinces proper. As a result the Slavs and Albanians learned more about modern business methods from the Ragusans than they did from the Greeks. *Zimmi* and Muslim merchants also learned much from their frequent visits to Dubrovnik. By the end of the sixteenth century the pupils were competing with their teachers. Bosnian merchants in particular imitated the Dubrovnik traders and became the first Slav businessmen to operate with modern business methods. Many other factors contributed to a revival of Balkan business in the sixteenth century,[13] but the importance of the example of Dubrovnik, at least in the western Balkans, should not be underestimated.

13. See the excellent and comprehensive article, Traian Stoianovich, "The Conquering Balkan Orthodox Merchants," *Journal of Economic History*, vol. 20, no. 2 (June, 1960), pp. 234-313.

Part Four

LIFE IN THE EUROPEAN "CORE" PROVINCES
OF THE OTTOMAN EMPIRE, 1574-1804

CHAPTER 9

The Change of Fortune

1. THE DECLINE OF THE OTTOMAN EMPIRE

ALTHOUGH the roots and first symptoms of the Ottoman Empire's decline are much older, the numerous problems became visible during the last third of the sixteenth century. An occasionally able sultan and the Köprülü dynasty of grand vezirs tried to reverse the trend, but decline continued practically unabated until the beginning of the nineteenth century. Scholars have given several reasons for this change in the fortune of the Ottoman Empire, and they disagree only in assessing the relative importance of the causes for this long period of steady decay.

The reasons most often cited for the Ottoman state's decline are: a drastic change in the training, personality, and activities of the rulers; the growing influence of the *enderun* on state affairs coupled with factionalism in the *birun* and the establishment of close ties between members of the inner and outer services; the growing corruption that resulted, in part, from the emergence of these factions; the sudden inflation at the turn of the sixteenth and seventeenth centuries, supposedly caused by the shift of world trade from the Mediterranean to the Atlantic and by the influx of silver from the Americas into the Ottoman Empire; a conflict between the old Turkish element (*beys*, *gazis*, and *sipahis*) and the descendants of slaves, which conflict split the rank of the "professional Ottomans;" changes in the organization and composition of the military establishment; and, finally, the inability of the Ottoman Empire to expand further. Each of these developments contributing to the steady decline of the Ottoman Empire's power both at home and abroad must be reviewed briefly.

During its first 266 years the House of Osman was unequaled in providing extremely able rulers. Their contributions to the growth and might of the empire were fundamental. It is unreasonable to assume, as some have done, that a mysterious biological change occurred suddenly, and

187

that beginning with Selim II (1566-74) only incompetents were born into the House of Osman. Even among the descendents of Ibrahim (1640-48) there were able men.

The ability of the ruler, given the Ottoman concept of the state, was fundamental to the empire's functioning. The role that the ruler was supposed to play in the state placed such a heavy load on his shoulders, that only an exceptional individual could carry it. As the empire expanded and the burden increased it surpassed the humanly possible. Mehmed II was the first to stop attending the councils of state simply because he could not afford the time. In his absence major office-holders became more important, opening the door to their future malfeasances. Selim I (1512-20) and Süleyman I (1520-66) were away from Istanbul most of the time, conquering the world. The void of leadership was filled by those who ran the state during their absence.

While the above factors partially explain the circumstances that made it difficult for the later sultans to be as effective as the earlier ones had been, and while they indicate why the power of the officials increased steadily, they do not account for the obvious individual weaknesses of most of the successors of Süleyman I. Here one must look to the deterioration of the sultan's training. Beginning with Orhan, Ottoman princes received the best education available; they served as governors of provinces under the tutelage of experienced administrators and in some cases even held other offices. Thus, when they ascended the throne they knew the problems and issues they had to handle and could rely on the personal loyalty of those men who had served with them. Prior to Süleyman the problem of succession had never been settled in the House of Osman. Every Ottoman prince was a candidate for the throne. This led to much competition among them and their followers and to frequent civil wars. In order to maintain their positions the sultans executed all their male relatives. While this system of fratricide took care of immediate threats, it did not diminish factionalism. The power of potential king-makers, especially the army, and the possibility of new clashes when the throne again became vacant only increased.

This situation changed abruptly when Süleyman I adopted the Arab-Islamic mode of succession through the oldest living male of the family. Although the new system was not embodied in legislation, it was followed more frequently than not. This more humane method of picking a ruler could have produced an even more complicated situation than the system of fratricide had if the numerous princes had continued to be placed, as they had been in the past, in administrative positions which were potential power bases. Fratricide ceased, but so did the training, both theoretical and practical, of the Ottoman princes; it was replaced by the *kafes,* known in western literature as the "golden cage system." All princes were kept from birth until death in the inner palace. Only the new sultan emerged into the real world. In the inner palace the princes spent their lives in a make-believe world of luxury among women and eunuchs. When they were elevated to the supreme dignity, often at a very ripe age and against their will, they lacked not only the necessary training for the difficult task they were supposed to perform, but any knowledge of real life as well.

The change in the succession pattern and in the training of future rulers also accounts for the growing power of the *enderun*, especially women and eunuchs. The mother of the ruler (*valide sultan*) became one of the most successful leaders of the many *enderun* factions. Being herself totally unfamiliar with the affairs of state, she was one of the least qualified people to become the most important and influential member of the "ruling establishment."

The growing power of the *enderun* accounts for the ties between *enderun* and *birun* factions, neither of which could have operated without the other. The first group not only supplied the ruler, but was also instrumental in selecting his successor. However, it could not rule without the cooperation of the latter group. That these factions also reflected the free-born or slave origin of their members is quite understandable apart from the fact that the *enderun* was manned entirely by slaves. In the days of Süleyman I the *birun*, too, was entirely in the hands of slaves who maintained a close relationship with those free men who were of slave origin. They, naturally, wanted to retain the power positions they had gained and favored those policies that had brought them to prominence. The descendants of the old "aristocracy," the *beys*, *gazis*, and *sipahi*, wanted to regain their lost position and advocated those measures that would have brought this about. What developed were large groups with members in both the inner and outer services who tied their future to the star of a prince or leading official with whom they rose and fell.

The backers of a given prince gained a great victory when he ascended to the throne, but their positon was by no means secure for the duration of his rule. Intrigues on a large scale became the main occupation of those "professional Ottomans" who served in Istanbul, and tenure became even less secure than it had been previously. Consequently, those in power tried not only to amass a fortune as rapidly as possible, but also to make certain that they, or at least their families, would retain it should the wheels of fortune turn. The establishment of fake *vakıfs*, which took large chunks out of the taxable segment of the economy, became the rule. Acts of this nature had occurred earlier, on a much smaller scale, but strong rulers like Mehmed II and Süleyman I had been able to abolish them. Weak rulers were unable to do so because they would have promptly alientated their supporters.

This desire to accumulate the maximum wealth as quickly as possible was one of the reasons for the growing corruption of men whose tenure in office was anything but secure, but it was not the only reason. Another important factor that contributed to corruption was inflation. It began during the reign of Murad III (1574-95) and is usually explained by the influx of silver, or rather by the decline in its value, making goods, especially those imported, extremely expensive. So far as the office-holders and other dignitaries were concerned, the inflation meant that the income from fiefs bought less, especially in terms of luxury goods, than previously, and the easiest way to find new sources of revenue was the "selling" of their services and "good will." There can be no doubt that the change in the price of silver contributed to the inflation and to the growth of corruption, but it does not explain the sudden huge deficits in the state budget. The explanation for the deficits lies elsewhere.

Chapters 4 and 5 explained that the Ottoman authorities fixed prices for domestically produced commodities that included basic food and other consumer items. Armaments, uniforms, and other military needs were either produced by slaves in state-owned arsenals or by craftsmen within the borders of the empire. The relatively small imports for which higher prices had to be paid could not account for the tremendous deficits with which the state was suddenly saddled. Their appearance points to another factor in the decline of the empire's fortunes that must be considered crucial both for the state and especially for the development of the Southeastern European lands under Ottoman rule.

One of the reasons for this sudden shortage of money has already been mentioned, the sudden growth in the number of *vakıfs* resulting in a serious loss of revenue for the treasury. In addition, there were major expenses that not even the extraordinary *bedel* taxes could cover. Of these the greatest were those connected with the "long war" with Austria (1593-1606) and the endless struggle with Persia. These wars contributed significantly to economic problems, not only inflation, and also created other difficulties leading to far-reaching consequences. Fought mainly by the feudal levies and the mercenary forces of the Ottoman Empire, militarily they accelerated the ascendancy of the *maaşlı* troops over the feudal-*gazi* forces and increased the influence of the former in Instanbul. They also decimated the ranks of the *sipahi* producing far-reaching economic and ethnographic changes of great importance for both the Ottoman Empire as a whole and the history of Southeastern Europe in particular.

The mention of the military aspects of the inflationary trend brings to mind the last usually cited reasons for the empire's decline. In most relevant accounts several interlocking developments are cited, including the ascendancy of the mercenaries in the military establishment, the lack of booty and especially newly conquered lands to support the *timarlıs*, and the resulting attempt of the *sipahis* to secure their personal and families' economic position. The explanation usually given can be summarized as follows.

The Ottoman Empire was first and foremost a military state that paid very little attention to trade, commerce, and production and relied on loot as its major source of income. This loot came from the conquest of large territories that were also used to satisfy the military's economic needs by being parceled out as *timars*. As long as large scale expansion was possible the system worked, but once expansion came to an end problems became unavoidable. Given the nature of Ottoman warfare—the army had to be under the sultan's personal command, and the soldiers had to be released around harvest time to return to their fiefs to collect their income—the campaign season was limited. It began in the Spring when the roads became passable and ended around harvest time. Only a certain distance could be covered within the time available for military operations, and once the empire's borders reached from the doors of Vienna to Azerbadjan and Iraq movements of armies had reached their limits. As a result loot did not fill the treasury any longer, and the holders of these benefices, no longer having land available for new fiefs, made certain of retaining them by converting them into private possessions.

To the superficial observer this explanation is satisfactory. Reaching the mentioned limits, the Ottoman Empire ceased to expand, and the transformation of fiefs occurred. Nevertheless, there are a few important factors that indicate different causal relations. In theory the sultan had to lead his army in person. In practice, however, several of the great sultans often sent out forces under another's command. Furthermore, by the end of the sixteenth century the feudal elements in the army had become secondary. Most of the fighting was carried on by mercenaries who did not have to return home in the fall. It should also be remembered that the need for new *timars* was in fact anything but pressing by the end of the sixteenth century because Timurid Persia absorbed new Turkish forces from Central Asia. As a matter of fact, the *timars* that became vacant in Europe as a result of the "long war" could not always be assigned because there were no qualified claimants around. Land had to be cultivated, and when the old feudal class declined it had to be replaced. Need, not the scarcity of land, created the new landholding pattern.

A completely different picture emerges if we take into consideration two more factors that have already been discussed: the Ottoman government's interest in commerce and that government's tendency to transform outlying provinces (Crimea, Moldavia, Wallachia, Dubrovnik, Transylvania) into vassal dependencies. The existence of vassal states and Süleyman I's attempt to transform central Hungary into such a dependency indicate that the central authorities in Istanbul realized that their ability to rule extended territories directly was limited, that they knew what and where these limits were, and that while they continued to pursue their "mission" of extending the *dar al-Islam*, they did not base the economic future of the state on steadily increasing income derived from loot. Vassal states were not supposed to be stripped of their goods; they were only to pay tribute. For these reasons one must look elsewhere for an explanation of the military and financial aspects of the Ottoman Empire's decline, and go beyond the usually given inability of the state to extend its borders further and further.

Other states during the same time suffered from inflation and from demographic problems connected with the regular recurrence of the plague and were able to overcome these difficulties and chart a new course that made the Western European states the leaders of the world. The Ottoman Empire did not react to the same problems in a similar manner. It is this difference that must be explained because in terms of both size and intrinsic wealth the Ottoman Empire's potential was at least as great as that of France, the Netherlands, or England. This is not the place to compare the institutions, economies, and basic principles of the West and the Ottoman state, but a few indications will, hopefully, suffice to make these differences clear.

There was a great difference between the positions of western rulers and of the sultan. The former began as the heads of feudal pyramids with limited powers; although their authority increased steadily, it was always limited. Just the opposite was true of the sultans. For this reason a weak ruler in a western state was a much lesser evil than a weak sultan. The growing freedom and strength of towns and cities, which permitted changes in the economy when necessary, was not paralleled by similar privileges granted to cities under Ottoman rule. Their position and internal organization were strictly regulated, and when any individual or group tried to introduce change, the extremely conservative authorities backed those who were opposed to innovation. Consequently, by the end of the eighteenth century, Western Europe's economy was already "modern," while that of the Ottoman Empire was still medieval. It was this conservatism in all phases of life that transformed the Ottoman state from a technological match for its enemies in the first half of the sixteenth century into a "backward" power by the end of the eighteenth. These are just a few factors that added up to economic backwardness, technological obsolescence, and an inability to cope with fiscal problems.

Differences in the role of the military are as important as economic differences when the Ottoman Empire is compared with the West after the middle of the sixteenth century. In both regions the importance of feudal forces declined and that of professional armies increased. At the end of the sixteenth century the feudatory soldiers (*sipahi* and *cebelü*) of Europe and Asia Minor could furnish 230,000 fighting men; by the end of the eighteenth century they could muster only 50,000 men. The decline in numbers was not tragic because with the development of modern warfare, there was a shift to infantry and technical troops. Given the administrative tasks performed by the *sipahi*, however, their disappearance called for the introduction of numerous civil servants. This was not done because the Ottoman Empire lacked the properly trained personnel and also the necessary funds. Instead of this new professional class taking over, the tasks of the *sipahi* were entrusted either to the by now corrupt existing officials, the clergy (both Muslim and *zimmi*), and tax farmers—all of whom had their own interests in mind and not the interests of a state that did not pay them.

The professional soldiers, the *maaşlı* forces, were mercenaries just as they were in the West, although the Ottoman forces were made up of slaves. The fact that the western forces were made up of free men made their relationship to the state and ruler simply that of employer and employee, even though they could create trouble, but the Ottoman sultans owned their soldiers and had to take care of them even when they were not needed. In addition to being a fiscal liability, this close affiliation of the *maaşlı* with the state made it impossible for the Ottoman government to "send them home" when they were not needed, making them a permanently armed power factor in the affairs of state. The result was that while in the West the rulers became the masters of their armies, in the Ottoman Empire the soldiery became the master of the state. By the end of the eighteenth century the number of those who claimed the privileges of janissaries, by then a closed hereditary corporation, had risen to four hundred thousand, but the number of those available for military service did not exceed twenty thousand. When the government tried to solidify its position by getting rid of these armed men in the capital by stationing them in the provinces it only shifted the problems to the provinces where law and order broke down completely. The result was further economic problems and a diminution of whatever loyalty the *zimmi* had had to the state.

Finally, there was a great difference between the basic concepts of the Ottoman Empire and the West. The Ottoman Empire's *raison d'être* and administrative organization was not only firmly established (see Chapter 2), but also almost by definition unchangeable: the realm of the House of Osman existed for the sole purpose of fulfilling God's will on earth by spreading Islam. What was right and wrong was known, and the difference between Muslim and *zimmi* was clear and could not be changed. The West had a certain freedom to think, to experiment, and to develop not only new philosophies, but even new interpretations of Christianity. The Ottoman world was rigid while the West was constantly changing and adapting to the socioeconomic and political requirements of a steadily expanding world whose center it became. In the West the modern state began to take shape and came to mean more and more even to the lowliest of its denizens. The Ottoman Empire went in the opposite direction. While in the West central, universally valid law replaced personal law, the Ottoman Empire remained a collection of individuals whose position, rights, and duties depended entirely on their religion and profession. The original difference in the Muslim ranks between the professional Ottomans and other true believers deepened when the former closed ranks to protect their privileges, thus making entry into their ranks more difficult. The government was not strong enough to stop this development. The *zimmi*, grouped in their *millet*s, became less and less interested in the continued survival of the Ottoman state when law and order broke down, to be replaced first with growing religious intolerance and later by the depradation of undesirable elements shipped from Istanbul into the provinces. Thus, the slow development of modern nations in the West was not only not occurring in the sultan's realm, but its previously existing vague cohesion began to disintegrate as well.

In summarizing the various interrelated causes for the sudden decline of the Ottoman Empire's might beginning in the last third of the sixteenth century, I would consider the concept of the state as "the divinely protected well-flourishing absolute domain of the House of Osman" to be the most relevant of all considerations. While this concept was the empire's greatest strength prior to the conquests of Selim I and Süleyman I, it became its greatest weakness when the state's size and the multiplicity of tasks its ruler had to perform became too great for even the ablest man to handle. Any change, which could occur in fact but was not admissable in theory, had to involve growth in the power and influence of those who were not entitled to power and influence and who, therefore, could be and were challenged constantly. Coupled with the shift in the succession pattern, this situation produced instability in government and made corruption possible. The divine mission of the state was never abandoned, but it prevented the integration of its population and even produced, after the decline of toleration and the breakdown of law and order, centrifugal tendencies. The old basic concept of the Ottoman state needed a revolutionary revision after the middle of the sixteenth century, but by this time conservatism, the previous successes that justified what had existed previously, and the absence of any important population segment that knew enough of other systems even to think of something different made reform a matter beyond speculation. Thus, the Ottoman Empire became ossified in its mid-sixteenth century shape, which it retained until the nineteenth century.

What happened around the middle of the sixteenth century when this ossification occurred could be debated; it could be considered as inevitable or as the result of an unlucky coincidence of developments. Was it inevitable that a state set in its ways could not cope with a suddenly emerging economic-fiscal crisis, or was it simply unlucky that this important problem faced the state when there were no able men to cope with it? Be that as it may, this crisis added to the growing corruption, the inefficiency of the government, and the centrifugal tendencies of those who were not "professional Ottomans."

Finally, the timing of the "long war" must be considered as a prime factor in the subsequent rapid decline of the fortunes of the Ottoman Empire. It was this war that increased the influence of the *maaşlı* forces, decimated the ranks of the European *sipahi*, made the already described wasteland out of the until then potentially rich Hungarian lands, deepened the economic crisis by the extravagant expenses involved in this war, and completely transformed the situation in the European "core" provinces, which until then had been the most solid foundation for the might of the empire. Once these "core" regions ceased to be the empire's economic and demographic mainstays, the decline accelerated and not even the Köprülüs were able to reverse the trend permanently. The changes that took place in Southeastern Europe were crucial for the fortunes of the Ottoman state and, obviously, are the most important occurrences for those interested in the history of this part of the continent. At no time were the fates of the Ottomans and the Southeastern Europeans interwoven so closely as they were in the seventeenth and eighteenth centuries.

2. WARS OF THE SEVENTEENTH CENTURY AND THE KÖPRÜLÜ PERIOD

THE first war that the Ottoman Empire fought after the death of Süleyman I, the war against the so-called Second Holy League (1571-81), is most famous for the Ottoman defeat at the naval battle of Lepanto (Naupactos, Inebahtı, Aynabahtı) in 1571. That battle was in fact unimportant because the Ottomans recouped their losses within a year, and their enemies were incapable of taking advantage of this victory. On the other hand, the Ottoman conquest of Cyprus, whose loss Venice recognized when she left the war in 1573, represented a significant military achievement. During this war the Ottoman army was still functioning very well, mostly under the able leadership of the future grand vezir Sinan *paşa*. It should not be forgotten that while this war was being fought in Europe, the Ottomans were also fighting a second war against Safavid Persia. The first serious signs of trouble with the military occurred after this war was concluded. In Istanbul the janissaries revolted in 1589, 1590, and 1591, and *maaşlı* cavalry in 1593, the same year in which the "long war" began. The first serious so-called *celali* revolt (there had been revolts previously, too) took place in Asia Minor in 1596, and its continuation in the next century weakened the empire's Anatolian power base just when its European base was also disintegrating.

Thus, while in 1571 a still relatively strong and reliable Ottoman army entered on campaign, by 1593 the reliability of the troops was already questionable. Although the Ottoman forces had able leadership in Sinan and then in Sultan Mehmed III, the long war indicates a change in their ability to take advantage of circumstances. For ten years, until Persia attacked in 1603, the Ottomans had to fight on only one front against poorly organized forces. Then, just when it appeared that the Habsburg-backed alliance between Moldavia, Wallachia, and Transylvania might gain a decisive victory, the instability of Sigismund Báthory coupled with the Habsburgs' emphasis on conquering Transylvania rather than on defeating the Ottomans and the poor quality of the leadership of their armies turned the tide. The Ottomans won a decisive victory at the Battle of Mezőkeresztes in October, 1596. Only fifty years earlier such a victory would have ended the war for the Ottomans would have secured important advantages, but at the end of the sixteenth century the Ottoman army was already unable to capitalize on its success. The war dragged on for another ten years. Both sides won minor victories, but the Ottoman Empire was economically destroyed, and it was faced with war on two fronts. When further janissary revolts occurred in 1603, the soldiers simply had had enough and did not wish to fight any longer.

By 1605 the Ottomans lacked the power to maintain their nominee, Steven Bocskai, on the throne of Transylvania, and the next year they had to make peace on the western front to turn their full attention to Persia. The Peace of Zsitvatorok left additional Hungarian lands waste and very insignificant gains in Ottoman hands, but it put an end to the Habsburgs paying tribute money. Using the strictest Muslim-Ottoman interpretation, the Ottomans released a "vassal," giving up land that at least in accordance with their theory had been part of the *dar al-Islam*. During this war the Ottoman forces occasionally still fought well, but were by no means always reliable. Moreover, the costs of the war, both in men lost and economic exhaustion, were not compensated by gains of equal value. Thus, while superficially victorious and in possession of additional territories, the Ottomans suffered losses that they could never make good.

Even after the peace Ottomans and the Habsburgs continued to engage in border skirmishes. One such skirmish brought the important city of Vácz under Ottoman rule in 1619, but this event was due more to the ineptness of the Habsburg commanders than to the ability of the Ottoman forces.

Of greater importance was the termination of the *devşirme* method of recruiting janissaries, an event often ascribed to the year 1638. While the child levy system had been used less and less frequently for at least the preceding half century, its official abolition was a clear indication of the growing influence of the janissaries on military policy-making. The end of recruiting secured them permanent membership in the corp by inheritance, leading to its final down-grading as a fighting unit and to its emergence as a dangerous and disrupting element.

The next important military action in Europe began when the Ottomans attacked Venetian-held Crete in 1645. This war, which lasted until 1670, reflected the decline of Ottoman fortunes, in spite of the fact that in the end Crete was conquered. The campaign consisted mainly of sieges and naval blockades that required a limited number of men. A hundred years earlier the Ottomans could have provided the needed force without weakening their main army, but now this operation tied down all the good forces they could muster. Thus, the Venetian commander, Francesco Morosini, was not only able to operate in the Morea, but also to induce the local population to rise in revolt. The Ottomans had to rely on auxiliaries drawn from Albania or on strong local lords to put up whatever resistance they could organize.

Chaotic conditions prevailed on this important peninsula for the entire duration of the war, and this situation, coupled with the slow progress of the operations on Crete and repeated defeats of the navy, brought about a crisis in Istanbul. In 1656 Mehmed IV (1648-87) was forced to appoint Mehmed Köprülü grand vezir with practically unlimited powers, thus ushering in the Köprülü period (see Appendix II). This appointment was well timed. George II Rákoczi's unfortunate Polish adventure (see Chapter 7) together with the poor showing of the Ottoman forces in fighting the Venetians encouraged the Habsburgs to attack the Ottomans in 1663. The newly gained important territories of the *Partium* (see Chapter 7) and much more were in danger. Unable to offer any serious resistance, the Ottomans suffered a crushing defeat at St. Gotthard in 1664. In spite of this great victory the Habsburgs proved to be as inept in taking advantage of great victories as the Ottomans had been a few years earlier after Mezőkeresztes. The ineptitude of general Raimondo Montecucculi played a large role in this failure of the Habsburg forces, but the main reason why the Ottomans did not have to pay dearly for their unpreparedness was the situation in Western Europe. Consequently, Vienna was glad to conclude the Truce of Vasvár with the Ottomans in 1664. This allowed them to complete the conquest of Crete and give the Köprülüs time to arrest the disintegration of the empire at least temporarily.

The Köprülü family, which furnished distinguished administrators, soldiers, and scholars to its country from the middle of the seventeenth century to the present, was of Albanian origin belonging to a group of Albanians that had been forcibly settled earlier in Asia Minor. Mehmed, the first distinguished member of the family, began his career in the *birun* as a pastry cook. From this humble beginning he rose rapidly in the service and subsequently served as governor of Damascus, Tripoli, Jerusalem, and Köstendil. He was seventy years old when Mehmed IV appointed him Grand Vezir. Mehmed *paşa* demanded full powers, and the sultan, a playboy interested in only his own pleasures, granted this request. While nothing can be said about this sultan that would be to his credit, the fact that he kept his word and did not interfere either with Mehmed Köprülü's or his son's, Ahmed's, administrations was certainly fortunate.

Determined to reverse the downward trend of the empire's fortunes, Mehmed Köprülü attacked what he considered to be the main cause of its decline, corruption. During his five years in office he is reported to have ordered the execution of about thirty thousand office-holders and *ulemas* accused of peculation or other misdeeds. This frightening example forced those still in office to toe the line. Revenues that had previously disappeared in the pockets of office-holders were again delivered to the treasury. Mehmed *paşa* also diminished the number of those who received salaries from the state. These measures reduced the budgetary deficit substantially from 160 million *akçes* in 1653 to 12 million by 1660.[1] Mehmed was mainly interested in restoring the administrative machinery of the Ottoman Empire and ending the corrupt practices of the various office-holders. He entrusted the military operations to his son and future successor, Ahmed, a very able military leader.

While it was Ahmed who lost the Battle of St. Gotthard, it was also he who finally brought the Cretan campaign to a successful conclusion and who, as his father's successor as grand vezir, took advantage of the relatively calmer times to continue the work begun by Mehmed. As a military man he also tried to reorganize the army by creating new units from the Anatolian peasantry to balance the growing power of the janissaries. In these moves can be found the beginning of the future Ottoman armies. These new forces, called *gönüllüs* (volunteers), never became powerful enough to serve the purpose Ahmed *paşa* had in mind, and when the strong hands of the Köprülüs disappeared the janissaries once again became a force for evil.

The war with Poland (1672-76), which occurred during the last years of Ahmed Köprülü's tenure as grand vezir, brought the last significant territorial gain in the history of the empire. It began when the Cossacks revolted against Poland and made common cause with the Crimean Tatars, asking for Ottoman protection. This was granted, and Ahmed himself led the Ottoman forces that gained the final victory. At the Peace of Żurawno the Poles ceded Podole and the Western Ukraine to the Ottomans and agreed to pay a yearly tribute of 220,000 ducats. The only other conquest, the island of Tenos in 1715, was insignificant.

The victory was fleeting. Established as they were in the Ukraine, for the first time the Ottomans faced the growing power of Russia, and the grand vezirate of Ahmed's successor, Kara Mustafa Köprülü, began with the first Ottoman war with Russian in 1677. That war lasted for four years and ended with the first permanent Ottoman loss of territory when, at the Peace of Radzyń, the Western Ukraine was handed over to the Tsar.

1. Gibb and Bowen, *Islamic Society and the West*, vol. 1, pt. 1, p. 26, n.1. These authors indicate that the deficit figures available for the years between 1653 and 1660 are not reliable.

Kara Mustafa chose the exact moment to renew the war against the Habsburgs. Why, it is not quite clear. He was an honest man, although not so talented as the first two Köprülüs. He was also a very ambitious man and somewhat insecure in his position because he did not belong to the main branch of the family and owed his position simply to the fact that he was a friend of the sultan. In view of the defeat in the Ukraine, and these considerations, he might have wanted a great and glorious victory to solidify his position. Be that as it may, hostilities were begun in 1682, and the grand vezir led a huge army, estimated to have been composed of as many as two hundred thousand men, including the numerous camp followers that always accompanied the Ottoman armies, to the gates of Vienna. The city was ably defended by the small forces of Count Rüdiger von Starhemberg, but the battle was decided by the bad generalship of Kara Mustafa. The general permitted German relief forces led by Charles of Lorraine and a large Polish army commanded by King John III Sobieski (1674-96) to take positions around his army unmolested. When attacked by his enemies on September 12, Kara Mustafa made several serious tactical mistakes. Defeat was inevitable. Although still involved in Western Europe, the Emperor Leopold I (1657-1705) decided to exploit this victory. This time his forces were under the command of three fine generals, Charles of Lorraine, Louis of Baden, and Eugene of Savoy.

Kara Mustafa was executed at the sultan's orders for his conduct before Vienna, and the decimated Ottoman armies faced the oncoming enemy without any strong leader. Encouraged by the events, Venice joined Poland and the Habsburgs and formed the third Holy League, thus splitting the forces of the Ottomans. Both the Habsburg and Venetian armies marched from victory to victory. In Hungary Buda fell in 1686, and a year later Charles of Lorraine won a decisive victory at the second Battle of Mohács.

At the same time the Venetians were advancing in the Morea. By the end of 1687 Morosini, again in command and supported by German units under Maximilian of Brunswick, by Swedish troops under Otto von Koenigsmarks, and by a few Italian units, had conquered the entire area. The next year the allies took Athens (it was their artillery that destroyed the Parthenon). The obvious inability of the Ottomans to fight brought the Russians back into the fray. They besieged Azov in 1687.

All these events, but especially the defeat at Mohács, infuriated the soldiers, who forced the sultan to abdicate while they rioted in Istanbul and partially destroyed that city. The new sultan, Süleyman II (1687-91), emerged from his *kafes* with no knowledge of the situation and no idea of what had to be done. The central administration practically ceased to function. The next year the Habsburg forces cleaned up in Hungary, and crossed the Danube, conquered Belgrade, and moved on along the river to Vidin, which fell in 1689. Moving south, they entered Niš during the same year. Naturally, their march added to the devastation of the Balkans and encouraged many *zimmis* to help the invaders. The situation was so critical that even the rioting soldiers were willing to submit to strong leadership once more, and this was supplied by the next grand vezir, Mustafa Köprülü.

Mustafa reconquered Vidin and Belgrade in 1690, which resulted in the mass migration, to be discussed in the next chapter, of Serbs into Hungary. Unfortunately for the Ottomans he lost his life the next year in the Battle of Novi Slankamen (Szalánkamén). This time the Ottomans were saved by the fact that the Habsburgs had become involved in the War of the League of Augsburg and could not press a full attack. Nevertheless, the wars continued and the Ottomans, once again, lacked leadership. During the next years all the remaining Ottoman fortresses in Hungary were lost, Azov fell to the Russians in 1696, and the Venetians continued to hold the Morea and occupied several islands. When Eugene of Savoy gained another decisive victory in 1697, this time at Zenta, the Ottomans once again turned to a Köprülü, Hüssein, and he began to work for peace.

On January 26, 1699, the most disastrous peace in Ottoman history, the Peace of Sremski Karlovci (Karlovitz, Karlóca), was concluded. The Ottomans were forced to give up all of Hungary and Transylvania, retaining only the Banat of Temesvár; they had to recognize the Venetian conquest of the Morea and most of Dalmatia and to return Podole to the Poles. The Russians tried to gain more, but finally concluded peace, too, in 1702, and retained Azov. After the peace with Russia Hüssein resigned. The Köprülü period had ended for all practical purposes (if we disregard the few months Numan held the office of grand vezir in 1710).

The Köprülü period (1656-1702) lends itself to several interpretations. It has been argued that it indicates that, in spite of ninety years of decline beginning with the death of Süleyman I, the empire was still viable by the time Mehmed *paşa* became grand vezir and needed only strong and honest leadership to reassert itself as a great power. Those who subscribe to this view stress that it was only the bad generalship of Kara Mustafa that brought a premature end to the recovery of the Ottoman state. At the other extreme we find experts who feel that the Köprülü period was nothing but a glowing testimony to the ability of Mehmed and Ahmed. The sultan at that time was so little interested in the affairs of state that even intrigues could not reach him, and the first two Köprülü grand vezirs took advantage of this situation to seize absolute power, which, in fact, was not rightfully theirs. This power together with their ability, honesty, and ruthlessness produced a sham recovery that would have collapsed, even without a great military defeat, as soon as the professional Ottomans had managed to get a sultan on the throne who was susceptible to the usual palace machinations and factional infighting. Both of these explanations assess the situation from the perspective of the central government and its functioning. Although an assessment of the Köprülü period simply in terms of the central authorities' efficiency has its merits, other criterion must be considered for a correct evaluation.

Between Mehmed Köprülü's elevation to the grand vezirial dignity (1656) and the attack on Vienna (1683) a new generation had grown up. In theory these young people should have been educated as professional Ottomans according to the strict principles enforced by the Köprülüs. Even if the grand vezirs could not always control every phase of Ottoman life and, therefore, the young generation had been subjected to the influences of the old corrupt school, they were able to fill the important administrative position of the state with their own men. Thus, the administration should have been strong and honest enough to face successfully a major crisis like the one that followed the defeat before Vienna. This, obviously, was not what occurred. While the Köprülüs were indeed able to place honest men in the most important positions and bring the budget almost into balance, they were unable to alter the fundamental ills of the state. These difficulties, and especially the attitudes that resulted from them, reasserted themselves as soon as the prestige of the Köprülüs had been destroyed and would probably have reappeared, sooner or later, even without a great defeat because they were fundamental.

The great economic and demographic changes that resulted from the "long war" were not reversed during the Köprülü period. Furthermore, they continued to alter the situation in the key European provinces, reinforcing the tendencies that began in the 1590s. The population continued to decline both in the cities and the countryside, creating serious shortages in manpower and production and leading to the transformation of the village and the city. The number of *timarlıs* was steadily declining; new relationships between "landowners" and the peasantry had to be worked out and the administration had to be restructured. Military reforms did not succeed, and the influence of the *maaşlı*, especially the janissaries, was not broken. Consequently, the situation that had made illegal action and corruption possible, especially in the provinces, was not altered, and the reasons for anti-Köprülü and antireform actions were not eliminated. This explains why a military revolt, after the second Battle of Mohács, was able to destroy not only the efficiency of the military, but also the entire reform work of the Köprülüs. The members of this family were indeed able to clear the worst offenders out of the central administration. Using their unlimited powers and the fear Mehmed's large-scale executions had created, they were also able to force the provincial administrators to obey Istanbul's orders and demands more closely than at any time since the death of Mehmed Sokollu (1579). Even the military behaved so long as it was ably led, regularly paid, and did not have to face disasters of major proportion. In a highly centralized and tradition-bound state greater efficiency at the center had to have a salutary effect and could produce temporary improvements without solving the basic socio-economic problems of the state. The Köprülüs accomplished much, but their work never touched the deeper problems. When it did, as in the case of military reform, it did so only unsuccessfully. None of the problems could have been solved by simply replacing one set of office-holders with another.

The conclusion that presents itself in assessing the Köprülü period when more than the efficiency of the central government is taken in account is the following. By the middle of the seventeenth century there were too many complicated problems to yield to reform attempts that concentrated simply on revitalizing the efficiency of the bureaucracy and the army. Consequently, the view that all that was needed to right the wrongs and re-establish the empire's position was strong and honest leadership cannot be maintained. What was needed were fundamental changes that no one, not even the Köprülüs, who had grown up in the professional Ottoman milieu could understand. Remarkable as the Köprülüs' accomplishment was it was doomed to ultimate failure. The most significant contribution of this family was that had it not ruled during a period in Ottoman history when the obvious weakness of the state could easily have brought on a determined attack from either her old foe, the Habsburg or her new enemy, the Russians, such an attack would have gone unchecked. While there are several reasons why these powers did not take determined steps against the Ottomans in the second half of the seventeenth century, one of them was the fact that the Köprülüs' administration successfully camouflaged the true state of affairs. When, in the eighteenth century, the impotence of the Ottoman Empire could not be hidden anymore, the fateful attack that could have destroyed it did not materialize because the great powers were carefully working against each other in the attempt to solve what became known as the "Eastern Question."

3. WARS OF THE EIGHTEENTH CENTURY

BETWEEN the Peace of Sremski Karlovci and the outbreak of the Serbian Revolution in 1804, the Ottomans were involved in six wars that affected their European provinces disregarding the Napolenoic wars that also influenced developments in this region although they were not fought there. All these wars were fought on Ottoman territory, which fact indicates clearly how drastically the balance of military power had shifted. By the eighteenth century the Ottoman Empire was clearly on the defensive. The one exception that brought territorial gains, the war with Venice, 1714-18, was fought against a state whose decline was as marked and rapid as was that of the Ottomans, on a terrain whose population, being Orthodox, resented the rule of a Catholic power and usually favored the Ottoman war effort. The surprising fact that during this entire century the only territory the Ottomans lost in Europe (besides the Crimea, which falls outside the scope of this volume) was the Banat of Temesvár in Europe can be explained by the jealousy among the great powers that worked against each other always giving the Ottomans a "friend" in the foe of their enemies or by European events that forced their opponents to leave their anti-Ottoman campaigns in order to turn to other problems.

The first war of the century, that of 1710-11 with Russia, has already been discussed in Chapter 6. It has been shown how Constantin Brîncoveanu's actions placed Peter the Great in a critical position which could have ended with his death in an Istanbul prison. The story of how he escaped by bribing the grand vezir is too well known to be repeated. The very fact that such a high official could have been bribed at a critical juncture of his country's history indicates the level the Ottoman Empire had fallen to only a few years after Hüssein Köprülü left office in 1702. It also explains why, from the point of view of both, the Ottomans and the people whom they ruled, the eighteenth was certainly the worst century in the long years in which they shared a common state. When we realize that over seventy years of mounting difficulties separate the capture of Peter the Great from the ascension of Selim III to the Ottoman throne (1789), we can understand the magnitude of the problem that this true would-be reformer faced.

The war with Venice was begun by the Ottomans who wanted to regain the Morea. This was an easy campaign, because Venice was not only weak, but several of her strong points were defended by mercenaries who were not interested in dying for the republic. Furthermore, the anti-Catholic sentiments of the population were stengthened by the Patriarch in Istanbul who excommunicated all Orthodox ready to help the Venetian forces. Venice, conscious of her weakness and trying to consolidate her forces, began the war by evacuating several fortresses, thus discouraging her partisans. The cowardly behavior of several commanders who were supposed to defend their positions but surrendered without fighting further weakened morale. Within a three-month period during 1715, most of the Morea was reconquered, but fighting continued in the Maina district and on several islands.

Seeing the Ottoman army occupied in the south, the Habsburgs believed that this was their moment and joined Venice in 1716, gaining an important victory at Petrovaradin (Peterwardein, Pétervárad) that year. The emperor's soldiers occupied Belgrade, the Banat of Temesvár, and Little Wallachia (Oltenia) the next year and were ready to move deeper into the Balkans. At this moment Great Britain offered her good services to Venice and the Ottomans. As seen from Western Europe the Eastern Question forced her to act, saving both the Ottomans and the Venetians but offering the Habsburgs more than acceptable terms. The Viennese conquests were upheld at the Peace of Požarevac (Passarowitz), and while these were not insignificant the Ottomans could console themselves with their own equally significant gains in southern Greece. Venice was saved from what might have become total destruction. Thus, the "balance" in the Balkans was temporarily saved.

For the next eighteen years the Ottomans and their European enemies remained at peace, but two important treaties were signed with Russia in 1720 and 1724. The first of these regulated commercial and diplomatic issues that had been unresolved in 1711, and also delimited in great detail the border between the two states. The second, a provisional document, drew lines for the partition of a troubled Persia between the Ottomans and the Russians.

In theory these treaties should have solved the problems between the two states. In practice the might of Russia continued to grow, as did her desire to reach the Black Sea. Before Russia moved she came to an agreement with the emperor in Vienna, proof once more of how in the eighteenth century no great power felt secure to act on her own. After the conclusion of the alliance the Russians started hostilities in 1736. They rapidly conquered the Crimea and occupied Azov. Following up these conquests, they demanded the transfer of all Ottoman lands from the mouth of the Danube to the Caucasus on the northern shores of the Black Sea.

Early in 1737 the Ottomans were threatened on yet another front. The Habsburg armies attacked and occupied Niš, Priština, and Novi-Pazar (Yeni-Pazar) south of the Danube, and Wallachia and parts of Moldavia north of the river. These large-scale conquests necessitated a scattering of the army. When the Ottomans counterattacked in 1738 this situation, together with poor leadership, forced a retreat and the evacuation of the Balkans with the exception of Belgrade, which was surrounded by Ottoman forces.

The emperor, confronted with this unfavorable military situation and concerned about the succession to his throne (he had no sons and was aged and ailing), welcomed the intervention of Great Britain, the Netherlands, and France, who were again concerned with the balance of power in the Near East. The French ambassador in Istanbul, the Marquis de Villeneuve, acted as peace maker. He concentrated on the Austrians, realizing that both the poor performance of their armies and the fear of the imminent death of Emperor Charles would force them to accept peace on almost any terms. He also knew that Austria's withdrawal from the war would force Russia, who could not face the "concert of Europe" on her own, to end hostilities. The resulting Peace of Belgrade (September, 1739) was amazingly favorable to the Ottomans, thanks to Villeneuve's understanding of the Austrian and Russian situations of which he wanted to take full advantage for his country. The Austrians returned Belgrade and Little Wallachia to the Ottomans, losing everything they had gained at Požarevac. Russia was permitted to retain Azov, but only as an unfortified city, and she had to promise not only not to maintain a fleet on the Black Sea, but even to use merchantmen flying the Ottoman flag for her trade there. While the Ottoman armies fought surprisingly well in 1738 against the Habsburg forces, the favorable outcome was really the result of the struggle of the great powers and their intervention.

The next war of importance, 1768-74, the first of the two brought about by the ambitions of Catherine the Great of Russia (1762-96), did not end so happily for the Ottomans. It was Frederick the Great of Prussia (1740-86) whose policy kept the Habsburgs from getting involved in this war and who finally diverted Catherine's attention from the Ottoman to the Polish problem saving the Ottomans from even greater losses than they in fact suffered. Not that the Austrians did not take advantage of the situation. At the end of the hostilities, in 1774, they occupied the Bukovina, which until then had been a part of Moldavia.

The war with Russia had two phases. The attack of the Russian army developed successfully. The Danubian Principalities and the great Ottoman fortresses of Kilia, Akerman, Izmail (Ismail), Bender, and Brăila (Ibrail) at the mouth of the Danube were soon occupied, and the army advanced into the Crimea. After these early successes in 1768-70 the Russian forces were involved in the organization of the occupied territories and plagued by supply problems and disease and did not procede further.

The famous naval expedition commanded by Gregory Orlov did not parallel these land victories. With the exception of Captain John Elphinstone none of the Russian commanders were capable men, and whatever the tsarina's forces gained they soon managed to lose. The Morea and the Islands, the scenes of this war, were divided. The traditionally anti-Ottoman regions like the Maina district helped the Russians, while others remained loyal to Istanbul. The Ottomans did not have regular forces available for this diversionary campaign, and fought with the help of locally raised forces who were often Christian and a large number of Albanian troops. These forces were sufficient to undo all the previous successes of the enemy on land, and by the middle of 1770 most of the Russian forces had returned to their ships and their local followers had been liquidated by the Albanians.

Naval action still offered chances of success, especially because the commander of the Ottoman navy, the *kapudan paşa* Hosameddin, was incompetent and a coward. It was he who in spite of good advice had twice placed the fleet in an impossible position in the battle of the Strait of Çeşme between the mainland and the Island of Chios (Sakĭz). In so doing he had practically insured the annihilation of his fleet as he watched the battle from the nearby shore. This happened on July 7, 1770, and a total disaster was averted only by the action of Hassan *paşa*, who subsequently became *kapudan* and later grand vezir. The battle gave the Russians a tremendous advantage, and Elphinstone suggested sailing through the Dardanelles and attacking Istanbul. The city was in turmoil.

Ravaged by plague and fearful of the approaching Russians, the citizenry panicked, and nobody knew what to do. The sudden appearance of the victorious Russian fleet would probably have delivered the city to the tsarina's forces. Orlov opposed the plan, however, and for two weeks nothing happened. Then it was decided to attack the island of Lemnos (Limni) at the entrance of the Dardanelles. The well-fortified island resisted for months and again the Russians did nothing. While the British recalled their officers who were serving with the Russian navy, the famous Francis de Tott, a Frenchman of Hungarian birth in the Ottoman service, fortified the Dardanelles, and Hassan *paşa* reorganized the Ottoman navy. In late October Hassan relieved Lemnos where the Russians abandoned all their equipment and artillery. Although the Russians continued to cruise in the Aegean until the end of the war, their fleet, short of supplies and devoid of good captains, ceased to be a danger for the Ottomans. Thanks to Orlov's incompetence, the Russians missed the one great chance any power had had since 1453 to occupy Istanbul.

Catherine, more and more involved in Polish affairs, agreed to an armistice at Giurgiu in May of 1772, but the peace negotiations that followed remained fruitless. After the first partition of Poland, the Russians resumed the war and late in 1773 crossed the Danube into Bulgaria. The Ottomans were forced to resume negotiations, and on July 30, 1774, the famous Treaty of Küçük Kajnarca was signed. Although the Russians gained only the relatively small region between the Dnester and the Prut and agreed to evacuate all other occupied territories, they temporarily upset the Balkan and Near Eastern balance of power and became a force that both the Ottoman government had to heed and the inhabitants of her European provinces wanted to follow. They forced the Ottomans to recognize the Crimea as an independent state and gained the political advantages described in the chapter dealing with Moldavia and Wallachia. Russia's navy and merchant marine were also freed from all restrictions, and her influence in Orthodox ecclesiastic circles of the Ottoman Empire became as important as her growing prestige in the political problems of the Christians, especially those in the Danubian Principalities.

A few years later, in 1783, the Russians violated this treaty and annexed the Crimea, forcing the Ottomans to acknowledge this change in a convention signed in Istanbul in January, 1784. These gains fell short of Catherine's goals, and after she and Joseph II of Austria (1780-90) came to an agreement on the partition of the European provinces of the Ottoman Empire, with the Russian portion including Istanbul destined to become the capital of a Greek state ruled by Grand Duke Constantine, the two powers only waited for an opportunity to begin hostilities. When the Ottomans protested against the illegal activities of Russia's consuls in the Danubian Principalities, Russia declared war in 1787. It was during this war that the tragic sultan Selim III (1789-1807) assumed the supreme dignity of the state and faced the first of the numerous wars that he was forced to fight against his will. Austria declared war shortly after Russia early in 1788. Ably led by Princes Alexander Suvarov and Nicholas Repnin, the Russian forces first captured Ochakov (Oczakow, Özü) and then moved into Moldavia, Wallachia, and the Dobrudja. The Habsburg forces began by penetrating into Serbia and Bosnia, but were pushed back in 1788. The next year they captured Belgrade and entered Wallachia again. In 1790 Joseph II died and was replaced by Leopold II (1790-92), who was opposed to the war and faced revolutionary situations in Belgium and Hungary, and a possible war with Prussia. He promptly began peace talks which ended, in 1791, with the Peace of Svishtov (Szisztova, Zištov). The *status quo ante* was re-established with only slight border rectifications in favor of Vienna around the Iron Gates on the Danube and the Bosnian border along the Sava. Thus, for all practical purposes the end of the last war that the Ottomans fought with their great neighbor on their northwestern border left the Danube-Sava line as the border.

Austria's defection as well as developments in Poland and France forced the Russians to conclude the war under conditions favorable to the Ottoman Empire. In January, 1792, the Treaty of Iaşi fixed the European border between the two states along the Dniester and Kuban rivers. Of these two the first is important for this study because it forced the Russians to return all Romanian lands to the Ottoman Empire. Although this was by no means the last Russo-Ottoman war, this border did remain fairly stable throughout the nineteenth century, with the exception of Bessarabia, which changed hands several times.

In all these eighteenth-century wars the Ottoman Empire's good fortune stemmed not so much from her ability to defend herself as from the balance-of-power game that repeatedly forced the Romanovs and the Habsburgs to deal with the Ottomans leniently. The price that Istanbul paid was not so much in territory as in freedom of action. After Küçük Kajnarca Russian influence became very strong in the decision-making process of the Ottoman government, and during the revolutionary period French influence became strong. In the nineteenth century first British and later German influence became paramount. It is worth noting that, beginning with the eighteenth centurry, Ottoman diplomacy proved to be as successful as the military leadership had been earlier. Unfortunately, this ability to adjust did not influence domestic policy in the eighteenth century. Selim III paid with his life for his attempts to change his realm's institutions. The effect of his efforts and the countermoves of his enemies on the European provinces will be discussed in the next chapters.

When the Ottoman Empire of 1804 is compared with what it had been in 1574, the territorial changes in Southeastern Europe—the loss of Hungary and Transylvania—might appear rather insignificant. Hungary had never been an economic asset, and Transylvania had contributed little to the strength of the Turkish state. Yet, this loss was significant because it not only indicated a growing Ottoman military weakness, but also brought the Habsburg forces to the Danube-Sava line whence they could and did repeatedly invade the "core" provinces of the Ottoman Empire. These raids contributed not only to the devastation of this economically important area, but also to its depopulation. The mass migration of Serbs in 1690 and 1694 created a second cultural center besides the Croats' in Habsburg lands. During the eighteenth century that center was to have increasing influence among the southern Slavs still under Ottoman rule. The penetration of western ideas and influences made possible by this shift of borders was as important for the national revival movements of the nineteenth century as was the breakdown of the efficiency of the Ottoman administrative and legal systems.

It was this deterioration of the Ottomans' ability to rule that makes the 1804 situation drastically different from that of 1574. During these slightly more than two centuries a strong, well-organized state had been transformed into one in which chaos reigned and local accomodations became more significant than the laws and edicts promulgated by the government. The Ottoman Empire's size was its only impressive feature in 1804, and nobody knew as well as its inhabitants how little the extent of the state contributed to its orderly functioning. Change had become inveitable, but the two bad centuries made it impossible for this transformation to occur. Ottoman reform was not what the *zimmi* of Europe were now demanding. They wanted at least home rule, but this was something the government could not have granted even if it would have been inclined to do so because it had lost control over those "professional Ottoman" elements that lived in the provinces and were opposed to granting more rights to the *zimmi* at their own expense.

The first of the successful revolutions, the Serbian of 1804, shows quite clearly how the demands of the inhabitants of the European provinces of the Ottoman Empire escalated rapidly from efficient government, to home rule, and finally to the conviction that only independence would satisfy their minimal demands for security of life and property. The Ottoman Empire did transform itself in the nineteenth century, but this transformation affected fewer and fewer of its former European subjects for whom the time had come for national revolutions and independence. The first man who led a successful revolt, Miloš Obrenović, has been called by his disgruntled countrymen the "Serbian *paşa*." The influence of Ottoman rule was lasting. Unfortunately, this influence was mainly that of the two bad centuries, and thus the memory that the people of this region have today of Ottoman rule is a very unpleasant one.

CHAPTER 10

The Changed World of
European Turkey

1. INTRODUCTION

DURING the period 1413-1574 the Ottoman Empire's institutions functioned well, and the individual subjects of the sultan—Muslim and *zimmi*, professional Ottoman and *reaya*—could be kept and were more or less willing to remain within the bounds set for them by their *hadd*. The great majority of people stuck to their social positions and occupations. The functions of the various professional Ottoman groups and of the urban and rural *reaya* as well as their interrelationship were clearly differentiated. Thus, it was not difficult, when writing about that period, to handle these three major elements of society as distinct units (see Chapters 2-5). Although it would make the task of the reader easier if this pattern could be maintained permitting him to turn, for example, from one chapter dealing with urban life to another covering the same topic and thus follow the history of the city from beginning to end, the author felt that this apparent advantage would involve so many drawbacks that the seeming help, that the parallel treatment could have represented, would, in fact, have made the reader's task more difficult.

After 1574 the changes that occurred were so closely interrelated that it is impossible to discuss the rural and urban components separately without obscuring the major lines of transformation. For example, economic changes that occurred in the countryside influenced those in the cities, and both the urban and rural modifications stemmed from the same causes. Economic changes were closely connected with demographic shifts and with new administrative patterns. Therefore, it was thought best to treat all these issues topically within the framework of a couple of chapters in order to present the history of the centuries that followed 1574 most comprehensively. In this and subsequent chapters developments will be treated topically, but within this framework an attempt will be made to separate, as much as possible, purely urban from purely rural phenomena

209

to help those who might be interested in the continuation of the story presented in the earlier chapter.

It is important to realize that in the post-1574 period, to use this arbitrary dividing line, theoretically everything remained exactly what it had been in the previous centuries. The central administration with its numerous branches, bureaus, and offices was not reformed. Although the boundaries of provinces and their subdivisions were changed and some of the office-holders acquired new titles, relationships between the central and provincial governments were supposed to have been the same. This was also true of the connections between the various social classes and the segments of the economy. What changed drastically was not only the quality of the office-holders, but also the attitude of practically everybody to radically different living conditions, and the relative importance of certain offices and practices. For example, the *mültezim* (tax farmer) became an official of great importance for the *reaya* in the seventeenth and eighteenth centuries. His position and the tax farm (*iltizam*) had existed since the beginning of the Ottoman state; what had changed was the number of these farms and the manner in which the *mültezim*s perceived and performed their duties.

There were other changes of great importance, first and foremost of which were those involving ownership of land. These far-reaching changes not only represented a shift in the relative importance of various preexisting patterns, but they were also clearly illegal. Even these cases had to be explained in terms of the law that was never changed, and the new patterns emerged simply because the government did not have the power to curb those who circumvented the regulations. Although these new arrangements became with time "traditional and accepted" and were eventually taken for granted, they were never legal and, in theory, they could have been abolished by a revitalized government. After Sultan Mahmud II destroyed the janissaries in 1826 and was able to initiate reforms, he moved against those whose position rested on illicit bases. Whatever he and his successors achieved in the way of reforms was made easier by the fact that even after centuries, during which certain practices became the accepted way of life, they could be attacked as illegal.

During the years following 1574 only the Köprülüs used the legality that did not correspond to reality to justify their actions, but the possiblity that someone else could use it in this manner always frightened those who were either forced by the circumstances or who took advantage of the situation to make a dishonest living. This fact explained some of their behavior patterns. The major aim of these people was to remove as much property as possible from interference by the authorities, or to create profitable undertakings, for example, illegally established guilds, which would not be prosecuted because of usefulness. These moves, irrespective of motivation—necessity or greed—violated someone else's *hadd* and often produced such violent reactions and counteractions that the social order was completely splintered. These pages deal only with events that influenced everyday life and created new socioeconomic patterns of lasting significance and not with the legal fiction of unchanged institutions and relationships that will not be investigated except in those cases where fiction influenced reality.

Although changes occurred everywhere and a general pattern of transformation becomes visible, the emerging "new order" was by no means uniform. This is not surprising because the new patterns reflected local conditions and not centrally enforced change. For this reason the common patterns will be presented first, and subsequently important local variations will be discussed. These locally conditioned developments added significantly to the fragmentation of the Southeastern European scene and created differences that survive to the present.

The present chapter ties together three closely interrelated aspects of communal life: the economic, the demographic, and the administrative. The basic economic change was the shift from the *timar* to the *çiftlik* system. Although it is impossible to determine what produced this change, it could be argued that the gradual diminishing of the *timarlıs'* military orientation coupled with corruption and greed affected them as much as it did the other professional Ottoman groups. It could also be adduced that this change was inevitable because the number of *timarlı* declined so drastically because of repeated plagues, lower birth rates, and heavy casualties during the "long war" that there were not enough of them to maintain the old land system or the position of this group within the circle of professional Ottomans.

Whatever the reason was for this change in landholding, it had to involve administrative change because the *timarlıs* were not only soldiers, but also administrators, and their gradual disappearance made the rise of other "civil servants" necessary. No new group was brought in; instead the functions performed by the *timarlıs* were assumed by the *ulema*, the Christian clergy, merchants, tax farmers, locally important strong families, and other groups that had existed previously. Such persons became much more important in society than they had been earlier, and the social and administrative patterns of the provinces were completely changed.

2. THE NEW VILLAGE

IN Chapter 2 the theory on which landownership rested had been explained. To recapitulate briefly, three types of landownership was recognized by the Ottomans. *Mırı* lands belonged to the sultan, *mülk* holdings were private property, while *vakıfs* denoted those possessions, by no means always land, whose income was reserved for the upkeep of pious institutions. When the government was strong an overwhelming proportion of the land was *mırı* and supplied the authorities with both the income derived from their produce and the taxes paid by those who worked on the land. All *timars* were *mırı* and could be reclaimed any time by the authorities. The *timarlı* received only a certain part of the income from the land in exchange for military service and the performance of some duties that in other states would have been performed by the civil service. The *timarlıs* had strictly limited authority over both the Muslim and *zimmi* peasantry. They could collect the goods and services to which they were entitled and could demand the obedience owed to them as civil servants. Apart from these obligations towards the *timarlı*, the *reaya* were free men and had their own *hadd* which was protected by the legal authorities. The *timarlı* was a soldier-administrator who benefited from the state's willingness to pay him in goods and services of *reaya* living on a defined piece or pieces of land, but he was not a landowner. Consequently, he had no interest in the land or in the men who worked it, and whenever he showed any interest the legal authorities were quick to inform him of the the limits of his authority. With the exception of *vakıf* properties, the state retained full control of the land and of the income it produced.

The establishment of *vakıfs* was considered a good deed, the duty of pious individuals, and was encouraged so long as they were set up legitimately with the permission of the authorities and served a truly worthy purpose. It has already been pointed out that each *vakıf* had a *mütevelli*, administrator. Several also had a *nazir*, who supervised day-by-day operations and for whose livelihood accounts were set aside in the deed that established the *vakıf*. This necessary proviso made it possible for unscrupulous individuals to take advantage of the system. A sizeable income set aside for a small project left large amounts available to support the *mütevelli*, and if the grant stipulated that this official had to be at all times the head of the donating family, the financial future of the family was assured. Abuses of this nature had occurred from the beginning. Under the strong sultans they were rectified by abolishing the fake *vakıfs* and making the income-yielding lands, markets, etc., once again *mırı*. Such was not the case in the two centuries now under review. The number of *vakıfs* that supported little more than the donor's family increased, and state revenue decreased correspondingly. So far as the peasants working the land of these establishments were concerned, this fake arrangement proved to be favorable. It spared them from becoming subject to the exactions of the emerging landlord class and tax farmers. Although the number of *vakıfs* increased considerably, the number of peasants protected from impositions remained small because anybody who wanted to establish a *vakıf* either had to own *mülk* property or had to have the right to dispose of *mırı* lands. Since only the sultans had this right, the number of those who held private property was small.

Although the sultans, in accordance with traditions, continued to establish *vakıfs*, the main loss of income for which the government itself was responsible stemmed from irregularities connected with corruption and the growing influence of the *enderun*. The city of Athens illustrates this development very well. In the first half of the seventeenth century the city was granted as a fief to the chief of the black eunuchs,[1] the *kızlar ağası*, who appointed his own representatives and collected a yearly income of 30,000 ducats.[2] While this income was lost to the state, Athens acquired virtual self-government because it was no longer subject to the *sancak beyi* of Euboea and the *kızlar ağası*'s and his representatives' interest was limited to the collection of revenues.

Athens also presents a good example of how economic and administrative change often went hand in hand. When the city became the fief of the chief black eunuch, the state lost revenue, the *sancak* to which Athens belonged lost authority, and two new administrations, those of the *kızlar ağası*'s appointees and the local government of the Athenian nobles, the *archons*, came into being.

To the above developments the third, the demographic aspect must be added. When the Venetians captured Athens they realized that they were unable to hold the city and decided to evacuate its population. During the last quarter of the sixteenth century, a contemporary, Simeon Kabasilas, estimated the number of males living in Athens at twelve thousand and numerous scholars agree that at the time of the Venetian attack on the city its inhabitants numbered around twenty thousand.[3] Although many of the deported inhabitants returned after 1715, Athens' population was still far below twenty thousand when Otto, the first king of modern Greece, entered his capital in 1832.

As long as Athens serves as an example of various developments and irregularities that occurred after the breakdown of the Ottoman administration, let two more events be added to the picture showing that even the differentiation between professional Ottoman and *reaya* and the privileges accorded to the *millets* were occasionally violated with impunity. Giving no date, William Miller mentions that on one occasion, when the Oecumenical Patriarch ordered the deposition of the archbishop of the city, the *kızlar ağası* had the order revoked at the demand of the Athenians. He also cites the case of the appointment of Demetrios Paleologos, whose family claimed but was unable to prove that it descended from the old imperial house, as the *kızlar ağası*'s chief administrative officer in 1712.[4]

1. The black eunuchs were a major faction in the *enderun*.
2. Several dates are given for the granting of this fief. The earliest is 1610, the latest 1645.
3. William Miller, *Essays on the Latin Orient* (Cambridge: Cambridge University Press, 1921), pp. 377, 387.
4. *Ibid.*, pp. 392, 416.

Significant as the changes were that resulted from the increasing number of *vakıfs* and irregularities like those mentioned in connection with Athens, their importance is almost negligible when compared with the significance of the transformation of the *timars* into *çiftliks*. That transformation meant the illegal conversion of *mırı* into *mülk* property, the introduction of landowning in the generally accepted sense, and drastic changes in both the peasants' lives and the patterns of agricultural production. This new proprietary and production pattern in the countryside influenced closely related changes in the cities, too, and in addition to creating new economic relationships contributed significantly to the emergence of a new social and demographic realignment.

The *çiftlik* was not a truly Ottoman innovation. It represented the extension and illegal application of a principle that had been recognized for many centuries. Muslim and *zimmi reaya* families could, under certain circumstances, own a *çift*, the smallest basic land unit necessary to support a family. This right supplied the theoretical justification as well as the actual basis for the name of the future *çiftlik*. The heart of every *timar* was the basic *çift* or *kılıç* that the *sipahi* cultivated for himself, and that was almost always assigned to his son on his death even when the heir's merits were so minimal that he got nothing else when the fief was redistributed. Thus, traditionally if not legally, this basic holding was considered to be private property. If the principles contained in these two established customs—one legal, the other traditional—could be extended from the smallest property size that made self-sufficient agricultural production and a minimal living standard possible to larger surfaces, true landed estates could be developed. This is what happened in the seventeenth and eighteenth centuries.

The problem of the *çiftlik*, which was called *hypostatika* in Greek-speaking provinces and *beylik* in Bosnia, has attracted the interest of several scholars whose findings helped this author greatly.[5] Busch-Zantner has defined the *çiftlik* as an estate similar to the well-known European holdings. A single individual owned and administered this land, either directly or with the help of a bailiff, and acquired an organization centered around the equivalent of a manor house. Not only is this definition the

5. The most comprehensive study is Richard Busch-Zantner, *Agrarverfassung, Gesellschaft und Siedlung in Südosteuropa unter besondeser Berücksichtigung der Türkeinzeit* (Leipzig: Harrassowitz, 1938) published as volume 3 in the *Beihefte zur Leipziger Vierteljahrsschrift für Südosteuropa* series. Short but valuable is Ömer Lutfi Barkan, "Çiftlik," *Islam Ansiklopedisi*, 3:392-97. There are two comprehensive Bulgarian contributions: Vera Mutafcieva and Strasimir Dimitrov, "Die Agrarverhältnisse im Osmanischen Reiche im XV-XVI Jahrhundert," and especially Bistra Cvetkova, "Quelques problèmes du féodalisme ottoman à l'époque du XVIe siécle au XVIIIe siècle." Both are in *Actes du Premier Congres*, vol. 3, pp. 689-702 and 709-20 respectively. By far the best, short, easily accessible study in English is Traian Stoinaovich, "Land Tenure and Related Sectors of the Balkan Economy," *The Journal of Economic History* 13 (Fall, 1953): 398-411.

generally accepted one, but it also corresponds to reality so far as both the peasants and landlords were concerned. While the more limited definitions of other scholars, for example, Cvetkova's, are technically more correct, Busch-Zantner's will be used.

Several factors contributed to the decline of the *timars* and the emergence of the *çiftliks*. From the point of view of Istanbul, two major causes appear to have been involved. Without the corruption that permitted those who acquired property not only to do so but also to have their actions "legalized" in documents issued by the offices in the capital and by several provincial *kadis*, the new landholding system could not have spread as rapidly or as widely as it did. The central authorities' need for money, the tremendous deficits in the budget caused by the inflation during the last quarter of the sixteenth century, and the tremendous expenses of the "long war" set into motion a trend that finally facilitated the establishment of *çiftliks*.

Needing the greatest possible revenues on a regular basis and being unable to rely any longer on the honesty of officials, the government began to lease the revenues of the state more and more frequently to individuals who were able to pay the treasury promptly in cash. These leases could be in the form of *mukataas* or *iltizams*, with the two expressions often used interchangeably. The *mukataa* involved basically the "cutting off" of a piece of property. For example, a large estate that belonged to the sultan could be handed over to an individual in exchange for a specified payment for a given number of years. The *iltizam* was more or less the farming out of the collection of revenues, mainly taxes, to a tax farmer who once again paid a fixed amount ahead of time for a given period during which he tried to make a profit on his investment. In theory this practice did not change the legal title to land or other income sources, but was a continuation of the old practice on which the *timar* system itself was based, namely, the bestowal of certain rights and benefices on individuals in exchange for the performance of certain duties.

As one moves away from Istanbul, one finds that the growing number of tax farmers who descended on the provinces rapidly came into conflict with the professional Ottomans because their interests often conflicted. The number of individuals who lived away from the capital and had the necessary funds to become the "creditors" of the government was not inconsiderable. The *tüccars* and *âyans*, as shown in Chapter 4, had acquired considerable wealth and invested it in many economic activities that brought them further income. Being capitalists interested in letting their money work for them, they were drawn to this new type of "business," which they claimed was part of their *hadd*. Furthermore, they insisted that many of the *mültezims* had no legal title to carry on these activities. In this endeavor to get a share of the new sources of wealth they were soon joined by the *beylerbeyis* and *sancak beyis*, who were not only increasingly corrupt, but also disposed of large revenues from their *has* holdings. These ranking officals either imitated the example of the central government by subdividing their holdings into *iltizams* and renting them out, or tried to become *mültezims* themselves. It was not long before all these individuals had coalesced into a single group which for all practical purposes acted as the bankers of the state. Several wealthy *zimmi* entered their ranks.

From its popularity it is quite clear that income farming was a very profitable venture. There were two reasons for this. The government, pressed for money, had to grant the *mültezims* favorable conditions; at the same time it had to leave the contribuables, who had to produce the rented-out revenues, to the tender mercies of the income collectors. This fact brought about numerous violations of the law and the disregard of privileges and rights not only of the *reaya* but also of *timarlıs* who were not rich enough to participate in the new enterprise and whose fiefs fell within or were near the region in which the powerful and rich *mültezims* were given practically a free hand.

There were three major causes for the next step that led from the *timar* to the *çiftlik*. The first involved the granting of fiefs to persons who were not entitled to them because they had not performed the necessary military-administrative duties. The case of Athens and the *kızlar ağası* illustrated this development. These absentee landlords not only farmed out their holdings, but by entering the ranks of the feudal lords they served as an example and encouraged others to claim rights to holdings without performing the concommitant duties. The trend weakened the military establishment and also reinforced the tendency toward acquiring claims to land on an individual and not on a service basis.

Equally important was the desire of the central government to increase the number of properties it could farm out to increase its revenue. The easiest way to do this was to increase the number of imperial *hases* and enlarge those already in existence. Thus, numerous fiefs were attached to the *havas-i hümayun* rather than reassigned at the death of their holders. This move diminished the number of *sipahi* and weakened both their power to resist encroachments on their rights and, indirectly, the military establishment.

The third factor, which stemmed from the other two, was the insecurity of tenure. This affected not only the holders of fiefs who were slowly evicted, but also those who profited from the new developments.

The *timarlı* who were not strong and wealthy enough to become *mültezims* in their own right tried to secure their financial future by transforming their fiefs into hereditary properties or into cash, which they could then invest in other forms of income-producing ventures. Obviously, both reactions were illegal in theory and had to be secured by "legal" papers issued by the corrupt judiciary. There exists documentary proof not only of the issuance of "title deeds" bestowing private ownership of land, but even of registered sales of fiefs.[6]

The tax farmers were also insecure. They invested heavily, paying in advance, in a venture that promised to be profitable. They could not, however, be certain that they would be able to make the expected gains. Intrigue in Istanbul and the continued need for cash tended to shorten the period during which they were free to collect revenues from the land or other income-producing property that they had leased. The tax farmers were mainly interested in lengthening this period, and they finally succeeded in obtaining *malikane* leases, which were granted for the lifetime of the appointee. Naturally, once a powerful individual acquired a *malikane* he tried to make it hereditary in his family. In this manner the remaining *timarlıs* and the *mültezims* worked for the same goal, the transformation of *mırı* property entrusted to them for a given period of time into *mülk* holdings. In the case of agricultural property this transormation meant the change from *timars* to *çiftliks*.

This change from one type of landholding to another was facilitated by far-reaching demographic changes that will be discussed later in this chapter. Suffice it to note at this point that the demographic trend consisted of a decline in Muslim and *zimmi* population, and a large scale migration of the *zimmis*. In the European provinces most *reaya* were *zimmi*, and their large-scale movements had serious economic consequences, which were closely related to the development of the new production pattern that emerged with the establishment of *çiftliks*.

The old fiefs consisted of the feudatory's *has çift*, which he cultivated pretty much on a subsistence basis, and the various holdings of the peasantry, which produced enough to keep them going, supply the "lord" with an income that raised his living standard above subsistence level, and permit them to pay taxes out of the revenue they earned by selling their surplus to nearby towns and cities. Thus, while the fiefs produced a surplus, their economy was not market-oriented, and the feudatory took no interest in the production pattern of the peasantry's choosing. Naturally, on a *çiftlik*, as on any other privately owned large estate, this pattern could not be followed if the owner was to earn considerable income. Production had to be centralized, rationalized, and adjusted to yield maximum income; it had to become market-oriented. This transformation involved the introduction of new crops, such as cotton and vegetables and later potatoes and maize, as well as increased meat production. The last-mentioned development was due to both the larger size of the average holdings and the scarcity of labor. For all these products and, naturally, for cereals, the domestic market proved to be too small, because the decline in population had not been restricted to rural areas, and because the

6. Cvetkova, "Quelques problèmes," p. 713 and Gălăbov and Duda, *Protokollarbücher*, Doc. Nos. 815 and 1135 on pp. 234 and 350.

shrinking urban population could not begin to absorb the agricultural goods that were produced. Profits from landholding had to be made by increasing exports that paid well and at the same time maintained the level of domestic prices.

This need for sales abroad contributed further to the weakening of the central administration's authority and to the corruption and growing independence of provincial officials, several of whom had become virtually local princelings by the eighteenth century. The exportation of strategic goods, such as lead, iron, and all agricultural products, was forbidden in the Ottoman Empire. True enough, these forbidden items had always been exported to some extent, but such exports had either been tied to special conditions like those of the *mezővárosok* of Hungary or to well-regulated treaties as in the case of Dubrovnik, or they had represented the minimal concessions made to international commercial contacts to secure much needed import items. During the seventeenth and eighteenth centuries these limitations disappeared. This is another example of the growing discrepancy between theory and practice, and of how unimportant the regulations of Istanbul were in the later centuries. The export regulations were never changed. Thus, most export activities were in theory illegal, but nobody could stop the *beylerbeyi*s or even the *sancak beyi*s, many of whom owned large *çiftlik*s themselves, from issuing local export licenses for a fee.

A new group of export merchants sprang up, many of whom were Albanians and Slavs. Together with the old *tüccar* group, which in later centuries come to be composed of more and more *zimmi* (predominantly Greeks) and fewer and fewer Muslims, the new merchants changed the structure of cities and grew into a force of considerable importance in the national revival movements of the eighteenth and nineteenth centuries. Several merchant families grew rich and important enough to become *mültezim*s and even minor local officials. They were often as hard on their conationals as the Turks were, and even less popular because they belonged to the same group as did those whom they often oppressed.

Irrespective of whether the new landlord was a *vakıf*, an ex-*timarlı*, the local *paşa* or *bey*, the court official residing in Istanbul, or the ex-*mültezim*, he was almost always an absentee landlord who administered his *çiftlik* with the help of the bailiff. It was this official who had to work out the new relationship between master and peasant. In establishing a *modus vivendi* several factors had to be atuned to each other. On paper the *reaya*s retained their rights. They had only certain obligations balanced by corresponding rights and were supposed to be free men who could sue and be sued in court, migrate, etc. The landlord, on the other hand, wanted to acquire the maximum possible control over the peasants' actions and movements—in other words, he wanted to strip them of their rights and tie them to the soil as serfs. Although legal considerations would hardly have stopped these powerful individuals from enserfing the Southeastern European peasantry, the scarcity of labor and the inability to force the return of a migrant from an equally powerful local potentate did. This does not mean that the situation of that peasantry did not change and that dependence on the lord did not increase significantly.

The breakdown of public security engendered by the depradations of the new lords, by the even worse behavior of the "undesirable elements" that were pushed out of Istanbul and settled in the provinces, and by the increasingly intolerant behavior of religious zealots whom the authorities were either unable or unwilling to check left the peasantry with three alternatives. They could migrate to safer locations, mainly into the mountains, and establish new settlements there on "free soil"; they could react by fighting fire with fire and form "patriotic bandit" units of *klephts* and *hajduks* for self-defense, thereby becoming outlaws; or they could turn to a strong man who could provide the security the authorities could no longer guarantee. They followed each of these paths. Naturally, those who selected the first two alternatives were lost to the new masters of the soil. Those who remained and were willing to work became even more valuable. This need for security increased the centralizing tendency required by market-oriented production. The manor house, which now made its appearance, often looked like a minor fortress and was frequently defended by the lord's private troops. To make this defense possible it was necessary to move people into more or less protected areas. Many old villages had to be relocated near to the manor house, and their inhabitants as well as other peasants whose villages had been destroyed by disorders became fully dependent on their lords.

This dependence was important for several reasons, but mainly because it was the means by which the lords kept their peasants from moving away. On most *çiftliks* the lords owned not only the houses of the peasants, but even their tools. There were cases of villages being built and equipped before tenants were recruited for them. Seeds, animals, and cash were loaned to the *reaya* at usurious rates secured by promises to produce. This relationship made it possible for the lord to prevent some peasants from migrating and force them to remain put by a "business contract" enforceable in court. The fact that the pre-existing group relationships were not destroyed and were even encouraged—entire villages continued to have group ties with their lords who discussed matters with them through their own officials—also tended to keep the restless individual in place. After all, his peers did not want to have to carry his share of the burden after his departure. Busch-Zantner goes so far as to state that it was the *çiftlik* system that gave the traditional *zadruga* its final form and full power over the lives of its members.[7] The village elected its

7. Busch-Zantner, *Agrarverfassung*, p. 135.

kmet who acted as local policeman and petty judge under the supervision of the *knez*, the head of the community.

The new landholding system transformed a Near Eastern type of relationship into an Eastern European one similar to that in Russia, Poland, Hungary, and Romania. This Eastern European system has often been severely criticized as backward and repressive when compared to that of Western and Central Europe, but it should be remembered that it was the breeding ground in Poland, Hungary, and to a lesser extent in Russia and Romania of the leaders of a great variety of reform and national movements during the eighteenth and nineteenth centuries.

Did the *çiftlik* have the same potential as the Eastern European landholding pattern had for becoming the basis for constructive developments? The answer most often given to this question is that the introduction of the *çiftlik* was harmful and one of the clearest indications that the Ottoman system, whose agriculture was based on the *timar*, had broken down. There are several reasons why this author does not share this view.

First, although the Ottomans had indeed originally diverted the Balkan landholding pattern from the European to the Near Eastern type when they took over as masters, in the process they had also arrested the full development of feudalism, which in this part of the world lagged several centuries behind its western European counterpart. The Balkan peasant did not become a serf. As has been shown in Chapter 5, he retained a number of rights and privileges, which together with his obligations were part of his *hadd*. The gulf between master and peasant never became as deep as it did in other parts of Eastern Europe.

The reason for the incomplete development of feudalism was that the arrival of the Ottomans eliminated the traditional ruling classes. Advantageous as this was to the peasant, the disappearance of the various people's leading elements had far-reaching and dire consequences. With the establishment of the *çiftlik* a new leadership group made its appearance in the form of landlords and peasant leaders. The *modus vivendi* between the *çiftlik* owner and the peasants was based on previously guaranteed rights. The peasants in the Serbian lands where the *zadruga* existed enjoyed more rights under the *çiftlik* system than did those in Macedonia and Bulgaria, and this is one reason why the Serbian lands were the first to revolt.

Second, in Eastern Europe the landholding system produced leaders in spite of the fact that for all practical purposes lords and peasants were isolated from each other, and the latter were denied even the right to complain. The potential of the *çiftlik*, whose lords and peasants shared some rights and had common interests, to become a force for change had to be even greater than that of the Eastern European estates. The Austrians understood this potential and introduced the rank and office of chief headman (*Ober-knez*) when they ruled Slav provinces between 1718 and

1729. Several powerful lords (see next chapter) understood it too, but Istanbul limited itself to confirming the *Ober-knezes'* position by *berats* issued by the local *paşas*. These new dignitaries facilitated dealings among all concerned—the authorities, landlords, and the peasantry. By the time Istanbul realized that they had acquired enough prestige, wealth, and leadership potential to be a social force it was too late. During the days of Selim III, when Istanbul turned to these men, the *çiftlik* too had already been destroyed.

Third, the *çiftlik* system of the seventeenth century had enough potential to produce drastic change and become the regenerating force of the Ottoman Empire. The people working in this new agrarian-landholding system were still Ottoman in their orientation, not national. The potential of the economic and social forces represented by the *çiftliks* would have profited the Ottoman Empire if the eighteenth century had not ruined them, too. Nothing indicates this possibility better than the first phase of the 1804 revolt in Serbia, where peasant rights were the strongest and the *çiftlik* was still powerful. The rapid transformation of this movement from one in favor of the sultan into one aimed at termination of Ottoman rule proves both previously presented contentions. The *çiftlik* was basically Ottoman-oriented, but during the eighteenth century those who lived in the countryside had learned a bitter lesson: Istanbul had no power to enforce its will and to protect its loyal subjects.

In summary, the important aspects that characterized the countryside in the seventeenth and eighteenth centuries were as follows. The dominant agricultural unit was the privately owned *çiftlik*. Its owner, who was Muslim and increasingly also *zimmi*, was an absentee landlord and exploited his estate with the help of a manager. The exploitation was market-oriented and involved the cultivation of new crops and a heavy increase in animal raising. The share of exports in the sales of goods increased. The countryside changed physically: larger and larger areas became depopulated and were used as pasture; villages clustered around fortified manor houses. In theory the inhabitants of the villages retained their legal freedom; in fact they were usually tied to the land because everything they needed to make a living was owned by the lord who was also their creditor, and because the community to which they belonged discouraged the migration of its members. The communities retained a large degree of internal self-government, and more and more power accumulated in the hands of their leaders. The result was a new leadership element among the peasantry.

3. DEMOGRAPHIC CHANGES

DEMOGRAPHIC changes not only influenced the village but also the city. Their influence was felt all over Eastern Europe and produced several significant transformations, the first of which was a decline in population.

No firm statistical data exist, but the tax rolls clearly reflect this trend. The decline of the Turkish-Muslim element, which was noted by contemporary travelers and observers, is not too difficult to explain. The plague and military campaigns incurred great losses of life. As mentioned, it was very difficult to replace these losses because the emergence first of Timurid and then of Safavid Persia cut off the Central Asiatic Turkish tribes from easy migration into Ottoman lands. Finally, it might be justifiable to conjecture that the Turkish element, which was fairly well-to-do financially and to a good extent urban, had relatively small families, much as did similar social groups elsewhere in Europe. The low birth rate among European Muslims has also been noted by contemporaries. Thus, high death rates from both natural and other causes, low birth rates, and the government's inability to replenish the Turkish element combined to diminish the percentage of the Turkish-Muslim population of the "core" provinces. In the countryside this decline in the number of Muslims was an additional factor contributing to the *timar-çiftlik* transformation, the increasing number of *zimmis* who managed to acquire land, and the growing reliance on *reaya* "officials" in the management of village affairs.

Not only were there fewer Muslims in Southeastern Europe than had been previously, but an even larger percentage of those who remained lived in towns and cities. The shift to outright landowning and the concommitant appearance of absentee landlordism explain this last demographic shift in the countryside.

In the increasingly Christian rural regions the total number of inhabitants also diminished. Once again most of the main reasons have already been mentioned: military campaigns and growing lawlessness forced people to migrate to safer regions including the cities; The Venetian conquest of the Morea and the Ottoman reconquest had the same results; the repeated campaigns and temporary rule of the Habsburgs in certain parts of the northeastern section of the Ottoman possessions, as well as the reestablishment of Ottoman rule in these areas produced large-scale emigrations. Of these population movements the best known are the two migrations of Serbs into Habsburg-held territories in 1690 and 1694. Under the leadership of the Metropolitan Bishop of Ipek (Peć), Arsenije III Černojević, some 200,000 Serbs moved northward with the retreating Habsburg forces in 1690 and were followed by a smaller number in 1694. Numerous smaller migrations occurred over the years.

Whenever people left others took their place, and thus the demographic map of Southeastern Europe was completely changed. At the end of the seventeenth century Southern Hungary gained a large number of Serbs, and Albanians filled the void in what is known today as the Kosovo-Metohija region in Yugoslavia. Albanians also settled in Epirus and even the Morea, while Bulgarians began to colonize larger and larger regions, moving out of their traditional areas of settlement toward the shores of the

Aegean and into Macedonia. Naturally, these and less important population movements did not represent violent conquest or a displacement of people. Some conationals had been living for centuries in the various regions into which several people moved, but the rather important population movements of the seventeenth and eighteenth centuries did give all these lands a new demographic profile, which became important when nationalism made its appearance. Although at first the new arrivals were usually less numerous than those whom they replaced, they rapidly became a majority.

Even though the *zimmi* also decreased in over-all numbers, they replaced not only Muslim elements, but also each other throughout Southeastern Europe. This change was at least as important in the cities as it was in the rural districts. In the urban settlements the Greeks and Slavs, and, to a lesser degree, the Albanians replaced not only the Muslims, but to a considerable degree even the Jews. In the seventeenth century, when religious intolerance began to grow in the Ottoman Empire, at least two western European states, England and Holland, were moving in the opposite direction, and a good many Southeastern European Jews migrated there. Salonika, the city with the largest Jewish settlement, offers the best illustration. The approximate number of Jews living in this city dropped from forty thousand in 1660 to about twelve thousand by 1792. A similar decline occurred in other places, such as Sarajevo, Zemun, Vidin, Skopje, and Belgrade, and a slightly less drastic one in Sofia, Monastir, and Edirne, all of which used to have strong Jewish communities.[8] In addition to growing Ottoman intolerance and growing tolerance in the West, internal dissention, which will be discussed in Chapter 12, also prompted many Jews to move to other countries.

In addition to the decline of established Ottoman and Jewish communities and the increase of native Christian elements, the appearance of a new Muslim group, the undesirables who had been expelled from Istanbul, had an important impact on the cities and towns. In Salonika the departing Jewish element was replaced not so much by Christians, who made up about 25 percent of the city's population in 1792, as by the "janissary" element, which furnished about 55 percent of the inhabitants.[9] In most other cities similar changes in the population pattern occurred.

Some cities suffered a heavy loss in population in the seventeenth century; although they regained some inhabitants during the next century, they did not reach their original size before the end of the period under investigation. Belgrade lost about half of its inhabitants in the last quarter of the seventeenth century, and Skopje nearly 80 percent. The case of Athens has already been presented (see p. 213). Other localities remained fairly stable so far as the total number of inhabitants was concerned, and

8. Traian Stoianovich, "The Conquering Balkan Orthodox Merchant," pp. 246-47.
9. *Ibid.*, p. 251.

some even grew, but the composition of their inhabitants changed drastically. Salonika, which remained fairly stable with approximately 60,000 inhabitants is a good example of this change, as are Plovdiv, whose Christian population increased from 240 people to 10,000 between the 1580s and 1680s, and Banjaluka in Bosnia where 6 percent of the inhabitants were Christians in 1655, but 80 percent by 1807.[10] Nikolai Todorov's recent study offers numerous examples of this kind.[11] Although no generalization could possibly do justice to the change in population or in the size of cities during this period, one general trend becomes clear: while the number of people living in cities decreased, the percentage of urban dwellers in the total population increased, making cities and towns and the economic activities centered therein relatively more important than they had been in previous centuries.

Most of the urban centers were renationalized during the two centuries under discussion, and the trend introduced by Ottoman occupation was reversed. Others again, those that were Ottoman establishments, lost their original Turkish character and took on that of the people who were in the majority in the surrounding countryside. Finally, some cities acquired a demographic composition that reflected internal migration patterns. These changes, together with those that occurred in the rural districts, created both the "heart lands" of the post-liberation nation-states, and also those regions—Northern Epirus, the Vojvodina, Bačka, Banat, Kosovo-Metohija, Macedonia, and Southern Thrace—that were to become the major centers of confrontation during the nineteenth and present centuries.

Coupled with demographic change went economic transformation, which has already been surveyed in the rural regions, including the emergence not only of new landholding patterns, but also of the new village, the large empty tracts used for raising animals, the introduction of new crops, and market-oriented production. The last-mentioned of these changes created a new merchant class that had great economic, administrative, and political significance. Most members of this new class lived in the cities.

4. THE NEW CITY

ALTHOUGH the new city was much less Turkish than the old had been, the upper layer of the population continued to be predominantly Muslim. Most took advantage of the transformation in rural areas and became absentee landowners, but as city dwellers they were joined by former rural

10. *Ibid.*
11. Nikolai Todorov, *Balkanskiat Grad, XV-XIX Vek. Socialno-Ikonomichesko i Demografsko Razvitie* [The Balkan city from the fifteenth to nineteenth centuries. Socioeconomic and demographic developments] (Sofia: Izdatelstvo Nauka i Izkustvo, 1972) is the best work on the subject. The author used the quantitative approach and the work is filled with excellent statistics.

elements who had taken advantage of this same development to acquire estates and had moved into the cities where they could enjoy their opulence. These people were joined by others, mainly merchants, who were often *zimmis* and whose numbers increased relative to the number of Muslims. Yet, because the Muslims had both old and new rich among them and had the easiest access to *çiftliks*, this group automatically enjoyed the highest prestige and gave the tone to "high society." This is proven by the fact that the richer a non-Muslim became and the more he could afford to circumvent the law, the more his home and his clothing resembled those of the Muslims.

Irrespective of religion, the number of the well-to-do segments in the cities increased. Todorov measures this increase quite clearly for the eighteenth century by using the tax valuation of dwellings whose sale or inheritance was registered in the cities of Vidin, Ruse, and Sofia. In a simplified form Todorov's data are as follows:[12]

Years	1700-10	1731-40	1771-80	1791-1800
Value of houses		Number/Percent		
up to 200 *kuruş*[13]	12/100	204/84.6	209/55.0	185/41.4
201 to 500 *kuruş*	0/0	33/13.8	112/29.5	152/34.1
501 to 1000 *kuruş*	0/0	3/ 1.2	38/10	73/16.4
over 1000 *kuruş*	0/0	1/ .4	21/ 5.5	36/ 8.1
Total	12/100	241/100	380/100	446/100

These figures indicate clearly that at least in these three cities the number of expensive dwellings increased considerably throughout the century because sale and inheritance figures are a fair indication of general real estate values. This impression is confirmed by the same author who states, in another work, that "the number of houses of high valuation had doubled during the second half of the eighteenth century."[14]

Although not all cities—and for most of them data comparable to those supplied by Todorov are lacking—show exactly the same pattern of size and composition of population as do these three, there is enough general information available to conclude that the number of truly rich individuals increased in most of them. Those persons whose wealth was based on real estate, including *çiftliks*, managed to acquire other functions, including "official positions," which were often on a hereditary basis. In this manner a new, capitalistic-bureaucratic upper class came into being. Most

12. Todorov, *Balkanskiat Grad*, p. 161. Unfortunately, the valuable population figures in this work deal only with the nineteenth century.

13. See Chapter 2, n. 3.

14. Todorov, "Population urbaine," p. 61.

of this class was still Muslim, but even among this group the number of *zimmi*s was increasing. These non-Muslims became the *çorbaci*, among other things, and became leaders in the nineteenth century.

Many members of the *zimmi* upper class made their original fortunes as *celep*s, but even more numerous among them were the members of the new commercial class. They emerged not only as a result of the new market-oriented agricultural activities and the already mentioned illegal export trade, but also because of a thorough change in the established economic pattern of the city itself.

The drastic transformation of the city that occurred in the seventeenth and eighteenth centuries was also tied to changes in the guild system. Up to the end of the sixteenth century Ottoman mercantilism, protectionism, and the government's ability to enforce its numerous regulations protected the structure of production in the cities, but in the later centuries orders issued from the capital were unable to counteract local forces. Just as in the case of agriculture, it is still impossible to establish, on the basis of studies already published, a clear causal relationship between changes in the guild system and the new order in the cities.

The changes occurred in such a short period of time that even the chronological sequence of events is hard to establish. Economic and political circumstances forced the guilds to make adjustments in their structure and policies, but these very changes were often the causes of important new developments. Political, social, and economic causes and effects were so closely interwoven that their mutual relationship can hardly be disentangled, although the results are quite clear.

To begin with, in addition to new trends that have already been discussed in this chapter, the first important development to be noted is that as a result of the decline in the population of the European provinces the market for goods produced by urban craftsmen shrank. This development coincided, as already noted, with two other developments that weakened the position of the urban producer. New possibilities for investment in land offered the *âyan*s, *tüccar*s, and other urban capitalists a chance to place their money into enterprises, tax farming, or outright acquisition of land, which yielded a much higher income than the strictly regulated and declining guilds could produce. The growing export trade, increasingly protected by the capitulations,[15] not only increased the economic importance and influence of the new merchant class, but placed the craftsmen, who needed new outlets for their goods, in the hands of this rising new urban element.

---

15. The capitulations were international trade agreements. As the Ottoman Empire weakened in relation to those states with which it had concluded them, the interpretation of the various clauses favored the latter more and more. Not only were customs rates fixed, but foreign states began to acquire the right to "protect" those traders in whose activities they became increasingly interested.

The guilds knew of the market situation and tried to adjust, but they were greatly handicapped by the strict regulations that had protected them in the past. When demand grew, for example, at the request of the merchants and the old guilds could not satisfy it, the obvious solution was either to increase the number of masters or to establish new guilds that paralleled the old. Most of these requests were denied by the authorities. The result was a group of illegal craftsmen and even a modest "putting out" system run by the merchants whose activities were not regulated like the guilds' and whose existence harmed the established craftsmen considerably. When new business opportunities presented themselves, for example with the appearance of tobacco, it took over a century to regulate handling and sale of the commodity. Only in the eighteenth century was a guild of tobacconists established, and then it was never able to eliminate from the market those who had handled this product previously but were not admitted into the new organization.

Working in a changing market with regulations that fitted a rapidly disappearing situation was very difficult, but what hurt the guilds even more was the deterioration of their internal organizations. In this case, too, there were several reasons for the complicated change. It will have to suffice to mention only the three that appear to be the most significant.

The least important cause is the demographic change that resulted in the increased number of *zimmi* in the cities and subsequently in the guilds. If the guilds could have maintained their old, tolerant approach and structure, the influx of *zimmis* could have been handled, but the growing religious fanaticism of the *ulema* influenced other organizations, including the guilds.

This second factor, intolerance, produced important changes. First, the guilds, while remaining nominally united, established *zimmi* and Muslim sections within their organization. Both groups began to meet separately, and by the end of the seventeenth century the *zimmis* were electing their own *yeğitbaşi* signifying, for all practical purposes, the splitting of the guilds. This split was formally recognized even by the authorities about a hundred years later when some of the *zimmi* branches obtained the right to have their own *kahyas*. At the same time the *zimmis* also began to hold their guild festivities separately from the parent body and organized their own welfare institutions. What emerged were two competing and often hostile organizations at a time when the shrinking market could hardly support more than one. The authorities continued to favor the Muslim guilds, but the emerging new merchant class favored the *zimmi* organizations, thereby aggravating the situation even further.

The third factor created the greatest difficulties: the growing association of the guilds with the janissaries, who appeared in the provincial cities either as garrison troops or as undesirables who were forced to leave Istanbul. The story of how and why these ex-soldiers were able to affiliate with most guilds does not fall within the scope of this study. Suffice it to say that it was accomplished by the guilds' and janissaries' common affiliation with certain *derviş* organizations and even more through the terror tactics of the ex-soldiers. These new guild members, who were as little interested in their craft as in their original military profession, escaped the authority of the guild officials because as "soldiers" they could only be disciplined or punished by their own officers. It became more and more difficult to force nonjanissary guild members to obey regulations when janissary members could flaunt them with impunity.

The influx of janissaries into the guilds increased the membership but not the productivity or the organizations. Their appearance also weakened the old *futuwwa* regulations and undermined the authority of the guild officers, whose religious and moral power declined as that of the *derviş*es grew. In this manner economic, demographic, and internal changes contributed to the undermining of the productive and social activities of the guilds, considerably diminishing their importance in the life of the city. The dominant role that the guild officials had played in previous centuries, even in the administration of the city, devolved more and more on local dignitaries, merchants, and a new and totally irresponsible element best personified by the number of n'er-do-wells whose claim to influence and a good living rested on nothing more than the fact that they were members of the janissary corps and as such could enforce their demands with the help of arms.

With the loss of internal cohesion and influence the guilds were no longer able to take care of their members. This is well illustrated by comparing the rise in the price of grain, which was still the basic staple in the diet of the average man, in Istanbul with the increase in wages. It should be remembered that the government paid great attention to prices in the capital (see Chapter 5) where it was easier to enforce regulations than it was in the provinces. Thus, it is fair to assume that the price-wage scissors was even less favorable in the cities of Southeastern Europe than the figures would indicate. In the capital grain prices rose 700 percent between 1550 and 1790, and the wages of skilled labor rose 800 percent; those of unskilled workers increased only 350 percent.[16] The number of masters and foremen whose income kept pace with prices was small; the majority of guild members saw their buying power cut in half. It is not surprising that they tried to organize themselves both within and outside the guild structure, thereby weakening the guilds even further.

All these economic and social changes were reflected in the physical appearance of the cities and towns, most of which began to contract not only as a result of the over-all decline in the population of the European provinces, but also because urban centers offered fewer chances for

16. Traian Stoianovich, "Factors in the Decline of Ottoman Society in the Balkans," *Slavic Review* 21 (December, 1962): 627.

making a living than in the days of the empire's glory. This contraction, which was most clearly seen in the gradual disappearance of suburbs, was also accelerated by the growing lawlessness and banditry that made the inhabitants of the outlying areas move towards the more secure centers. Within the towns the growing number of imposing structures erected by the wealthy was accompanied by an increase in the number of poor neighborhoods.

At all levels of income the polarization between Muslim and *zimmi* increased, in spite of the fact that the physical appearance of the dwellings and clothing of the richest non-Muslims began to resemble that of the Muslims. Contributing to this growing chasm between Muslim and *zimmi* were: the venality of most officials; the inability of the few who were honest to enforce the law; the growing number of those who placed themselves beyond the law by acquiring *berat*s which, in accordance with the capitulations, placed them under the jurisdiction of foreign consuls; the decline of the power and efficiency of the guilds and growing power of the janissaries in both the economic and social management of the urban centers; and, last but not least, the contracting market for the goods produced in the cities. This centrifugal development was much more marked and in the long run much more significant in the cities than it was in the countryside.

In rural areas the absentee landlord and his local representative were foreign elements whose growing power was resented by the peasantry. Yet these *reayas* lived in their own compact communities, and most of them dealt only with their own elected representatives. The "outsider" was master; he was resented and feared, but he was not a visible day-to-day force in the peasant's life. Finally, the landlord could not press the peasant beyond a certain limit because he might lose much needed manpower. After all, the peasant still had the legal right to migrate.

In urban areas Muslim and *zimmi* elements lived together in close daily contact. The growing power and lawlessness of the janissaries could not be checked either by the inefficient authorities or by the guilds. The new masters, absentee landlords living in towns, merchants, and janissaries, had no interest in preventing the departure of people whose labor they did not need, but they had every interest in making the maximum profit in a steadily shrinking, increasingly competitive market. Consequently, it was impossible to work out a *modus vivendi* between them and the economically lower placed elements of the population. Even within the narrow circle of the upper class in the city, divisions were sharp and went beyond the less and less satisfactory but at least traditional relations between Muslim and *zimmi*.

Among the Muslims the "old" ruling elements—*âyans*, *tüccar*s, officeholders—could and did merge into a new upper class with the absentee landlords, the *mültezim*s, and the Muslim element of the new merchant group forming something akin to a Muslim provincial aristocracy. This group faced other Muslims, like the janissaries, who appeared among them with sufficient immunities and power but without clearly defined economic interests and positions and tried to take their sinecures and offices. The resulting confrontation produced, as will be seen, a great variety of accommodations.

The provincial aristocracy was interested in re-establishing social stability, although on a new basis. In rural areas they were fairly successful in achieving their goal with the help of the *çiftlik* system. This was not the case in the cities where their adversaries, the "Muslim proletariate with status," could not be tamed. When the problems of the city spilled over into the countryside the lawless element became victorious and the Ottoman Empire was doomed. Splits similar to those among the Muslims also occurred within the *zimmi* ranks.

Although the number of Jews among the *zimmi* declined, as did their influence, new splits developed within the ranks of the Orthodox Christians. In part these new splits had purely ecclesiastic reasons closely tied to linguistic problems, but they were also closely related to the emergence of a new Orthodox merchant class, which had to develop the numerous business ties built up over centuries by the older trading element, mainly the Greeks and the merchants of Dubrovnik. That individuals of common origin who knew and understood each other worked together in this effort against the old-established and competing newer groups is not surprising. In their attempt to capture parts of the local market and export trade, they learned to value not only the business techniques, but also the education of those with whom they began to compete. They began to imitate the organizations and educational institutions around them in the cities, adding cultural elements to the financial power they were acquiring. In so doing they lay the foundations for the cultural and even national rebirth of the various Southeastern European nations.

All these changes produced a new city, which was often smaller than its sixteenth-century counterpart. In this city the *zimmi*, and in particular the Christians, grew steadily in number, although ethnically this group was not always the same as the one that the conquering Ottomans had displaced a couple of centuries earlier. Wealth was accumulating often in new hands at the same time that the living standard of the majority was declining. Old regulations remained officially in force, and the dignitaries who were supposed to enforce them kept their positions, but the life of the city was regulated by both the new socioeconomic realities and the new holders of power.

Not only did the rich become richer and the poor become poorer, but each social and economic group became less and less cohesive. Gradually the city became an agglomeration of people who, although in the same place, lived more and more within their own little worlds according to their own rules.

Although both the country and city changed for the worse, rural and urban life continued to be half-way tolerable until the new masters were finally displaced by the janissary and other lawless elements. Then even this system was destroyed. With this last transformation in the second half of the eighteenth century, whatever hope there was for the Ottoman Empire was lost. Yet even the development surveyed so far indicates that Ottoman social structure was able to adjust—even if imperfectly—to change. The state and its laws, however, remained ossified, became anachronistic, and ceased to command the allegiance of its inhabitants. For this failure the administrative inability of the Ottomans to create a state-oriented society is always blamed, and the *millet* system is invariably cited as the greatest stumbling block to the creation of an integrated society. Before other aspects of the last two centuries covered by this volume are discussed, mention must be made of the state's failure to sell itself to its inhabitants in times of prosperity, and especially of the importance of the *millet* system in bringing about this fundamental weakness of the Ottoman state.

According to most scholars Ottoman institutions worked very well so long as the situation for which they were created prevailed and poorly when new circumstances arose. Thus, the *millet* system permitted the Ottomans not only to handle the affairs of those for whom Muslim law was not applicable, but also to save large amounts of money because, together with the *timar* system, it obviated the need for a large, paid civil service. In the long run, however, it created separate organizations for the different *zimmi* groups. As time went on, these groups came to look on their *millet* organizations as their "government," and developed separate loyalties and authority structures, which became centrifugal forces when the empire ceased to function properly.

This standard evaluation of the *millet* system, although correct, places too much emphasis on the importance of the *millets* during the centuries of decline. It is important to recognize that this system never worked exactly as planned. In theory it was designed for two purposes: to identify and group together people with similar interests under authorities they all recognized, and to insure the loyalty of the *zimmi* toward the state. The *millet* system could not fulfill the first of these two purposes for the simple reason that it was based on an erroneous assumption. Although the Orthodox *millet*, which dominated the European provinces, was united in its distrust and hatred of Roman Catholics, it was by no means united internally. Linguistic, ecclesiastic, and even proto-national differences that predated the Ottoman conquest, and equally long-standing regional and professional differences not only survived, but were sharpened when the

Orthodox *millet* was placed under the Patriarch at Istanbul and the Greeks and the Greek language became dominant. There never was a group with common goals and interests with whom the central authorities could deal as a unit. What emerged in the seventeenth and eighteenth centuries was not the disintegration of the Orthodox *millet* opening the door to new foci of loyalty. What emerged were old differences and antagonisms that could not be expressed openly so long as the *millet* leadership was protected by the power of a strong state and could not be challenged.

Once this fragmentation within the Orthodox community is considered, it becomes obvious that the *millet* system could not insure the loyalty of the *zimmi* because its authorities were not considered representative. It is perfectly true that up to roughly the end of the sixteenth century the *zimmi* of Europe were if not necessarily loyal to the Ottoman Empire then at least more or less satisfied with living within its borders. This satisfaction, however, did not stem from their pleasure at having to deal mainly with "their own authorities," but from the fact that their lives and property were secure and that they could live fairly well-regulated lives within the limits set for them by the laws that were known and to a considerable extent respected by everybody. Whatever "loyalty" the people of Southeastern Europe might have felt did not stem from satisfaction with either the state of the *millet* authorities, but from the "Pax Ottomanica." When this relative internal peace ceased the reason for satisfaction disappeared. The loss of relative well-being and security, and not the fact that the *millet* system became dated, accounts for the fact that all *zimmi* whose economic fortunes were not tied to the continued existence of the state moved from indifference to growing hostility. The *millet* system's failure was not the cause of this growing hostility; rather the reasons lay in the changes brought about by a state suffering from almost total administrative paralysis and unable to prevent local civil strife.

CHAPTER 11

The Final Disintegration
of Provincial Order in
Ottoman Southeastern Europe

---

1. INTRODUCTION

GREAT as the changes presented in the preceding chapter were, they would not have led to the final disintegration of the administrative, social, and economic structures of the "core" provinces without further developments stemming from the corruption of the central authorities and their inability to exercise effective control over events in the provinces. The drastic changes that occurred in the cities and the countryside were unfavorable to the masses and were therefore resented, but they could possibly have led to the establishment of a new socioeconomic equilibrium capable of future development.

As already stressed, the change that occurred in the countryside simply established the same system in the "core" provinces that characterized the organization and rural life in practically all of contemporary Europe. Most of the land was in the hands of large estate owners, usually absentee landlords, who ran their holdings with production for the market in mind. Besides these large units, a few smaller holdings survived in the hands of the peasantry. The landlords, although oppressive and arbitrary, had less power over their peasants than did Russian, Hungarian, or Polish nobles whose lands were worked by serfs and whose needs for field hands could be satisfied more easily than those of the Ottoman lords. This circumstance, together with the fact that the Ottoman estate with its frequently export-oriented production became more and more dependent on the world market, could possibly have directed the further development of the Ottoman agrarian system into the same channels along which it developed if not in all then at least in Eastern Europe. Although Eastern European agrarian systems were certainly not satisfactory from the point of view of the peasantry who, like their Ottoman counterparts, often belonged to a creed and nationality different from those of their lords, the gradual transformations that occurred in these other parts of Europe in the nineteenth century were certainly very different and relatively more satisfactory for those who worked the land than was the case under the Turkish and Christian *paşas* in Southeastern Europe. The fact that this different development went beyond the market-oriented estate stage can be explained by the total disintegration of the provincial administrative order in the European provinces of the empire, which destroyed the orderly landlord-peasant relationship that had slowly began to develop after the *çiftlik* system had become the dominant method of agricultural production in the Balkans.

The problem of the cities is somewhat more complicated because there the fragmentation of the old order was much more marked. In the cities, unlike the rural districts, no new pattern of life developed, and urban developments did not begin to parallel that of the rest of Europe in freedoms, local rights, social mobility, and economic activity in spite of the fact that visible class differences began to emerge. Consequently, one cannot even speculate, as was done in the case of rural developments, that with time the development of Southeastern European cities could have approached that of the rest of Europe. Nevertheless, it seems admissible to assume that some form of order would have emerged from the growing chaos, out of necessity. For any stability to occur two preconditions had to exist: strong local leadership and a power structure broader than the city to support that leadership. Although the first precondition was indeed emerging in the urban areas, the second was totally lacking in the eighteenth century.

It was this absence of an effective government that in the final analysis determined the direction in which city and country moved, and fostered the emergence of forces that in the nineteenth century brought about the re-emergence of independent states in Southeastern Europe. In simple terms, the absence of an effective government left decision-making in the hands not of local officials, who were just as inefficient as were the central governmental agencies, but of local power centers. Naturally, these differed markedly from region to region, but everywhere during the eighteenth century three major powers confronted each other: the well-established upper strata of society, the "undesirables" streaming into the provinces in greater and greater numbers, and the local forces that opposed them both. The first of these groups was not united. It consisted of office-holders, landlords, merchants, and other political and economic Muslim and *zimmi* dignitaries who were often antagonistic and yet had vested interests and desired stable conditions. Their main adversaries, who for simplicity's sake will be identified from now on as the janissaries, were either members of the professional Ottoman establishment or claimed other privileges that "entitled" them to what could be called sinecures, but who in fact owned absolutely nothing except numerous legal immunities and, unfortunately, arms. They could not gain what they considered to be their legal due, a living (*dirlik*) comensurate with their *hadd*, without destroying the well-established upper strata.

Like the second group, the third, the "bandits," had no means of making a decent living. Both groups represented the growing demand of the have-nots to be given a share of the material and legal benefits enjoyed by the well-to-do. The bandits differed from the janissaries not only in religion, but also in having no rights to claim inclusion in the "establishment" among the professional Ottomans, and they often hated the janissaries more than they did their legal masters. Many became bandits in reaction to the janissaries. To this third group belonged the awakening members of the *millets*, the forerunners of patriots and freedom fighters. The eighteenth century can be legitimately viewed as a period in which the first two groups fought a civil war in the empire's European provinces and at the same time struggled against the third. It was this confrontation that determined the future of Southeastern Europe.

2. THE CIVIL WAR WITHIN THE ESTABLISHMENT

MOST confrontations leading to civil strife result from the dissatisfaction of those who have no share in the political and economic decision-making process. This was not the case with the endemic civil war in the Ottoman Empire. Those who fought each other were all members of the ruling group, with the great difference that one faction belonged to it by virtue of its position and power while the other simply claimed the right to be part of the ruling elite. The war that they fought was a struggle for the right to control the rest of the population. Their struggle brought a third element onto the scene, those who fought on behalf of the population, and toward the end of the eighteenth century even the sultan began to interfere.

The bandits represented those who paid the price for the civil war. They reacted both physically and intellectually to the events, and while these reactions were as important as the power struggle within the establishment in determining the history of the Balkans from the end of the eighteenth century to at least the end of World War II, they had a negligible influence on eighteenth century developments. The action of the outs will be discussed in the next section of this chapter that will end with a few words about the reaction of Sultan Selim III to the chaos in his provinces.

The two factions of the civil war fought by professional Ottoman cannot simply be labeled "heroes" who stood for law and order and the preservation of their rights, and "villains" whose behavior came close to being that of mere criminals and murderers. Often those who protected "rights" had no legitimate claims to what they were defending because they had acquired their wealth and position illegally. Legal proofs showing that they were entitled to privileges were often fraudulent documents issued by bribed officials.

On the other hand, members of the janissary element frequently had legitimate claims as far as legislation, custom, and their *hadd* were concerned, even if they had long ceased to perform the functions and duties that corresponded to their privileges. A curious contradiction resulted: the law breaker was on the same side as those who fought for order and stability, while people with legitimate demands were in the camp of those who destroyed the empire with their lawless and inhuman behavior. Yet, those who dug the empire's grave were neither revolutionaries nor Robin Hoods. They were not working for a progressive or constructive transformation of the political and social order. They were the most selfish and oppressive elements that ever influenced Ottoman historical developments. Consequently, whenever it took sides the population of Southeastern Europe, including those who were indeed revolutionaries with constructive changes in mind, backed their masters and lords in their fight against those who tried to strip them of their illegally gained positions.

There was a second contradiction in the civil war. Wherever the new masters had illegally acquired control or where those who had enjoyed local power for centuries were able, in the eighteenth century, to increase their importance by illegal means to match that of the new lords, the local population suffered least. These strong power centers could be more or less permanent or only temporary, and they could be based on strength of a group or of a single individual.

The Muslim *beys* of Bosnia are a good example of a long-established group in power. Descended from people who converted soon after the Ottoman conquest, these *beys* had enjoyed power in Bosnia for centuries and had supplied the central government with many important vezirs, *paşas*, and other high dignitaries. Yet, their base and their prime loyalty continued to be local. Being natives of the province, they spoke the language of their fellow Bosnians, understood the local traditions, customs, superstitions, and mores, and retained a much greater religious tolerance than did their fellow Muslims. When the efficacy of the central authorities began to decline, the *beys* took it upon themselves to maintain order in their province, and their influence increased to the point where, by the eighteenth century, practically every official appointed to a post in Bosnia was native to the province. The governor was often nothing more than a highly honored guest. It was the local lords who ran the province as they pleased. Although the steady increase in the *beys'* power also meant that their hand rested much more heavily on the peasantry and other *reaya* than it had earlier, the fact that the *beys* had never lost contact with the masses and understood them made coexistence of the two groups easier and more acceptable. They were able to keep janissary types out of their province and thus avoid some of the tribulations that other regions suffered. Geography also helped the *beys*. They were far from Istanbul and close to reviving Crna Gora, which offered refuge and occasionally even help, and to Albania, where local chieftains also regained much of their former power and influence at the expense of the central authorities. The nearness of Dalmatia and Croatia also helped. But when all these elements are considered, the major force that created the relative peace and stability that Bosnia enjoyed was the strong, local, Muslim aristocracy.

Numerous local "chiefs," mainly in Albania, Central Greece, and the Morea, provide a good example of more limited but equally long-established power centers. In these districts the Ottomans had never been able to establish their power fully, and while they introduced their own administrative system they continued to work mainly through existing leaders. In some cases the arrangement was totally informal; in others the local potentates were transformed into important Christian *sipahi*. The importance of these local lords increased sharply during the war with Venice of 1684-99, during the subsequent period of Venetian rule in the Morea, and especially during the war of 1714-18 which led to the reconquest of the Peloponnesus. By the time this war had ended, the Ottomans lacked the power to displace local leaders, particularly those who had supported the sultan during the war.

These local lords had soldiers, armed *zimmi*. Although illegal, the use of such forces was not new; the difference between these armed *zimmi* and previous ones was, nevertheless, significant. In earlier centuries their presence had been tolerated because in a given region the Ottomans had been unable to enforce regulations or had felt that it would cost too much to do so and was not really necessary because of satisfactory arrangements with local masters. By the early eighteenth century these *zimmi* soldiers constituted little private armies over whom the Ottomans had no control. They could fight with or against the troops of the empire, depending on what their local masters decided was to their advantage. Trained, although often badly organized, these troops became, besides the rising new merchant class, an important force in the national movements of the nineteenth century. Those who are familiar with that century know that during the Greek War of Independence these local forces fought each other as frequently as they fought the Ottomans.

The difference between the situation in Bosnia and in other regions in which individual families and not a social group became the real center of power during the eighteenth century goes beyond this obvious contrast. The Bosnian lords were Muslims and were soldiers themselves besides being landlords, while some of the lords in Albania and all of those in Greece were Christians and commanders of local forces. In Bosnia it was easy for Istanbul to appoint the most important local people to leading positions. Although some Aegean Islands had almost hereditary Christian governors, the mainland did not, and it was not possible to turn around and institute this practice in the eighteenth century when antagonism sharpened constantly. Consequently, the Bosnian masters' position was often quasi-legal, while that of the other local overlords usually was not. Thus, the janissary element could move more easily against the Christian potentates than against the Bosnians. Furthermore, the Bosnian Muslims were strong and numerous enough to make any venture directed against them appear very risky; it was more tempting to attack a solitary figure fighting with limited local forces. Consequently, the population under strong lords—although their rule could be and often was very oppressive— usually was not subject to the worst features of the general chaos. Life was more peaceful under the *de facto* rule of local masters than it was in the other parts of the Balkans.

Very strong new lords constituted the third major variation. They were the most successful of the many people who acquired wealth and power in the manner described in the preceding chapter. Some slowly built up huge estates until they virtually owned little provinces. Others ruthlessly used either their official position or their leadership in a janissary group to force the local lords to turn over their possessions. The former tried to acquire official positions to "legitimize" their "lordships," while the latter added possessions to existing titles. These men were known as *âyans*, and while the word still meant notable, it was applied very differently than it had been in the earlier centuries (see Chapter 4) and was used to describe local rulers. Some of the *âyans* established petty dynasties. The Buşatlis, who supplied *sancak beyi*s for Shkodër (Skutari, Işkodra) for eighty years (1752-1832) have already been mentioned, but people like them were the exception. In most cases the *âyan* owed his eminence to his own talent and savage determination, and to the support of a group of people who were tied to and often loyal only to him.[1] At the death of these *âyans* loyalties ceased and the struggle for succession developed, of which even the weakened state could take advantage.

The two most famous *âyans* were Osman Pasvanoğlu, *Paşa* of Vidin (1799-1807), and Ali, *Paşa* of Ioannina (Janina) (1788-1822). They were not isolated phenomena. Another Ali was master of Albania for a while, Mehmet *paşa* played the same role in northern Bosnia, and Ilukoğlu was in Silistra, Ibrahim in Serres, and similar *âyan* rulers in other regions for

1. For the end of this period Stanford Shaw's list of various local chieftains gives a good idea of how prevalent their presence and power was. Besides the Buşatlis, Ali of Janina, and Osman Pasvanoğlu, he lists the following: Vejsoğlu Halil Usta in the region of Dimotica, Dağdevirenoglu around Edirne; Tokatjikli Süleyman *ağa* whose seat was Gümülcine; Yillikzade Süleyman *ağa*, who ruled over Silistria and Deliorman, the region between Brăla and Ismail, and obeyed the orders of Nazir Ahmed *ağa*; Tirsinikli-oğlu Ismail *ağa* in the area around Nicopolis, Sistova, and Rusçuk; and Ibrahim *paşa* in Central Albania. Stanford J. Shaw, *Between Old and New: The Ottoman Empire under Sultan Selim III, 1789-1807* (Cambridge, Mass.: Harvard University Press, 1971), pp. 227-28.

longer or shorter periods. The difference between the first two and the others lay in length of rule and especially in importance of actions.

Pasvanoğlu made the region around Vidin his "realm," protected it well, and although the citizens of Vidin paid heavy taxes to a tyrant, they lived in relative peace. All in all the city was fairly prosperous because Osman *paşa* controlled trade along the Danube and further enriched his little domain with loot. He was one of the great "protectors" of janissaries and other bands, many of whom he organized and used to raid far and wide. His forces caused serious damage in Wallachia in 1802, and as a protector of the janissaries he played an important part in the outbreak of the Serbian revolt in 1804. When his behavior brought about his dismissal from his official position, he threatened to march on Istanbul. Nothing is a better indication of the sad state into which the central government had fallen than the government's response to Pasvanoğlu's threat: it "made peace" by reappointing him to his *paşalik*. Although Vidin was not happy with his rule (most other places controlled by the *âyan*s were not either), it was certainly better off than the regions, including parts of Wallachia and the Belgrade *paşalik*, that were constantly subject to his raids.

Ali of Janina is an even more interesting figure than Osman of Vidin.[2] Born in Tepelenë (Tepelen, Tepedelen) in southern Albania, he entered the Ottoman service and was appointed *Paşa* of Janina in 1788. He held this position until his death, at the age of eighty, in 1822. It would be hard to find another individual who understood the conditions in the Ottoman Empire at the end of the eighteenth century better than he did. He used every available means to expand his territory, and additional appointments, local arrangements, and pressure to extend his sway. He managed to have three of his sons appointed as *bey*s and *paşa*s to neighboring areas. In this manner he forged a state within a state controlled either directly or through "vassals." The western border of this domain were the Adriatic and Ionian seacoasts beginning just south of Durrës. His lands, bordered on the south by the Mediterranean and on the east by the Aegean, included all of the Morea and all of mainland Greece with the exception of Attica-Boeotia and Euboea (Eğriboz, Negroponte, Evvoia). In the north the border ran from a few miles south of Durrës eastward, south of Bitola to the Aegean a few miles west of the mouth of the Vardar River.

This was the largest single area controlled by an *âyan* in Europe, and Ali, a cruel, treacherous, but able man, knew how to take advantage of the French and Napoleonic wars to play a small role on the international scene. He dealt with the British, Russians, and French directly. His end came years after this survey ends, in 1822, when the Mahmud II's armies

2. Two biographies of Ali were published more than a hundred years apart: Richard A. Davenport, *The Life of Ali Pasha of Janina* (London: Lupton Relfe, 1822) and William C. F. Plomer, *The Diamond of Janina: Ali Pasha, 1741-1822* (London: Cope, 1970).

attacked him after he had refused to go to Istanbul and had declared himself an independent ruler in 1819. By that time the Greeks were fighting for independence. Ali's defeat released the Ottoman army and represented an important turning point in the Greek struggle. Thus, Ali not only exemplifies the extreme to which the power of local masters could be developed, but he also influenced events in Serbia and Greece. While anything but benevolent and beloved, he realized that he "ruled" over a mixed population and therefore sought support in all quarters, Christians and Muslims alike fought in his armies, but were also used to fight each other. A good number of those who fought subsequently for Serbia and Greece learned the art of warfare in his service.

There were âyans or other lords, both Muslim and Christian, in practically all parts of the Balkan Peninsula. Not only did they train certain segments of the population in the use of arms, but they also served as models for others, including some clergymen and knezes, of how much a strong man could get from the established authorities. Thus, in more ways than one they prepared the soil from which the uprisings and independence movements of the nineteenth century grew. They were a disruptive element and posed a serious problem for the central authorities, but one may ask how the Ottoman Empire's European provinces would have fared without them. If nothing else, the âyans and other lords performed a police function of some value.

It is also possible to look at these local chieftains as a potential nucleus for the birth of a reconstructed Ottoman Empire. As has been seen, Ali of Janina built his domain by obtaining official titles from the central government for himself, his family, and followers, and Pasvanoğlu ceased to fight Istanbul when the government reappointed him to "his" paşalik. They might not have been loyal to the sultan in the sense in which loyalty is defined today, but they understood the need for a "legal" power basis and knew who could provide it.

With certain local variations this recognition of the need for an overlord, if only to ratify local situations, was present everywhere. Every chieftain, hereditary master of a region, and small or large lord irrespective of his religion faced others who were trying to take their place. On a smaller scale çorbacis and other local minor office-holders were in the same position. All of them performed functions neglected by the state, and what was left of law and order, production, tax paying, and other manifestations of communal life was due to their greater or lesser ability. Had there been two or three generations of such men, it is quite conceivable that the informal states within the state could have become basic units of a restructured, federated state. Such a state would have been Ottoman in name only and could have represented the real ethnic, economic, and other forces that were developing quickly in the Balkan Peninsula.

Unfortunately, there were too many local enemies, and the central authorities continually tried to weaken the local lords while they were alive and to destroy what they had built once they died. The result was that few local power centers survived their creators, leaving this possible development and the question of the *âyans'* loyalty in the realm of speculation. What remains unchallenged is the fact that they were the only effective and efficient local administrators in the Balkans in the eighteenth century.

The stronger the local administrator, the more capable he was of keeping the enemy away from his domain, either by raising enough local forces to act as a deterent or, as Pasvanoğlu did, by using the enemy for his own purposes. Many janissaries were quite satisfied to make a living in the service of a local master, but not all of them felt this way. Apart from the fact that there were not enough men willing and able to employ them or to risk admitting this unruly element into their domain, there were simply too many janissaries, a great number of whom were interested in becoming their own masters rather than in service.

As is well known the janissaries were originally recruited through the child levy (*devşirme*). They were the slaves of the sultan and served as infantrymen. Their power grew steadily. They were instrumental in bringing Selim I to power, and Süleyman I was forced to pay them an "accession gift" when he ascended the throne. During the reigns of these great rulers the janissaries numbered around twelve thousand men and represented the best fighting force of the empire, and possibly of Europe. By the end of the reign of Murad III their number had increased to around twenty-seven thousand. By the end of the eighteenth century, the reign of Selim III, there were fifty thousand men still serving in janissary units, but about four hundred thousand claimed the rights and privileges belonging to members of the corps.

As the number of janissaries increased, their influence also spread not only in military and political affairs, but also throughout society as a whole. The process was gradual. Originally the janissaries were not allowed to marry until their fighting days were over, but early in the sixteenth century they were given this right. To support their families they began to demand "gifts" more frequently, and when the great inflation began clamored successfully for repeated increases in basic pay. During the centuries of decline few people had any fixed income, and the janissaries understandably wanted to keep this boon for their own families. Around the middle of the seventeenth century they finally secured the abolition of the *devşirme*, thus securing the privilege to serve in the corps for their own sons.

As members of the professional Ottoman class the janissaries enjoyed numerous privileges besides fixed basic pay, including tax exemption. To gain these advantages many people of nonjanissary origin bribed officials and had themselves listed on the janissary rolls, thus swelling the number of those "legally" belonging to this elite corps. Yet, the growing financial troubles of the state touched the janissaries, too. They had power to black-mail the government, but what they could gain was limited by the author-ities' ability to pay. To make it possible for the janissaries to earn a living .they were allowed to join guilds which they in turn subverted (see Chapter 10). Most of these "new janissaries" did not serve as soldiers, al-though they were armed, something of an artisan-militia, and drew pay from the treasury. By the end of the seventeenth century they were the masters of Istanbul, and the government began to disperse them, as much as possible, as garrison forces. This pattern was repeated in the provincial towns. A few active janissaries on military duty maintained close connec-tion with a group of armed petty traders and artisans who were consid-ered their auxiliary forces and were called *yamaks*.

The meager opportunities offered by the business communities of the provincial cities and towns could not support the growing number of greedy *yamaks*. Following their own leaders, called *dahis*, they descended on the countryside where they became the scourge of landlord and peasant alike. Recognizing no authority but their own, they defied the officials of the state, disobeyed even the sultans' orders, and instituted a reign of terror. Whenever they could they forced the peasantry to pay ar-bitrary taxes, murdered peasant leaders, and tried to eliminate the land-lords whose fortified manor houses and armed retainers were the only force that could oppose them. Although the peasantry suffered the most, landlords and office-holders were also constantly threatened by these roving *yamak* bands. In Serbia prior to the 1804 revolt, for example, alli-ances of leading *dahis* created forces strong enough to become practically the masters of entire provinces. However, unlike the areas in which strong *âyans* had made themselves petty rulers, the *yamak*-dominated regions knew no peace or order. The inability of the authorities to check these lawless men illustrates the impotence of the once all-powerful Ottoman state. It also created the circumstances that had to lead to that state's final disintegration.

3. POPULAR FORCES

IN response to this chaotic situation in the provinces and to the murderous *yamak* rule, in the late seventeenth and in the eighteenth centuries, the number and activity of "bandits" increased. Known locally as *hajduks*, *klephts*, *uskoks*, and *morlaks*, these armed men had been operating in the Balkans almost since the appearance of the Ottomans.[3] Their actions be-

---

3. The first volume of a comprehensive history of the *hajduks* and *klephts* containing numerous relevant documents is Bistra Cvetkova, *Hajdutstvoto v Bulgarskite zemi prez 15/18 vek* [Hajdutism in the Bulgarian lands from the fifteenth through eighteenth centuries] (Sofia: Nauka i izkustvo, 1971). In a western language see the same auth-or's "Mouvements anti-féodaux dans les terres bulgares sous domination ottomane du XVIe au XVIIIe siècles," *Études Historiques* (Sofia: Historical Institute of the Bul-

came endemic, increased in scope after the 1630s, and became really large-scale after the 1680s as the janissary corps deteriorated and the *yamaks* appeared in the Balkans.[4]

In calling these groups and men "bandits" no pejorative meaning is implied. They were not criminals in the usually accepted sense of the word, although the authorities considered them in this light. High and often arbitrary taxes, strict economic regulations that did not change when the economic structure altered, devastation produced by war, and other reasons drove these men to make a living by robbery. Undoubtedly, religious and other social factors also contributed to the bitterness that sent these men into the mountains. Today, the people of the Balkans look at them as heroes, freedom fighters, and fathers of their wars of liberation. Cvetkova sums up her splendid study with the following.[5] The *hajduks* represented: (1) a permanent resistance movement; (2) a reaction to the "injustice of the Ottoman feudal system"; (3) a significant force in opposition to the Ottomans beginning with the seventeenth century; (4) an expression of national conscience; (5) a movement whose strength lay in the support of the bulk of the population; and (6) a force that tied all Balkan resistance movements together.

Hobsbawn appears to agree with her. He considers banditry to be the expression of "the resistance of entire communities or peoples against the destruction of its way of life . . . the precursor of revolution."[6] Speaking of the *hajduks*, he states that they "were robbers by trade, enemies of the Turks and popular avengers by social role, primitive movements of guerilla resistance and libertation," which represented "the highest form of primitive banditry, the one which comes closest to being a permanent and conscious focus of peasant insurrection."[7]

Close as these two opinions are, they differ significantly. They agree that, at least from the middle of the seventeenth century onward, *hajduks* operated almost constantly, but there is a significant difference between Cvetkova's claim that they were reacting to the "injustice of the Ottoman feudal system" and Hobsbawn's assertion that they were reacting against "the destruction of [a] way of life." If the Ottoman system was feudal in the sense in which this expression is used to describe the economy of the Middle Ages in Western Europe, then it was feudal both in the town and in the countryside. Yet the *hajduk* movement was almost exclusively a rural movement. Apart from geographic and strategic reasons, two facts explain this: the Ottoman system changed the known "way of life" in the

garian Academy of Sciences, 1965), 2: 149-68. One chapter in Eric Hobsbawn, *Bandits* (London: G. Weidenfeld and Nicolson, 1969) also deals with these people.

4. These dates are given by Cvetkova, "Mouvements anti-féodaux," pp. 158, 160.
5. Cvetkova, *Hajdutstvoto*, p. 391.
6. Hobsbawn, *Bandits*, pp. 18, 19.
7. *Ibid.*, p. 62.

countryside much more drastically than in the city, and the shift from *timar* to *çiftlik*, which coincided with intensification of *hajduk* activity, represented the real and thorough change that Hobsbawn considers essential for permanent, large-scale "social banditry."

Unlike Cvetkova, Hobsbawn does not speak of a "resistance movement," a "national conscience," or a Balkan-wide action when he discusses the *hajduk*s. The last of Cvetkova's three contentions can be accepted with some reservation. If her statement simply means that "banditry" was an area-wide phenomenon which, by its mere existence, created similarities in the chain of reactions that occurred in Southeastern Europe, she is right. On the other hand, if she wishes to indicate that the movement had anything like a regional unity she is probably wrong. There is no known indication that even at the end of the century the various *hajduk* groups cooperated systematically on such a scale.

Although today *hajduk*s are considered national heroes and forerunners of the successful revolutionaries of the nineteenth century, attribution of modern nationalistic feelings and motivations to them appears unjustified, as does speaking of a resistance movement in the sense in which this expression is used to describe nineteenth and twentieth century phenomena. True enough, folk songs and tales of considerably earlier origin also treat them as champions of the downtrodden, the Christian masses suffering under the misrule of the Muslims. No doubt, by the end of the eighteenth century something like a national consciousness existed among the various Balkan people, and the difference between them—let alone the feeling that separated them from the Turks—became clearer and clearer. It would be reading present-day concepts into the past, however, to attribute national motives to the *hajduk*s as early as in the early eighteenth century. This is not to question their love for their native land in a narrower sense or their sympathy for the people who inhabited it. For the movement to have been possible, a mutual understanding between these people and the fighting men had to exist.

The resistance of these fighting peasants was mainly local and stemmed as Hobsbawn has indicated, from their unwillingness to accept drastic change in their way of life. This resistance generated its own dynamics: the escalation of revolt and countermeasures leading to endemic civil war and involving the authorities, the local potentates, the *yamak*-janissary forces, the various popular *hajduk* units, and in many cases locally recruited police forces known as *armatoles* or *Kirdžhalis*. As the chaos and magnitude of this multifaceted civil war increased, cooperation between the *hajduk* forces and the large masses of the peasant population increased giving the former a broader and more solid base for their operations. It was at this stage that the *hajduk* became indeed the "nuclei of possible liberators, recognized by the people as such."[8] When the official

8. *Ibid.*, p. 71.

authorities backed this coalition against their major enemy, the *yamak*-janissary group, the stage was set for a major revolt.

The man who brought about this novel alignment of forces was the tragic reforming sultan, Selim III (1789-1807). He was not a "westernizer" in the sense of accepting western values. Educated as a traditional Muslim-professional Ottoman, Selim believed that it was his duty as supreme master to rid society of its imperfections and bring it back to the perfectly functioning level of the mid-sixteenth century. He sought to clean house, to eliminate innumerable corrupt practices including the acquisition of "rights" that were not at all in accordance with the strict concepts of Muslim-Ottoman jurisprudence. He realized, furthermore, that even if he were to succeed, the Ottoman Empire would be unable to resist Russian and Austrian encroachment because of its relative technical, and in particular military, backwardness. This realization made the sultan a limited technological "modernizer."[9]

Selim was no "democrat" interested in giving "equal rights" to the *reaya*. Both major thrusts of his reform endangered the position of those whose claims to prominence, wealth, social status, and privilege were not well founded or those, mainly in the military establishment, who would lose their positions as a result of the technological changes the ruler contemplated. The janissary-*yamak* forces that rampaged throughout the Balkans were threatened by Selim's goals. They became his major adversaries and the natural allies of his enemies, of whom Pasvanoğlu was the most powerful in the same geographic region.

When Selim III became sultan, the Ottoman Empire was at war with both Russia and Austria. The year he assumed power the tsar's armies invaded Moldavia and Wallachia, and the emperor's armies Serbia and Bosnia. In the latter provinces the *yamak* forces were among the first to flee, giving the population a welcome relief from their depradations. Forced by the events in France and by the death of Emperor Joseph II, Austria made peace with the Ottoman Empire (Peace of Svishtov, 1791) and agreed to evacuate all the conquered Ottoman lands. At this point the sultan and the population had a common interest, although for different reasons, in preventing the return of the *yamak*s. For the next seven years Selim's forces battled the various local lords and *yamak*s in the Balkans. Although they were not able to eliminate them, they were at least occasionally successful, raising some hopes among the population. When the Ottoman Empire joined the European war against Napoleon in 1798, large numbers of soldiers had to be withdrawn from the Balkans. This gave Pasvanoğlu a chance to gain supremacy in Serbia.

When Pasvanoğlu began his operations by sending *yamak* forces who had sought sanctuary in his lands into Serbia, the chain of events that trig-

9. By far the best work on Selim III and his time is Stanford J. Shaw, *Between Old and New*.

gered the 1804 revolt of the Serbs began. In 1799 the forces of the *Paşa* of Belgrade, Hajji Mustafa, defeated the *yamaks* at Šabac (Sabácz, Bögürdelen). Aware that these men, who fled this time to Bosnia, would attempt to return and that his forces would not be sufficient to defeat them every time, he came to an agreement with the *knezes* of Serbia to arm their own men to fight as auxiliary forces under the governor's command. This was the first instance in Ottoman history of the legal arming of *reaya*. It was natural for the *knezes* to turn to *hajduks* first when looking for "trained" warriors, but in so doing it gave these men a "legal" status. The following year this Christian-Serbian-*hajduk* force defeated troops sent by Pasvanoğlu and *yamaks* before Belgrade and saved that city and its governor.

This battle supplied ammunition to Selim's enemies, who objected to the use of non-Muslim troops against Muslims by Muslim authorities. Selim, in the midst of a foreign war, tried to compromise and allowed the *yamaks* to return to Belgrade on condition that they submit to and obey the governor. These men did not keep their promise and in August of 1801 murdered Hajji Mustafa. Their leader, Halil *ağa*, supported by four *yamak dahis*, became the master of Serbia and instituted the reign of terror that finally led to the revolt of 1804.

Although subsequent events are described in detail in volume VIII of this series, it must be noted here that between 1801 and 1804 the *hajduk* units were transformed into major national resistance armies, illustrating the transition from "banditry" to national liberation forces. This transformation also explains, at least in part, why the Serbian revolt of 1804, which originally aimed only at the expulsion of the *yamaks* and the re-establishment of Hajji Mustafa's system, rapidly turned into a Serbian War of Independence. Old-fashioned *hajduks* would have been delighted with the sultan's order reaffirming their right to bear arms and their fight against the *yamaks*, but a national force closely allied to the powerful leaders of the population at large, the *knezes*, could not be satisfied with the sultan's decision, revolutionary as it was in the traditional Ottoman context. When the Serbs' demands went beyond the request of legitimate Ottoman rule with a greater voice in deciding local issues for themselves, Selim had to safeguard the integrity of his realm. The success of the Serbian War of Independence encouraged the other Balkan people and led to other successful uprisings and wars of liberation that brought to an end the Ottoman rule in Southeastern Europe.

The events in Serbia and those in other Balkan lands during the nineteenth century were the result of the steady decline in the Ottomans' ability to enforce the laws and to control the *yamak*-type elements of the professional Ottoman class. This lack of authority was not limited to European provinces of the empire, but here religious differences between ruler and ruled were more pronounced than elsewhere; here the change that

the lack of law enforcement created brought about a more drastic altera-
tion in the patterns of daily life; and here the Ottomans faced a West that
not only was able to fight them more and more successfully, but also was
able to transmit new ideas to the population of the border regions that
had conationals living across it. These ideas contributed to its self-aware-
ness and facilitated the transformation of *hajduks* into freedom fighters.

This and the previous chapters summarized the transformation, the
changing of the life patterns of the population, that made revolt inevitable, and determined that the last, roughly century-long phase of the Ottoman Empire's disintegration began in its European provinces. The empire's meteoric rise to greatness began with the conquests in Southeastern
Europe. For centuries it was here that the power-center of the state was
located, and it was also in this area that the empire's decline began both
in terms of loss of territory and as a result of massive popular rejection
resulting from the breakdown of law and order.

Part Five

GENERAL CONSIDERATIONS

CHAPTER 12

Cultural Life

1. INTRODUCTION

THE only lengthy discussion of cultural activities thus far was the one devoted to Dubrovnik, the most independent of the Ottoman-dominated lands and the one with more contacts with western civilization than any other province. A few remarks were also made about cultural activities in the Romanian Principalities. The inhabitants of these lands were also able to keep certain aspects of public life in their own hands, and although they did not have the direct access to Western Europe that Dubrovnik had, they were stimulated by western ideas indirectly, mainly through Poland and to a lesser extent through Hungary and Russia.

The inhabitants of the other Ottoman provinces in Europe were by no means less gifted than those of Dubrovnik, Moldavia, and Wallachia, but they did not develop a flourishing intellectual life. There are many reasons for this failure, the first being isolation. The Greeks certainly had a longer, higher, unbroken cultural heritage to safeguard and to develop further than had those who lived in the three vassal states. While some Greeks remained in touch with non-Ottoman Europe by either living under Genoese or Venetian rule for shorter or longer periods of time or through their trading activities, the majority was cut off from the West as effectively as were all others whose lands did not border directly on Christian-ruled states or who had not retained some rights of self-government. The large majority of the people lived in a Muslim-Near Eastern milieu that was alien to them and were hermetically sealed off from the cultural and intellectual world to which they had belonged until the arrival of the Ottomans. This isolation was not at all conductive to the activities that interest the intellectual historian.

The strict, formalistic orthodoxy of the Ottoman authorities has to be added to isolation from the non-Ottoman world as the second major reason that stifled intellectual activities in Southeastern Europe. The Ottomans were tolerant masters for two hundred years, but several circumstances made them hostile to those who manifested the independence and originality of the mind necessary to a true cultural life. By the time they appeared on the historical scene as a state-creating and sustaining force, the Muslim civilization of the Near East had passed its glorious phase and for political, but mainly theological, reasons had limited the scope of inquiry and intellectual freedom. Poets, artists, and even architects, including numerous Turks, adhered strictly to the accepted styles and norms, and although their works were of great and lasting beauty, they lacked novelty and were mainly imitative in style. When under Orhan, but especially under Murad I, the Ottomans accepted high Sunni Islam with all its beliefs and institutions, they inherited all the features of intellectual orthodoxy as well. The somewhat freer and even experimental intellectual climate that had existed during the reign of Mehmed II produced a sharp reaction in the days of Bayezid II. The growing influence of the Arab lands that began with Selim I's conquest led, under his successors, to growing religious intolerance, and any chance for original artistic or intellectual activity disappeared.

Other reasons also account for the relative paucity of cultural manifestations in the European provinces of the empire. Being the most crucial power center of the state and relatively close to the capital, these lands were more closely supervised by the authorities in Istanbul than were some of the sultan's distant and less important possessions. It is important to remember that in these crucial lands of Southeastern Europe[1] the overwhelming majority of the population was Orthodox Christian and that the Ottomans distrusted them more than any other religious group in the realm. Moreover, it was against these people that the Ottomans had fought their most crucial battles ever since the days of Osman I. The Orthodox *millet* was always more closely surveyed than were the others. This explains why in the lands surveyed the Jews had somewhat more freedom than did the Christians. Jews were trusted somewhat more because they were not feared. Thus it was that the very people, the Orthodox Christians, who were in the majority and could have advanced the intellectual and artistic life of the provinces were the ones whose activities were the most closely watched and discouraged.

Dissention within the ranks of the Orthodox also played a significant role in limiting cultural activities. During the past two centuries Serbian, Bulgarian, and occasionally even Romanian historians, referring to this dissention, have repeatedly dubbed this the period of the Turkish-Greek

1. At the beginning of the seventeenth century the lands under direct Ottoman rule in Europe (232,400 square miles) and those of the vassal states (112,600 square miles) amounted to 21.6 and 10.5 percent respectively of the empire's total territory (1,-071,000 square miles). The surface of the vassal lands was calculated by the author. The other two figures are given in Donald E. Pitcher, *An Historical Georgraphy of the Ottoman Empire* (Leiden: E. J. Brill, 1972), pp. 134-35.

yoke. Greek historians have rejected this interpretation, pointing out that the Greeks were subjected as much to the oppression of the Ottomans as were their fellow Christians.

The controversy centers around the role of the church, and more specifically around that of the Patriarchate throughout the period of Ottoman rule and particularly during the Phanariot-dominated eighteenth century. The defenders of the ecclesiastical policy point out, quite correctly, that the Patriarch and the bishops had the duty, especially after the establishment of the *millet* system, to administer the affairs of the Orthodox Christians, to speak on their behalf before the sultan and other Ottoman authorities, and to protect them from injustice. In order to perform these duties, many of which had been performed by lay office-holders, the church had to establish a highly centralized administrative structure, which paralleled that of the Ottoman authorities and went beyond the old purely spiritual organization. More importantly, the hierarchy of the church had the supreme duty to protect the faith and its purity under extremely adverse circumstances. Therefore, it had to insist on doctrinal conformity and even on purely ritualistic aspects of religious services to save the church from annihilation. Even if some of its members were occasionally influenced by considerations of a less lofty character, there can be little doubt that the higher clergy had these tasks in mind and performed its duties accordingly.

The difficulty arose from the fact that, as already noted previously, the Orthodox *millet* did not correspond to an ethnic or linguistic unit. Rather it represented a variety of people who, in the long-gone days of their independence, had insisted on the establishment of national churches, following the Byzantine model whenever they could. They did not understand that the patriarch was simply carrying out the sultan's orders for a "unified church." In their eyes the new order represented simply a return to "Greek" supremacy and the disappearance of their own ecclesiastical institutions. Few were sophisticated enough to think of even these basic considerations, but everybody noticed the gradual replacement of Church Slavonic by Greek in the services, the steady replacement of Serbian and Bulgarian bishops by Greek nationals, and the increase in church taxes. The last mentioned fact was inevitable, resulting as it did from the steady inflation of the late sixteenth century. The other abuses came mainly in the late seventeenth and eighteenth centuries but were, subsequently, considered to have characterized the entire Ottoman period.

It is as easy to condemn the church for its insistence on a liturgical language that finally made the services unintelligible to many faithful, for its destruction of Church Slavonic books, and for the elimination of the vernacular from its schools as it is to defend these measures. This is why the controversy between the Greeks and their Slavic coreligionists is beyond resolution. These measures did indeed hurt the Slavs grievously, but they can be defended as inevitable measures once the hierarchy was charged with enforcing uniform laws at the same time that it had to perform its supreme duty, the saving of the faith, under the most difficult circumstances.

What cannot be denied is the fact that the grecification of the church and its educational institutions cut the Slavs off from the sources of their civilization, which was beginning to grow along original lines just when the Turkish attacks on Southeastern Europe began. This fact separated the non-Greek Orthodox from the cultural life of Europe even more than the general isolation had already done. What these people could develop they did. Their folk culture flourished, but learning and the arts languished and were left almost entirely to the Greeks. Dubrovnik and the Romanian Principalities were the only places where non-Greek Christians could and indeed did pursue intellectual and artistic careers.

Finally, a few introductory remarks must be made about the Turks. They too lived in Southeastern Europe and left their marks on the countryside. The magnificent Selimiye Mosque at Edirne, the masterpiece of the great Turkish architect Sinan (1491-1588), is only the best known of numerous architectural remains of Turkish rule, which include other mosques, mausolea, tomb-stones, the homes of the rich, covered markets, public baths, and some fortifications. Yet, very few of these buildings can be considered to be truly original expressions of a creative genius or to bear the stamp of a "European-Ottoman," regional style.

The meagerness of the Muslims' contribution to the culture of the region should not be surprising. The Turks were even more restricted by the ossified cultural codes of Muslim-Near Eastern civilization than were the Christians and Jews. With the exception of those who lived in the easternmost regions of the Balkans (today's European Turkey), most of the Turks in Southeastern Europe were administrators, soldiers, landlords, or artisans and lived in relative isolation. Those with talent gravitated to the major centers of Ottoman culture—Istanbul, Edirne, and Bursa—where their talents had wider scope. Thus, significant Ottoman works of art and literature were created outside the regions with which this volume deals. Southeastern Europe was important to the Ottomans economically and militarily, but it was "foreign soil" ethnographically and was not conducive to the creation of lasting contributions to Ottoman-Turkish civilization.

These circumstances and considerations explain why the intellectual-artistic achievements of people living under Ottoman rule in Southeastern Europe were relatively meager, and why this chapter, which will touch only on the most significant aspects of cultural life, is relatively short. Nevertheless, it should be remembered that what has been accomplished by the creative minds in this region was produced under extremely unfavorable circumstances. When this fact is kept in mind, the results are much more impressive than would appear at first glance.

2. THE GREEKS

OF the various advantages the Greeks enjoyed in comparison with the Ottomans' other European Christian subjects, their long cultural tradition and the fact that important segments of their lands remained for centuries under the rule of the Italian city states are the most important when their cultural activities are considered. Prior to the eighteenth century most of the important Greek cultural achievements came from lands outside the empire. Although speaking strictly they do not fall within the purvue of this study, a few words must be said about those achievements because of their importance for the history of the Greek people.

These extra-empire cultural activities may be divided into two distinctive groups: the achievements of those Greek scholars, writers, painters, and men of science who migrated, as is well known, by the hundreds into Italy and even further to the West after the fall of Constantinople, and the cultural contributions of those who continued to live in traditionally Greek lands, mainly Cyprus, Crete, and the other islands. The first of these groups will not be discussed because it belongs more properly to the history of Western Europe and is fairly well known. It will suffice to stress the Greeks' great contribution to the Renaissance as teachers of Greek at the various universities and courts, and as transmitters, translators, and commentators of the great works of Classical Greece to the West. They also played a significant role as scientists, editors, and publishers and made a lasting mark on the development of modern Europe.

Although the contribution of the Greeks living in the West to the cultural history of the world was tremendous, the contributions of those who stayed in their homeland was more significant for the development of Greek culture.[2] Contact with Italy, mainly with Venice, the overlord of the most important Greek cultural centers, and the Venetian-controlled University of Padua were of great importance for knowledge and new literary forms.[3] The work done by Greek men of letters in Greek lands not under Ottoman control is of great significance because it was these men who kept their people's culture alive and even growing. Among those who lived under Ottoman rule not only the literary tradition of their long history was lost, but literacy declined catastrophically to the point that most parish clergymen were practically illiterates. The literary activity of the

2. For satisfactory surveys of the development of Greek culture written in western languages, see Börje Knös, *L'histoire de la littérature néo-grecque. La période jusqu'en 1821* (Uppsala: Almquist and Wihsell, 1962); A. Mirambel, *La littérature grecque moderne* (Paris: Presses Universitaires de France, 1953); Linos Politis, *A History of Modern Greek Literature* (Oxford: The Clarendon Press, 1973). The following pages rely heavily on the work of Politis.

3. For the significance of Venice for Greek culture in the Ottoman period, a good short survey is offered by William H. McNeill, *Venice; The Hinge of Europe, 1081-1797* (Chicago and London: University of Chicago Press, 1974). Another work to be consulted is Oliver Logan, *Culture and Society in Venice, 1470-1790; The Renaissance and Its Heritage* (New York: Scribner, 1972).

Greeks on the Turkish-dominated mainland practically disappeared for two centuries. What was left was folk literature expressing itself first in the demotic songs and later in the *Klephtika*, ballads sung to celebrate the deeds of the *kelphts*.

Crete was the first center of Greek literature after the fall of Constantinople. During the first half of the sixteenth century, several poets who followed the literary models of Renaissance Italy were active on this island. Stefanos Sachlikis, a lawyer by training, wrote poetry describing mainly accidents that he had encountered. His contemporary, Marinos Falieros, wrote on a greater variety of topics including religious and erotic themes. During the same period another poet known only as Bergadis wrote the poem *Apokopos*, which described a trip to the underworld and was the first modern Greek literary work to be printed (Venice, 1519). According to Politis, it was "the most poetical work of the sixteenth century."[4] Simultaneously, in Cyprus an unknown poet wrote excellent love poetry also on the Italian model.

Although most of the important prose writers of this period worked in the West, some legal texts were published in demotic in Cyprus, and somewhat earlier, in the fifteenth century, Leontios Machairás wrote a history of the island in popular prose. The only prose from Ottoman-occupied lands in modern Greek that is worth mentioning is the correspondence from the patriarchate to German protestant scholars while Jeremais II was Patriarch (1572-95).

During the next century prose works became more numerous. Meletios Pigás (1535-1602) a Padua-educated Cretan who became Patriarch of Alexandria in 1590, wrote sermons in demotic. His pupil Kyrillos Loukaris (1572-1639), the first Patriarch of Constantinople ever to be executed on the sultan's orders, founded the first press of the patriarchate, had the Gospels translated into demotic, and placed great emphasis on improving education. It was Loukaris who invited Theophilos Karydaleos (1560-1645) to teach in his school, and the influence of this scholar was soon felt in the reviving Greek school system throughout the empire.

All these cultural manifestations must take a back seat to the activities of the Cretans, who dominated the Greek intellectual scene for about a hundred years beginning with the 1570s. During that time not only literature, but also painting had a "golden age" on Crete. Michael Damaskinos (1535?-91) and Domenico Theotocopoulos (1540?-1614), better known as El Greco, were the two giants of the Cretan school. The icon painting of the island had far-reaching and long-lasting influence in the entire Orthodox world. Nevertheless, it was in literature that Crete made its greatest contribution to Greek culture.

The first major figure was the playwright Georgios Chortatsis, who was born sometime in the middle of the sixteenth century. In his hands de-

4. Politis, *Modern Greek Literature*, p. 42.

motic became a full-fledged literary language. His three plays, the tragedy *Erofili*, the comedy *Katzourbos*, and the pastoral *Gyparis* were based on Italian models, but thematically, linguistically, and structurally they had a high degree of originality, which marked him as a creative talent of the first rank. Probably the most important of all Cretan writers was the play-wright Vitsentzos Kornaros, who lived toward the end of Crete's great literary century. Nothing is known about him but his name and the fact that he wrote *The Sacrifice of Abraham* in his youth and *Erotokritos* as a mature poet. The first play, using the well-known biblical story, enjoyed great popularity for centuries. Beautifully written, it is a highly original work that disregarded all the accepted rules of writing for the stage yet managed to create the dramatic unity that made it a fine piece. *Erotokritos* is modeled on the usual theme of chivalry. The hero, a simple knight, is in love with his king's daughter and must perform great feats, often unknown, before he is permitted to marry her. The scene is thoroughly Balkanic; the heroes are Athenians, the enemies are Vlachs and people from the East. This play receives highest praise from the experts, and its popularity has lasted into the present century. There were also lesser talents who wrote plays. Although this great century of Crete ended with the Turkish conquest of the island in 1669, its literary tradition survived.

During the late seventeenth century Greek literary activity continued in Venetian-dominated lands, mainly the Ionian Islands, and later spread even to Vienna, but the most important developments occurred in the Ottoman lands and were closely connected with the rise of the Phanariots. Thanks to the Phanariots' influence at the Sublime Porte, part of the Greek population gained some privileges, and this development had its cultural results. The already mentioned Alexandros Mavrocordatos, the second Phanariot to hold the office of imperial dragoman (great interpreter), was a learned man who had taught at the patriarchal school and written several studies. His son, Nikolaos (1670-1730), the first Phanariot prince in the Romanian principalities, was also a writer of note. His novel *Parerga of Philotheos* is considered the first manifestation of the Greek revival.[5] The importance of these works lay in their content, which reflected new ideas emerging in Western Europe, and not in their language and style, which were inferior to what had been written in the earlier periods. Voltaire's ideas were mirrored in the early writings of Eugenios Voulgaris (1716-1806), although this writer became a conservative especially after moving to Russian in 1770.

Two other writers prior to the 1770s, when the influence of the Enlightenment really became strong, merit mention: Konstantinos Dapontes and Kosmas. When Dapontes was born is not known; he became a monk at Mt. Athos in 1757 and died in 1784. As a stylist he was not distinguished, but he wrote much on any subject about which he acquired some knowl-

5. *Ibid.*, pp. 74-75. Written in 1718, the work was not published until 1800.

edge, and because much of what he wrote was published in his life time he became important as a popularizer. Kosmas (1714-79), thought to have been a pupil of Voulgaris, was an itinerant preacher whose sermons were written down by his listeners. He combined "the highest form of the spirit of education and enlightenment and religious faith and national consciousness," and "may be considered as one of the precursors of the awakenment [sic] of the nation."[6]

This growing spirit of enlightenment and national rebirth produced its first great figures at the end of the eighteenth century in writers thoroughly influenced by the events in France. Among them was Josephus Moisiodax (d. 1790) who taught in the Phanariot courts of Iaşi and Bucharest. Mainly involved in the sciences, he was also interested in education and in the creation of a popular literary language. More important in every respect was Dimitrios Katartzís (1725?-1807), who wrote in the popular language because he wanted to make the views of the modern world known to as many people as possible. The giant of the period was undoubtedly Adamantios Koraïs (1748-1833). A Medical doctor who lived in Paris after 1788, Koraïs is a major figure of the Greek political enlightenment. He accepted the ideas of the French Revolution, and played a major role in the birth of modern Greece. In this context, however, only one of his accomplishments must be noted. He was the first Greek to be trained as a linguist and was able to influence at least a generation of Greek writers and linguists. Beyond doubt, he was the father of the modern Greek literary language.

In ending this short survey of Greek intellectual activities under Ottoman rule, Rigas Velestinlís must be mentioned (1757?-98). Rigas served Phanariot princes and even the Turkish administration before moving to Vienna around 1790. It was in this city that his publishing activities, including translations, the publication of maps, the writing of patriotic brochures and songs, short stories, and a handbook of physics, were cut short by his arrest by the Austrian police. The Habsburg authorities handed him over to the Ottomans who executed him. He was a great Greek patriot, and a hero-martyr, but as a literary figure he was only of secondary importance.

3. THE SLAVS

THE Slav people also lived under both Ottoman and Christian rulers. As in the case of the Greeks, among the Slavs, too, most cultural activity took place in those lands that were not under Ottoman domination. Dubrovnik was the only Slav region ruled by its inhabitants. Dalmatia was under Venetian rule for most of the centuries with which this volume deals, while the Slovenes were subjected to the Habsburgs and wealthy and

6. *Ibid.*, p. 77.

educated Croats of Croatia-Slavonia also retreated into Habsburg-held territory when the Ottomans occupied part of their homeland.

The Bulgarians, all of whom lived under Ottoman rule and in close proximity to the major administrative centers of Istanbul and Edirne, had the least opportunity to express themselves in the written word, in painting, or in architecture. The Serbs were in a situation similar to that of the Bulgarians for centuries, but during the last hundred years before the revolt of 1804 they developed rapidly an educational establishment of considerable size and built a cultural life around it. The center of this movement was the Metropolitanate of Karlovci (Karlowitz, Karlócza) in Habsburg-held Slavonia. It had been established and protected by Emperor Leopold I's (1657-1705) two letters of privilege of 1690 and 1691 as the religious, cultural, and even national center of the Serbs when they migrated into his land under the leadership of the Patriarch of Ipek (Peć), Arsenije III Crnojević, in 1690. This cultural revival of greatest importance for the rebirth of the entire nation occurred outside the realm of the sultans and, is, therefore, not of direct concern for a survey of activities that took place in the Ottoman Empire.

If the Ottoman-dominated lands were the only ones to be considered, there would hardly be any justification for speaking about Slavs in this chapter, apart from folk songs, the popular poetry celebrating the deeds of the *hajduks*, and, first and foremost, the *Kosovo Epic*. That epic developed slowly over the centuries, with each generation contributing to the creation of one of the greatest epic poems in world literature dealing with the famous Battle of Kosovo in 1389. The Slovenes, who never had any contact with the regions of Southeastern Europe, must be omitted, but the Dalmatians outside of Dubrovnik and the Croats had enough contact with our region to justify a short survey of their cultural activities together with those of the Serbs and Bulgars.[7]

Most of the literature in Dalmatia and Croatia during the centuries under study was written in Croatian. It should be remembered that in these years there was no single Croatian literary language, and that each writer used the dialect with which he was the most familiar. The authors whose names and works will be listed wrote not only in the three major dialects (čakavski, kajkavski, and štokavski), but even in a fourth that can be considered a "language" in its own right, Bosnian štokavski. The development of a unified Croatian literary language, let alone that of modern Serbo-Croatian, did not occur until the nineteenth century.

In Dalmatia the first writer of real importance who worked outside of Dubrovnik was Marko Marulić (1450-1524) of Split. Although this author wrote in both Latin and Croatian, it was his Latin works that earned him a European-wide reputation. Marulić was a prolific writer and deeply re-

---

7. The following pages are based mainly on Antun Barać, *A History of Yugloslav Literature.* For full reference see Chapter 8 n. 9.

ligious. He was also a humanist who understood the problems that the Ottoman occupation created for his countrymen, and his best works concern their lives. Among his short poems his *Prayer against the Turks* is the best known. His major work, written in 1501 and printed in Venice twenty years later, was the epic *Judita*. Although the story is the biblical tale of Judith and Holofernes, the enemy can easily be identified with the Turks. Marulić does not rank high as a master of the poetic form, but his understanding of his people's problems enabled him to write with deep insight and feeling.

Two authors who lived on the island of Hvar deserve mention. Hanibal Lucić (1485-1553) is remembered for his drama *Slave Girl*. The story and the poetic form imitate Italian models, in particular Petrarch, but there are forms derived from folk poetry, too, in his play. The story is routine: a noble girl is captured by pirates, sold into slavery, and freed by her lover. The details, however, clearly reflect the troubled times and conditions of the Dalmatian coast during the poet's lifetime. Petar Hektorović (1487-1572) was the first writer to use folk poetry extensively as his model. He wrote mainly love poems, but also verses dealing with the life of the people around him. His best known poem, *Fishing and Fishermen's Talks* (published in 1568), belongs to the latter category.

The city of Zadar produced Petar Zoranić (1508-50?), the author of the first Croatian novel, *Mountains*, published posthumously in 1569. The work gives a realistic description of the life of people of different social classes in Dalmatia during the author's lifetime. Brno Krnarutić (dates uncertain, middle of sixteenth century) wrote the poem *The Capture of Szigetvár* (published in 1584), a theme used repeatedly by Croatian and Hungarian poets. It dealt with the capture of Szigetvár by the Ottomans in 1566 during which both Süleyman I and the defender Count Nikola Zrinski (Miklós Zrinyi) lost their lives.[8]

During the next century, the greatest in Dubrovnik's cultural history, the rest of Dalmatia produced no first-class writer. Nevertheless, two of the lesser lights merit mention. Bartol Kašić (1575-1650) of the island of Pag, a clergyman during the Counterreformation, was interested in using books to advance his work. Trying to reach the widest possible audience, he discovered that štokavski was the most commonly spoken dialect and wrote in it. He authored the first grammar of Southern Slav language, the *Institutiones linguae Illyricae*, published in 1604. Kašić's purpose, to

---

8. The Zrinski-Zrinyi family is a good example of the high Croatian nobility's position within the Habsburg lands. Not only did they spell their names in three different ways (Croatian, Hungarian, and Latin), but they were usually equally fluent in these languages as well as in German. They were not quite sure of their ethnic identity. Although they certainly did not consider themselves Germans, their feelings towards Croatia and Hungary were ambivalent, and both people consider them national heroes and leaders with equal justification.

spread the Catholic message, was most successfully pursued by a native Bosnian clergyman, Matija Divković (1563-1631). Divković was not original and took his subject matter from a great variety of sources, but he is important because he set an example for several other clergymen-writers and because of his ability to mingle religious message with popular tales. He was the first to use the Bosnian štokavski dialect in writing.

In the eighteenth century, when Dubrovnik's greatest son was not a writer but the scientist Rudjer Bošković (1711-87), two writers of importance worked along the coast. Both were Franciscans interested in missionary work in the Ottoman Empire. Filip Grabovac (1695-1750) was not a great writer, but he was a dedicated patriot and excellent social observer. His description of the life of the people are valuable, but his reforming zeal displeased the Venetians who arrested him and he died in captivity. Much more significant was the work of Andrija Kašić Miošić (1704-60) who worked in numerous parishes in Dalmatia and Bosnia. A born democrat who loved everybody, he felt close to the common people and discovered their art and poetry, but he also became convinced that the stories they told were false. Considering all Southern Slavs as one people, he set out to tell them the "truth" in a form all would understand. He wrote two "histories," *The Pleasant Story of the Slav Nation* (1756) and *The Little Ark* (1760). *The Pleasant Story* is more important because it attempted to tell the entire history of all Southern Slavs with emphasis on the Ottoman period. Of some literary significance, his works are simple in language because he wanted to reach the greatest possible number of readers, and his poetry, based on folk poetry, created a truly Croatian poetic form. He became very popular and influential.

In Croatia-Slavonia the first writer of any significance was a Jesuit secondary school teacher in Zagreb, Juraj Habdelić (1609-78). He did not consider himself a writer, but his collections of sermons (*The Mirror of Mary* and the *Original Sin of our Father Adam*) are written in excellent Croatian and contain many valuable and exact observations of life around him.

Completely different were the contributions of two of his contemporaries, sons of the highest nobility: Petar Zrinski (Péter Zrinyi, 1621-71) and his brother-in-law Fran Krsto Frankopan (1643-71). Both were highly educated men in the western tradition, but both were familiar with Dalmatian literature and folk poetry and blended these elements in their writings.

Petar Zrinski was a soldier and Ban of Croatia. He joined the Hungary-wide conspiracy organized by his older brother Nicola Zrinski (Miklós Zrinyi), great-grandson of the hero of Szigetvár, who saw the day of the Ottomans' expulsion from Hungary-Croatia-Slavonia as imminent, but predicted (together with his fellow conspirators) that Habsburg rule would hardly be an improvement over the Ottomans. His only work, *The*

Siren of the Adriatic, deals with the Battle of Szigetvár and is merely a Croatian version of his brother's epic, a classic in Hungarian called *Szigeti Veszedelem*. Its only merit is its language.

Frankopan, who was executed as a fellow conspirator with Petar although he was at best marginally involved in the plot, was a writer of great talent who translated Molière, but was totally unknown to the reading public. His writings were confiscated by the authorities and first published in the nineteenth century. Of his works the collection of lyric poems, *The Garden of Rest*, dealing with a great variety of subjects such as love, war, description of his times, and the sorrows of a young man who knew much tragedy in his life, is the most remarkable. Many of these poems were written in prison. His form of expression and use of the language mark Frankopan as one of the most remarkable poets of the seventeenth century.

Croatia produced two more important figures during the same century; Juraj Križanić (1618-83) and Pavao Ritter Vitezović (1652-1712). Križanić was born near Zagreb, joined the Jesuit order, and was educated in Rome. In connection with his interest in healing the Great Schism, he made two trips to Russia. Traveling to numerous Slav-inhabited lands, Križanić added their union to that of the churches as his goal and became the first "Pan-Slav." During his second visit to Russia he was arrested and sent to Siberia. It is not known when he was released, but he found death with the Poles at the walls of Vienna in 1683. In his numerous works he preached his ideals to all Slavs, but particularly to the Russians, criticizing, admonishing, and calling the Slavs to greatness. He is mainly important as a "political theorist," but his talents as a writer were far from negligible.

Vitezović was born in Senj, but worked mainly in Zagreb. Neither a nobleman nor a cleric, he was the first Croatian who tried to live from his writing and publishing activities. He was a prolific and multitalented intellectual, but died in great poverty in Vienna. A "Yugoslav" who dreamed of the unification of all Southern Slavs under Habsburg rule, his concern extended to linguistics and orthography and he tried to create a unified literary language for all Southern Slavs. His longest poem picked up the old theme and described the *Resistance of Szigetvár*, while his *Serbia Illustrated* was the first history of Serbia ever written using documents and the other tools of the modern historian.

Among those writing in Croatian in the eighteenth century, Tito Brezovački (1757-1805) of Zagreb was the most talented. A Pauline monk, he turned to writing after his order was dissolved. He was a social critic who opposed corruption, superstition, and the political situation in Croatia. He wrote to teach, and his characters represent the various social classes and their shortcomings with great clarity. He became most important as a playwright for an amateur company in Zagreb. Two of his pieces, *The*

Sorcerer's Apprentice and *Diogenese* (the story of a servant who simultaneously serves two masters who do not know they are brothers) are timeless enough to be performed even today.

The only other author of any significance during this century was Matija Antun Reljković (1732-98), a son of Slavonia. As an officer serving in the seven years war, he was captured and lived in various German cities. There he had the chance to compare life with that in his native province. Recently liberated from the Turks, Slavonia lived in great misery under the jurisdiction of ecclesiastic and laic masters who apparently did not understand the problems of the people whom they served. The result of this comparison was *The Satyr*, written in the verse form of folk poems and published in Dresden in 1762. Reljković addressed himself to the problems of Slavonia critically, but also constructively. The work rapidly gained popularity among both the educated and uneducated, but it displeased the authorities. It deserves to be remembered both for its versification and content. Reljković's other literary works did not live up to the promise of this first publication.

The long centuries of Ottoman rule prevented the Serbs from creating a literature comparable to that of the Croats. With the exception of folk poetry, the literary activity of this nation was limited to the work done by monks in several monasteries and produced nothing of significant importance. The only important cultural figure prior to the migration into Habsburg-held lands was Pajsije (1550?-1647), one of the first metropolitans of the See of Ipek after it was re-established by the Ottomans in 1557. His own work, a biography of Stefan IV Uroš (1355-71), the last ruler of Serbia, is worthless, but his activities as a collector of manuscripts and his encouragement of monks to do the same and to produce copies yielded significant and long-lasting results. The situation changed after the migration into Habsburg-held lands, and a great number of writers appeared. Most of them, however, were still clergymen who began to use a somewhat artifical language, a mixture of Church Slavonic, the popular idiom, and extensive borrowings from Russian. This new "literary language" became the vehicle for the earliest examples of modern Serbian literature, but was understood only by the clergy, the thin layer of educated laymen in the cities, and a handful of people who lived in rural areas.

The first center of this new Serbian literature was the monastery of Szentendre, north of Buda on the Danube, which had been established by the monks from Rača (on the Sava River west of Belgrade) who had followed Arsenije III in 1790. One of the monks, Kiprijan, wrote the first study on Serbian poetic forms. The real center of Serbian cultural, including literary, activities developed further to the south, in today's Vojvodina district. It was here that the three writers who deserve mention began working: Zaharije Orfelin (1726-85), Jovan Rajić (1726-1801), and Dositej Obradović (1742-1811).

Orfelin was a layman. He was well educated, mainly as a result of his own efforts, and held a wide range of jobs during his life, which was spent in the major cities of the Vojvodina and in Vienna and Venice. His literary activities were as varied as his occupations and ranged from elementary text books to studies in viniculture. Most of his works were published anonymously or under pseudonyms, and all of them sought to instruct in one form or another. He was certainly the best Serbian poet of the century, and he also published a biography of Peter the Great and edited, in 1768 in Venice, *The Slavo-Serb Magazine*, which published articles on a great variety of subjects and was the first journal of this kind.

Rajić was a Kiev-educated priest. He traveled widely collecting materials for a historical study, *History of the Different Slavonic Nations, Especially the Bulgarians, Croats and Serbs*, which was finally published in four volumes in Vienna in 1794-95. Unlike the Bulgarian Father Paisii, whom he befriended at Mt. Athos, Rajić was not so much interested in his own people as in an "attempt to view the history of the various Southern Slavs as one."[9] He used the new, artificial literary language, found few readers, and his influence was extremely limited. Yet his work, based on many years of documentary research, remains the first attempt at a scientific history of the Southern Slavs.

Obradović was by far the most remarkable of the Serbian writers. He learned to read at a tender age and as a young man became a monk in order to learn more and to become a saint. Monastic life disappointed him. He was especially repulsed by the ignorance of the monks and set out to acquire knowledge. For more than thirty years he traveled across Europe from England to Istanbul and then into Asia Minor. He became knowledgable not only of many languages, but of philosophy, mathematics, sciences, and literature, and was the first writer to spread the ideas of the Enlightenment and to plead for unity, brotherhood, and religious toleration among the Southern Slavs. Like Orfelin, Obradović wanted to combat the influence of the monasteries, by teaching modern methods and thus advancing the development of his people. He had much to say, and because he wrote in the popular and not in the new, artificial language his influence was great. His themes were not original—he borrowed freely from world literature, from Aesop's *Fables* to modern works—but his style was original and skillful. It became the example of modern popular Serbian raised to the literary level and was imitated by many. Two of his most popular works, *Life and Adventures* (an autobiography) and *Fables* (an adaptation of Aesop containing much practical and timely advice), were published in the eighteenth century, in 1783 and 1788 respectively, together with several other less popular volumes. In Obradović the Serbs gained a very influential literary giant whose activities extended beyond

9. Hans Kohn, *The Idea of Nationalism* (New York: Macmillan, 1961), p. 550.

writing into politics toward the end of his life, making him one of the great men of modern Serbian history.

If much less could be said about Serbian than about Croatian writers, even less can be written about the Bulgarians. The Ottoman conquest cut short the beginnings of a literary school of high quality whose influence had reached not only into other Slav lands, but also into the Romanian principalities by the eve of the conquest.[10] The Bulgarians suffered, as did the Serbs, from centuries of direct Ottoman rule, but they were located much closer to Edirne and Istanbul than were their fellow Slavs to the West. This proximity to the Ottoman capitals had two results; the majority of the Bulgarian population was probably the most closely supervised of all those who inhabited the Ottoman Empire; at the same time there were also more opportunities to cooperate with the conquerors. No other people of the "core provinces" developed a quasi-middle class similar to the Bulgarian *çorbacis*, who enjoyed certain economic privileges and by the eighteenth century even held minor administrative posts. Thus, although the great majority of the Bulgarians were not able to express themselves, the small minority, the *çorbacis*, were. Unfortunately, these were people who looked after their own interests, cooperated with the Ottomans, and were linked to the masses by nothing more than the language they spoke.

It is quite understandable that under these circumstances whatever culture survived did so behind the protective walls of monasteries in Bulgaria proper, in Macedonia, and on Mt. Athos. Here documents were preserved and copied, and "cell-schools" were set up mainly for the purposes of instructing young monks. Occasionally, however, other people also received some education in these schools which served as models for small centers of lay learning whose curriculum rarely went beyond the teaching of the basic requirements of literacy needed by craftsmen who served both as teachers and students in these lay establishments. All these schools taken together did not produce enough learning to make it the basis of a real cultural life. What little learning there was, mainly in the monasteries, was scholastic and medieval and was important only because it preserved a language that in later centuries could serve as the basis for modern literary Bulgarian.

A few isolated developments occurred outside the Bulgarian lands, but these were of more historical than cultural importance. In 1508 the first printed Bulgarian work, a liturgy, appeared in Romania, and in 1651 a work that was primarily a prayer book, *Abagar*, was printed in Rome. The latter is considered to be the first publication to contain some hints of modern Bulgarian.[11]

10. See Petar Dinekov, "L'école litteraire de Tărnavo," *Études Balkaniques* 8 (1972): 5-111.
11. Two works in English contain some information on Bulgarian cultural life. Ni-

The true Bulgarian Renaissance did not occur until the nineteenth century, but the eighteenth did produce Father Paisii (1722-98) and Stoiko Vladislavov (1739-1815?), who indicate the birth of the new spirit and who deserve to be included in this chapter. Paisii was born in Bansko (Blagoevgard), in nothern Macedonia. At the age of twenty-three he became a monk at the Hilendar Monastery on Mt. Athos. Working in the libraries at Mt. Athos, Paisii collected material relating to his people, and after nearly twenty years he published, in 1762, his *Slavo-Bulgarian History*.[12] This short volume, written in cumbersome and archaic Church Slavonic, was as novel in its approach and spirit as it was dated linguistically. It was the work of a conscious Bulgarian patriot saddened by the political oppression of the Ottomans, by the ecclesiastic supremacy of the Greeks, and by the lack of his people's national awareness. The great tsars of Bulgaria's past, the giants Cyril and Methodius, and the cultural and political accomplishments of his people are presented in glowing terms. His main goal was to make the Bulgarians realize that they were a people with a great past and should work diligently for an equally glorious future. The book speaks of Bulgaria, the love of the fatherland, and the native language. Although the work was not printed for some eighty years, it had an impact on the Bulgarians who followed the author's advice: "Copy this history, and pay everybody who knows to write and copies it and keep it."[13]

One of those who was impressed by Paisii's work and who did more than anyone else at the end of the eighteenth and the beginning of the nineteenth century to publicize his views was Stoiko Vladislavov, one of the few Bulgarians who rose to the rank of bishop. Born in Kotel, he met Paisii in 1765. Subsequently, under the name of Sophronii he became Bishop of Vratsa. His life was not a happy one and ended in exile in Wallachia. His volume of sermons, *Sunday Book* (1806), and his autobiography, *The Life and Sufferings of Sinful Sophronius*, did much to popularize Paisii's ideas and goals, but they are also among the earliest works written in good modern literary Bulgarian and are therefore significant. Paisii and Sophronii mark the beginning of the Bulgarian Renaissance and are important historical and cultural figures in their own right.

---

kolai Todorov, Lyubomir Dinev, and Lyuben Malnishki, *Bulgaria; Historical and Geographical Outline* (Sofia: Sofia Press, 1968) and D. Kossev, H. Hristov, and D. Angelov, (*A Short History of Bulgaria* (Sofia: Foreign Languages Press, 1963).

12. The best work dealing with Paisii and his work is D. Kosev, Al. Burmov, Hr. Hristov, V. Paskaleva, and V. Mutafchieva, *Paisii Hildendarski i negovata epoha* [Paisii of Hilendar and his time] (Sofia: BAN, 1962). The work is useful for the general reading public because each of the chapters is followed by a summary in western languages.

13. Hans Kohn's translation, *The Idea of Nationalism*, p. 544.

4. THE JEWS[14]

WHEN the Ottoman conquest began Greek-speaking Jews known either as Romaniots or Gregos lived in several of the cities conquered. They were not too numerous and after the arrival of the Sephardim were absorbed into these more advanced and skilled communities. These new arrivals found not only Greek-speaking coreligionists but also some Ashkenazi communities, which had come from Central Europe and had begun to arrive somewhat earlier in the fifteenth century than had the Sephardim and continued their migration well into the sixteenth century. By the second half of the century there were active Ashkenazi communities in several cities, including Istanbul, Edirne, Sofia, Pleven, Vidin, Trikala, Arta, and even the Sephardic stronghold of Salonika. These communities, which originated during the reign of Mehmed II (1451-81), found life under Ottoman rule so much better than it had been in their old homes that they sent letters back to the German-speaking world, actively encouraging their friends to join them. [15] Although the Ashkenazi communities remained separate, it was the Sephardim who became the dominant Jewish element in the Ottoman Empire.

The best known Sephardic Jew living in the Ottoman state was Joseph Nasi (1515?-79). Born João Miguez in Portugal, he first migrated to Antwerp whence he moved to Istanbul with a considerable fortune in 1554. He became a friend of Mehmed Sokollu and Sultan Selim II (1566-74) and was appointed Duke of Naxos. In addition to this position he had numerous commercial interests in the capital and great influence in foreign affairs. It was he who urged more strongly than did anybody else the war against Venice that brought the empire the island of Cyprus in 1570. Less well known but also influential in the shaping of foreign policy was Solomon Abenayish (1520?-1603), born Alvaro Mendes. He received the Dukedom of Lesbos (Mytilene) and advocated the empire's anti-Spanish naval policy.

The most influential of the Ashkenazi was Solomon Askenazi (1520-1603), the personal physician and friend of Mehmed Sokollu. Born and trained in Italy, he had practiced in Poland before moving to Istanbul, and his knowledge of these two countries was as much appreciated by the

14. The following pages rely mainly on the following works: Abram Leon Sacher, *A History of the Jews* (New York: Alfred A. Knopf, 1937); two books by Gershom G. Scholem, *Major Trends in Jewish Mysticism* (New York: Schocken Books, 1941), *Sabbatai Sevi; The Mystical Messiah* (Princeton: Princeton University Press, 1973); Israel Halpern, "The Jews in Eastern Europe," and Itzhak Ben-Zvi, "Eretz Yisreal under Ottoman Rule, 1517-1917," both of which are in Louis Finkelstein, ed., *The Jews; Their History* (New York: Schocken Books, 1972); H. Z. Hirschberg, "The Oriental Jewish Communities," in A. J. Arberry, ed., *Religion in the Middle East*, 2 vols. (Cambridge, The University Press, 1969), vol. 1—*Judaism and Christianity*.

15. See H. Z. Hirschberg, "The Oriental Jewish Communities," p. 146.

Sublime Porte as was his medical knowledge. He greatly influenced the state's policy towards Poland and served as its ambassador to Venice.[16] Although there were many other very important physicians, statesmen, tradesmen, and artisans, the European provinces of the Ottoman Empire were not too significant intellectually for the Jews who lived under the scepter of the sultan. Material security was not matched by intellectual accomplishments like those achieved by Jews in the Near East. Jerusalem, Safad, Gaza, and even Cairo became much more important cultural centers for the Jews than did even Salonika. Although old tales and songs as well as their languages survived among the Jewish communities, their activities remained focused on their traditional scholarship.

Among the scholars of the Near Eastern provinces the study of the Kabbalah became popular in the seventeenth century, producing the controversial figure Sabbatai Zevi (1625-76). Born in Izmir (Smyrna), Zevi was a sickly man, although the often voiced contention that he was a maniac-depressive cannot be proven. He first spoke of having received a "message" in 1648, but he did not make his message public. As a matter of fact he never wrote anything, and his fame is due to Nathan of Gaza (1644-89), whom he encountered after he moved to Jerusalem in 1662, having wandered from town to town since 1651 when he had been banished from Izmir. It was Nathan who discovered Sabbatai's "law" and proclaimed him the Messiah. The message preached by Sabbatai and Nathan was basically a mystic antinomianism, which was always expressed in exalted ritual. In 1663 the Jerusalem community, in dire need of funds, sent Sabbatai to Cairo for help. There he met his third wife, Sarah. Of Polish origin, she was to become the most fervent (albeit not always honest) propagator of his teachings in the West after his death.

Although Zevi's teachings were never clearly formulated, his messianic mysticism attracted many followers, released deep emotions, and was highly disturbing to the orthodox rabbinate. In the words of Gershom G. Schalom, "Sabbatianism represents the first serious revolt in Judaism since the Middle Ages; it was the case of a mystical idea leading directly to the disintegration of the orthodox Judaism of the 'believers.' Its heretical mysticism produced an outburst of more of less veiled nihilistic tendencies among some of the followers. Finally, it encouraged a mood of religious anarchism on a mystical basis. . . ."[17] No wonder that the rabbinate turned to the sultan who ordered Zevi to appear before him in 1666.

Before leaving Jerusalem this self-proclaimed master of the world divided the globe among twenty-six of his followers. He was arrested in Istanbul and sent to prison at Abydos (on the Asiatic shores of the Dardanelles). There he lived as a little prince, holding court to as many as a

16. Cecil Roth, "The European Age in Jewish History," in Louis Finkelstein, *The Jews*, pp. 255-56.

17. Gershom G. Scholem, *Major Trends*, p. 299.

thousand followers. Finally, he was brought before the sultan who offered him apostasy or death. Zevi chose the former, and as Mehmed *effendi* became the sultan's royal door-keeper. Although he died in disgrace in Ulcinj (Dulcingo), his influence was amazingly long-lasting. It gravely affected the Jewish communities in the empire's core provinces where his teaching was popular, and his apostasy created consternation and division, adding to other problems the Jewish inhabitants faced.

Some of these problems were as old as the Sephardic and Ashkenazi settlements themselves. Not only was there a division between these two major communities, but within each of them there existed sharp lines, drawn in accordance with the origin of the settlers. For example, among the Aragonese further rifts developed along ritualistic and even merely professional lines. In a sense the Jewish group never formed true communities, but was a mosaic of small segments united by origin, profession, and ritual. The splintering tendency was reinforced by the Ottoman system, which grouped all Jews together without taking into account even the basic division between the Sephardim and Ashkenazis.

The Ottoman's growing intolerance of non-Muslims in the late sixteenth and seventeenth centuries only reinforced the latent discontent and rivalry within the Jewish community, although not as much as it did among the Christians. In the seventeenth century the Jews could, if they so chose, emigrate to either Holland or England and thus change their lot.

To this already splintering Jewry Sabbatai Zevi's message offered the best solution for all problems—messianic or individual salvation. The Sabbatian teachings were eagerly received in the European "core provinces" and added significantly to the disintegration of the Jewish communities. Zevi's apostasy was regarded by some of this Balkan followers as the "supreme mystical act" and perfectly consistent with Judaism. In Salonika four hundred families followed his example, and they and their descendants to the present day are known as the *dönme*, Muslims of Salonika-Jewish origin living in Turkey. After Zevi died the decline of the Jewish population in the Southeast European lands began in earnest.

Despite this decline, the long residence of the Jews, especially the Sephardim, in these provinces had helped them to maintain their traditions, rituals, language, and communal life under circumstances that were far better than elsewhere in Europe during these long centuries. It was this tradition, together with some wealth, that the Jews took with them when they again began to move westward. According to Scholem, they also carried ideas that stemmed from Sabbatianism, became important in the eighteenth and nineteenth centuries, and helped to create reformed Judaism.[18]

Although the Jews were able to preserve for the future what was dearest to them, they differed from the other people of Southeastern Europe only

18. *Ibid.*, p. 301.

in degree. They were less numerous than the other ethnic groups, and not being indigenous and with a history and tradition not tied to the area, their contribution to posterity was much narrower than was that of the Slavs or the Greeks.

Even among the Greeks most of the political and administrative institutions and traditions were lost as was the great majority of their visual arts and architecture, which "offended" Ottoman-Muslim tastes and values. They saved only their tradition and languages and added folk poetry depicting their life under Ottoman rule. The progress made by the Slavs occurred in areas over which the Turks had no control—at least no direct control. Only the Greeks were able to advance their culture, even if only very slightly, living in the "core provinces." It should be remembered, however, that large areas of the lands they inhabited were often under Venetian rule or were administered, for all practical purposes, by local Greek magnates whose rule the Ottomans had to tolerate. These circumstances, together with the high development of Greek culture at the time of the Ottoman conquest and Greek control of the Orthodox church, created somewhat more favorable circumstances for them which they were able to exploit. Although the very nature of Ottoman administration accounts to a large extent for the centuries' long survival of all the people they ruled in Southeastern Europe, these peoples' love for their tradition and culture, some of which was expressed by the men whose works have been mentioned in this chapter, furnished the force and the visible marks of the identities that survived.

CHAPTER 13

Conclusions

1. THE OTTOMAN PERIOD

THE first, but especially the second chapter discussed the nature and organization of the Ottoman administration and society. In order to evaluate what this empire's domination over Southeastern Europe produced, it is necessary to return shortly to these topics and stress some of their features and their significance.

The Ottoman state was an empire, but it was very unlike the Romans' or the later imperial nations' of Western Europe. When the old Roman proudly declared *civis Romanus sum*, he was not expressing the pride that a modern-day nationalist would have felt. What he was referring to, very proudly, was a body of fully codified rights and privileges that set him apart from all other people. The fact that these laws were those of Rome and that the empire was the creation of this city whose citizen he was gave the *civis Romanus sum* statement a clearly defined local, quasi-national meaning, even if the individual who uttered it was somebody who had never even seen the imperial city. There was not only one Rome, and later a second and third, but there also were Romans.

The Ottoman Empire was not a national empire, nor was it identified with a locality and its citizens. The capital moved from Söğüt to Bursa to Edirne and finally to Istanbul, and the empire had no citizens, nor did it have a language like Latin, Greek, English, French, or Dutch. Osmanlica, the language of administration, was incomprehensible to the majority of Turks. The Ottoman Empire was a dynastic state whose justification for existence was based on certain religious assumptions. In this respect it demands comparison with the Arab empires and even with China and Japan.

The Arab empires were certainly based on religious assumptions, but, in spite of the long rule of the Ummayads and 'Abbāsids, they were not dynastic by definition. As a matter of fact, strictly speaking these and all

271

other caliphates were illegal. The Arab states after Muhammad were Islamic, but were not tied to a specific dynasty. The Chinese emperors also based their rule on the "mandate of heaven," but, quite apart from the fact that heaven was not clearly tied to any specific deity, the mandate could be transferred from one ruling family to another. In neither the Arab nor the Chinese empires were religion and a given family's rule the equally important bases for the existence of the state that they were in the Ottoman case. Nor was the Ottoman double base of legality the same as that in Japan. The sultan was not the "son of heaven" as was the emperor of the island empire, where the origins of people, state, religion, and imperial house went back to the same mythological past. The Ottoman Empire was a multiethnic, multilingual, and even multireligious state held together by the rule of a given family whose right to reign was based on Turkic tradition, but whose duties and obligations were determined by religious considerations. These two elements of different origin determined the state's structure and the place of every individual in it.

This structure assigned supremacy to the two elements without which the state could not have existed, the ruler and Islam. All that had to be added to these basic considerations were administrative and social institutions that assured their proper place in state and society. It is important to realize that these two divisions, the social and administrative, were not identical and were run independently from each other.

Politically, the sultan was in theory absolute. He delegated some power to the professional Ottoman—the Osmanlica speakers, the Ottoman equivalent of Christian-feudal Europe's "political nations," the nobility—who ran the various administrative offices described in the first two chapters. Unlike the European nobility, the professional Ottoman class had no legal rights, although tradition gave them extensive power. They could be recruited from practically any element in society and could be dismissed and even killed at the will of the ruler. When the members of this group became too powerful, the sultan simply recruited from new sources to reestablish his own political supremacy. When he proved unable to act in this manner, the political structure of the empire began to decline. The professional Ottoman was a member of the Ottoman "political nation," but only at the sufferance of the sultan, and his rights and functions derived from the ruler's appointment and not from rights that he himself possessed. Yet all political and administrative functions were concentrated in the hands of this class, which was broken down into higher and lower echelons within the parallel functional organizations already described. In a sense the Ottoman Empire had a functional administrative structure whose offices were manned by specially trained bureaucrats of various ranks who were simply the temporary executors of political decisions that remained the exclusive right of the ruler.

The professional Ottoman class was created for a specific reason: the administrative and political management of the state. It was the importance of this function, not ethnic origin, language, or religion, that placed this class at the apex of the social pyramid. The lower layers of this structure were constructed according to the same criterion: functionalism. Peasant, tradesman, guild merchant, craftsman, clergyman, or day laborer —in short anybody who lived in the Ottoman Empire—performed a duty that was directly useful to the state. From the point of view of the central government the relative importance and usefulness of a profession determined the social and class status of its practioners. Each socioprofessional group was strictly regulated, and its members had certain duties and rights. Because the proper functioning of society had only one goal, the support of the state, the stability of the class division of the population along socioprofessional lines had to be assured. In this respect the Ottoman Empire, with its numerous rules and regulations governing the economic activities and the professional division of its population, achieved the type of highly centralized and regulated imperial order that the reforms of the Emperor Diocletian (284-305) had tried to introduce into the Roman Empire. Attempts were made to make marginally useful men fully useful, as in the case of the nomads, but once any given individual was enrolled in a socioprofessional class he and his descendants were supposedly fixed for eternity.

It should also be remembered that military service was included in the duties that the administrative-political class had to perform. Thus, governors and lower ranking provincial officials who belonged to this class had no right or power to change the regulations that governed the lives of those who belonged to the other professions. This compartmentalization of society ensured a certain internal freedom and flexibility within the framework of the law and permitted classes to adjust to the local requirements of a given area. It was another sure sign of the empire's decline when, in the later centuries, this strict division of functions broke down. The rich could then acquire interests in professions other than their own, and the professional Ottomans could acquire "membership" in the lower classes, neglecting their own activities and diverting income from the treasury to their own pockets.

Viewed from the administrative-political angle, the Ottoman Empire was organized into horizontal layers of social classes in accordance with their professional activities. The duties and rights of each class reflected the degree of importance that the government attached to its economic activities.

The population was also divided vertically along legal-religious lines. In addition to the Muslims there existed the *millets* of the Orthodox, the Armenians, and the Jews. These were parallel organizations, and each was independent within the limits of its own competence. The Ottomans had no concept corresponding to national lines of differentiation, and although Islam was certainly superior in their eyes to any other creed, they did not subordinate the latter to the former. The *millet* system did not establish a division between ruler and ruled; that division was established by the difference between professional Ottoman and *reaya*, which was not based on religion although practically all professional Ottomans were Muslims. The purpose of the *millet* system was simply to create a secondary imperial administrative and primary legal structure for the *zimmi*. Through this system a great and universal empire could be ruled without the primary duties and responsibilities of the administrative-political class being altered. At the same time acceptable living conditions and legal structures for the non-Muslims were created. Given the power of the early sultans, I agree with Professor Kemal Karpat's statement, that "had the Ottoman government accepted the idea of minority-majority or developed a political sense of nationality it could easily have liquidated the patchwork of races and religions under its rule transforming them into one homogenous Muslim or Turkish group."[1] The *millet* system was the solution devised by a government that did not know what nationality meant and, therefore, was unfamiliar with the majority-minority concept. "The *millet* linked," to quote Professor Karpat again, "the individual to the ruling authority as far as basic administration was concerned and complemented the social estates in the religious-cultural field."[2]

The vertical and horizontal divisions of society coexisted with equal force and, superimposed on each other, produced a grid. Each individual belonged within one of the squares in this grid and could move relatively freely within that square. Horizontal movement from one *millet* into another was possible through conversion for all except Muslims, while vertical movement within a given *millet* was much more difficult and rarer because too much movement along these lines would have upset the socioeconomic balance on which the existence of the state depended. This grid concept is a convenient tool for investigating the effects of Ottoman rule in Southeastern Europe.

One of the first results of Ottoman conquest was the elimination of princes and nobles. The majority of the old ruling class was quickly liquidated by the Ottomans, who sought to remove the most likely source of revolt and resistance. Furthermore, the princes and the nobility could not be fitted into the Ottoman social grid because they performed no useful functions for the state. Whenever any of these men could not be liquidated they were, at least in theory, absorbed into the professional Ot-

1. Kemal Karpat, *An Inquiry into the Social Foundations of Nationalism in the Ottoman State; From Social Estates to Classes, from Millets to Nations*, Research Monograph No. 39 (Xeroxed) of the Center of International Studies of the Woodrow Wilson School of Public and International Affairs of Princeton University (Princeton, 1973), p. 39.
2. *Ibid.*

toman class by being given functions usually reserved for members of this class. The local lords accepted this arrangement because it assured continued enjoyment of rights they had had under pre-Ottoman rulers, albeit within a different legal system and under the guise of new titles, and they often became good Ottoman bureaucrats. These cases were not too numerous.

The destruction of the old ruling element was not resented by the masses who had little in common with it and had often suffered grievously from arbitrary rule. The pre-Ottoman sociopolitical order collapsed with the elimination of those who had created and maintained it and made the introduction of the Ottoman system possible. This system not only appeared to be working smoothly, but the absence of a native leadership element appeared to go unchallenged for about two centuries.

Two additional factors contributed significantly to the initial stability of the Ottoman order. The so-called Pax Ottomanica, coupled with a relative economic stability and even improvement when compared with the previous centuries, eliminated the ills, insecurity, and extreme hardship that usually caused popular discontent and revolt. Furthermore, the constant movement of people during the first two centuries kept the population structure fluid enough to prevent the formation of solidly established local interest groups. Several factors produced this demographic change: the influx of Turks in Southeastern Europe; the already discussed internal migration of the local population; the immigration of Jews; and the massive involuntary transportation of people from one location to another ordered by the authorities to populate cities, to supply agricultural laborers, or to transport recalcitrant elements from their native habitat to strange surroundings where they could no longer cause trouble. Even when these massive demographic shifts occurred almost all who moved, whether voluntarily or involuntarily, remained in the same square of the Ottoman social grid to which they had always belonged. Those who came from outside the state were also assigned a place in this over-all structure.

This structure was considered immutable, especially after it had proved that it fulfilled its purpose. Its major weakness was that those who devised it disregarded the most basic features of human nature and social living. Even among the most dedicated professional Ottomans selfish considerations were always a motivating force, as attested by the creation of the numerous illegal *vakıfs*. Among the majority of the population, the *reaya*, whose fortune was not tied to that of the state, the desire to take care of self and family was even harder to eliminate. In order to ensure the proper functioning of the socioeconomic units, the Ottomans had to create new local leaders such as the officials of the guilds presented in Chapter 4, and the *knezes*, *kmets*, and *çorbacis*, who performed similar functions in the villages.

All of these men were in fact community leaders whose position carried status and prestige transforming them into a new leadership element on the local level. They were not members of a "new aristocracy" but firsts among equals, who not only spoke for their fellows but also began to lead them in the later centuries when the Ottoman order was breaking up. When, especially during the eighteenth century, these local leaders began to cooperate with each other, the people of Southeastern Europe at long last regained the leadership that they had lost with the disappearance of their own nobility. Those members of the old nobility who survived the long Ottoman rule, either as recognized local tribal leaders or as holders of Ottoman titles, had to make common cause with the new leaders unless they wanted to be considered little better than the Ottomans by the emerging popular movements.

The discontent that these new leaders voiced in the name of their followers indicates that the communities for which they spoke were not as united and monolithic nor as satisfied with their lot as they should have been if the ideal on which the Ottoman social structure was based were more than theory. There were two major reasons for this difference between theory and reality. The first of these was economic.

As we know, Ottoman society was broken up into classes in accordance with economic functions (with the exception of the professional Ottoman group), and each profession's size, activities, production ratios, profits, and all other aspects of its activity were strictly regulated. In the earlier centuries this limitation produced the goods, services, and tax income needed by the state and guaranteed a fair return for the producers, but it also froze the economic life of the state into a strictly determined mold.

So long as the Ottoman economic system did not differ too much from that of the rest of Europe, especially regarding nonagricultural activities, it worked. Nevertheless, even during this period one significant difference did exist between the Ottoman and western systems. The fiscal policies of all European states were to a large extent dependent on the rulers' ability to wrest income in the form of taxations, tolls, custom revenues, and monetary policies from the population, in addition to the income from the royal domain. This struggle for additional income was part of that for overall power and is crucial in the story of the well-known transition from the medieval to the modern state. The situation was very different in the Ottoman Empire where the royal domain was, at least in theory, identical with the state. The central government simply assumed that all income, over and above the amounts assigned to different segments of the population as profits or salaries, belonged to it, and so it never developed a true fiscal policy.

After the discovery of the Americas, when all of Europe began to suffer from inflation and a price revolution that lasted for centuries, the states were able to adjust more or less their fiscal policies and production patterns to fit the new circumstances. They did this throughout the sixteenth to eighteenth centuries in spite of constant wars that were as demanding as the Ottoman campaigns. The Ottoman Empire was unable to make a similar adjustment. Having no fiscal policy, it could only repeatedly devalue its currency when in financial trouble. Not until the nineteenth century were modern fiscal measures and a budget introduced.

Nor did the Ottoman authorities change the regulations that governed production and trade, thus preventing their adjustment to changed market conditions. When the growing weakness of the empire forced its government to accede to the various economic demands of the Western European states, the competition of foreign goods ruined the guilds. The agricultural sector tried to adjust by turning to the *çiftlik* system and new crops, but by the time this occurred the state lacked not only the understanding of what this new system signified but also the power to protect it. Consequently, the horizontal borders of each social grid became intolerable for those who were supposed to live within it, and they turned more and more from the authorities and officials to their own dignitaries for leadership.

Just as the barrier created by the socioprofessional organization of the empire became less and less suited for the realities of every day life as time passed, so did those created by the *millet* system. Here the difference between theory and reality had existed from the very beginning and was not the result of the inability of the Ottomans to adjust to changing circumstances. From the moment of their creation the *millets* were supposed to stand for units that were as meaningful for the various *zimmi* as the unity of the Sunni Muslim community was. Although this group was less unified in fact than it was in theory, it was more closely knit than were those created by the *millets*. To a considerable extent Islam became the first loyalty of those who followed this creed, and Arabs could, to a large extent, consider the Ottoman-Islamic state their own. The situation was very different in the case of the *millets*, the organizations that were supposedly created to correspond to the prime loyalty of those who belonged to them.

The Armenian *millet* presents the clearest example of this difference between assumed unity and reality. Although all those belonging to this *millet* were monophysites, the difference between Copts and Armenians, and Chaldaeans and Georgians, to mention only a few of those included in this "unit," was tremendous. Fortunately, most of these groups were relatively small, rarely constituted majorities, and lived in areas that were of no crucial economic or strategic import. The one exception was Egypt. Furthermore, the Armenian Patriarch, realizing that "his flock" consisted of a variety of different churches, never tried to dominate them and dealt with them with the help of their recognized leaders. Thus, the Ottomans had relatively little trouble with this *millet* during the centuries surveyed by this volume.

Theologically, the Jewish *millet* was much more closely united than the Armenian, but, as we have seen in Chapter 12, even in this *millet* serious differences existed, not only between the followers of different rites but even among those of the same rite, depending on their geographic origin. Although considerable numbers of this *millet*'s members lived in Southeastern Europe, where their economic importance was great, the Ottomans had no problems with this group. For centuries the Jews had nowhere to go where they would have been welcome, were separated from the other *zimmi* among whom they lived, were always a minority except in a few cities, and began to leave the Ottoman Empire in considerable numbers by the time the situation became critical for its inhabitants.

The most important problem was presented by the Orthodox *millet*, because the majority of the population was Orthodox in the Southeastern European part of the empire. In their case the theological unity was real, but the question of primary loyalty presented problems. Although theology meant very little to the great majority of the Orthodox, whose belief was mainly of the folk religion variety, the church was a symbol of their identity but only coupled with other considerations.

Prior to the arrival of the Ottomans the Byzantine Empire had been fighting the rising Slav states for about eight centuries. Although the emperors were repeatedly forced by political and military considerations to grant varying degrees of independence to these states and high-sounding titles to their rulers, the church authorities, under the leadership of the Patriarch of Constantinople, were always interested in maintaining the unity of the religious establishment. The correct faith was not, as far as they were concerned, a political or national issue. Yet, seen from the vantage point of the Slavs, the Orthodox was a Byzantine-Greek church, and because their model for a state was that of Eastern Rome the really powerful Slav rulers always strove to create national churches headed by their own patriarchs. In this manner the church became a symbol of independence, if not of nationhood.[3]

The weaker Byzantium became the easier it was for local ecclesiastic and laic dignitaries to assert their independence. On the religious plane most of these claims were clearly illegal. Ironically, it was the Muslim state of the Ottomans that re-established the unity of the Orthodox church when it created the Orthodox *millet*, but this move did not erase the memory of centuries of fighting between Greeks and Slavs nor the role played by ecclesiastic establishments in this struggle. With the Southeast European states eliminated only the church remained to represent the continuation of previous loyalties but also of sharp differences. The Otto-

---

3. The best explanation for both the political and ecclesiastic relationships between Byzantium and the Slav states is offered by Dimitri Obolensky, *The Byzantine Commonwealth; Eastern Europe, 500-1453* (New York and Washington: Praeger, 1971).

mans never understood that for the Orthodox the church represented more than just their spiritual institution. Therefore, they were unable to deal with the problems within this *millet*.

Ottoman conquest destroyed the larger units represented by the states of Southeastern Europe. In its place a multitude of theoretically self-contained units which were small enough to be powerless but large enough to be functionally useful were created by the socioprofessional structure with its clear distinctions represented in the cities by the *mahalles* and in the countryside by the village attached to its *timarli*'s estate only. Most of these new communities retained little from the past but their Orthodoxy, onto which they now transferred the traditions, beliefs, or other self-identifying values that had survived.

This new set of meaningful communal values added to the spiritual ones came to stand for the church for the majority of the Orthodox. The ecclesiastic authorities for whom, naturally, the basic theological values and the spiritual functions of the church remained paramount fought this trend. As the Phanariots came to dominate the patriarchate, church action began to appear more and more as Greek action to the Slav. A situation vaguely similar to the pre-Ottoman struggle in church matters between Greek and Slav began to reappear. Just as the economic crisis forced the population to turn away from its appointed laic leaders and replace them with those of their own local chiefs, so did this different interpretation of the meaning and significance of the church that separated the higher clergy from the masses of the faithful. The chief ally of the local dignitary became the parish priest, who was elected from the community whose values he understood and shared. It was this "popular church" that helped to bring together the leaders of the various communities and reshape them, mainly in the eighteenth century, into new, larger units comparable to those that had disappeared with the arrival of the Ottomans. Only now they were national.

The organization of the Ottoman Empire corresponded perfectly to its self-conceived character expressed by its official name, "The divinely protected well-flourishing absolute domain of the House of Osman." Divine protection was self-evident given the Islamic character of the state; nobody questioned the absolute right of the ruling house to own and administer the state's domain; and the entire social structure was designed to make the empire "well flourishing." To insure this last mentioned goal, the population had to be strictly organized and when needed transferred from one location to another. Beyond that, the state had little interest in the people as long as they remained obedient, did not revolt, and performed the assigned duties. The result was a very strict, overorganized socioeconomic structure that soon ossified and was, at the same time, amazingly lenient. This lenience prevented the enserfment of the Southeastern European peasantry and allowed the population, both urban and rural, to reorganize on a small communal basis under the leadership of its own elected officials. Although political, and to a considerable extent even cultural, life came to a standstill for centuries once the Ottoman rule descended on Southeastern Europe, and economic progress was made very difficult by the strict regulations imposed by the government, the possibility of people to retain at least parts of their freedom and organize as self-regulating communities assured their survival and facilitated their rebirth in the form of modern "nations."

Obviously, the evaluation presented so far applies to the Slav-, Greek- and Albanian-inhabited parts of the "core provinces." For reasons given in Chapter 5 the Ottomans were unable to introduce their own social grid system in the Hungarian-Croatian lands. In these lands the *mezőváros* and frontier societies developed a social order that was not Ottoman, but was imposed by circumstances beyond the control of the sultan's government. The questions that must be asked concerning these lands belong, therefore, more properly in the next section of this chapter.

In turning from the "core provinces" to the vassal territories, Dubrovnik holds a unique position. The models for local development were western, mainly Italian, and there was no Ottoman influence. Yet, it should not be forgotten that Dubrovnik owed both its prosperity and, in large measure, its security to its connection with the Ottoman Empire. Potential enemies of Dubrovnik realized that an attack on the republic might easily involve them in a war with the Ottoman Empire. This knowledge dampened their desire to acquire this prosperous piece of real estate. Thus, Dubrovnik was the only region that did not suffer—and even profited—from Ottoman "overlordship."

While Dubrovnik's independence was safeguarded by its connection with the Ottomans, the Principality of Transylvania owed its independence to Ottoman-Habsburg hostility. Ottoman "protection" of the principality was not as perfect as was that of Dubrovnik, and Transylvania suffered repeatedly from the invasion of Habsburg armies. The incursions of Ottoman armies were the result of the policies of some of Transylvania's princes, which were often reckless and certainly never as enlightened and clever as those of the Dubrovnik Senate. Although the principality remained western-oriented and its social problems stemmed from its own "seven deadly sins" rather than from the introduction of the Ottoman system, the connection with the Ottomans brought significant changes to these lands, too. Most important among these was a reorientation of trade toward the east, especially toward the Danubian Principalities, which created lasting ties among these three lands. The years of independence, a creation of the Ottomans, also increased the difference between Transylvania and the rest of Hungary in social and political matters as well, a development that would probably not have taken place to such a marked degree under other cirumstances. In the case of Transylvania Ottoman influence was indirect but of great and lasting significance.

The relationship between the Danubian Principalities and the Ottomans during the centuries predating the Phanariot period is the hardest to assess. Vassal status prevented the introduction of the Ottoman socioeconomic system in Moldavia and Wallachia, but did not exempt these lands from contributing their share to the well-being of the Ottoman state. The amount of money in taxes and bribes as well as the quantity of goods shipped from the Romanian lands into the empire proper was considerable. It is very unlikely that direct Ottoman rule could have placed a larger economic burden on the principalities than did vassalage. While Moldavia and Wallachia retained their leading social classes and the freedom to elect their princes, they had to defend themselves without Ottoman help against the Hungarians and Poles. In exchange for this military burden they were able to maintain economic and cultural contacts with the Christian world producing something like a Romanian cultural renaissance, especially in the seventeenth century. Yet, by the same century political life had become chaotic, the peasantry had been enserfed and lived under much worse conditions than did that of the "core provinces," and the cities were more dependent on the nobility than anywhere else in Europe.

In the opinion of this author Moldavia and Wallachia paid an enormous economic and social price for political semi-independence and cultural autonomy. The following unanswered questions arise. To what extent was the connection with the Ottomans responsible for the unhealthy development—beginning with the free-for-all for the princely titles at the top of the social pyramid to the total enserfment of the peasantry on the bottom —that plagued Romania even after it regained its unity and independence? Would these developments have taken place even without Ottoman overlordship and to the same extent? It would be misleading to blame the Ottomans too much by pointing out that their rapacity and corruption encouraged office seekers and also forced them, as well as the nobility at large, to treat the peasants increasingly harshly, because unhealthy trends in the principalities began *before* the corrupt period of the Ottoman administration. Undoubtedly, once corruption appeared in Istanbul it reinforced the nefarious developments in Moldavia and Wallachia.

Whatever the answers are to the questions just raised, the Romanian lands, miserable as they were, were still Romanian when the first Phanariot princes ascended the thrones of Moldavia and Wallachia. It was the Phanariot period that introduced if not Ottoman then Istanbul practices into the life of the Romanians (see section 4 of Chapter 6). The result was as unhealthy for the political life of the principalities and the Romanian character of the upper classes as the previous developments had been for the economy of these lands and the life of the lower classes. There can be no doubt that the decision to hand over Moldavia and Wallachia to Phanariot *hospodars* was made by the Ottoman government and that, therefore, that government can be held responsible for the results of this move. Yet, it should also be remembered that the regime introduced into the Danubian lands was not the Ottoman system described earlier in this chapter, but one that did not fit into it and existed only because a totally inefficient government could no longer run its own house without the help of a politically influential element whose very existence proved that the Ottoman social and state system had ceased to perform its duties. The decision to move Phanariots into the principalities was a purely defensive measure and indicated how low the might of the state, which used to be the strongest military power of Europe, had sunk. By introducing the *hospodars* into Moldavia and Wallachia the Ottomans hoped to counteract the growing influence of Russia in these lands. It is ironic to compare those—in the long run harmful—developments that occurred in the Danubian Principalities while the Ottoman Empire was strong with those similarly unhappy changes that took place there when the Istanbul government was practically powerless. The Ottomans cannot be blamed unequivocally for unhealthy trends in Moldavia and Wallachia prior to the eighteenth century. They were, however, fully responsible for those that appeared after the first decade of that century, although these were the result of the behavior of Christian, non-Turkish office-holders.

2. THE OTTOMAN LEGACY

"BACKWARDNESS" is the term most often used to describe the result of Ottoman rule in Southeastern Europe. The Ottomans are blamed for cutting off their European provinces from the great intellectual trends of the rest of the continent beginning with the Renaissance and ending with the Enlightenment. They are accused of retarding educational and economic changes and progress, and denounced for depriving those under their rule of the means of self-expression and self-government. Although each of these charges contains some truth, they are stressed much too heavily, especially when we ask ourselves the following questions. How important was the Reformation's effect in non-Ottoman Orthodox lands? What was the educational level and the rate of literacy of the great peasant masses elsewhere in Europe on the eve of the nineteenth century? What rights of self-expression did the serfs of the continent enjoy? To what extent did populations contribute to government prior to the French Revolution? The answers to these questions show that most non-Ottoman lands were only slightly better off than those ruled from Istanbul, and that the standard evaluations of Ottoman "backwardness" are exaggerated when applied to the end of the eighteenth century. The differences become much more impressive when later developments are considered. Intellectually, economically, and even politically the "Balkans" lagged further behind "civilized Europe" and appeared much more "backward" in 1880 than they had in 1780. In this respect it was the nineteenth that became "the critical century," whether national governments or the Ottomans were in charge of the fate of Southeastern European people. Some of the factors that prevented more satisfactory developments were indeed the results of previous Ottoman overlordship.

In the opinion of this author the most important change that Ottoman rule brought to Southeastern Europe was the large scale demographic transformation of the area, the consequences of which still determine the relationship of its people to each other. It was during the centuries of Ottoman rule that Serbs settled in great numbers north of their traditional homeland in what is today called the Banat, in the Vojvodina, and even in northern Serbia together with certain regions in Slavonia and the Bácska. Romanians moved in equally important numbers into the Banat and the regions of the Crişana, and the Albanians expanded into the Kosovo-Metohija district of present day Yugoslavia and into Epirus and even Macedonia. Although the pattern of Greek habitation did not change as significantly, Greeks did settle in cities where they had previously been a small or nonexistent segment of the population. Where these migration patterns overlapped they created "modern" problems like the famous issue of Macedonia. Forced settlements by the Ottomans, and after 1699 by the Habsburgs in the regions acquired as a result of the Peace of Karlovci, added to the demographic changes brought about by the movement of people. These migrations, as already pointed out, were the results of Ottoman actions and must,therefore, be considered part of the Ottoman legacy.

Even though the heartlands of each people remained the same, the areas in which its individual members lived were much larger than they had been prior to the arrival of the Ottomans. Naturally, the regions into which the different people moved had been inhabited historically by others who, once they regained independence, were to claim them. The historic argument advanced in a period dominated by nationalism was simple: each nation claimed those regions it had inhabited or ruled prior to the establishment of Ottoman overlordship. This argument was often labeled unrealistic, visionary, or archaic by the spokesmen of other people who based their counterclaims on the "modern" theory of self-determination of nations in accordance with "the will" of those who inhabited a given region. The trouble was that the supposedly unrealistic historical claims to any place did not take into account demographic realities. The migrations during the Ottoman centuries had not produced homogenous ethnic areas, but rather a mosaic of hopelessly interwoven population patterns corresponding to the small communal organizations produced by the Ottoman social grid system. Even if the over-all pattern produced the major changes previously mentioned, it was these small units, and not large masses, that moved at any given moment. Thus, Ottoman social organization and the migratory patterns created by the forces that the Ottoman had set in motion were responsible for the appearance of Southeastern Europe's major, modern international problem: large areas inhabited by ethnically mixed populations.

Less clear-cut is the economic result of Ottoman rule. In the agricultural sector the problem of the great Hungarian plain, discussed in Chapters 4 and 5, was the most important because of the large area involved. There can be no doubt that this large region became a desert in the sixteenth century, that the soil deteriorated to a degree that even at present it is not as fertile as it once was. Nor can there be a doubt that the resulting loss of population opened the door to a migration and settlement that completely changed the demographic composition of the population living in this area. Blame for this development has always been assigned to the campaigns of the Ottomans beginning with 1526, and to their inability to take care of the land once it became an Ottoman *eyalet*. That the long period of constant warfare between 1526 (Battle of Mohács) and 1606 (Peace of Zsitvatorok) had a devastating effect on the Hungarian plain cannot be disputed, but it was certainly not Ottoman policy to force the population to emigrate from the lands over which their armies marched and which they finally conquered. Nowhere did mass emigration parallel hostilities to the extent that it did in central Hungary. For this the Ottomans cannot be blamed; they would have preferred to rule a well-populated area suitable for the establishment of *timars*. The depopulation of the plain must be blamed either on the Hungarian nobility, which not only fled but induced its peasants to do the same, or on the fact that by 1526 the agricultural potential of the land had become so marginal that a type of warfare that did not destroy the land permanently elsewhere had this effect in central Hungary forcing the population to move to more fertile regions. Because the nobility and the peasantry were in sharp conflict in the decades immediately preceding 1526, the second alternative appears to be the correct explanation for the drastic changes that occurred in central Hungary in the years following that date.

If this explanation is accepted, it becomes obvious that the catastrophic development that hit the region between the Danube and Tisza rivers would have occurred even if the Ottomans had not invaded the plain. Neither the nobility nor the peasantry had the necessary knowledge or means to arrest the steady deterioration of the soil, which had reached the critical point by the early sixteenth century. What would have happened if this final exhaustion of the land had occurred under the rule of non-Ottoman masters is anybody's guess, but under the Ottomans it produced the growth of the *mezővárosok*, still the larger cities on the plain, and the introduction of the pastural-type animal husbandry as the major economic activity of the region. This pursuit remained the basis of the economy of the Hungarian plain well into the nineteenth century.

Agricultural pursuits in the rest of the "core provinces" did not appear to have changed drastically once the wars ceased and orderly production resumed. The old landlords were gone and the tax system had changed, but the peasant continued to work as before. He must have done a very good job, judging by the amount of taxes he was able to pay and the quantity of produce he made available to the lord, the market, and the *celep*. He was able to learn the techniques needed to grow new crops when they finally were introduced, mainly in the days of the market-oriented *çiftlik* system.

Nor can it be argued that Ottoman rule produced technological backwardness in the agricultural sector of the economy. Although the peasantry's tools were primitive, so were those used by cultivators elsewhere in Europe. On the eve of the French Revolution, approximately the terminal date of this volume, the wooden plow, for example was still used all over continental Europe still untouched by the agricultural revolution that had already begun to transform England. Statistics are not available to prove this contention, but travelers' reports and general descriptions dating from the eighteenth century would indicate that the Ottoman lands were worse off than the agricultural lands of Western Europe only in the availability of draft animals. Once again, it was during the nineteenth century that the agriculture of Southeastern Europe began to fall behind that of the other parts of the continent.

It was in the realms of transportation, especially navigation, and manufacture where the Ottoman's successors were greatly handicapped. Even as late as the seventeenth century the Ottoman merchant marine, manned mostly by Greeks, was still important, but it then declined rapidly because of the same considerations—the ability of the powers to enforce their will on the Ottomans in economic matters—mentioned in connection with manufacture and trade. The decline of this trade also contributed to the decline of shipping. Manufacture, however, suffered not only from foreign competition, but also from the Ottomans' inability or unwillingness to alter their system. By the seventeenth century the guild system was woefully inadequate, and its transformation into a modern industrial production system using machinery simply did not occur. Although an occasional factory did make an appearance, [4] the Ottoman period must be held responsible for bequeathing a totally inadequate, medieval manufacturing sector to the economies of the empire's successor states. In this respect the legacy of Ottoman rule created the gravest difficulties for the people of Southeastern Europe.

Turning, finally, to political considerations, to the often mentioned diffi-

4. See Nikolai Todorov, *Balkanskiat Grad*, especially Chapter 4.

culties that the people had in taking care of themselves after centuries during which they had been excluded from the decision-making process and from administrative activities, the conclusions warranted by this study differ somewhat from those offered in the past. It is perfectly true that, with the exception of the Ragusan oligarchy and the Romanian boyars, the "political nations" of those people who came under Ottoman rule had been eliminated. The number of local notables who were able to maintain their position in Greece, Albania, Bosnia, and elsewhere was not significant enough to replace the former "native leadership," although in certain regions, especially Albania and Bosnia, such notables played a significant role. Nevertheless, none of the people who were able to establish independent states in the nineteenth century lacked qualified personnel for the offices of the newly established governments. Ironically, only in the case of the last people to establish their own state, the Bulgarians, did one of the great powers, Russia, feel that the absence of politically qualified elements in the population justified the staffing of the new state's offices with her own nationals. Even in this case, Russia quickly learned that her assumptions had been incorrect.

That those who lived for centuries under Ottoman rule could care for themselves when given a chance should not be very surprising. The social grid system not only compartmentalized the population, but also left each little professional-confessional unit free to run its own internal affairs. Those whose duty it became to perform these tasks also acted as the groups' spokesmen and negotiators with the outside world, including the authorities. In this manner the population acquired a relatively large number of individuals with some administrative and executive experience and some elementary knowledge of those governmental regulations, functions, and offices that touched on life within their communities. These communal office-holders, including in many cases the local clergy, did not make political decisions, but they did acquire a good knowledge of practical politics so far as the functioning of the various branches of government was concerned. They learned much about local administration, basic finances, and the problems of social groups, and they became used to leadership, decision-making, and assuming responsibility.

It was this element of society that took over political leadership with relative ease prior to or just after the establishment of the various independent Southeast European states. Compared to the old "political nations" that had disappeared or to the Romanian nobility, this new leadership was both more numerous and much more variegated in background and interests, even if it was not as well educated and sophisticated. They were able to furnish real popular leadership. This had certain advantages, but it was also easier for those with whom they had to deal, especially the diplomats of the great powers, to fool them than it was to hoodwink a Romanian boyar or a Greek trader. Because, in this manner, the Ottoman legacy had both its advantages and disadvantages, the final evaluation of its importance in the political-administrative domain cannot be made without one additional consideration, the performance of the leadership element.

When, during the past and present centuries, people from all walks of life have spoken caustically of "Balkan conditions," and "Balkanization," they have been referring not so much to the economic conditions in Southeastern Europe as to the manner in which the leaders there have performed their duties. In this respect there was no difference between Romania governed by its traditional upper-class leaders and the other states whose statesmen and bureaucrats emerged from the Ottoman-created leadership group. It was not the lack of political and administrative training, as had been often assumed, that forced the leaders of the Balkan states to act in the manner that earned them the scorn of the rest of Europe. It was the Ottoman legacy and training that was reflected in their actions. This aspect of the Ottoman past was the most damaging of all the legacies bequeathed to the people of Southeastern Europe by their former masters.

It is ironic that the Ottoman Empire, the most strictly and thoroughly organized state imaginable, should have spawned others in which chaotic conditions prevailed. It is sad to contemplate that the successors of the professional Ottomans, a dedicated, hard-working, and often selfless group of people, should have been politicians and administrators known for their laziness, selfishness, and venality. It is painful to recognize that a state in which law was so important that the *millet* system was developed to make certain that everybody's life was strictly regulated by a given set of laws was replaced by others in which laws were honored more in their breach than in their enforcement. Yet these were the characteristics of public life that were understood when "Balkan conditions" were mentioned.

There can be no doubt that Southeastern Europe became "Balkanized" under Ottoman rule. The process began early, in the centuries during which Ottoman administration was exemplary. While members of the *millets* lived side by side and were not subordinated to the Muslim population, and while the relatively lenient treatment of the various communal groups was exemplary for its time, there was, nevertheless, a clear difference between Muslim and *zimmi* and professional Ottoman and *reaya*. The people of Southeastern Europe were both *zimmi* and *reaya*, and, therefore, suffered from many disadvantages, which might have been relatively minor but were sufficient in number to encourage people to attempt to circumvent them. Dissimulation, evasive tactics, and white lies became part of daily life.

The need to act evasively, if not dishonestly, became a necessity when the well-organized and governed Ottoman state was transformed into the chaotic and corrupt polity described in Part IV of this volume. For something like two hundred years economic and even physical survival depended on the ability of the people and especially their leaders to outwit the authorities. It was the most corrupt, ruthless, selfish lawbreaker among the bureaucrats who prospered the most, and it was this type of "politician" who served as an example for those who replaced the Ottoman functionaries. Unfortunately, it was the "system" introduced by the unscrupulous office-holders of the latter Ottoman periods and not the earlier well-functioning system, that became the political-administrative legacy of the long years of foreign rule, and it was this nefarious inheritance that became infamous under the label "Balkan conditions."

These conditions not only meant the continuation of misrule, although now by "Christian *paşas*," but also made Southeastern Europe truly backward compared to the rest of the continent in the nineteenth century. The West and even the Hungarian lands of the Habsburgs and Russia were undergoing rapid changes and progress, industrialization and urbanization, agricultural innovation, and drastic changes in the educational establishment. Only the ex-Ottoman lands, the "Balkans," continued to live in the past because it suited an elite that put its selfish aims above all other considerations. Because this elite, its values, and methods of rule were a continuation of what the Ottomans had to tolerate toward the end of their rule in Eastern Europe, the Ottoman political legacy must be considered the greatest problem faced by peoples who, once again, had become masters of their own destiny.

Bibliographic Essay

1. INTRODUCTION

UNTIL fairly recently historians of those Southeast European people who lived, for longer or shorter periods, under Ottoman rule have evaluated these centuries of foreign domination in a uniformly negative and often hostile manner. They have pointed out that their people were cut off from the rest of Europe and from the important developments that occurred there and were also prevented from expressing themselves and from developing their own civilizations and institutions. When describing the centuries during which the Ottoman system functioned well, these scholars have stressed the strict enforcement of regulations that favored the conquerors and exploited the native population, and when dealing with the later centuries they have stressed the lawlessness and arbitrariness of local satraps. Such an approach was quite understandable on the part of historians of newly liberated nations and new states during the nineteenth and early twentieth centuries. These men were under the influence of recently gained freedom and virulent nationalism and had a psychological need to justify centuries of national impotence and the far from satisfactory developments within the newly independent nation-states, which were frequently attributed to the baneful Ottoman heritage.

The historiography of the interwar period in these countries was still nationalistic and rather narrow in focus. Its emphasis was on political history at the expense of social, economic, and demographic analysis. The Ottoman period, during which the native populations' political activities were practically nonexistent, was either passed over by the political historian because "nothing happened" or evaluated negatively because the people had had no experience in government under the Ottomans to prepare them for liberation.

Since the end of the Second World War, and especially since the middle of the 1950s, the situation has changed. The historians of Southeastern Europe have begun to utilize their archives much more extensively than was the case in earlier periods, and they have moved away from the emphasis on political history. The result has been much more scholarly and objective works, which have shed new light on the Ottoman period. The Ottomans are still considered to have brought mainly disaster to the people of Southeastern Europe, but this evaluation is now based on the study of the records and events and is not ascribed to the planned, inhuman, willfully destructive behavior of barbaric Asiatic hordes.

When the Ottomans passed from the chronicler to the historian stage they wrote, as did the historians of all other empires, mainly from a centralistic point of view. Events that occurred in the capital and elsewhere were all evaluated from the point of view of the central authorities. The first Turkish historians, after the establishment of the republic, were possibly even more nationalistic and political in their approach than were those of Southeastern Europe. The transformation of the Ottoman Empire—which was never a nation-state—into nationalist Turkey, the loss of the empire, and the metamorphosis of an Islamic into a laic state produced a trauma that had to be overcome by self-justification explaining some of the excesses of early Turkish historiography. Toward the end of the interwar period changes became visible, and since 1945 much good work has been done by Turkish scholars.

Some of the early western studies were excellent and are still useful. This period was followed by one during which those who wrote had no access to Ottoman sources or were linguistically unqualified to use them. Relying on previous studies, on each other, on the work of the Southeast European historians, and on material available in Western European archives in languages they had mastered, these authors produced some solid but very limited works. In the West fully qualified scholars also began to write toward the end of the interwar period, and their number has increased steadily since then.

The works of all these scholars was either monographic and biographic, or, when broader in scope, political and administrative and written from a central, imperial point of view. No general history of the Ottoman Empire has been written from a regional point of view. While this volume is not a detailed history of Southeastern Europe under Ottoman rule, but simply a general survey of life in this part of the empire, an evaluation, in equally general terms, of the main features of Ottoman overlordship and its consequences can, nevertheless, be presented based on the material it contains.

2. PRIMARY SOURCES

THE major collections of documents containing information on Ottoman rule in Southeastern Europe are in national and municipal archives of the region. With the exception of those in Albania and Greece, I have worked in major archives of every country although I visited those in Turkey before beginning work on this volume. While no references to archival material appear in the footnotes, it was the study of documents that formed my views and served as the basis for the general evaluation of Ottoman rule and its effects on the subject people presented in this volume.

The most important archives are the *Baş Vekâlet Arşivi* and the *Top Kapı Sarayı Müzesi ve Arşivi* in Istanbul. Unfortunately a good portion of the millions of documents is still inadequately catalogued making research difficult. Two works give good information on the content of these archives: Midhat Sertoğlu, *Muhteva Bakımından Başvekâlet Arşivi* [Survey of the content of the Başvekâlet Archives] (Ankara, 1955) describes the first mentioned depository, while for the second a catalogue was prepared by Tahsin Öz, *Arşiv Kılavuzu*, 2 vols. (Istanbul, 1938-40).

Next in importance are the Turkish language holdings in Bulgaria. The Romanian scholar, Mihail Guboglu estimated that there are "about one million Ottoman-Turkish documents together with several million printed texts and oriental manuscripts" in Bulgaria.[1] These documents belong to various collections of which those in the *Orientalski Otdel kim Narodnata Biblioteka "Kiril i Metodii"* [the Oriental Section of the Cyril and Methodius National Library] are the most important. By 1966, the most recent date when exact figures are available, 138,399 documents belonging to this section had been properly identified and described.[2] I am certain, given the excellence of Bulgarian Turkologists and the energy with which they work, that by now this number has at least doubled.

In Yugoslavia the largest collection of Turkish materials is that of the *Orijentalni Institut* housed in the *Zemaljski Muzej* [National Museum] in Sarajevo with smaller collections in Dubrovnik, Skopje, and other cities. The Sarajevo collection is well organized and catalogued, and contains a wealth of material of great importance. Together with the *Gazi Husref Bey Arhiv* in the same city, containing mainly material concerning the Bosnian Muslims, the Oriental Institute's collection makes Sarajevo the most important center for Ottoman studies in Yugoslavia. The *Državni Arhives* [National Archives] of the various constituent republics of Yugoslavia have most of the remaining Ottoman material, but none of them has a really important collection.

North of the Danube-Sava line the most important collections of documents are in Romania. These include not only material in Turkish, but

1. Mihail Guboglu, "Les Documents Turcs de la Section Orientale de la Bibliotheque 'V. Kolarov' de Sofia et leur importance pour l'Histoire des Pays Roumains," *Studia et Acta Orientalia* (Bucharest), 3 (1960-61): 93. The entire article is of great help to anyone interested in this library, renamed the *Narodnata Biblioteka "Kiril i Metodii"*, because it describes the organization of the collection and also gives the bibliographies of several important Bulgarian specialists.

2. Elena Savova, ed., *Les Etudes Balkaniques et Sud-est Européennes en Bulgarie; Guide de Documentation* (Sofia: BAN, 1966), p. 40. On pages 36-47 there is information on all Bulgarian archives, several of which contain materials relevant to the Turkish period.

also a much larger number of documents in Romanian dating from the centuries surveyed in this volume. They are housed in the various state archives as well as in those of most major cities. The Turkish material available in Romania amounts to about 225,000 documents and 600 *defters*. For those housed in the State Archives [*Arhivelor Statului din Republica Socialista România*], the Library of the Academy of Sciences [*Bibliotecii Academici R. P. R.*], the Archives of the Academy of Sciences [*Arhivelor Academici R. P. R.*], and Museum for Archeology and History in Bucharest [*Muzeului de Arheologie şi istorie din Bicureşti*], all in the capital city, Mihail Goboglu published a *Catalogul Documentelor Turcesti*, 2 vols. (Bucharest, 1960-65) describing 5,048 documents.[3] Both volumes have excellent indexes and are of great help to scholars.

In Hungary most of the relevant documents are housed in the *Magyar Országos Levéltár* [Hungarian National Archives] in Budapest. Only a relatively small portion of the material is in Turkish with the rest in Hungarian, Latin, and German. A wealth of material dealing with Transylvania is also in Budapest. Organized into various collections, the documents are well catalogued and easily accessible. An excellent description of these collections can be found in Domokos Kosáry, *Bevezetés Magyarország történetének forrásaiba és irodalmába*, [Introduction to the sources and Literature of Hungarian history] 3 vols. (Budapest, 1951-58) and also in the first volume (only one published so far) of a planned five volume expanded study by the same author under the same title that appeared in Budapest in 1970.

Finally, there is much relevant material in a great variety of languages, including Turkish, in the *Haus,- Hof und Staatsarchiv* in Vienna. Collections dealing with the countries of Southeastern Europe can easily be identified with the help of Ludwig Bittner et al., eds., *Gesamtinventar des Wiener Haus,- Hof und Staats-archives*, 5 vols. (Vienna, 1936-40). Much older, but extremely well done and important for the Turkish period is Gustav L. Flügel, *Die arabischen, persischen und türkischen Handschriften der Kaiserlich-Königlichen Bibliothek zu Wien*, 3 vols. (Vienna, 1865-67) dealing with the material in the National Library in Vienna.

Publication of documents contained in the numerous archives of Southeastern Europe was begun in the nineteenth century. While not as systematic and sustained as desirable, a great amount of material is already available in print. The major problem facing those who are interested in these documents is that the collections have been printed in numerous, rather obscure journals. Most of the documents have appeared either as appendixes to monographs or as articles or special issues in an incredible number of periodicals published by the various academies of science, universities, archives, and museums. I am certain that in spite of my interest,

3. The initials R.P.R. were changed to R.S.R. in 1965 when Romania changed its official name from Romanian Peoples Republic to Romanian Socialist Republic.

I am unaware of many important documents already in print somewhere. A simple listing of only the titles of the possible journals to be kept in mind would take up several pages and would not serve the purpose of a bibliographic essay. Thus, I must limit myself to bringing to the reader's attention the fact that in looking for documents in print a great number of journals must be consulted, most of which are not indexed. Even the number of special volumes devoted to the publication of primary materials has by now become too large to permit a full listing. I will list only those that I consider the most important and present them as samples of what is available.

In Bulgaria the publication of *Dokumenti za Bulgarskata Istroriia*, under various editors, has begun. Volumes 3 and 4 contain Turkish materials. Since 1958 another series, *Fontes Historiae Bulgaricae*, is also being published in Sofia. Volumes 4 and 5 of this series are volumes 1 and 2 of *Fontes Turcici Historiae Bulgaricae*, edited by Christo Gandev and Gălăb Gălăbov (Sofia, 1959-60). Gălăbov was also the editor of *Turski izvori za istoriiata na pravoto v bulgarskite zemi* [Turkish sources for the legal history of the Bulgarian lands], (Sofia, 1962). Less specialized but very important is the publication prepared by a team of editors, *Turski izvori za bălgarskata istoriia* [Turkish documents relating to Bulgarian history]. Two other collections are of great interest: Petŭr K. Petrov, ed., *Asimilatorskata politika za turskite zavoevateli: Sbornik ot dokumenti za pomokhamendanchvaniia i poturchvaniia, XV-XIX v.* [Assimilatory policy of the Turkish conquest: Collection of documents concerning conversion to Islam and turkification, 19-20 centuries] (Sofia, 1962), and Nikolai Todorov, ed., *Polozhenieto na bulgarskiia narod pod tursko robstvo. Dokumenti i materiali* [The status of the Bulgarian nation under the Turkish yoke. Documents and materials] (Sofia, 1953).

In Yugoslavia it is the Oriental Institute of Sarajevo that leads in publishing Turkish materials in the very important series *Monumenta turcica historiam Slavorum meridionalium illustrantia*, which began to appear in 1957. Extremely well edited and covering a great variety of documents carefully grouped, the *Monumenta* is a publication of real merit. Scholarly institutions located in other cities also publish Turkish documents. A few examples will show the variety of topics to which Yugoslav scholars have addressed themselves: Hazim Šabanović, ed., *Turski izvori za istorije Beograda* [Turkish sources for the history of Belgrade] (Belgrade, 1964); Dušanka Šopova, ed., *Makedonija vo XVI i XVII vek—Dokumenti od Carigradskite arhivi, 1557-1645* [Macedonia in the 16th and 17th centuries—Documents from the Istanbul Archives, 1557-1645] (Skopje, 1955); Hasan Kalesi, ed., *Najstariji vakufski dokumenti u Jugoslaviji na arapskom jeziku* [The oldest Vakıf documents in Arabic in Yugoslavia] (Priština; 1972).

Romania has three major collections of documents the majority of which were originally in Romanian. The earliest of these retained the name of its original editor, Euxodiu Hurumzaki, ed., *Documente privitoare la istoria Românilor* [Documents relating to the History of the Romanians], 24 vols. (Bucharest, 1876-1962), and is a storehouse of information. Equally valuable is the series that began to appear in 1929, Andrei Veress, ed., *Documente privitoare la istoria Ardealului, Moldovei și Țarii Rominesti* [Documents relating to the history of Transylvania, Moldavia, and Wallachia], 11 vols. (Burcharest, 1929-39). The most ambitious was the venture begun under the over-all editorship of Andrei Oțetea and David Prodan in 1951. So far over sixty volumes of the *Documenta Romaniae Historica* have appeared in Bucharest. Not only is this series broken down into subseries (A for Moldavia, B for Wallachia, and C for Transylvania) but each volume carefully groups documents relating to a selected topic, such as economic history and agriculture, for a specific time period. This collection is the most useful of all and will continue to provide a great amount of information. Smaller collections have also been published. Once again, only a few examples will be cited to illustrate the variety of topics covered: I. C. Filitti, ed., *Lettres et extraits concernant les rélations des Principautés Roumaines avec la France, 1728-1810* (Bucharest, 1915); D. Z. Furnică, ed., *Documente privitoare la comerțul romînesc, 1473-1868* [Documents relating to Romanian trade, 1573-1868] (Bucharest, 1931); and the two collections dealing with Bucharest, Florian Georgescu, Paul I. Cernovodeanu, and Iana C. Panait, eds. *Documente privind istoria orașului București* [Documents concerning the history of the city of Bucharest] (Bucharest, 1960) and Gheorghe Potras, ed., *Documente privitoare la istoria orașului București* [Documents relating to the history of the city of Bucharest] (Bucharest, 1961).

Hungary has published more documents than any other country under study. By 1930 Emma Bartoniek could list 3,109 titles of either source-material catalogues or document publications in her *Magyar Történeti Forráskiadványok* [Publication of sources for Hungarian history] (Budapest, 1930), and much more has been published since that date. The largest collection, for which a number of editors are responsible, is the *Monumenta Hungariae Historica* published in five series. It includes a series dealing with Transylvania in the 1540-1699 period, Sándor Szilágyi, ed., *Monumenta comitiala regni Transylvaniae, 1540-1699*, 21 vols. (Budapest, 1875-92). Publication of this series began as early as 1857, and by now several hundred volumes are available. The publication of Turkish materials also started quite early. Áron Szilády and Sándor Szilágyi were the general editors of *Török-Magyarkorú Történelmi Emlékek* [Historical relics of Turkey's Hungarian period] published in Budapest between 1863 and 1916. The first series of nine volumes contains documents, and the second series of five volumes includes the work of relevant Turkish chroniclers. Lajos Thallóczy, János Krecsmárik and Gyula Szekfű, eds.

brought out in the same city in 1914 the Hungarian translation of many Turkish documents in their *Török-Magyar Oklevéltár, 1533-1789* [Turkish-Hungarian Archive, 1533-1789], but only the first volume of a projected multivolume work, Sándor Takáts, Ferenc Eckhart, Gyula Szekfű, eds., *A budai basák magyarnyelvű levelezése, 1553-1589* [The correspondence in Hungarian of the Paşas of Buda, 1553-89] (Budapest, 1915) has appeared. Andrew Veress, already mentioned previously in connection with Romanian publications, brought out his *Fontes Rerum Transylvanicarum*, 5 vols. (Budapest, 1911-21). An extremely valuable volume is Lajos Fekete and Gyula Káldy-Nagy, eds., *Rechnungsbücher Türkischer Finanzstellen in Buda (Ofen), 1550-1580* (Budapest, 1962) giving the original texts and excellent explanations. As indicated, the published material is voluminous and the cited titles only indicate the magnitude of the enterprise. Other publications include smaller collections, archives of counties, cities, families, as well as memoirs and travelers' notes.

There are several document collections dealing with specific people who have been mentioned in this volume. They are not of primary importance for those interested in the main topic of this study and for that reason only three examples will be given. Károly Szabó, ed., *Székely Oklevéltár, 1211-1750* [Székely Archives 1211-1750], 7 vols. (Kolozsvár, 1872-98) contains important material for the events touching on the Székelys. The fourth volume of Franz Zimmermann, Carl Werner, Friedrich Müller, and Gustav Gündisch, eds., *Urkundenbuch zur Geschichte der Deutschen in Siebenbürgen*, 4 vols. (Nagyszeben/Sibiu, 1891-1937) does the same for the Transylvanian Germans.

Documents published outside the region under study include: Franz Babinger, *Das Archiv des Bosniaken Osman Pascha* (Berlin, 1931); Gălăb Gălăbov and Herbert W. Duda, eds., *Die Protokollarbücher des Kadiamtes Sofia* (München, 1960), I. Hudiţa, ed., *Repertoire des documents concernants les négotiations diplomatiques entre la France et la Transylvanie au XVIIe siècle* (Paris, 1926); and Gustav Bayerle, ed., *Ottoman Diplomacy in Hungary; Letters from the Pashas of Buda, 1590-1593* (Bloomington, 1972). Very important is Franz Babinger, ed., *Sultanische Urkunden zur Geschichte der osmanischen Wirtschaft und Staatsverwaltung am Ausgang der Herrschaft Mehmeds II, des Eroberers* (München, 1956), which is supplemented by Nicoară Beldiceanu, ed., *Les actes des premiers sultans conservés dans les manuscrits turcs de la Bibliothèque Nationale à Paris. I- Actes de Mehmed II et de Bayezid II du MS fond turc ancien 39* (Paris, 1960). The diffusion of Turkish manuscripts is well illustrated by M. J. Blašković, ed., *Arabische, türkische und persische Handschriften der Universitätsbibliothek in Bratislava* (Bratislava, 1961).

These few titles must serve as indications of the amount of documents and other primary sources already available in print. Although it is not always possible or easy to work in the archives themselves, the interested scholar can do much research on the basis of material printed in these publications and in the numerous journals.

3. GENERAL WORKS AND BIBLIOGRAPHIES

THE period of Turkish rule is covered by the national histories of the individual peoples. The space devoted to the Ottoman centuries may be rather lengthy, as in volumes 3 and 4 of Bálint Hóman's and Gyula Szekfü's *Magyar Történet* [Hungarian history] 1st ed. (Budapest, 1928), and in volumes 2 and 3 of the collective work *Istoria Rominiei* [History of the Romanians], 4 vols. (Bucharest, 1960) edited by a committee, or in the first four volumes of *Osmanlı Tarihi* [Ottoman history], 8 vols. (Ankara, 1960) which were written by Ismail Hakkı Uzunçarşılı and contain very useful narrative, copious footnotes, and bibliographies. In each of these works, however, the story is told entirely from the point of view of the authors' country.

Until Uzunçarşılı, and beginning with the fifth volume Enver Ziya Karal, began to write *Osmanlı Tarihi*, the best Ottoman histories were the old works of Joseph Hammer-Purgstall, *Geschichte des osmanischen Reiches*, 10 vols. (Pest, 1827-35), J. W. Zinkeisen, *Geschichte des osmanischen Reiches in Europa*, 7 vols. (Gotha-Hamburg, 1840-63), and Nicolae Iorga, *Geschichte des osmanischen Reiches*, 5 vols. (Gotha, 1908-13). Of these three Hammer-Purgstall's is the most detailed and scholarly, Zinkeisen's the most relevant to the subject of this volume, and Iorga's the most carelessly written but full with excellent insights and interpretations. Uzunçarşılı worked with the Turkish archives, but unfortunately he is somewhat careless on details and often even contradicts himself.

For the average reader, especially for one not too familiar with the Ottoman Empire, Halil Inalcık, *The Ottoman Empire; The Classical Age, 1300-1600*, trans. Norman Itzkowitz and Colim Imber (New York and Washington, 1973) is the recommended work. Of other Ottoman histories, including E. Creasy, *History of Ottoman Turks from the Beginning of the Empire to the Present Time*, 2 vols. (London, 1854-56), George J. Eversely, *The Turkish Empire, its Growth and Decay* (London, 1917), A. de la Jonquière, *Histoire de l'empire ottoman*, rev. ed., 2 vols. (Paris, 1914), Harry Luke, *The Old Turkey and the New; From Byzantium to Ankara*, rev. ed. (London, 1955), the following three are the most useful without being distinguished: William Miller, *The Ottoman Empire and its Successors* (Cambridge, 1927), Charles Eliot, *Turkey in Europe*, new ed. (London, 1908), and Léon Lamouche, *Histoire de la Turquie* (Paris, 1934). There is a great need for a comprehensive one- or two-volume Ottoman history in one of the major western languages.

The institutions of the Ottoman central government were well presented recently by Inalcık in his above mentioned volume, but there are several other excellent studies on this topic. The observations of Ogier

Ghiselin de Busbecq, contained in his letters written from the Ottoman Empire between 1555 and 1562, have been edited by C. T. Forster and F. H. B. Daniell in *The Life and Letters of Ogier Ghiselin de Busbecq* (London, 1881), which was reissued by the Clarendon Press in 1968. The earliest work of note on this subject was again written by Joseph Hammer-Purgstall, *Staatsverfassung und Staatsverwaltung des Osmanischen Reiches*, 2 vols. (Vienna, 1815) and is still very useful. To these can be added two outstanding and indispensible modern works: A. D. Alderson, *The Structure of the Ottoman Dynasty* (London, 1956) and H. A. R. Gibb and Harold Bowen, *Islamic Society and the West*, one volume in two (London, New York, and Toronto, 1957). Uzunçarşılı's *Osmanlı Devleti Teskilatına Medhal* [Introduction to the administration of the Ottoman state] (Istanbul, 1941) presents the advantages and weaknesses noted in connection with his previously cited work.

Turning from Turkish institutions to those of the *zimmi*, we find a rather unsatisfactory situation. Although the literature on the Orthodox chuch is extensive, most histories of this church concentrate on the patriarchate and on the Russian church. There are few specialized works dealing with Orthodoxy in the Balkans under Ottoman rule. Of those general church histories that pay attention to the Balkans, B. J. Kidd, *The Churches of Eastern Christiandom from A.D. 451 to the Present Time* (London, 1927) and A. K. Fortescue, *The Orthodox Eastern Church* (London, 1927) are the most satisfactory. Although very badly translated, N. J. Pantazopoulos's *Church and Law in the Balkan Peninsula during the Ottoman Rule* (Salonika, 1967) is interesting. The two most important relevant monographs are T. H. Papadopoullos, *Studies and Documents relating to the History of the Greek Church and People under Turkish Domination* (Brussels, 1952), which is somewhat biased against the Slavs, and the more specialized work by H. Scheel, *Die Staatsrechtliche Stellung der ökumenischen Kirchenfürsten in der alten Türkei. Ein Beitrag zur Geschichte der Türkischen Verfassung und Verwaltung* (Berlin, 1942). The best works dealing with aspects of the Orthodox problem under Turkish rule are László Hadrovics, *Le peuple serbe et son église sous la domination turque* (Paris, 1947) and Ivan Snegarov, *Istoriia na Ochridskata arkhiepiskopiia patriarshiia ot padaneto i pod turtsite do neinoto unishtozhenie (1394-1787 g.)* [History of the Ohrid Archdiocese Patriarchate from its fall to the Turks to its abolition (1394-1787)], (Sofia, 1931), Steven Runciman, *The Great Church in Captivity* (Cambridge: Cambridge University Press, 1968), and Mirko Mirkovič, *Pravni položej i karakter srpske crkve pod turskom vlašću, 1459-1766* [The legal position and character of the Serbian church under Ottoman rule, 1459-1766] (Belgrade, 1965).

The earliest and still valuable study of Jews in the Ottoman Empire is Moise Franco, *Essai sur l'histoire des Israélites de l'Empire Ottoman depuis les origines jusqu'à nos jours* (Paris, 1897). Very comprehensive but somewhat carelessly written is Solomon A. Rosanes, *Divre yeme Yisrael bo-Togarma* [History of the Jews in Turkey], 6 vols. (Sofia, 1934-44; Jerusalem, 1945). Isaac S. Emmanuel and Abraham Galante wrote numerous works on the Jews under Ottoman rule, and all their writings are recommended. The former published, among other works, *Histoire des Israélites de Salonique* (Paris, 1935) and the latter *Histoire des Juifs d'Istanbul* (Istanbul, 1941).

In addition to the works of Zinkeisen, Miller, and Eliot there are several others than can be considered "regional histories." F. W. Ebeling, *Geschichte des Osmanischen Reiches in Europa* (Leipzig, 1854) was one of the earliest, followed by: K. Roth, *Geschichte der christlichen Balkanstaaten, Bulgarian, Serbien, Rumanien, Montenegro, Griechenland* (Leipzig, 1907); Ferdinand Schevill, *History of the Balkan Peninsula from Earliest Times to the Present Day* (New York, 1922); Nicolae Iorga, *Histoire des états balkaniques jusque'à 1924* (Paris, 1924), of which the first four chapters are relevant; Jacques Ancel, *L'unité de la civilization balkanique* (Paris, 1927); and Georg Stadtmüller, *Geschichte Südosteuropas* (München, 1950). All these studies are dated with the exception of Stadtmüller, who includes Hungary in his work, but sadly neglects the Ottoman period. Fortunately, there are two works that can be considered classics: Ferdinand Braudel, *La Méditerranée et le monde méditerranean à la époque de Philippe II*, 2 vols. (Paris, 1949) and Leften S. Stavrianos, *The Balkans since 1453* (New York, 1958). Braudel's famous volumes cover the entire Mediterranean basin. It is a highly imaginative and original piece of work based on thorough scholarship. His general ideas and theories as well as his findings relating to the Ottoman world are of great value. Stavrianos's volume is *the* regional history for the Balkans. Well researched, organized, and written, it is by far the best study in print. Good basic bibliographies enhance the value of this study.

There are many other categories that could be listed, including travelers' accounts, biographies, and topical histories, but limitations of space preclude inclusion of them all, and the mention of a few would unjustifiably neglect the others. It would be more useful to list some of the lesser known but important bibliographies that would lead the interested scholar to this material.

Gerhard Teich, "Bibliographie der Bibliographien Südosteuropas," *Wirtschaftswissenschaftliche Süd-osteuropa Forschung* (1963), pp. 177-213 gives a rather complete listing of the most relevant bibliographies. Léon Savadjian, *Bibliographie balkanique, 1920-1938*, 8 vols. (Paris, 1931-39) is also useful and comprehensive. For earlier writings J. D. Pearson and Julia F. Ashton, eds., *Index Islamicus, 1906-1955* (Cambridge, 1958) and J. D. Pearson, ed., *Index Islamicus Supplement, 1956-1960* (Cambridge, 1962) are helpful. Numerous bibliographies of this type are easily found in most libraries. More important for detailed work are the special bibliographies prepared by scholars of the Southwest European countries.

The Romanians have undertaken the most ambitious and comprehensive bibliographies. Under the editorship of Ioan Lupu, Nestor Camariano, and Ovidiu Papadima the publication of *Bibliografia Analitica a Periodicelor Româeşti* was begun in 1967. Up to the present six volumes have appeared covering the years 1790-1858. The thoroughness of this well-organized work leaves nothing to be desired, and it is the basic reference for Romanian periodical publications. An equally impressive undertaking got under way in Bucharest in 1970 when the first volume of *Bibliographia Historica Romaniae* covering the years 1944-69 appeared under the editor-ship of Ştefan Pascu, Ioachim Crǎciun, and Bujor Surdu. While this first volume was only a selective bibliography, volume 2, the first of several dealing with nineteenth-century publications, which appeared in 1972 under the editorship of Cornelia Bodea, is already comprehensive. Well organized and fully indexed with subtitles in French, this is an extremely important volume.

The most useful of the contemporary Bulgarian bibliographies are the supplements to volumes 2 and 5 of *Études Historiques, La Science Historique Bulgare, 1960-1964, Bibliographie* (Sofia, 1965) and *La Science Historique Bulgare, 1965-1969, Bibliographie* (Sofia, 1970). The first of these volumes was edited by Lilija Kirkova and Emilija Kostova-Jankova, and the second by Lilija Kirkova. In both the original titles are transliterated in Latin script and a French translation is given for each entry.

Under the editorship of Jorjo Tadić *Ten Years of Yugoslav Historiography, 1945-1955* was published in Belgrade in 1955. This long bibliographic essay is organized in a topical-chronological manner which makes it somewhat difficult to use. Titles are given in English with the original also given in the Latin script. The same editor was responsible for the next volume published in French in Belgrade in 1965, *Historiographie Yougoslave, 1955-1965*. The same essay form was used, but the titles are easier to find because they are listed in footnotes on the bottom of each page and are not placed in the text itself.

Bibliographie d'oeuvres choisies de la science historique hongroises, 1945-1959 (no editor given) was published in Budapest in 1960. Organized chronologically with topical subdivisions, the original titles, their French translations and a short explanation for each entry in French is given for 2,059 titles. Under the editorship of M. Sz. Gyivicsán, L. Makkai, et al., *Bibliographie d'oeuvres choisies de la science historique hongroise, 1964-1968* appeared in 1970 as volume 2 of *Études Historiques.* The 2,309 titles are organized in exactly the same manner as the first volume.

In 1966 a similar volume was published in Athens under the editorship of C. Th. Dimaras, *Quinze ans de bibliographie historique en Grèce, 1950-*

1964 avec une annexe pour 1965. The organization of this volume is topical with chronological subdivisions for each topic. The titles are given in Greek with a French translation for each of the 5,500 entries. It is hoped that more bibliographies of this kind will soon appear so that they may be presented either at the meetings of the Association Internationale d'-Études du Sud-Est Européen (A.I.E.S.E.E.) that will meet in 1974 or of the Comité International des Sciences Historique (C.I.S.H.) meeting in 1975.

A publication of great value is one that the Institute for Balkan Studies of the Bulgarian Academy of Sciences began to issue yearly beginning with 1966 under the editorship of N. Todorov, K. Georgiev and V. Traikov, *Bibliographie d'Études Balkaniques.* These volumes cover all publications that refer to the Balkan Peninsula in all disciplines published anywhere. The indexes are also of great help; in addition to one giving the names of the authors, another lists subject matter and geographic names, and a third enumerates all the periodicals that were consulted. This section ends with a listing of collective works and newly published bibliographies. These appendixes alone would make this Bulgarian publication indispensable. The above bibliography used in conjunction with the four-volume *Südosteuropa-Bibliographie* (München, 1943-73), each volume of which is in two parts, covers everything of importance in the Southeast European field. The first volume of the German publication was edited by Fritz Valjavec and the subsequent volumes by Gertrud Krallert-Sattler. Recently, a very important specialized bibliography appeared in the Netherlands: Hans Jürgen and Jutta Kornrumpf, eds., *Osmanische Bibliographie, mit besonderer Berücksichtigung der Türkei in Europa* (Leiden, 1973). This thick volume is somewhat difficult to use because it is organized both topically and by author but has no index. Unless the scholar is interested in a specific topic that corresponds to one of the divisions or subdivisions of the volume, it is rather difficult to find titles.

I will end this section with a short reference to some collective works, namely, those issued for the congresses of the A.I.E.S.E.E. and C.I.S.H. The titles are somewhat confusing, but these volumes always contain important articles and often include bibliographies dealing with the Turkish period of Southeastern Europe. For the C.I.S.H. congresses of 1955, 1960, and 1970 the Hungarians issued special collections under the title *Études Historiques,* and for 1965 under the title *Nouvelles Études Historiques.* Some confusion arises because the five volumes published by the Bulgarians for the 1960, 1965, and 1970 congresses also have the title *Études Historiques,* and the four Romanian volumes for 1955, 1960, 1965, and 1970 are entitled *Nouvelles Études d'Histoire.*

Although the above volumes contain important studies, they are not as significant for students of the Ottoman period as are the *Actes du Premier*

Congrès International des Etudes Balkaniques et Sud-est Européennes (Sofia, 1967-70). In volumes 3 and 4 some 500 pages are devoted to historical studies of the fifteenth through the eighteenth centuries and include some studies of major importance. Scholars working in other disciplines have also contributed. This collection must be consulted by anyone studying Ottoman rule in Europe. The materials presented at the second congress are at present being edited for publication.

No summary of general works on our subject would be complete without mentioning four invaluable studies: M. Z. Pakalın, *Osmanlı Tarih Deyimleri ve Terimleri Sözlöğü*, [Dictionary of terms and expressions of Ottoman history], 3 vols. (Ankara, 1946-55); the old edition of the *Encyclopaedia of Islam*, four volumes in eight (Leiden-London, 1913-29); the new edition of the *Encyclopaedia* (Leiden and London, 1960-), which goes to the beginning of Ka in 66 fascicles; and finally, *Islam Ansiklopedisi* (Istanbul, 1940-) which had reached words beginning with Tug by 1974 in 125 fascicles.

4. JOURNALS

BIBLIOGRAPHIC essays usually do not include a section on journals. However, I felt that a few words must be said about them in this essay because they contain so much important material and because the majority are obscure to the kind of audience to which this volume is directed.

The major American and the Western European historical journals are of relatively little use to the scholar interested in the Ottoman period of Southeastern Europe, although occasionally, an important article does appear in these publications. This is quite understandable because these journals are devoted primarily to the national histories of the countries in which they are published. Only slightly more important are specialized journals such as the *Slavic Review*, the *East European Quarterly*, *Canadian Slavic Studies*, *Slavic and East-European Studies*, *Slavonic and East European Review*, *Jahrbücher für Geschichte Osteuropas*, *Revue des Études Slaves*, and several others devoted to the Slavic world. These specialized journals cover the entire historical scope of the region, including Russia/Soviet Union. Infrequently, they include articles dealing with the problems of Ottoman history. The same is true of the various journals devoted to Muslim and Oriental studies. Nevertheless, these publications must be checked carefully because they contain relevant articles more often than do the major historical journals. The most important of these journals is the *International Journal of Middle East Studies*.

Consequently, a familiarity with at least the most important journals published in the countries that were for some time under Ottoman rule becomes absolutely necessary. Up to 1965 the most important Albanian publication was *Universiteti Shtetëror Buletin* [The Bulletin of the State

University], but since that date the more specialized *Studime historikë* [Historical studies] has become more important. Greece has no really specialized major historical journal. Most of the relevant material appears in the history section of the *Praktika tis Akademias Athenon* [Proceedings of the Athenian Academy] or in *Deltion tis Istorikis kai Ethnologikis Etairias tis Elladis* [Bulletin of the Greek Historical and Ethnographic Society]. Of the Greek journals published in western languages *Balkan Studies* is the most important.

There are also relatively few publications of importance in Turkey. The most important is *Belleten* [Bulletin] of the Turkish Historical Society, which in 1937 replaced the *Türk tarih encümeni mecmuasi* [Journal of the Turkish Historical Committee]. The older journal is also worth close attention. To these must be added *Istanbul Üniversitesi Iktisat fakültesi mecmuasi* and *Istanbul Üniversitesi Edebiyat fakültesi tarih dergisi* [Journal of the Economic Faculty of Istanbul University and Historical Journal of the Literature Faculty of Istanbul University], as well as *Ankara Üniversitesi Dil ve Tarih-Coğrafya fakültesi dergisi* [Journal of the Language, History, and Geography Faculty of Ankara University] in which numerous very important articles were published. Finally, relevant articles can also be found in *Vakıflar Dergisi* [Journal of the *Vakıfs,*] which publishes both documents and articles, while *Belgeler* [Documents] of Ankara is devoted only to documents. Recently, a new journal, the *Archivum Ottomanicum* has begun to appear. This is the only one in a western language devoted entirely to Ottomans history. Unfortunately, no really scholarly journal in a western language is published in Turkey.

As we move from these three countries to the other four of our area, the number of important publications increases. Bulgaria has several historical journals of which *Istoricheski Pregled* [Historical review], *Izvestiia na Instituta za Istoriia pri BAN* [Journal of the Bulgarian Academy of Sciences' Historical Institute] are the most important. The very valuable *Études Balkaniques* has been published in Sofia since 1964, and since 1973 the *Bulgarian Historical Review* has been published in English and French. A few important articles are published in the other Bulgarian journals.

Romania's major historical journal is *Studii: Revistă de istorie* [Studies: Review of history]. The two other historical publications that must be kept in mind are the *Anuarul Institutlui de Istorie din Cluj* [The yearbook of the Historical Institute in Cluj] and *Studii şi cercetăi ştiinţifice. Sectia Istorie, Iaşi* [Scientific studies and investigations. Historical Section, Iaşi]. *Studie et acta orientalia* is more specialized and deals to a large extent with Ottoman material. In western languages there appears the *Revue roumaine d'histoire*, which often publishes material from the Romanian language journals. More specialized, as its title indicates, is the

Revue des études sud-est européennes, which has at least one relevant article in each issue. Since 1963 the *Bulletin de l'Association Internationale des Études du Sud-Est Européen* has also been published in Bucharest. It publishes articles in addition to news of the association.

In Yugoslavia every constituent republic has a historical periodical. *Istorija* is published in Skopje; *Istorijski Zapisi* [Historical Notes], in Titograd; *Godišnjak društva istoričara Bosne i Hercegovine* [Yearbook of the Historical Society of Bosnia-Hercegovina] and the *Glasnik Zemaljskog muzeja u Sarajevu* [Messenger of the National Museum in Sarajevo], appear in Sarajevo, *Zbornik Filozofske fakultete* [Collection of the Philosophical Faculty], in Ljubljana. The two largest republics publish the oldest journals: *Istorijski časopis* [Historical Review] in Beograd, and *Historijski pregled* [Historical Review] in Zagreb. There are numerous *Zborniks* and *Radovi* published by the various universities and academies. Of the more specialized journals the *Prilozi za orijentalnu filologiju i istoriju* [Contributions to Oriental Philology and History] of Sarajevo is the most relevant. Given the importance of Dubrovnik, the *Anali Historijskog instituta JAZU i Dubrovniku* [The Annals of the Historical Institute of the Yugoslav Academy of Sciences and Arts in Dubrovnik] must also be consulted regularly. Since 1970 an excellent publication in western languages, *Balcanica,* has appeared in Beograd.

Like Yugoslavia, Hungary has a great number of historical publications. Of these *Századok* [Centuries] and *Történelmi Szemle* [Historical Review] are the most important. Although their focus is on more recent centuries, articles dealing with the Ottoman period of Hungary also appear in these journals. In addition to these major journals the following are also important: *Annales Universitatis Scientiarum Budapestinensis de Rolando Eötvös nominatae, Sectio Historica, Acta Universitatis Debreceniensis,* and *Acta Universitatis Szegediensis.* More specialized is the very important *Acta Orientalia Academiae Scientiarum Hungaricae.* Of the two publications in western languages, the *Acta Historica* and the *New Hungarian Quarterly,* the latter is not strictly speaking a scholarly publication because it is written for the general educated public. Both do occasionally contain excellent articles dealing with the Ottoman period.

This listing of relevant journals is far from complete. I do not wish to extend it by listing Russian, Italian, and other periodicals, but will only add five more titles because of their special import. These are the Dutch publication *Journal of the Economic and Social History of the Orient,* the *Archiv Orientálni* of Prague, the Polish publications *Folia Orientalia* of Kraków and *Przegląd Orientalistyczny* [Oriental Review] of Warszawa, and *Naroda Asii i Afriki* of Moscow. Those who wish to go beyond this basic but admittedly arbitrary selection should turn to the periodical indexes of the cited bibliographies.

5. References to a few selected authors and titles

A listing of monographs and articles that would be comparable to even the above, sketchy selection of journals and periodicals would be impossible because it would exclude numerous excellent scholars. Instead of an arbitrary selection from several thousand titles, what follows is a listing of scholars whose work has profited me the most. This approach also omits more notable authors than it includes, and to them I offer my sincere apologies.

Of the Turkish authors Ömer Lutfi Barkan must be mentioned first. It was he who began to use Turkish census figures and similar data systematically to study demographic and economic developments in the Ottoman Empire. As far as I know, he published only one book, *XV. ve XVI. asırlarda osmanlı imperatorluğunda zirai ekonominin hukuki ve mali esasları* [Judicial and financial principles of the agricultural economy of the Ottoman Empire in the fifteenth and sixteenth centuries], (Istanbul, 1943), but the number of important articles he has published makes him the most important scholar in his field. Included among his articles are: "XV asır sonunda bazı büyük şehirlerde eşya ve yiyecek fiyatlarının tesbit ve teftişi hususlarının tanzim eden kanunlar" [Laws regulating the fixing and inspecting particulars of prices for goods and food in some large cities at the end of the fifteenth century] in *Tarih Vesikaları* [Historical Documents] (1941); "1079-80 (1669-70) mal yılına ait bir osmanlı büçesi" [An Ottoman budget concerning the fiscal year 1079-80 (1669-70)] and "1070-71 (1660-61) tarihli osmanlı bütçesi ve bir mukayese" [The dated Ottoman budget of 1070-71 (1660-1661) and a comparison] in the 1955-56 issue of the *Istanbul Üniversitesi Iktisat fakültesi mecmuasi*. Barkan published "Edirne Askerı Kassamına âit Tereke Defterleri (1545-1659)" [The inheritance register of the Edirne military Kassam (fixer of inheritance shares), 1545-1659] in *Belgeler* (1968), and "894 (1488/1489) yılı Cizyesinin Tahsilâtına âit Muhasebe Bilânçoları" [The book-keeping balances of the *cizye* tax for the year 894 (1488-89)] in 1964. In volume 14 of *Sosyal siyaset Konferansları* (Istanbul, 1963) can be found his "XVI-XVIII asırlarda Türkiyede Inşâat Işçilerinin Hukukı-Durumu" [The legal position of construction workers in Turkey in the sixteenth-eighteenth centuries]. This list could be extended. The bibliographic work of the Kornrumpf cited earlier lists thirty-one of his studies and is still not complete. Therefore, only the titles of his three most important non-Turkish studies will be added to this list: "Quelques observations sur l'organisation économique et sociale des villes ottomanes des XVIe et XVIIe siècles" in *Receuils Société Jean Bodin, VII.* (Bruxelles, 1956); and "Essai sur les données statistiques des registres de recensement dans l'Empire Ottoman aux XVe et XVIe siècles" in *Journal of Economic and Social History of the Orient* (1957); and "Research on the Ottoman Fiscal Surveys" in Michael E.

Cook, ed., *Studies in the Economic History of the Near East* (London: 1970).

Halil Inalcık is the leading Turkish historian of the Balkans today. His incredible output of books, articles, and contributions to encyclopaedias runs around a hundred titles. Everything Inalcık has written is of value, the scope of his interest is wide-ranging. His provocative study "XV asırda Rumelide hıristiyan sipahiler ve menşeleri; Stefan Duşandan Osmanlı Imparatorluğunda" [Christian *Sipahis* in Rumelia in the fifteenth century and their origins; from Steven Dušan to the Ottoman Empire] in *Fuad Köprülü Armağanı* (Studies presented to Fuad Köprülü) deals with the beginning of Ottoman rule, while his key note paper given at the second international congress of A.I.E.S.E.E. in Athens, which was printed as a separatum in 1970, *The Ottoman Decline and its Effects upon the Reaya* deals with the end of Ottoman rule. There is hardly any topic in the periods falling between those discussed in these two studies on which Inalcık has not written.

Uzunçarşılı, who has already appeared in this bibliographic essay, is another amazingly prolific Turkish historian for whose name one looks in all bibliographies. Of great interest is his *Osmanlı devleti teşkilâtindan: Kapıkulu ocakları* [From the organization of the Ottoman state: The Corps of the Slaves of the Porte], 2 vols. (Ankara, 1943-44), which deals with the extremely important problem of recruiting and organizing slave manpower. To leave Turkish scholars aside for a moment, the same topic is discussed in Baslike D. Papoulia's very interesting *Ursprung and Wesen der "Knabenlese" im Osmanischen Reich* (München, 1963). Two works that deal with the most famous of the *devşirme* recruits from different points of view should be mentioned in this connection: Ahmed Refik, *Sokollu (911-987)* (Istanbul, 1924) sees the great grand vezir very differently from the Yugoslav biographer, Radovan Samardžić, *Mehmed Paša Sokolović* (Beograd, 1967).

Among the Bulgarians Nikolai Todorov and Bistra Cvetkova hold the same position as Barkan and Inalcık do among the Turks, from the point of view of both the quality and quantity of their writings. The bibliography of Todorov's works for the period 1951-64 includes 107 titles, and it should be remembered that it was *after* 1964 that he published most of his major works. Between 1964-69 alone he published 34 additional titles. Although his range takes him from archival source publications to popular articles and from one historical period to another, his main interest is the Ottoman period and his major specialization is economic and urban history. He is somewhat of an economic determinist, but his works are indispensible for anybody studying the Ottoman rule in Southeastern Europe. Given the number of his articles and books, it is almost impossible to pick the best or most representative among them. Clearly those titles cited in the footnotes and in this essay were used more extensively in writing this volume than some of his other publications.

Bistra Cvetkova's interest is narrower than Todorov's; she is an Otto-manist and one of the best in the world today. The bibliography of her works is also incredibly extensive and includes documentary publications, monographs, long essays published in installments, as well as numerous shorter articles. She deals with administration, the urban and rural econ-omy, and practically all other aspects of Ottoman rule, but her major in-terest is her own people and their life under that rule. Once again, without citing any titles apart from those already mentioned, I can recommend her studies without reservation.

The works of the Bulgarian authors Gălăb Gălăbov and Vera Mutaf-chieva are also solid and useful, but do not rank with those of Todorov or Cvetkova. I have always found the work of Ivan Snegarov of great interest because of his concentration on cultural and religious history. His own countrymen have also found his contributions valuable enough to publish "Nauchnoto delo na akademik Ivan Snegarov" [The Scientific Work of Academician Ivan Snegarev] by D. Angelov and J. Nikolov in *Izvestiia na Instituta za Istoriia pri BAN* (1964). He was eighty years old at that time. A bibliography of his most important works was published in the same issue of this journal. One title will serve as an example of his contribu-tions: *Turskoto vladichestvo prechka za kulturnoto razvitie na bulgarskia narod i drugite balkanski narodi* [The obstacle of Turkish rule for the cul-tural life of the Bulgarian nation and other Balkan nations] (Sofia, 1958).

It is impossible to list all Bulgarian historians whose work is of value. A few additional examples will have to satisfy the reader. Among Khristo Gandev's works is *Faktori na bulgarskoto Vzrazhdene, 1600-1830 g.* [Factors (causes) of the Bulgarian renaissance in the years 1600-1830] (Sofia, 1943) which was picked as an example of his writing because it too refers to cultural history. Those interested in a systematic economic history should turn to part 1 of Zhak Natan, *Istoriia Ekonomicheskogo Razvitiia Bolgarii* [The history of Bulgarian economic development] (Moscow, 1961). Unique for the entire Balkan region is a venture begun under the editorship of Asher Khananel and Eli Eshkenazi, *Evrejski izvori za ob-shtestveno-ikonomicheskoto razvite na balkanskite zemi prez XVI vek.* [Jewish sources for the socioeconomic development of the Balkan lands in the 16th century] (Sofia, 1960-).

It remains to note, not so much for the scholarship involved but rather as an indication of the interest in the topic, the attempts made to write the history of Bulgaria under Ottoman rule. The first was Iordan Georgiev, *Bolgarite pod turskoto robstvo (Ot krai na XIV do krai XVIII vek.)* [Bul-gars under Turkish rule (from the end of the 14th to the end of the 18th centuries)] (Sofia, 1901). Next came Alois Hajek, *Bulgarien unter der Tür-kenherrschaft* (Stuttgart, 1925). In the 1930s Ahmed Refik published *Türk idaresinde Bulgaristan, (973-1255)* [Bulgaria under Turkish rule (973-1255)=1565-1840] (Istanbul, 1933), while in the next decade Michel Leo, *La Bulgarie et son peuple sous la domination ottomane, tels que les ont vus les voyageurs anglo-saxons (1586-1878)* (Sofia, 1949) appeared. These titles illustrate the variety and richness of the work done on Bulgaria under Ottoman rule mainly by Bulgarian scholars.

It is equally difficult to select among the many excellent scholars in Yugoslavia. It should be noted that most of the studies of interest to readers of this volume were published in the form of countless articles, often with summaries in the major western languages, and that a search in the bibliographies is required before any detailed work on a given subject is undertaken. These articles are often minor monographic studies. Two examples show the importance of these studies because of the topics and the detailed manner in which they are handled: Branislav Djurdjev, "O vojnucina. S osvortom na razvoj turksog feudalizma i na pitanje bosankog agaluka," [About the Vojnuks. The development of Turkish feudalism and the question of the Bosnian Agaluk], *Glasnik Zemaljskog muzeja*, 2 (1947): 75-137; and Nedim Filipović, "Pogled na osmanski feudalizam (sa naročitim obzirom na agrarne odnose)" [A review of Ottoman feudalism (with special emphasis on Agrarian relations)], *Godišnjak Istoriskog društva Bosne i Herecegovine*, 4 (1953): 1-146. Among Filipović's numerous other works is one of great interest for the little explored period of the civil war following the defeat of the Ottomans at Ankara in 1402: *Princ Musa i šejh Badreddin* (Sarajevo, 1971).

The two scholars mentioned above are among the major students of the Ottoman period of the Yugoslav lands. Djurdjev is extremely prolific and has very strong Marxist beliefs that color most of his writings. Although one does not have to agree with all his interpretations and views, the basic scholarship of his work is excellent and warrants close attention. It is impossible to do justice to Djurdjev's breadth of interest. His above article dealt with economics but he has also published *Uloga crkve u starijoj istoriji srpskog naroda* [The role of the Church in the ancient history of the Serbian people] (Sarajevo, 1964), which is in fact the history of the Peć see up to 1766. Djurdjev has also edited several collections of documents. For example, together with some colleagues he has published *Kanuni i kanunname za Bosánki, Hercegovački, Zvornički, Kliški, Crnogorski i Skadarski sandžak* [Laws and law codes of the *sancaks* of Bosnia, Hercegovina, Zvornik, Kliš, Montenegro, and Skutari] as the first volume of *Monumenta turcica* (Sarajevo, 1953). As a result of his editorial efforts, Djurdjev conceived an original way to present Ottoman material to the general public, and together with Miloje Vasić edited *Jugoslovenske zemlje pod turskom vlašcu, do kraja XVIII stoljeća* [Yugoslav lands under Turkish rule to the end of the eighteenth century] (Zagreb, 1962) in which documents, explanations, and connective essays form part of an integrated story. Moving into a different area of Yugoslavia, Djurdjev published *Turska vlast u Crnoj Gori u XVI i XVIII veku* [Turkish rule in Montenegro in the sixteenth and eighteenth centuries] (Sarajevo, 1953). The same topic was treated by Gligor Stanojević, who has also published a great deal, in *Iz istorije Crne Gore u XVI i XVII vijeku* [About the history of Montenegro in the sixteenth and seventeenth centuries] (Titograd, 1959), and by Tomica Nikičević and Branko Pavičević, *Crnogorske isprave, XIV-XIX vijeka* [Montenegrin Documents, fourteenth to nineteenth centuries] (Cetinje, 1964).

Just as Barkan served as the main example for Turkish scholars, so Djurdjev does for the Yugoslavs. Several other scholars whose work is of great importance, including Nedim Filipović, could have served the same purpose, but space permits the naming of only a few.

Ivan Božić wrote the relevant *Turska i Dubrovnik i XIV u XV veku* [Turkey and Dubrovnik in the fourteenth and fifteenth centuries] (Beograd, 1952). In addition to those authors cited in the footnotes of the Dubrovnik chapter, the following titles show the variety of topics that have been studied in connection with the city republic: Dragan Roller, *Dubrovački zanati u XV i XVII stojeću* [The Dubrovnik crafts in the fifteenth and seventeenth centuries] (Zagreb, 1951); Josip Luetić, *Mornarica Dubrovačke republike* [The marine of the Dubrovnik Republic] (Dubrovnik, 1962); and Vuk Vinar's almost endless flow of articles dealing with every conceivable aspect of the Dubrovnik economy. There is a wealth of literature on Dubrovnik's cultural activities, and in thinking about them the name of Jorjo Tadić comes automatically to mind. Among his numerous studies his *Gradja o slikarskoj školi i Dubrovniku, XIII- XIV veka* [Contributions of the Dubrovnik school of painters in the thirteenth and fourteenth centuries], 2 vols. (Belgrade, 1952) is possibly the best known. For the last centuries one can turn to Kuno Prijatelj, *Umjetnost XVII i XVIII stoljeća u Dalmaciji* [Art in seventeenth and eighteenth century Dalmatia] (Zagreb, 1956), while a short survey of literature is offered by D. Pavlović, *Iz književne i kulturne istorije Dubrovnika* [Contributions to the Literature and Culture of Dobrovnik] (Sarajevo, 1955).

Other scholars from whose works I profited greatly include Hazim Šabanović, Hamdija Kreševljaković, Gliša Elesović, and Hamid Hadžibegić. Among Šabanović's publications are *Bosanski Pašaluk; Postanak i Upravna podjela* [The Paşalık of Bosnia; Its formation and administrative organization] (Sarajevo, 1959), while Kreševljaković's *Kapetanije i kapetani u Bosni i Hercegovini* [Captaincies and captains in Bosnia and Hercegovina] (Sarajevo, 1954) has already been discussed in this volume. Another interesting work of his is *Esnafi i obrti u Bosni i Hercegovini* [Guilds and crafts in Bosnia and Hercegovina] (Sarajevo, 1957). These three scholars and many others have published much good work, mainly in the form of lengthy articles.

A few other authors and titles dealing with economic history must be mentioned next. The oldest of the still useful works is M. Ninčić, *Istorija agrarnopravnih odnosa; srpskih težaka pod Turcima* [History of the agrarian-legal relationships; The Serbian peasants under the Turks] (Belgrade, 1902). Konstantin Bastaić turned to the same problem in *Timarsko vlasništvo u feudalnom sistemu osmanlijska Turske, od XV do XVII stoljeća* [*Timar* holdings in the Ottoman Turkish feudal system from the fifteenth to the seventeenth centuries] (Zagreb, 1958). The number of works, especially long articles, dealing with practically every economic aspect of the Turkish period is very impressive. On the other hand, the work most readily available, Mijo Mirković, *Ekonomska historija Jugoslavije* [Yugoslavia's economic history] (Zagreb, 1958) is basically a text book and pays little attention to the Ottoman centuries.

Of the various works on the *zadruga*s Emile Sicard, *La Zadruga Sudslave dans l'évolution des groups domestiques* (Paris, 1943) is the easiest to use for an introduction to this subject. Interesting special cases are discussed by Milenko S. Filipović, *Nesrodnička i prevojena zadruga* [The *zadruga* of non-relatives and the split *zadruga*] (Beograd, 1945).

Several works of interest deal with the great migration of 1690 that affected every aspect of Serbian, Yugoslav, ecclesiastic, and even Hungarian history. These include: Dušan J. Popović, *Velika seoba Srba 1690* [The great Serbian migration of 1690] (Beograd, 1954), and the older but more comprehensive work of Aleksa Ivić, *Migracije Srba u Hrvatsku tokum 16, 17, i 18 stoleća* [The Serbian migration into Croatia in the course of the sixteenth, seventeenth and eighteenth centuries] (Subotica, 1926).

Finally, it should be noted that Djurdjev was not the only one dealing with the church. The oldest work, although published posthumously, is Ilarion Ruvarac, *O pećkim patriarsima od 1557 do 1690* [About the Patriarchate of Peć from 1557 to 1690] (Sremski Karlovci, 1931). In the nineteenth century Miljenko Vukčević, *Srpski Narod, crkva i sveštenstvo u turskom carstvu od 1459-1557 god.* [The Serbian nation, church, and clergy within the Turkish Empire in the years 1459-1557] (Belgrade, 1896) appeared. More specialized is the work of Svestislav Davidović, *Srpska pravoslavna crkva u Bosni i Hercegovini (od 960 do 1930 god.)* [The Serbian Orthodox church in Bosnia and Hercegovina from 960 to 1930] (Sarajevo, 1931).

The historiography of the remaining two countries, Romania and Hungary, differs markedly from those surveyed so far. This is quite understandable. Although tied to the Ottoman Empire, the Danubian Principalities lived under their own rulers and, in this sense, had an uninterrupted political history. Although a large part of their country was under Ottoman rule for a century and a half, the Hungarians also had a king, a diet, and an uninterrupted political history. Consequently, the emphasis has been on national history in these countries, and studies dealing with Ottoman rule and its various aspects are scant.

Romanian history has always been written by good scholars. The tradition begun by the great historians of the nineteenth century has continued and flourished after the First and especially after the Second World War, producing an almost endless stream of publications. The most miniscule issue has been treated in at least a few articles, local histories have been stressed as much as national problems, and practically every individual who has contributed something in any field of human endeavor has been remembered. Naturally, this prodigous activity has produced not only exemplary publications of documents and excellent bibliographies, archival catalogues, and other primary materials, but also numerous articles and collective works. Several of these have already been mentioned either in footnotes or in this essay. In the next few paragraphs, I will concentrate mainly on subjects connected with Ottoman influences and will limit myself to major monographs as much as possible. As a result of this approach the names of some very important people, including Andrei Oțetea, Ştefan Ştefănescu, Constantin C. Giurescu, Mihail Berza, and the excellent economic historian of the Ottoman centuries Marie M. Alexandrescu-Dersca will be omitted or only rarely mentioned in spite of what I learned not only from their writings but also from long talks with them. Because this essay is based on the criterion of "utility to my education," their names must be listed with my gratitude.

The relationship between the Ottomans and Moldavia has been discussed by N. A. Constantinescu, *Începuturile şi stabilirea suzeranității turcesti în Moldova* [Origins and establishment of Turkish suzerainty in Moldavia] (Bucharest, 1914), and treated by C. Giurescu, *Capitulațiile Moldovei cu Poarta Otomană* [Capitulation agreements of Moldavia with the Ottoman Porte] (Bucharest, 1908). Also closely related to the Ottoman problem are H. Dj. Siruni, *Domnii romîni la Poarta Ottomană* [Romanian lords at the Ottoman Porte] (Bucharest, 1941), and Georg Müller, *Die Türkenherrschaft in Siebenbürgen. Verfassungsrechtliche Verhältnisse Siebenbürgens zur Pforte* (Bucharest, 1938).

In connection with Ottoman studies two Romanian names stand out: Mihail Guboglu and Carl Göllner. Guboglu has published those catalogues already mentioned and others, documents, a handbook of Ottoman paleography, and several articles. He is an outstanding Turkologist. Jointly with his younger colleague, Mustafa M. Mehmet, he has translated and published the provocative *Cronici turcești privind țările române (Extrase, sec. XV—mijlocul sec. XVIII)* [Turkish chroniclers dealing with the Romanian lands (Selection from the 15th to the middle of the eighteenth century)] (Bucharest, 1966). This is the first of a projected series.

Carl Göllner became widely and deservedly known for his *Turcica, die europäischen Türkendrücke des XVI Jahrhunderts,* 2 vols. (Bucharest-

Berlin, 1961; Bucharest-Baden-Baden, 1968), and although his interests and writings now cover a great variety of subjects, his articles dealing with the Ottoman period deserve close attention.

Naturally, the major figures of Romanian history, like Michael the Brave, Steven the Great, or Dimitrie Cantemir, are the subject of several biographies, as are lesser personalities, but some studies deal with individuals who made their name outside of Romania. Among these, for example, are Camil Mureşan, *Iancu de Hunedoara* [John Hunyadi] 2nd ed. (Bucharest, 1968) and the work on the important Mavrocordatos family, Alexandru A. C. Sturdza, *L'Europe Orientale et la Role Historique des Maurocordato (1660-1830)* (Paris, 1913).

Three books, one for each of the major Romanian lands are examples of the extremely rich literature dealing with economic history: Valeria Costăchel, P. P. Panaitescu, and A. Cazacu, *Viaţa feudală în Ţara Romanească şi Moldova (sec. XIV-XVII)* [Feudal life in Wallachia and Moldavia (fourteenth to seventeenth centuries)] (Bucharest, 1957); V. Mihordea, *Relaţiile agrare din secolul al XVIII-lea în Moldova* [Agrarian conditions in eighteenth-century Moldavia] (Bucharest, 1968), and, last but not least, one of the works of Samuil Goldenberg, the excellent economic historian of Transylvania, *Clujul în sec. XVI. Producţia şi schimbul de mărfuri* [The city of Cluj in the sixteenth century. The production and exchange of goods] (Bucharest, 1958).

This last title is indicative of city histories that exist for almost all places of any significance. Two works dealing with Bucharest will indicate the variety of topics treated: Milan Popovici, *Aspecte din istoria finanţelor oraşului Bucureşti* [Aspects of the Financial History of the City of Bucharest] (Bucharest, 1960) and Panait I. Panait, *Aspecte din lupta populaţiei bucureştene împotriva regimului turco-fanariot (1716-1821)* [Aspects of the fight of the people of Bucharest against the Turkish-Phanariot regime (1716-1821)] (Bucharest 1962). Of the various city histories I prefer, Dan Berindei, *Oraşul Bucureşti, reşedinţă şi capitală a Ţării Româneşti (1459-1862)* [The city of Bucharest, residence and capital of Wallachia (1459-1862)] (Bucharest, 1963) because it has the best bibliography.

Transylvania's history has also been studied from every possible angle. For her economy, in addition to the already cited Goldenberg title, the best example is the monumental study of David Prodan, *Iobăgia în Transilvania în secolul al XVI-lea* [Serfdom in sixteenth century Transylvania], 3 vols. (Bucharest, 1967-68). For the diplomatic history of the critical period following the Battle of Mohács in 1526, a good study was written by Rodica Ciocan, *Politica Habsburgilor faţă de Transilvania în tempul lui Carol V (1526-56)* [Habsburg policy toward Transylvania in the days of Charles V (1526-56)] (Bucharest, 1945), while the history of the independent principality was presented by Ştefan Pascu, *Transilvania în epoca principatului. Timpul suzeranităţii turçest, 1541-1691* [Transylvania in the period of the Principality. The time of Turkish suzerainty, 1541-1691] (Cluj, 1948).

The best introductions to religious and cultural history are a collective study published by Bible Study and Orthodox Missionary Society, *Istoria bisericii române* [A history of the Romanian church], 2 vols. (Bucharest, 1957-58), and P. P. Panaitescu, *Introducere în istoria culturii românești* [Introduction to the cultural history of the Romanians] (Bucharest, 1969).

Finally, the already mentioned foreign language publication series, *Bibliotheca Historica Romaniae*, has published to date three volumes relevant to the period covered by this study. Number 7 is the already cited *Der Transsilvanische Volksaufstand, 1437-38* by Ştefan Pascu (Bucharest, 1964). This was followed by number 36, V. Mihordea, *Maîtres du sol et paysans dans les Principautés Roumaines au XVIIIe siècle* (Bucharest, 1971) and by number 41, Paul Cernovodeanu, *England's Trade Policy in the Levant, 1660-1714* (Bucharest, 1972) concentrating on trade with the Romanian lands.

In many respects the case of the Hungarian scholars and their works parallels that sketched in the case of the Romanians. A prodigious amount of work exists in articles or in monographs that cannot be cited because, in spite of their importance, they touch on topics tangental to this volume. Lack of space prohibits more than a mention of Zsigmond Pál Pach, Kálmán Benda, László Makkai, Klára Hegyi, and many others from whose works I benefited greatly.

Hungarians have long been interested in Turkish affairs, and, beginning with Ármin Vámbery, there have been several scholars of international repute including Gyula Németh, Lajos Fekete, and Gyula Káldy-Nagy. Most of their work, however, was either pure Turkology, methodology, and an extensive program of document publications prior to the issuance of numerous materials relevant to counties and cities, besides those dealing with the occupied region as a whole. A great number of excellent articles dealing with these topics have also appeared. Even family archives have been combed for Turkish material which has subsequently been published.

These are works of great value, but studies dealing with purely historical subjects have quite understandably been relatively rare. Until the importance of the *mezővárosok* and a few other issues were discovered, Hungarian historians found little of interest in the Turkish-held lands when they compared life and developments there with what had occurred in Habsburg-ruled Hungary, Slovakia, or Transylvania. Thus, few concentrated on the period of Turkish rule. Sándor Takáts published *Rajzok a török világból* [Sketches of the Turkish days], 3 vols. (Budapest, 1915-17). His work is surpassed by Mária Schwab *Az igazságszolgáltatás fejlödése a török hódoltság idején az alföldi városokban* [The development of the dispensing of justice in the cities of the Great Plain during the period of the

Turkish occupation] (Budapest, 1939), and Zsolt Pákay, *Veszprém vármegye története a török hódoltság korában a rovásadó összeirása alapján, 1531-1696* [The history of Veszprém County under Turkish rule based on the Cizye records, 1531-1696] (Veszprém, 1942). To this same group of studies concentrating on the Turkish period belongs Pál Z. Szabó, *A török Pécs* [Turkish Pécs] (Pécs, 1958). The importance of the periodical literature cannot be stressed strongly enough because it contains a great wealth of fine studies. Gyula Káldy-Nagy's article, "Statisztikai adatok a török hódoltsági terület nyugat felé irányuló áruforgalmáról" [Statistical data concerning the flow of goods toward the West from the territory under Turkish rule], *Történeti Statisztikai Évkönyv* [Yearbook of historical statistics] (1965-66), pp. 27-97 must serve as the example for such articles.

The monographic literature concentrates either on Habsburg Hungary, which is discussed in another volume of this series, or on Transylvania. Concerning this principality some of the numerous documentary collections issued have already been mentioned. There is at least one work written about every major historical figure, policies under different princes have been analyzed; and military campaigns have been described and dissected—in short someone has studied every aspect of the public life of Transylvania. A few examples will have to suffice to indicate the variety of topics that have been treated: Lajos Szádecky-Kardoss dealt with the problem of the Székelys in his *A székely nemzet története és alkotmánya* [The history and constitution of the Székely nation] (Budapest, 1927), while the curious duality of the position of this nation was discussed by György Bónis, *Székely jog, magyar jog* [Székely law, Hungarian law] (Kolozsvár, 1942). The most detailed history of the Székelys is István Rugonfalvi Kiss, *A nemes székely nemzet képe* [The image of the noble Székely nation], 3 vols. (Debrecen, 1939-40).

An interesting study dealing with the problem of the accepted nations and religions of Transylvania is Miklós Endes, *Erdély Három nemzete és négy vallása autonomiájának története* [The history of the autonomy of Transylvania's three nations and four religions] (Budapest, 1935). For the period of Transylvania's history surveyed in this volume, the following titles are of particular interest: Károly Lám, *Az erdélyi országgyülés szervezete, 1541-1848* [The organization of the Transylvanian diet, 1541-1848] (Kolozsvár, 1918); Gyula Vajda, *Erdély viszonya a portához és a német császárhoz mint magyar királyhoz a nemzeti fejedelemség korában, 1540-1690* [The relationship of Transylvania to the Porte and to the German emperor in his capacity as Hungarian King during the period of the National Principality, 1540-1690] (Kolozsvár, 1891); Johann Lipták, *A portai adó törénete az erdélyi fejedelemségben* [The history of Turkish taxes in the principality of Transylvania] (Késmárk, 1911); Vencel Biró, *Erdély követei a portán* [Transylvania's ambassadors at the Porte] (Kolozsvár,

1921); Imre Lukinich, *Erdély területi változásai a török hóditás korában, 1541-1711* [The changes in Transylvania's territory during the period of the Turkish conquest, 1540-1711] (Budapest, 1918); Mária Szentgyörgyi, *Jobbágyterhek a XVI-XVII. századi Erdélyben* [The obligations of the serfs in Transylvania in the sixteenth and seventeenth centuries] (Budapest, 1962). F. Gabriella Gáspár, *Az erdélyi fejedelmek törekvései a lengyel tronra* [The Attempt of the Transylvanian princes to gain the Polish throne] (Debrecen, 1943) is well researched, but her conclusions are questionable.

Most of these titles are dated, but because recent scholarship has concentrated on other topics they must still be remembered. Although more recent studies are very important, they are either too specialized to be cited or they deal with issues that were not handled in this volume. It would be desirable if Hungary's excellent contemporary historians would publish a study that would finally do justice to the topic that the French scholar A. Lefaivre attempted, rather unsuccessfully, in his *Les Magyars pendant la domination ottomane en Hongrie (1526-1722)*, 2 vols. (Paris, 1902).

The Czechs have a long tradition of writing about Southeastern Europe, beginning with the famous Josef Konstantin Jireček who published *Dějiny naroda bulharskeho* [History of the Bulgarian Nation] (Praha, 1876) and the even better known *Geschichte der Serben*, 2 vols. (Gotha, 1911-18), both of which have been translated and reissued. His worthy successor Josef Kabrda has written numerous articles on Turkish and Balkan studies and the excellent work in French, *Le système fiscal de l' Église orthodox dans l'Empire ottoman d'après les documents turcs* (Brno, 1969). Younger scholars in Czechoslovakia are doing excellent work at present.

Poland also has its outstanding Ottomanists, including the most famous of them all, Jan Reychmann, who together with Ananiasz Zajączkowski has published *Zarys Dyplomatyki Osmánko-Tureckiej* (Warszawa, 1955) which has been translated into English by Andrew Ehrenkreutz, *Handbook for Ottoman-Turkish Diplomatics* (The Hague, 1968). Together with Zygmunt Abrahamowicz, Zayączkowski also edited *Katalog dokumentów tureckich. Dokumenty do Djzeijów Polski i krajów ościennych w latach 1455-1672* [Catalogue of Turkish Documents. Documents relating to Poland and her neighbor states, 1455-1682]. vol. 1 (Warszawa, 1959). To these two examples only one more will be added: Wladislaw Konopczyński, *Polska u Turcija, 1683-1792* [Poland and Turkey, 1683-1792] (Warszawa, 1936) to indicate that in Poland too work continues to be done on Turkish subjects.

In conclusion, a few general comments must be made about the scholarship of the western world. The authors and works concerned are rather well known and easily available, so it is hoped that the following summary treatment will be excused by the reader.

A desire to understand and study the life of the Ottomans began a long time ago with the best of the travelers of whom one, de Busbecq, has been mentioned in this essay. With the work of Hammer-Purgstall began the writing of Ottoman history by western scholars. This tradition continues to the present. Historians who wrote about the Ottomans can be grouped, roughly, into two categories: the true specialists and those who became interested in a Ottoman topic and wrote something of value in spite of the fact that most of their work had been done on other aspects of history.

Among the Ottoman specialists we have men like Claude Cahen or Paul Wittek whose major interests were either the pre-Ottoman Turks or the beginnings of the Ottoman Empire. Others, like Franz Babinger, Harold Bowen, Alexandre Bennigsen, Bertold Spuler, Carl Brockelmann, and Gotthard Jäschke have dealt with a great variety of topics covering various periods of Ottoman history. Their works are indispensible for persons dealing with any aspect of history in which the Ottomans were involved, but touch on the problems of Southeastern Europe under Ottoman rule only marginally. The same is true of the Russian specialists. Vasilii V. Barthold (also known as Wilhelm Barthold) who is among those scholars working on the early Turks, and Anatolii F. Miller who is among those whose work deals with the later Ottoman Empire.

Barnette Miller, Sydney N. Fisher, Albert Lybyer, Harold Lamb, Hester D. Jenkins, Roger B. Merriman, and others have written one or more valuable volumes based mainly, and in many cases entirely, on western language sources. It is younger scholars, of whom Stanford J. Shaw and Speros Vryonis, Jr., are the best examples, who combine a thorough Ottomanist training with a knowledge of area languages and a breadth of interest and are working on studies of equal value for those interested in the Ottomans or in people who lived under Ottoman rule.

Turning from the Ottomanists to the Balkanists, most of the scholars mentioned in this essay (men like Gewehr or Schevill) relied primarily on western language sources. Scholars like Hugh Seton-Watson or the Hungarian scholar Emil Niederhauser who have mastered all the languages and histories necessary to write about Southeastern Europe under Ottoman rule are not too numerous and so far have concentrated on the nineteenth and twentieth centuries when dealing with this area. Although there are many excellent specialists of the region who are familiar with more than one of the regional languages—Charles and Barbara Jelavich, Wayne Vuchinic, Michael B. Petrovich, Gale Stokes, Georges Castellan, Georges Haupt, and many others fall into this group—they either lack the knowledge of Ottoman Turkish or have concentrated their work on the last two centuries. Men like Leften S. Stavrianos and Traian Stojanovich are rare in the West. This is why it is so important to familiarize onself with the work of the scholars of Southeastern Europe. It is, once again, among the younger scholars that one finds individuals whose training and interest as well as their already proven ability indicate that specialized work on Southeastern Europe under Ottoman rule will go on. These younger scholars include, besides several Europeans, John V. A. Fine, Jr. in the United States.

For every name mentioned in the above essay at least a dozen others had to be omitted, and for each title cited another twenty-five were sacrificed. Just as the entire volume is a broad survey, so is this essay, which has tried to indicate that enough sources and secondary works are already in print to permit an in-depth investigation of most of the issues touched on in this volume. If access to archives and libraries in Southeastern Europe could be secured, even more could be accomplished, but the material already available in print permits the scholar living outside the area to study most topics in great detail.

Appendixes

APPENDIX 1

THE HOUSE OF OSMAN

	Date of Birth	Accession Date	End of Reign
1. Osman I	ca. 1258	1281/1300[a]	1324[1]
2. Orhan	1288	1324	1360
3. Murad I	1326	1360	1389
4. Bāyezid I	ca. 1360	1389	1402
Interregnum[3]			
5. Mehmed I	1389	1413	1421
6. Murad II	1404	1421	1444[1]
		1446[2]	1451
7. Mehmed II	1432	1444	1446[b]
		1451[2]	1481
8. Bāyezid II	1448	1481	1512[b]
9. Selim I	1470	1512	1520
10. Süleyman I	1494	1520	1566
11. Selim II	1524	1566	1574
12. Murad III	1546	1574	1595
13. Mehmed III	1566	1595	1603
14. Ahmed I	1590	1603	1617
15. Mustafa I	1592	1617	1618[b]
		1622[2]	1623[b]
16. Osman II	1604	1618	1622[b,c]
17. Murad IV	1609	1623	1640
18. Ibrahim	1615	1640	1648[b,c]
19. Mehmed IV	1642	1648	1687[b]
20. Süleyman II	1642	1687	1691
21. Ahmed II	1643	1691[c]	1695
22. Mustafa II	1664	1695	1703[b]
23. Ahmed III	1673	1703	1730[b]
24. Mahmud I	1696	1730	1754
25. Osman III	1699	1754	1757
26. Mustafa III	1717	1757	1774
27. Abdülhamid I	1725	1774	1789

28. Selim III	1761	1789	1807[b]/1808[c]
29. Mustafa IV	1779	1807	1808[b,e]
30. Mahmud II	1785	1808	1839
31. Abdülmecid I	1823	1839	1861
32. Abdülaziz	1830	1861	1876[b, c]
33. Murad V	1840	1876	1876[b]
34. Abdülhamid II	1842	1876	1909[b·]
35. Mehmed V Reşad	1844	1909	1918
36. Mehmed VI Vahdeddin	1861	1918	1922[b]
37. Abdülmecid II[e]	1868	1922	1924

a. Became feudal lord in 1281 and independent ruler in 1300
b. Reign ended with deposition
c. Murdered
d. Died by suicide
e. Held title of Caliph only

1. Year of abdication
2. Resumed reign
3. *Devir Fetret* (The Great Interregnum): July 28, 1402 - July 5, 1413

Name of Prince	Seat of Power	Held Power From	Until
Isa	Balıkesir/Bursa	1402	1403
Musa	Bursa	1403	1404 (took Bursa from Isa)
Mehmed	Amasya	1402	1404
	Amasya/Bursa	1404	1413 (took Bursa from Musa uniting Anatolia)
Süleyman	Edirne	1402	1411
Musa	Edirne	1411	1413 (moved to Europe, took Edirne from Süleyman)

In 1413 Mehmed defeated Musa, took Edirne, and reunited the empire.

APPENDIX 2

GRAND VEZIRS

ACCORDING to tradition, which is not supported by documentary evidence, Sultan Orhan appointed his brother and later one of his sons as the first two grand *vezirs*. Counting these two officials, a total of 178 individuals held the position until it was abolished in November, 1861, by Sultan Abdülaziz. Several of these grand vezirs served in this position more than once.

The position carried much prestige and often great power, but it was also fraught with dangers. Besides being subject to the sultans' changing moods and favors, holders of the position were exposed to numerous dangers. Six grand vezirs died in battle, three were assassinated, and twenty-one were executed at the order of the ruler. Only twenty-two died in office.

Most grand vezirs had short tenures in office. It was not unusual to serve less than a year, and in a few cases only a few hours. Those who held the position the longest without interruption were the following:

Kara-Halil Cenderli (under Murad II)—25 years
Ali Cenderli (under Murad II and Bayezid I)—18 years
Mehmed Sokollu (under Süleyman I, Selim II, and Murad III)—15 years
Ahmed Köprülü (under Mehmed IV)—15 years
Ibrahim (under Süleyman I)—13 years

Two families, the Cenderli and the Köprülü, were able to establish vezirial dynasties.

Cenderli Grand Vezirs

Kara-Halil—1359-85
Ali (son of Kara-Halil)—1386-1404
Ibrahim (son of Ali)—1411
Bāyezid—1418
Halil (son of Ibrahim)—1429-53
Ibrahim (son of Halil)—1497-99

Köprülü Grand Vezirs

Mehmed—1656-61
Ahmed (son of Mehmed)—1661-76
Kara Mustafa (nephew of Mehmed)—1676-83
Mustafa (son of Mehmed)—1689-91
Hüssein (nephew of Mehmed)—1697-1702
Numan—1710

APPENDIX 3

MAJOR MILITARY CAMPAIGNS, PEACE TREATIES, TERRITORIAL GAINS AND LOSSES
OF THE OTTOMAN EMPIRE IN EUROPE, 1345-1801.°

1345	First Ottoman campaign in Europe
1349	Second Ottoman campaign in Europe
1352	Conquest of Çimpe (Tzympe)
1354	Conquest of Gelibolu (Gallipoli, Kallipolis)
1354-56	Conquest of Eastern Thrace along the western shores of the Marmara (Propontis) Sea including the cities of Tekirdağ (Daidestos, Rodosto) and Çorlu (Tsorulon, Tsouroullos), Didymoteichos (Dimetoka, Dimotika)
1360-66	Conquest of Thrace east of the lower Maritsa (Evros, Hebros, Meriç) river including Stara Zagora (Eskizağra)
1365	Conquest of Edirne (Adrianoypolis, Adrianopol, Odrin) and Plovdiv (Philippopolis) Dubrovnik (Ragusa) agrees to pay tribute
1366	Ottomans defeated at Vidin; lose Gallipoli
1366-69	Conquest of Central Bulgaria between the Rhodope (Rodopi, Rodope) and the Balkan (Stara planina) ranges
1371	Ottoman victory at Chirmen (Chernomen, Chermanon, Çirmen) followed by the conquest of Elkhovo (Kızılağaç), Jambol (Yanbolu), Aitos (Aetos, Aydoz), Poljanovgrad (Karnobat, Karınabad), Sozopol (Sosopol, Sözebolu), Ihtiman, Samakov by 1375.
1371	Crna Gora (Montenegro) declares her independence
1372	Bulgarian ruler accepts vassal status
1376	Byzantines return Gallipoli to Ottomans
1380	Crossing of the Vardar (Axios) River, conquest of Bitola (Bitolj, Manastir)
1383	Conquest of Serres (Seres, Serré, Serrai)
1385	Conquest of Sofia
1386	Conquest of Niš (Nish)
1387	Defeat on the Topolnica (Toplica) River; First conquest of Thessaloníki (Salonika, Selānik)
1388	Defeat at Pločnik (Plotchnik); Crossing of the Balkan range and conquest of Kolarovgrad (Šumen, Şumnu), Provadija (Pravadi), Novi Pazar
1389	First Battle of Kosovo; First raids into Hungary
1390-91	First naval raids on Khíos (Híos, Chios), Halkís (Chalkis, Negroponte), and Attiki, (Attiké, Attica, Attika)
1391	Conquest of Skopje (Skoplje, Skopije, Shkupi, Üsküb, Üsküp)
1391-98	First siege of Constantinople (Istanbul, Byzantium)
1393	Conquest of Silistra (Silistre)
1394	Conquest of Tŭrnovo (Tarnovo, T'rnovo) and Nikopol (Nikopolis, Niyebol); raids into the Peloponnesos (Morea)
1395	Battle on the Argeş River—Wallachia agrees to pay tribute Raids into Hungary

°Whenever possible all names of a given location are given. Unless a city is very well
known the name indicated on contemporary maps is given first, but when the name is
repeated the one used in most historical texts is mentioned. For example: 1656 Bozca
Ada (Tenedos), but 1716-18 Tenedos.

320

1396	Battle of Nikopolis
1398	Conquest of Vidin
1397-99	Raids into Thessalía (Thessaly), Doris, Locris, N.E. Morea, S. Albania, and Epirus
1403	Salonika lost
1416	Inconclusive war with Venice
1419	War with Wallachia, capture of Giurgiu
1420	First Attack on Transylvania
1421	Attack on Transylvania with Braşov (Brassó, Kronstadt) destroyed
1422	Second siege of Constantinople
1423-30	War with Venice
1430	Reconquest of Salonika; Conquest of most of Epirus, S. Albania; New raids into the Morea
1432	Raids into Transylvania
1437	War with Hungary
1438	Raids into Transylvania
1439	Smederevo (Semendriye, Szendrö) conquered; Bosnia agrees to pay tribute; Victory in the first Battle of Szalánkemén (Slankamen)
1441	Ottoman defeat at Beograd (Belgrade, Nándorfehérvár)
1441-42	Raids into Transylvania
1442	Attack on Hungary; Ottoman defeat at İalomiţa (Jalomica)
1443	Hungarian counterattack reaches Vidin and Sofia. Truce of Szeged gives Hungarians free hand in Wallachia and Serbia
1444	Hungarians break truce; Great Ottoman victory at Varna
1446	Raids into the Morea
1448	Hungarians defeated in the second Battle of Kosovo; Ottomans invade Serbia, attack central Albania
1450	Attacks on Albania
1453	Conquest of Constantinople
1454	Attacks on Serbia
1455	Conquest of Novi Brod and Kruševac (Alacahisar); Moldavia agrees to pay tribute
1456	Attack on Belgrade
1459	Final defeat of Serbia
1460	Conquest of the Duchy of Athens and much of the Morea
1461	Conquest of the Genovese holdings in the Aegean Sea
1462	Invasion of Wallachia
1456-63	Wars with Scanderbeg (George Kastriote) in Albania
1463	Conquest of southern and central Bosnia (northern Bosnia is Hungarian); loss of the Morea to Venice
1464	Morea reconquered
1465	Conquest of Hercegovina
1467	Conquest of Albania except fortresses in Venetian hands.
1463-79	Long war with Venice
1468	Raids into Dalmatia and Croatia
1470	Conquest of Negroponte (Euboea, Évvoia)
1471	Raids into Croatia
1473	Raids into Croatia
1474	Siege of Shkodër (Shkodra, Scutari, Işkodra); Raids into Transylvania
1475	Crimean Tatars become vassals of the Ottomans
1476	Campaigns against Hungary and Wallachia Wallachia becomes vassal state

1477-78	Raids into Italy; conquest of the Venetian forts in Albania—Krujë (Kroja, Croia, Akçahisar), Lezhë (Leş, Alessio), Drishti (Drivastum, Drivasto, Drivost)
1479	Peace with Venice; Ottomans keep their conquests and get Shkodër and the Island of Límnos (Lemnos)
	Raids into Hungary and Transylvania—Ottoman defeat at Kenyérmezö
1480	Landing at Otranto
1480-81	Siege of Rhodes
1481	Evacuation of Otranto
1483	Conquest of Hercegovina (Herzegowina)
1484	War with Moldavia, conquest of Kilija (Kilia, Chilia-Nouă), and Bilhorod Dnistrovskii (Akerman, Akkerman, Cetatea Albă)
1494	Attack on Montenegro
1497	Final subjugation of Albania
1499	Conquest of Montenegro
	Venice gets Cyprus from its last king leading to:
1499-1503	War with Venice resulting in Ottoman conquest of Návpaktos (Lepanto, Inebahtı), Methóni (Modon, Moton), Koróni (Koron), and Navarino (Pylos, Anavarin)
1512	Moldavia becomes vassal state
1520	Conquests in northern Bosnia
1521	Conquest of Belgrade, raids into Hungary and Austria
1522	Conquest of Rhodes and of Orşova (Orsova, Orschowa)
1526	First Battle of Mohács, first occupation of Buda
1527	Conquest of Jajce (Yayçe) and all of N. Bosnia
1528	Second conquest of Buda (Ofen)
1529	First siege of Vienna
1532	Conquest of Köszeg (Güns), but withdrawal from Hungary
1533	Armistice of Istanbul, both Ferdinand and Zápolyai agree to pay tribute
1535	Ottoman-French alliance
1537-40	War with Venice
1538	First Holy League (Charles V and the Pope join Venice)
1540	Venice gives up Navplion (Nauplion, Anabolu) and all her holdings in the Morea
1541	Third conquest of Buda where *paşalik* is established
1543	Ottomans conquer Pécs (Fünfkirchen), Siklós, Esztergom (Gran), Székesfehérvár (Stuhlweissenburg)
1544	Ottomans conquer Visegrád, Nógrád (Novigrad, Neugrad), Hatvan, Simontornya
1547	Ferdinand recognizes *paşalik*, continues to pay tribute
1551-62	War with Austria
1551	Conquest of Zrenjanin (Nagybecskerek), Oradea (Oradea Mare, Nagyvarád, Grossvardein), Csanád, Lipova (Lippa)
1552	Conquest of Timişoara (Temesvár), Veszprém, Drégely, and Szolnok, but defeat at Eger (Erlau)
1554	Conquest of Kaposvár and Filakovo (Fülek)
1556	First attack on Szigetvár
1557	Conquest of Tata
1560	Naxos conquered

1562	Peace; Austria recognizes all Ottoman conquests, the independence of Transylvania under Ottoman suzerainty, and continues to pay tribute
1565	Siege of Malta
1566	Gyula and Szigetvár conquered, but Veszprém and Tata lost; conquest of Khíos
1570	War with Venice (backed by Spain); conquest of Cyprus
1571-81	War with the Second Holy League
1571	Naval battle at Lepanto
1573	Venice leaves war, recognizes the loss of Cyprus, and pays war indemnity; Ottomans attack Nagykanizsa (Kanizsa, Grosskanischa)
1593-1606	War with Austria
1593	Veszprém reconquered
1594	Györ (Raab, Yanık) conquered, but several small forts lost
1595	Esztergom lost
1596	Ottoman victory at Mezőkeresztes; conquest of Eger
1598	Veszprém lost; Buda under attack
1600	Nagykanizsa conquered
1601	Székesfehérvár lost
1602	Austrians attack Buda, Ottomans reconquer Székesfehérvár
1603	Austrians attack Buda
1605	Esztergom reconquered
1606	Peace of Zsitvatorok; both sides keep what they hold, but Austria stops paying tribute
1619	Vácz (Waitzen) conquered
1638	(approximate end of the *devşirme*)
1645-70	War with Venice
1645	Ottomans attack Crete
1651	Ottomans defeated in naval battle at Páros (Para)
1656	Ottomans defeated in naval battle near Dardanelles; Venice conquers Límnos and Bozca Ada (Tenedos)
1658	Ottomans attack Austrian troops in Transylvania
1660	Conquest of Nagyvárad
1663	Austria joins Venice in war
1664	Ottomans defeated at St. Gotthard
	Twenty years' truce concluded at Vasvár with Austria
1669	Ottomans conquer Iraklion (Candia) on Crete
1670	Peace; Venice returns everything she conquered, and the Ottomans get Crete with exception of three fortresses.
1672-76	War with Poland
1673	Ottomans defeated at Khotin (Hotin, Chocim)
1676	Ottomans defeated at Lwów (L'viv, Lemberg)
	Ottomans victorious at Żurawno
	Peace of Żurawno gives Ottomans the Eastern Ukraine and Podole (Podolia)—*At this point the Ottoman Empire reaches its maximum extent in Europe*
1677-81	First war with Russia
1681	Peace of Radzyń; Ottomans give up the Eastern Ukraine
	First permanent loss of territory
1682-99	War with Austria
1683	Second siege of Vienna

1684	Third Holy League (Venice and Poland join Austria); Visegrád, Vácz lost
1686	Ottomans lose Siklós, Pécs, Buda, Veszprém, Szeged, and the Battle of Zenta to Austria; Venice conquers most of the Morea
1687	Ottomans lose Eger and the second Battle of Mohács to Austria First Russian siege of Azov
1688	Ottomans give up Székesfehérvár, Lippa, and Belgrade
1689	Ottomans give up Szigetvár, Vidin, and Niš
1690	Ottomans give up Nagykanizsa, but reconquer Belgrade and Vidin and defeat Austrians in Transylvania
1691	Ottomans lose second Battle of Szalánkamén
1694	Gyula lost
1696	Lippa reconquered Azov lost to Russians
1697	Ottomans defeated again at Zenta
1699	Peace of Sremski Karlovci (Karlowitz, Karlóca) Poland gets Podole back Venice gets the Morea and most of Dalmatia Austria gets all of Hungary with the exception of the Banat of Temesvár (Timişoara, Timişvar)
1710-11	War with Russia
1711	Ottomans win Battle of the Prut; In Peace of Prut get Azov back
1714-18	War with Venice; The Morea, Límnos, Tenedos, and Corinth reconquered by the Ottomans
1715	Conquest of Tenos (last Ottoman conquest)
1716	War with Austria; Ottomans defeated at Petrovaradin (Petervardein, Pétervárad)
1717	Austrians conquer Belgrade
1718	Peace of Požarevac (Passarowitz) with Austria; Ottomans lose Banat of Temesvár and Little Wallachia (Oltenia)
1736-39	War with Austria and Russia
1736	Russians conquer Azov
1739	Russians invade Moldavia
1739	Treaty of Belgrade with Austria; Ottomans regain Belgrade Russia obliged to raze the fortifications of Azov and promise not to keep a fleet on Black Sea
1768-74	War with Russia
1769	Russians conquer Iassy (Iaşi) and Bucharest (Bucureşti)
1770	Russians capture but give up Navarino, win a great naval battle near Khíos and subsequently conquer eighteen Aegean Islands, and occupy the cities of Kilija (Kilia, Chilia-Nouǎ), Bilhorod Dnistrovskii (Akkerman, Ackerman, Akerman, Cetatea Albǎ), Izmail (Ismail), Bender (Bender'i, Tighana), and Brǎila (Ibrail)
1774	Treaty of Küçük Kajnarca; Russians get freedom at Azov, the Kerch Peninsula, the fortresses of Kinburn, Yenikale in the Crimea, the mouths of the Dnieper and Bug rivers; the lands of the Tatar Khan become a Russian protectorate; all other Russian-held lands returned to Ottomans; Austrians occupy the Bukovina.
1783	Russia annexes the lands of the Tatar Khan
1787-92	War with Russia
1788	Austria joins the war
1788	Russians conquer Ochakov

1789	Austrian armies invade Bosnia and Servia
	Russian armies invade Moldavia and Wallachia
1790	Russians conquer Izmail
1791	Peace of Svishtov (Ziştov) with Austria re-establishing the borders of 1788
1792	Peace of Iaşi with Russia; Ottomans give up territory on the north shore of the Black Sea making the Dniester the Russian-Ottoman border

APPENDIX 4

RULERS (EMPERORS, KINGS, PRINCES, BANS, ETC.) WITH WHOM THE OTTOMANS CAME INTO CONTACT EITHER AS ENEMIES OR AS OVERLORDS, 1282-1804

Byzantine Emperors (Paleologi family)

Andronicus II - 1282-1328
Andronicus III - 1328-41
John V - 1341-91
John VI (Cantacuzene) - coregent - 1341-55
Manuel II - 1391-1425
John VII - 1425-48
Constantine XI - 1448-53

The last Seljuqs of Rum

Mas'ūd II - 1284-93; 1294-1301; 1303-05
Kay-Qubādh III - 1293-94; 1301-03; 1305-07
Ghiyāthal-Dīn Mas'ūd III - 1307

Rulers of Serbian states (titles change)

Stefan (Steven) II Uroš - 1282-1321
Stefan III Uroš - 1321-31
Stefan Dušan - 1331-55
Stefan IV Uroš - 1355-71
Lazar Hrebeljanović - 1371-89
Stefan Lazarević - 1389-1427
Djuradj Branković - 1427-56
Lazar Branković - 1456-58
Stefan Tomašević - 1459

Rulers of Bosnia

Stepan Kostromanić - 1314-53
Stepan Tvrtko I - 1353-91
Stefan Dabiša - 1391-95
Jelena (Helen) Gruba (wife of the above) - 1395-98
Stefan Ostoja - 1398-1404
Stefan Tvrtko II Tvrtković - 1404-9
Stefan Ostoja - 1409-21 with counterkings - Stefan II Tvrtko - 1414-15; Radivoj Ostojić - 1432-35 and 1443-46
Stefan Tvrtko II Tvrtković - 1421-43
Stefan Tomaš - 1443-63

Bulgarian Rulers

John (Ivan Aleksandur) - 1331-71
John Shishman (ruler of Turnovo after his father's death and division of state) - 1371-93
John Stratsimir (ruler in Vidin after division of state) 1365-96

Rulers of Crna Gora (Montenegro) - Zeta Balšić Family

Balša I - dates unclear, died 1360 approx.
Stratimir - ca. 1360-72
Djuradj (George) I - 1372-78
Balša II - 1378-85

326

Djuradj II - 1385-1403
Balša III - 1403-21

Cernojević family

Stefan (Steven) - 1427-65
John (Ivan) - 1465-90
Djuradj - 1490-96

Petrović family

Danilo - 1696-1737
Sava - 1737-82
Petar (Peter) I - 1782-1830

Rulers of Moldavia (beginning with 1388 when Ottomans cross the Balkans and reach Danube)

Petru (Peter) I - ca. 1374-92
Roman I - ca. 1392-94
Ştefan (Steven) I - ca. 1394-99
Iuga - 1399-1400
Alexandru cel Bun (Alexander the Good) - 1400-31
Iliaş - 1432-33
Ştefan II - 1433-35
the above two corulers - 1435-42
Ştefan II (coruler with Petru II) - 1444-45
Ştefan II - 1445-47
Petru II (coruler with Roman II) - 1447
Roman II - 1447-48
Petru II - 1448-49
Bogdan II - 1449-51
Petro Aron - 1451-55 (alternating with Alexăndrel)
Alexăndrel - 1452-55 (alternating with Petru Aron)
Petru Aron - 1455-57
Ştefan cel Mare (Steven the Great) - 1457-1504
Bogdan III - 1504-17
Ştefăniţa - 1517-27
Petru Rareş - 1527-40
Ştefan Lăustă - 1538-40 (challenger)
Alexandru Cornea - 1540-41
Petru Rareş - 1541-46
Iliaş Rareş - 1546-51
Ştefan Rareş - 1551-52
Ioan (John) Joldea - 1552
Alexandru Lăuşneanu - 1552-61
Ioan Despot - 1561-63
Ştefan Tomşa - 1563-64
Alexandru Lăuşneanu - 1564-68
Bogdan Lăuşneanu - 1568-72
Ioan Vodă cel Viteaz (the Brave) - 1572-74
Petru Şchiopul - 1574-91 (not continuously on throne)
Ioan Potcoavă - 1577 (interrupting rule of above)
Iancu Sasul - 1579-82 (interrupting Petru Şchiopul)

Aron Tiranul - 1591-95 (not continuously on throne) interrupted by
Alexandru cel Rău (the Bad) - 1592-93
Petru Cazacul - 1593
Ştefan Răzvan - 1595
Ieremia Movilă - 1595-1600
Mihai Viteazul (Michael the Brave) - 1600 (see Wallachia)
Ieremia Movilă - 1600-6
Simon Movilă - 1606-7
Mihai Movilă - 1607
Constantin Movilă - 1607-11
Ştefan II Tomşa - 1611-15
Alexandru Movilă - 1615-16
Radu Mihnea - 1616-19
Gaspar Graţiani - 1619-20
Alexandru Iliaş - 1620-21
Ştefan II Tomşa - 1621-23
Radu Mihnea - 1623-26
Miron Barnovschi-Movilă - 1626-29
Alexandru Coconul - 1629-30
Moise Movilă - 1630-31
Alexandru Iliaş - 1631-33
Miron Barnovschi-Movilă - 1633
Moise Movilă- 1633-34
Vasile Lupu - 1634-53
Gheorghe (George) Ştefan - 1653-58
Gheorghe Ghica - 1658-59
Constantin Şerban - 1659
Ştefăniţa Lupu - 1659-61
Constantin Şerban - 1661
Ştefăniţa Lupu - 1661
Eustratie Dabija - 1661-65
Gheorghe Duca - 1665-66
Iliaş Alexandru - 1666-68
Gheorghe Duca - 1668-72
Ştefan Petriceicu - 1672-78 (not continuous)
Dumitraşcu (Dimitri) Cantacuzino - 1673, 1674-75, interrupting rule of Ştefan
     Petriceicu
Antonie (Anthony) Ruset - 1675-78, interrupting rule of Ştefan Petriceicu
Gheorghe Duca - 1678-83
Ştefan Petriceicu - 1683-84
Dumitraşcu Cantacuzino - 1684-85
Constantin Cantermir - 1685-93
Dimitrie Cantemir - 1693
Constantin Duca - 1693-95
Antioh Cantemir - 1695-1700
Constantin Duca - 1700-3
Mihail Racoviţă - 1703-5
Antioh Cantemir - 1705-7
Mihail Racoviţă - 1707-9
Nicolae (Nicholas) Mavrocordat - 1709-10
Dimitri Cantemir - 1710-11

Beginning of Phanariot Regime

Nicolae Mavrocordat - 1711-15

Mihail Racoviță - 1715-26
Grigore II Ghica - 1726-33
Constantin Mavrocordat - 1733-35
Grigore II Ghica - 1735-41
Constantin Mavrocordat - 1741-43
Ion Mavrocordat - 1743-47
Grigore II Ghica - 1747-48
Constantin Mavrocordat - 1748-49
Constantin Racoviță - 1749-53
Matei Ghica - 1753-56
Constantin Racovița - 1756-57
Scarlat Ghica - 1757-58
Ioan Teodor Callimachi - 1758-61
Grigore Callimachi - 1761-64
Grigore III Ghica - 1764-67
Grigore Callimachi - 1767-69
Constantin Mavrocordat - 1769 (followed by five years of Russian occupation)
Grigore II Ghica - 1774-77
Constantin Moruzi - 1777-82
Alexandru C. Mavrocordat - 1782-85
Alexandru I. Mavrocordat - 1785-86
Alexandru Ipsilanti - 1787-88
Emanuel Giani-Ruset - 1788-89 (followed by three years of Russian occupation)
Alexandru Moruzi - 1792
Mihail Suțu - 1792-95
Alexandru Callimachi - 1795-99
Constantin Ipsilanti - 1799-1801
Alexandru Suțu - 1801-2
Alexandru Moruzi - 1802-6

Rulers of Wallachia (beginning with 1388 when Ottomans cross the Balkans and
    reach the Danube)

Mircea cel Bătrîn (the Old) - 1386-1418 (rule interrupted by Vlad Uzurpatorul,
    1394-97)
Mihail - 1418-20
Dan II - 1422-31 (interrupted by Radu II in 1421, 1423, 1424, 1426, and 1427)
Alexandru I - 1431-36
Vlad Dracul - 1436, 1442, 1443, 1446
Mircea (son of Dracul) - 1442
Basarab II - 1442-43
Vladislav II - 1446-56
Vlad Tepeş - 1456-62
Radu cel Frumos (the Fair) - 1462-75
Basarab-Laiotă - 1473-74
Vlad Tepeş - 1476
Basarab-Laiotă - 1476-77
Basarab cel Tînăr-Țepeluş - 1477-81
Mircea - 1481
Vlad Călugărul - 1481
Basarab cel Tînăr (the Young) - 1481-82
Vlad Călugărul - 1482-95
Radu cel Mare (the Great) - 1495-1508
Mihnea cel Rău (the Bad) - 1508-09

Mircea - 1509-10
Vlad cel Tînăr (the Young) - 1510-12
Neagoe Basarab - 1512-21
Teodosie - 1521
Vlad Căugărul - 1521-22
Radu de la Afumaţi - 1522-29 (ruled with one interruption)
Vladislav III - 1523-25 (ruled with interruptions by Radu Bădica - 1523-24)
Moise - 1529-30
Vlad Înecatul - 1530-32
Vlad Vintilă de la Slatina - 1532-35
Radu Paisie (Petru de la Argeş) - 1535-45
Mircea Ciobanul - 1545-59 (with two interruptions)
Radu Ilie - 1552-53
Pătraşcu cel Bun (the Old) - 1554-57
Petru cel Tînăr (the Young) - 1559-68
Alexandru II Mircea - 1568-77
Mihnea Turcitul - 1577-83
Petru Cercel - 1583-85
Mihnea Turcitul - 1585-91
Ştefan Surdul (the Deaf) - 1591-92
Alexandru cel Rău (the Bad) - 1592-93
Mihai Viteazul (the Brave) - 1593-1601
Simion Movilă - 1600-1
Radu Mihnea - 1601-2
Radu Şerban - 1602-11
Radu Mihnea - 1611-16
Gavril Movilă - 1616
Alexandru Iliaş - 1616-18
Gavril Movilă - 1618-20
Radu Mihnea - 1620-23
Alexandru Coconul - 1623-27
Alexandru Iliaş - 1627-29
Leon Tomşa - 1629-32
Radu Iliaş - 1632
Matei Basarab - 1632-54
Constantin Şerban - 1654-58
Mihnea III Radu - 1658-59
Gheorghe Ghica - 1659-60
Grigore Ghica - 1660-64
Radu Leon - 1664-69
Antonie din Popeşti - 1669-72
Grigore Ghica - 1672-73
Gheorghe Duca - 1673-78
Şerban Cantacuzino - 1678-88
Constantin Brîncoveanu - 1688-1714
Stefan Cantacuzino - 1714-15

Beginning of Phanariot Regime
Nicolae Mavrocordat - 1715-16
Ion Mavrocordat - 1716-19
Nicolae Mavrocordat - 1719-30
Constantin Mavrocordat - 1730
Mihail Racoviţă - 1730-31

Constantin Mavrocordat - 1731-33
Grigore II Ghica - 1733-35
Constantin Mavrocordat - 1735-41
Mihail Racoviţă - 1741-44
Constantin Mavrocordat - 1744-48
Grigore II Ghica - 1748-52
Matei Ghica - 1752-53
Constantin Racoviţă - 1753-56
Constantin Mavrocordat - 1756-58
Scarlat Ghica - 1758-61
Constantin Mavrocordat - 1761-63
Constantin Racoviţă - 1763-64
Ştefan Racoviţă - 1764-65
Scarlat Ghica - 1765-66
Alexandru Scarlat Chica - 1766-68
Grigore II Ghica - 1768-69
Emanuel Giani-Ruset - 1770-71 (three years of Russian occupation follow)
Alexandru Ypsilanti - 1774-82
Nicolae Caragea - 1782-83
Mihail Suţu - 1783-86
Nicolae Mavrogheni - 1786-90
Mihail Suţu - 1791-93
Alexandru Moruzi - 1793-96
Alexandru Ypsilanti - 1796-97
Constantin Hangerli - 1797-99
Alexandru Moruzi - 1799-1801
Mihail Suţu - 1801-2
Constantin Ypsilanti - 1802-6

Kings of Hungary

Sigismund (Zsigmond) of Luxemburg - 1387-1437
Albert of Habsburg - 1437-39
Władysław (Ulászló) Jagieło - 1440-44
János (John) Hunyadi (Iancu de Hunedoara), Regent - 1446-52
László V (Ladislas) of Habsburg - 1452-57
Mátyás (Matthias) Hunyadi - 1458-90
Władysław II (Ulászló) Jagieło - 1490-1516
Lajos (Louis) II Jagieło - 1516-26

Habsburgs

Ferdinand I - 1526-64
János (John) Zápolyai, counterking - 1526-40
Maximillian (Miksa) I - 1564-76
Rudolph - 1576-1608
Matthias II - 1608-19
Ferdinand II - 1619-37
Ferdinand III - 1637-57
Leopold (Lipót) I - 1657-1705
Joseph (József) I - 1705-11
Charles (Károly) III - 1711-40
Maria Theresa - 1740-80
Joseph II - 1780-90
Leopold II - 1790-92

Francis (Ferenc) I - 1792-1835

Princes of Transylvania

John (János) Zápolyai (King of Hungary) - 1526-41
Isabella - 1541-51
Under Habsburg rule - 1551-56
Isabella - 1556-59
John-Sigismund (János-Zsigmond) Zápolyai 1559-71
Steven (István) Báthory - 1571-86 (after 1576 King of Poland residing in Kraków)
Christopher (Kristóf) Báthory - 1576-81
Sigismund (Zsigmond) Báthordy - 1581-99 (abicated in 1593, resumed rule in 1594; abdicated 1598, resumed rule in 1598)
Andrew (András), Cardinal Báthory - 1599
Mihai Viteazul - 1599-1600
Sigismund Báthory - 1601-2 (abdicated and resumed rule in 1601)
Habsburg occupation (General George Basta) - 1602-3
Moses Székely - 1603
Habsburg occupation (General George Basta) - 1604
Steven (István) Bocskai - 1604-6
Sigismund (Zsigmond) Rákoczi - 1606-08
Gabriel (Gábor) Báthory - 1608-13
Gabriel (Gábor) Bethlen - 1613-29
Catherine of Brandenburg (widow of Gabriel Bethlen) - 1629-30
Steven (István) Bethlen - 1630
George (György) I Rákoczi - 1630-48
George (György) II Rákoczi - 1648-57 (claimed title until 1660)
Francis (Ferencz) Rhédey - 1657-58
Ákos Barcsay - 1658-60
John (János) Kemény - 1661-62
Michael (Mihály) I Apafy - 1662-90
Emery (Imre) Thököli - 1690 (appointed by Ottomans, ruled for one month)
Michael (Mihály) II Apafy - 1690 (elected by Transylvanians, never took power)
George (György) Bánffy - Habsburg governor of Transylvania, 1692-1704
Francis (Ferencz) II Rákoczi - 1704-11

Kings of Poland

Casimir IV Jagiełło - 1447-92
John Albert Jagiełło - 1492-1501
Alexander I Jagiełło - 1501-6
Sigismund I Jagiełło - 1506-48
Sigismund II Jagiełło - 1548-72
Henri de Valois - 1572-75
Steven Báthory - 1575-86
Sigismund III Vasa - 1587-1632
Władysław IV Vasa - 1632-48
John Casimir Vasa - 1648-68
Michael Wisniowiecki - 1669-73
John III Sobieski - 1674-96
Interregnum - 1696-97
Augustus II of Saxony - 1697-1733

Tsars of Russia

Theodore III - 1676-82
Sophia, Regent - 1682-89 for co-Tsars Ivan V (1682-96) and
Peter I - 1682-1725
Catherine I - 1725-27
Peter II - 1727-30
Anna - 1730-40
Ivan VI - 1740-41
Elizabeth - 1741-62
Peter III - 1762
Catherine II - 1762-96
Paul I - 1796-1801
Alexander I - 1801-25

Doges of Venice

Andrea Contarini - 1368-83
Michael Morosini - 1383-84
Antonio Venier - 1384-1400
Michael Steno - 1400-13
Tommaso Mocenigo - 1413-23
Francesco Foscari - 1423-57
Pasquale Malipiero - 1457-62
Cristoforo Moro - 1462-71
Niccolò Tron - 1471-74
Niccolò Marcello - 1474
Pietro Mocenigo - 1474-76
Andrea Vendramin - 1476-78
Giovanni Mocenigo - 1478-85
Marco Barbarigo - 1485-86
Agostino Barbarigo - 1486-1501
Leonardo Loredan - 1501-21
Antonio Grimani - 1521-23
Andrea Gritti - 1523-38
Pietro Lando - 1538-45
Francesco Donato - 1545-53
Marcantonio Trevisan - 1553-54
Francesco Venier - 1554-56
Lorenzo Priuli - 1556-59
Girolamo Priuli - 1559-67
Pietro Loredan - 1567-70
Aloise (Luigi) Mocenigo - 1570-77
Sebastian Venier - 1577-78
Niccolò Da Ponte - 1578-85
Pasquale Cicogna - 1585-95
Marin Grimani - 1595-1606
Leonardo Donà - 1606-12
Marcantonio Memmo - 1612-15
Giovanni Bembo - 1615-18
Niccolò Donà - 1618
Antonio Priuli - 1618-23
Francesco Contarini - 1623-24
Giovanni Corner - 1624-30

Niccolò Contarini - 1630-31
Francesco Erizzo - 1631-46
Francesco Molin - 1646-55
Carlo Contarini - 1655-56
Francesco Corner - 1656
Bertuccio Valier - 1656-58
Giovanni Pesaro - 1658-59
Domenico Contarini - 1659-74
Niccolò Sagredo - 1674-76
Aloise Contarini - 1676-83
Marcantonio Giustiniani - 1683-88
Francesco Morosini - 1688-94
Silvestro Valier - 1694-1700
Aloise Mocenigo - 1700-9
Giovanni Corner - 1709-22
Aloise Sebastian Mocenigo - 1722-32
Carlo Ruzzini - 1732-35
Luigi Pisani - 1735-41
Pietro Grimani - 1741-52
Francesco Loredan - 1752-62
Marco Foscarini - 1762-63
Aloise Mocenigo - 1763-79
Paolo Renier - 1779-88
Ludovico Manin - 1788-97

APPENDIX 5

Glossary of Geographic Names

A great number of cities, rivers, islands, regions, and mountains mentioned in this volume are known by several names. Many of them are also relatively unknown and hard to find in a standard atlas. This glossary contains the names of only those places, listed in accordance with the present-day official names, that have had several names during the past centuries, and gives the most important of these. When not too easily found on maps, the approximate locations are also given.

Well-known geographical names such as Vienna, Istanbul, the Carpathian and Balkan ranges, the Danube River, and the Aegean Sea are not listed. They appear in the index of this volume.

A

Abydos (Çanakkale) — City on the eastern shore of the Dardanelles

Alba Iulia (Apulum, Gyulafehérvár, Karlsburg) — City in southeastern Transylvania

Amasya (Amaseia, Amasia) — City in north-central Asia Minor

Argeş — City west of Bucharest

Arta (Ambracia, Narda) — Bay and city in Greece on the Ionian Sea

Astarea — Mainland possession of Dubrovnik

Axios (Vardar) — River flowing through Yugoslavia and Greece

Aytos (Aydos, Aitos) — City north-northeast of Burgas

Azov (Azak) — City on northeastern shore of Azov Sea

B

Bácska (Bačka) — Region in southern Hungary W. of the Danube

Baia — Battlefield near Suceava in northern Moldavia

Balıkesir — City in Western Asia Minor, S. of Marmara Sea

Banat (Bánát) — Region of northeastern Yugoslavia and western Romania

Banjaluka (Banyaluka) — City in northern Bosnia

Bansko (Blagoevgrad) — City in southwestern Bulgaria

Baraolt (Barót) — City in southern Transylvania

Benderi (Bender, Tighin) — City near the mouth of the Dnester River

Beograd (Belgrade, Belgrad, Nándorfehérvár, Singdunum) — City at confluence of the Danube and Sara rivers

Bihor Mountains (Bihar hegység, Munţii Bihorului) — Range in western Transylvania

Bilhorod Dnistrovskii (Bielgorod, Akerman, Akkirman, Moncastro, Cetatea Albă)
Port city at the mouth of the Dnester River

Bistriţa (Beszterce, Bistritz)
City in northern Transylvania

Bitola (Bitolj, Monastir, Manastir)
City in southern Yugoslavia

Blaj (Balázsfalva, Blasendorf)
Small town south of Cluj

Bobâlna
Village in northern Transylvania

Bosna (Bosnia, Bosnien)
Province in present-day Western Yugoslavia

Bozca Ada (Tenedos)
Aegean island near Dardanelles

Brăila (Ibrail)
Danubian port in Romania

Braşov (Brassó, Kronstadt)
City in southeastern Transylvania

Bratislava (Pozsony, Pressburg)
Capital of Slovakia

Bucureşti (Bucharest, Bükreş)
Capital of Romania

Buda (Budin, Ofen)
One of the two cities that became Budapest

Burgas (Pyrgos, Burgaz)
Bulgarian port on the Black Sea

Bursa (Prusa, Brusa)
City in western Asia Minor south of the Marmara Sea

C

Călgău
Small town in northern Transylvania

Căpălna
Village near Călgău

Cavtat
Small city part of the Dubrovnik city republic

Cegléd
City in the center of the Hungarian plain

Chirmen (Chermanon, Chernomen, Çirmen)
City near Plovdiv

Cluj (Kolozsvár, Klausenburg)
City in western Transylvania; capital of Transulvania

Codrului Culmea
Mountain in western Transylvania

Crişana
Region of Romania, west of Transylvania

Csanád
City in southeastern Hungary

Csepel
Danube island S. of Budapest

Ç

Çanakkale (Abydos)
Town on the eastern shore of the Dardanelles

Çeşme
Strait in the Aegean between the mainland and the island of Khíos

Çimpe (Tzympe)
Town on the western shore of the Dardanelles

Çorlu (Tsourlon, Tzouroullos)
Town on the western shore of the Dardanelles

D

Damascus (al-Dimashq, Dimişh)
Capital of Syria

Debrecen
City in northeastern Hungary

Deliorman
Town in northeastern Bulgaria

Dibra Mountains
Range north of Lake Ohrid

Didymoteichos (Dimetoka, Dimotika) — City in eastern Thrace (Greece)

Dobrudja (Dobruca, Dobrogea) — Province on the Black Sea, half in Romania, half in Bulgaria

Drégely — Town in north-central Hungary

Drishti (Drivastum, Drivasto, Drivost) — City near Shkodër in Albania

Dubrovnik (Ragusium, Ragusa) — Port city on the Adriatic north of Montenegro

Durrës (Diraç, Drač, Durazzo) — Port city in central Albania

Ė

Ebros (Hebros, Maritsa, Meriç) — River flowing through Bulgaria, Turkey, and Greece

Edirne (Adrianopolis, Adrianople, Adrianopol, Odrin) — Turkish city on the Maritsa River

Eger (Egri, Erlau) — City in northern Hungary

Elkhovo (Kızılagaç) — City in southeastern Bulgaria

Epidaurus — Ancient Roman city near Dubrovnik

Esztergom (Gran, Estergon) — City on the Danube, northern Hungary

Euboea (Eğriboz, Negroponte, Evvoia) — Large Greek peninsula in the Aegean Sea north of Athens

F

Filakovo (Fülek) — City in southern Slovakia

G

Gaza (Gazze, Ghazza) — City on the Mediterranean northeast of Port Said

Gelibolu (Kallipolis, Gallipoli) — City on western shore of the Dardanelles

Giurgiu (Yergögü) — Romanian port city on the Danube

Győr (Raab, Yanık) — City in northwest Hungary

Gyula — City in southeast Hungary

H

Hatvan — City in the northern part of the Hungarian Plain

Hvar (Pharus, Lesina) — Adriatic island, central Yugoslav Coast

I

Ialomiţa (Jalomica) River — Southeastern Romania

Iaşi (Jassy) — Capital of Moldavia on the Prut River

Ikhtiman (Ihtiman) — Town in west-central Bulgaria

Ioannina (Janina, Yanina, Yanya) — City in northwestern Greece

Iráklion (Candia) — Capital of Crete

Izmail (Ismail) — Soviet port city on the Danube

Izmir (Smyrna) — Anatolian port on the Aegean Sea

Iznik (Nicaea) — City in northwestern Anatolia near Bursa

J

Jajce (Yayce)	City in northern Bosnia
Janów	City in southeastern Poland
Jerusalem (Quds, Yerushalayim, Kudüs)	Capital of Palestine

K

Kamieniec Podolski (Kaminiec, Kamnice)	City in the Ukraine on the Dnester River
Kanizsa (Nagykanizsa, Grosskanizsa, Kanije, Kanişa)	City in southwestern Hungary
Kaposvár	City in southwestern Hungary
Karlovci (Sremski Karlovci, Karlócza, Karlowitz)	Yugoslav city on the Danube west of Beograd
Kecskemét	City in the center of the Hungarian Plain
Khíos (Chios, Scio, Sakiz)	Large island in the Aegean Sea off Izmir
Khotin (Hotin, Chocim)	City in the Ukraine on the Dnester River
Kilia (Kili, Kiliya, Kilija, Chilia-Nouă)	Soviet port on the Danube
Kolarovo (Kolarovgrad, Sumen, Şumnu)	City in northeastern Bulgaria
Koločep	Island in Adriatic belonging to Dubrovnik
Komotine (Gümülcine)	City in eastern Greece
Konya (Iconium)	City in south-central Asia Minor
Kórinthos (Korintos, Corinthia, Corinth)	City in the Peloponnesos at the eastern end of the gulf
Koróni (Koron)	City in southwest Morea
Kosovo (Kosova)	Battlefield near Prištna in Yugoslavia
Kőszeg (Güns)	City in western Hungary
Kotel	City in eastern Bulgaria
Kotor (Cáttaro)	Port in southwestern Yugoslavia
Koyunhisar (Baphaeum)	City near the eastern end of the Gulf of Iznik
Kriti (Crete, Candia, Girid)	Island in the Mediterranean
Krujë (Kroja, Croia, Akçahisar)	City in Albania north of Tirana
Küçük Kajnarca	Village in Bulgaria near Silistra
Kyustendil (Köstendil, Velbuzd)	City southwest of Sofia
Kýpros (Cyprus, Kıbrıs)	Island in the Mediterranean

L

Larisa (Larissa, Yenişehir)	City in east-central Greece
Lastvo (Lastovo, Lagosta)	Island in the Adriatic belonging to Dubrovnik
Lesbos (Mytilene, Mitilíni, Midilli)	Large island in the Aegean north of Khios
Lezhë (Leş, Alessio)	City in northern Albania
Limnos (Limni, Lemnos)	Island in the Aegean north of Lesbos
Lipova (Lippa)	City in the Crişana (Romania)

Lokrum	Island in the Adriatic belonging to Dubrovnik
Lopud	Island in the Adriatic belonging to Dubrovnik
Lviv (Lwów, Lemberg)	City in the western Ukraine

M

Maínalon (Maina)	Mountains and peninsula in southern Morea
Manisa (Magnesia ad Maeanderum)	City in central Asia Minor
Manzikert (Malazgirt)	City in Asia Minor, north of Lake Van
Maritsa (Ebros, Hebros, Meriç)	River flowing through Bulgaria, Turkey, and Greece
Methóni (Modon, Moton)	City in southwest Morea
Mezőkeresztes	Battlefield in northeast Hungary
Mljet (Meleda)	Island in Adriatic belonging to Dubrovnik
Mohács	City in south-central Hungary
Mostar	Capital of Hercegovina
Munţii Meseşului (Meszeshegység)	Mountains in western Transylvania
Munţii Metaliferi (Érchegység)	Mountains in western Transylvania

N

Nagykőrös	City in central Hungary
Nagyvárad (Oradea, Varad, Grosswardein)	City in the Crişana (Romania)
Najran	City in Southeast Arabia
Navarino (Anavarin, Pylos)	City in southwestern Morea
Navpaktos (Naupaktos, Lepanto, Inebahtı, Aynabahtı)	City on the north shore of the Gulf of Corinth
Navplion (Nauplion, Anabolu)	City on the Gulf of Argolis (Morea)
Nicaea (Iznik)	City in Northwestern Anatolia near Bursa
Nikopol (Nicopolis, Nikopolis, Niğbolu, Niyebol)	City on the Danube in Bulgaria
Niš (Niş, Nish, Naissus)	City in central Serbia on the Morava River
Nográd (Novigrad, Neugrad)	City in north-central Hungary
Novi Brdo (Novabırda)	City near Priština, Yugoslavia
Novi Pazar (Novibazar, Yeni-Pazar)	Cities, one in southern Serbia, the other in northeastern Bulgaria

O

Oczakow (Ochakov, Özü)	City on the Black Sea east of Odessa
Ohrid (Lichnida, Ochrid, Okhrida, Ohri)	City in southwestern Yugoslavia
Olt	Romanian river flowing into the Danube
Oltenia (Little Wallachia)	Southwestern Romania
Orăştie (Szászváros, Broos)	City on the Mureş River, Transylvania

| Orşova (Orsova) | City on the Danube, western Romania |

P

Pag (Pago)	Island in Adriatic, northwest Yugoslavia
Páros (Para)	Cycladic Island, Greece
Pazardzhik (Tatarpazarcik)	City on the Maritsa, central Bulgaria
Peć (Ipek)	City in Serbia, near Albanian border
Pécs (Fünfkirchen)	City in southern Hungary
Pelješać (Sabbioncello)	Peninsula belonging to Dubrovnik
Pelopónnesos (Peloponnesus, Morea)	Peninsula making up southern Greece
Petrovaradin (Pétervárad, Péterwardein)	City in Yugoslav Banat
Pleven (Plevna)	City in north-central Bulgaria
Pločnik (Plotchnik)	City in central Serbia
Plovdiv (Philippopolis, Filibe)	City in central Bulgaria
Poiana Ruscăi (Pojána Ruszka)	Range in western Transylvania
Poljanovgrad (Karnobat, Karınabad)	City in east-central Bulgaria
Požarevac (Passarowitz)	City in south-central Yugoslavia
Prilep (Prelepe)	City in southern Yugoslavia about fifty miles east-northeast of Lake Ohrid
Priština (Prishtinë, Priştine)	City in south-central Yugoslavia
Provadiya (Pravadi)	City west of Varna

R

Rača	Monastery town on the Sava River
Radzyń	City in east-central Poland
Rhodos (Rodos, Rhodes, Rhodus, Rodi)	Island in the Mediterranean south of western Anatolia
Ruse (Russe, Ruščuk, Rusçuk)	Bulgarian port on the Danube

S

Şafad (Safed, Zefat)	City in northern Israel
Sakarya (Sangarius)	River in Asia Minor
Sarajevo (Bosna-Saray, Saray-Bosna, Saray, Vrhbosna)	Capital of Bosnia
Satu Mare (Szatmár, Sathmar)	City in northwest Romania
Senj (Zeng)	Port city on northern Yugoslav coast
Serres (Seres, Siris, Sérrai)	City northeast of Salonika
Semenicul (Szemenek) Mountains	Range in western Transylvania
Shkodër (Scutari, Skutari, Shkodra, Scodra, Işkodra)	City in northern Albania
Sibiu (Nagyszeben, Hermannstadt)	City in southern Transylvania
Siklós	City in southern Hungary
Silistra (Durostorum, Silistre)	Bulgarian port on the Danube
Simontornya	City in central Hungary west of the Danube
Skopje (Skoplje, Üsküp, Üsküb, Shkupi)	Capital of Yugoslav Macedonia on the Varda River
Slankamen (Szalánkamén)	City north of Beograd

Smederevo (Semendire, Semendriye, Szendrő)	City on the Danube east of Beograd
Sofia (Serdica, Sofya)	Capital of Bulgaria
Söğüt	Town in northwest Asia Minor near Bursa
Sozopol (Sözebolu)	Town south of Burgas
Split (Spalato)	Dalmatian port northwest of Dubrovnik
Stănileşti	Village on the Prut River south of Iaşi
Stara Zagora (Eskizagra)	City in central Bulgaria
Struma (Strimon)	River flowing through Bulgaria and Greece
Suceava	City in northeastern Romania
Svishtov (Sistova, Ziştova)	Bulgarian port on Danube
Szeged (Szegedin)	City in southern Hungary
Székesfehérvár (Stuhlweissenburg)	City west of Budapest
Szentendre (Sankt Andrae)	City north of Budapest
Szent Gotthárd	City in western Hungary
Szigetvár (Sigetvar, Sigeth)	City in southwest Hungary
Szolnok	City on the Tisza River in Hungary

Š

Šabac (Sabácz, Böğürdelen)	City on the Sava River west of Beograd
Šibenik (Sebenico)	Port city on central Yugoslav coast
Šipan (Guippana)	Island in Adriatic belonging to Dubrovnik

T

Ṭarābulus (Tripolis, Trablus, Tripoli)	City in northern Syria
Târnava Mare (Nagy Küküllö, Grosse Kokel)	River in central Transylvania
Tata	City in northwestern Hungary
Tekirdağ (Daidestos, Rodosto)	Turkish city on the European shore of the Marmara Sea
Tenos (Tínos, Istendil)	Cycladic Island, Greece
Tepelenë (Tepelen, Tepedelen)	City in southern Albania
Thessaloníki (Saloniki, Salonika, Selānik)	Greek port near the mouth of the Varda River
Timişoara (Temesvár, Tımışvar)	City in southwestern Romania
Tîrgovişte (Târgovişte)	City northwest of Bucharest
Tisza (Theiss) River	River on the Hungarian plain
Topolnica (Toplica)	River in central Serbia
Trabzon (Trebizond, Trapesus, Travzon)	Turkish Black Sea port in eastern Anatolia
Transylvania (Erdély, Ardeal, Siebenbürgen)	Part of present-day Romania west of the Carpathians
Trikala (Trikkala, Tırhala)	City in central Greece
Tripolís	City in central Morea
Trogir (Tragirium, Trau)	Port city on central Yugoslav coast

Tŭrnovo (Veliko Tŭrnovo, Tirnovo, Tărnovo, Tirnova) — City in north-central Bulgaria

U

Ulcinj (Olcinium, Dulcigno) — Port city in Crna Gora (Montenegro)

Ü

Üzünköprü — City in western European Turkey

V

Vácz (Waitzen) — City on the Danube north of Budapest

Vardar (Axios) — River flowing through Yugoslavia and Greece

Varna (Odessus, Warna) — Bulgarian port on the Black Sea

Văslug — Town south of Iaşi

Vasvár — Town in western Hungary

Velbužd (Küstendil) — City not important today on the upper course of the Struma River about forty-five miles south-southwest of Sofia

Veszprém — City in west-central Hungary

Vidin (Bononia) — Danubian port in northwestern Bulgaria

Visegrád — Town on the Danube in northwestern Hungary

Vize (Bizya) — City in European Turkey

Vratsa (Vraca) — City in northwestern Bulgaria

Y

Yambol (Jambol, Yanbolu) — City in eastern Bulgaria

Yerevan (Erevan, Erivan, Revan) — Capital of Soviet Armenia

Yerushalayim (Jerusalem, Quds, Kudüs) — *See* Jerusalem

Z

Zadar (Iadera, Zara) — Dalmatian port

Zagreb (Zágráb, Agram, Zagrabia, Gric, Mons Grech) — Capital of Croatia on the Sava River

Zefat (Şafad, Safed) — City in northern Israel

Zemun (Semlin, Zimony) — City on the Sava River facing Beograd

Zenta (Senta) — Town on the Tisza River in northern Yugoslavia

Zsitvatorok — The mouth of the Žitava River near Komárno (Komárom)

Zrenjanin (Nagybecskerek, Veliki Bečkerek) — City near Novi Sad (Ujvidék, Neusatz)

Żurawno (Zuravno) — Town on the upper Dniester River

APPENDIX 6

Glossary of Foreign Terms and Expressions

A

Adat	*See urf*
Ağa	Chief; officer; master
Agıl resmi	Fold fee for wintering of herds
Ahdname	Pact conferring vassal status on dependent rulers
Akçe	Basic silver coin of account in the Ottoman Empire
Akhi	1) Mystic fraternity; 2) Leader of mystic fraternity; 3) Trade or craft guild member
Akıncı	Irregular soldier used as scout or raider
Akritoi	Byzantine border warrior; fighter for Christianity
Alay beyi	Military rank, roughly equivalent to colonel; these men also served as local provincial administrators
Archon	Greek nobleman and/or city administrator
Armatoles	Locally recruited Christian policemen in seventeenth and eighteenth centuries
Arus resmi	Marriage fee
Avariz	Extraordinary (special, temporary) tax

Â

Âdet-i ağnam	"Sheep" tax paid on all small, four-legged animals
Âlim	Muslim learned man
Âmme	General or public law
Âşar	Tithe
Âyan	1) Muslim notable; 2) Local (regional) lord or petty ruler

B

Baba	Father; Holy man
Bán (banus)	Hungarian viceroy administering Croatia
Bazirgan	*See tüccar*
Bedel	Sum paid for exemption from military service (originally an *avariz* tax [which see] that has been transformed into a regular tax)
Bedestan	"Bazaar"; covered market, the fortified section covering luxury shops
Benak	Tax on Muslim married householders; one of the three dues making up the *raiyyet rusmu* (which see)
Berat	Ottoman imperial warrant conferring dignities or privileges
Bey (beğ)	1) Ruler; 2) governor; 3) gentleman
Beylerbeyi	Highest ranking governor
Beylerbeylik	Province (up to sixteenth century)
Beylik	1) Area governed by a *bey;* 2) In Bosnia name for a *çiftlik* (which see)
Birun	"Outer service"; Collective term describing all those members of the *Mülkiye* (which see) who served in the

343

Ottoman imperial palace outside of the residence of the imperial family

C

Călăraşi	Free Romanian peasant
Caliph	Ruler of the Arab-Muslim states
Cebelü	Armed man serving under a *sipahi* (which see)
Celali	Rebel of Asia Minor
Celep	Agent entrusted with buying and delivering forced purchases of food to designated places
Celepkeşan	Celep (which see) also charged with raising some of the livestock he had to deliver
Cizye	Poll tax, paid by non-Muslims

Ç

Çarsı	Market
Çavuş	Originally, a courier at the imperial court; later (eighteenth century) an official charged with executing orders or judgments
Çavuşbaşi	Head of the *Çavuş* Corps
Çerisürücü	1) Police officer; 2) Military policemen
Çift	Basic unit of landholding with size depending on fertility of soil
Çiftlik	Farm or privately owned estate
Çift resmi	One of the three dues making up the *raiyyet rusmu* (which see)
Çirak	Apprentice
Çorbaci	Rich non-Muslim holding a minor office

D

Dahi	Leader of Janissary-*yamak* group
Dar al-Harb	All lands not under Muslim rule; enemy territory
Dar al-Islam	The domain of Islam
Defterdar	Chief Treasury official
Defter emini	Keeper of records
Derbentci	Guard of a bridge, pass, or other strategic location
Derviş	Wandering Muslim holy man
Devşirme	Child levy
Dhimmah	See *Zimme*
Dhimmi	See *Zimmi*
Diniye	Class of religious dignitaries
Dirlik	1) Income, livelihood; 2) Minimum guarantee for a decent livelihood
Divan	1) Council of state; 2) Council of Romanian rulers
Divan-i hümayun	Imperial council
Doğanci	Raiser of hunting falcons
Domn	Traditional title of the rulers of Moldavia and Wallachia
Dorobanţi	Romanian peasant tied to the land
Dönüm	Ottoman land measure equaling 1,124.24 square yards

E

Ehl-i hibre	Guild official charged with quality and price controls

Emir	High Arab dignitary; "Prince"
Enderun	"Inner service"; Collective term describing all those members of the *Mülkiye* (which see) who served in the inner section of the Ottoman imperial palace containing the ruler's residence
Erkan-i devlet	"Pillars of the realm"; Members of the imperial council
Esnaf	Class of artisans and small merchants
Evliya	Friend; in Folk Islam—saint
Eyalet	Ottoman province (after the sixteenth century)

F

Ferman	Imperial edict
Fetva	Written ruling of the *şeyhülislam* (which see) or lower ranking *müftis* (which see)
Frengi	Ottoman expression for Christian inhabitants of the *dar al-Harb* (which see)
Funduki	Ottoman gold coin
Futuwwa	1) Mystic fraternity; 2) Ethical code of mystic fraternity; 3) Ethical code of artisan and trade guilds

G

Gaza	Holy war
Gazi	1) Ottoman border warrior; 2) Fighter for Islam
Gedikli	Journeyman; licensed craftsman or shopkeeper
Gönüllü	Volunteer; soldier recruited from Anatolian peasantry

H

Hadd	"Limit" or "border" defining the rights and duties of any given individual
Hadith	Muslim religious tradition
Hajduk	1) Bandit; 2) Resistance fighter
Hanafī	One of the four "accepted" Sunni legal schools
Hanbalī	One of the four "accepted" Sunni legal schools
Haraç	Land-use tax; sometimes used as a synonym of *cizye* (which see)
Has	"Fief" of the largest size
Has çift	The core section of a *timar* (which see) cultivated by the *timarlı* (which see) himself
Havas-i hümayun	Imperial estate
Hijra	The flight of Muhammad from Mecca to Yathrib (Medina)
Hisbe	Section of ihtisāb (which see) important for regulating commerce
Hospodar	Title of Phanariot rulers of Moldavia and Wallachia
Hükümet sancak	Self-governing, sometimes hereditary, province
Hypostatika	Greek expression for *çiftlik* (which see)

I

Ihtisāb	Body of laws regulating fair trade and public morals
Ijma'	Concensus of the Muslim learned men
İjtihād	Right of doctrinal interpretation
İlmiye	Class of jurist and teachers

Iltizam	Tax farm
Imaret	A building complex that serves a variety of purposes and is supported by the income of a pious foundation
Iqta'	Military fief
Ispence	Equivalent of *Çift resmi* (which see) paid by non-Muslims
Iştira	Forced purchase of foodstuffs

J

Jihad	Holy war

K

Kadi	Judge
Kadiasker	Military judge; Highest rank in Ottoman judiciary
Kafes	"Golden cage"; The custom that kept Ottoman princes for their entire life in the "inner palace" unless they became sultans.
Kâhya	1) Steward, supervisor, agent, assistant (used in numerous connections with these meanings); 2) Representative of groups before the central government
Kalemiye	Class of scribes; men of the pen
Kalfa	Guild member with master's qualifications, but not owning his own business
Kanun	Law based on the ruler's authority
Kanunname	Law code
Kapı Kâhyasi	Representative of vassal princes or privileged communities dealing with Ottoman central government
Kapı kulu	"Slave of the Porte"; serving as soldier, administrator, or in a variety of other positions; a salaried officer of the Ottoman government
Kapudan-i derya	Chief admiral of the Ottoman navy
Kara Kuruş	Ottoman name for Austrian silver Grossus
Kaza	1) Smallest provincial administrative district; 2) Judicial district
Kethüda	1) Agent; 2) Chief officer of guilds dealing with the authorities; 3) "Second-in-command" serving under governors and other major office holders; 4) Agent of the city dealing with the central government; 5) Supervisor of a borough in a city
Khalifa	See *Caliph*
Kile	Name of several weights (presently one Istanbul Kile equals about 82 pounds (36.5 k); 88 pounds in earlier centuries
Kirdžhali	Locally recruited Muslim policeman in the seventeenth and eighteenth centuries, often disorderly
Kılıç	"Sword"; the basic minimum land supporting a warrior
Kızlar agası	Chief of the black eunuchs in the imperial palace
Klepht	1) Bandit; 2) Resistance fighter
Kmet	Petty judge and policeman elected from their midst by the villagers
Knez	1) Leader; 2) Village head man; 3) Leader of *zadruga* (which see)

Kul	Slave
Kuruş	Ottoman monetary unit introduced in the seventeenth century

L

Liva	Alternate name for *sancak* (which see)

M

Maaslı	Salaried; Especially salaried Ottoman soldier
Mahalle	Borough, city section
Mal	Wealth
Mal defterdari	1) Provincial treasurer; 2) Registrar of property
Malikane	Tax farm or other lease granted for the recipient lifetime
Mālikī	One of the four "accepted" Sunni legal schools
Medrese	Muslim school of higher learning
Mevkufcu (*Mevkufatçı*)	Registrar and administrator of real estate and properties without legal owners
Mezőváros	"Prairie town"; self-governing peasant-town on the Hungarian plain
Millet	A group of non-Muslim people considered as a legal-administrative unit by the Ottomans
Mırı	Government owned possessions, mainly land
Mogoriš	Title of Slav chiefs in early centuries
Morlak	1) Bandit; 2) Resistance fighter
Mubayaa	Wholesale purchase; sometimes forced purchase of foodstuffs
Muhtar	Bailiff of a city district
Muhtesib	Government official responsible for the application of *ihtisab* laws (q.v.); especially market inspector
Mukataa	1) To rent out; 2) The land rented; 3) A tax form of government revenue rented out to individuals; typical after 1550.
Mukayese	Forced purchase of foodstuffs
Mücerred	Bachelor's tax; one of the three dues making up the *raiyyet rusmu* (which see)
Müderris	Professor at the *medrese* (which see)
Müfti	Jurisconsult
Mülk	Private property, mainly land
Mülkiye	Class of administrators serving in the imperial palace
Mültezim	1) Tax collector; 2) Tax farmer
Müsellem	A person serving in the army in exchange for tax exemption
Mütevelli	Administrator (bailiff) of a *vakıf* (which see)

N

Nahiye	1) Subdivision of the judicial *kaza;* 2) Subdivision of a *mahalla* (which see)
Naib	Low ranking judge serving under kadı
Nazir	Supervisor
Nişancı	Affixer of the official imperial signature to documents and secretary of the imperial council

O

Ober-knez	District headman; title of Christian official introduced in eighteenth century by Austrians
Oka	Ottoman weight; 1/100 of a *kile* (which see)
Oppida	Other name for *mezőváros* (which see)
Otlak resmi	Pasturage fee

Ö

Örf	See *urf*

P

Palanka (*Palánka*)	Palisade, small fortification
Para	Ottoman monetary unit introduced in the seventeenth century in the Eastern Provinces, then spreading into general imperial usage.
Paşa	High honorific title of rank
Paşalik	Region (province) governed by a *paşa*
Pekmez	Grape juice boiled to thick syrup
Pencik	1) Title deed to a slave; 2) The sultan's right to receive one-fifth of all prisoners of war
Peşcheşurile	Accession gift paid by Moldavia and Wallachia whenever a new prince ascended their thrones
Piyade	Irregular (auxiliary) infantryman

Q

Qijās	Analogy
Qur'ān	The sacred book of Islam

R

Raiyyet rusmu	Main personal tax paid by Muslims
Reaya	"The Flock"; originally all subjects of the state, later only the non-Muslims
Resmi duhan	Unspecified tax paid at wedding by the bride's father
Resmi kovan	Tax on bee hives
Rüsum	Cash paid as tax in place of deliveries in kind

S

Sadrazam	Grand vezir
Salariye	Tax levied on must, barley, millet, oats, and rye
Salyane	Annual remittance to central government of taxes collected in a province wherein no *timar*s were assigned
Sancak	Provincial administrative unit, major subdivision of *beylerbeylik* or *eyalet* (which see)
Sancak beyi	Governor of a *sancak* (which see)
Seyfiye	Class of military men; men of the sword
Shāfi'i	One of the four "accepted" sunni legal schools
Sharī'a	Islamic law
Sipahi	Cavalryman, either feudal or salaried
Subaşı	Police chief
Sufi	Muslim mystic

Sunni	Muslim follower of the four "orthodox" legal schools
Sūra	Chapter of the Qur'ān
Sürsat zehiresi	Forced deliveries of foodstuff and raw materials to the army in times of war; considered a tax

Ş

Şerifi	Ottoman gold coin
Şeyh	1) Chief; 2) Religious leader; 3) Trival leader; 4) Nominal over-all and *de facto* religious leader; of artisan and merchant guilds; 5) Holy man
Şeyhülislam	Chief of the Ottoman *ulema* (which see)

T

Tahrir	Census and property record
Tapu	1) Title deed; 2) Fee paid by peasant for title deed to his *tasarruf* (which see)
Tarikat	*Derviş* orders; also used occasionally for the order's rules
Tasarruf	Property and tenancy rights of the peasantry
Tekke	House of *derviş* orders
Timar	Ottoman "fief"
Timarlı	Beneficiary of the income of a *timar* (which see)
Törü	The ruler's right to issue decrees
Tuğ	Horsetail, the number of which carried before an official indicated his rank
Tuğra	The highly stylized official signature of the sultan
Tuğralı	Ottoman gold coin
Tüccar	Large-scale merchant

U

Ulema	The class of learned men; doctors of law, theology and jurisprudence
Urf	Customary law
Usta	1) Teacher; 2) Guild master
Uskok	1) Bandit; 2) Resistance fighter

V

Vajda	Title of the royal Hungarian governor of Transylvania
Vakfiye	Donation deed establishing a *vakıf* (which see)
Vakıf	A trust established with a grant of land or other income-producing property to support a pious foundation in perpetuity
Valide sultan	Title of the sultan's mother
Végvár	Border fortress
Vekil	Agent, representative, proxy
Voievod	Traditional title of the rulers of Moldavia and Wallachia
Voynuk	Raiser of horses for imperial stables

Y

Yamak	Auxiliary janissary
Yaya	Irregular (auxiliary) infantryman
Yaya başı	Janissary officer in charge of *devşirme* (which see) recruitment

Yiğitbaşı	Man responsible for enforcement of guild regulations; Also raw material buyer of the guilds
Yerli	1) Local, especially local janissary recruit; 2) Herdsman, raiser of animals
Yürük	Turkic nomad living in Ottoman Empire, considered part of the military class

Z

Zadruga	Serb consanguinal family (clan)
Zaim	Beneficiary of the income of a *zeamet* (which see)
Zaviye	Hostel maintained by *dervişes*
Zeamet	Medium-size Ottoman "fief"
Zer-i mahbub	Ottoman gold coin
Zimme	Guarantee of security
Zimmi	"Protected person"; Any non-Muslim living in a non-Muslim state and obeying its laws
Zincirli	Ottoman gold coin

Index

351

Ottoman policy of, 66; and Székelys, 149
Mavrocordatos, Alexander, 128, 129, 257
Mavrocordatos, Constantine, 136-37
Mavrocordatos, Nicholas, 132, 275
Mavromikhalis family, 92
Manzikert, Battle of, 9, 10, 18
Maximillian of Brunswick, 199
Maximillian I of Habsburg, 152, 156, 157
Mecca, 4, 41
Medina, 41
Medrese, 40, 43, 52, 53, 83
Mefkufcu, 43, 99
Mehmed I, 16, 25, 26, 27, 28, 63, 64
Mehmed II, 16, 27, 29, 30, 40, 44, 45, 46, 47,
   48, 49, 56, 57, 65, 66, 67, 95, 98, 109, 115,
   116, 124, 188, 189, 253, 267
Mehmed III, 195
Mehmed IV, 197
Mehmed Sokollu, 58, 64, 122, 201, 267
Méliusz-Juhász, Peter, 153
Menčetić, Šiško, 180
Mevlevi, 53
Mezőkeresztes, Battle of, 158, 196, 197
Mezőváros, 218, 280, 284. *See also* Oppida
Mihai Viteazul, 122, 124, 158; and Georg
   Basta, 119, 159
Milescu, Nicolae, 129
"Military border," 106
Military class, 17, 18, 33, 36. *See also Seyfiye*
Military organization of Ottomans, 37-40
Miller, William, 213
Millet, 5, 6, 252, 253; Armenian, 49, 277; ex-
   planation of, 44; Jewish, 278; functioning
   of, 273-74; Orthodox, 278-79; role of, in
   city government, 85; role of, in guilds, 78,
   79; role of, in *mahalle*, 75, 76; in theory
   and practice, 49, 277-79. *See also* Jewish
   millet; Orthodox millet
Millet başi, 44, 45, 46, 47, 49
Minor Council of Dubrovnik, 171
Mircea cel Bătrîn, 21, 22, 26, 27, 28, 115
Mırı , 90, 98, 211, 212; converted to *mülk*,
   214, 217; explained, 93
Mogoriš, 170
Mohács: first battle of, 69, 70, 89, 284; second
   battle of, 199, 201
Moisiodax, Josephus, 258
Moldavia, 41, 42, 63, 70, 73, 196, 281, 282;
   Austrian occupation of, 204; Gabriel
   Báthory attacks, 160; boyar cliques in, 123-
   24, 125; cultural developments in, 128-29,
   130, 135; cultural decline in, 137; Divan of,
   121; economic problems of, 121-26; gifts
   given by, in Istanbul, 122-23; Greek influence in, 128, 129; Hungarian attacks on,
   115-16; illegal Ottoman actions in, 126;
   "new nobility" of, 133-34, 135, 136; peasantry of, 137-38; *peşcheşurile* paid by, 122;
   Phanariot period in, 132-41; Polish and
   Tatar attacks on, 116, 131, 158; relations of,

with Ottomans, 121-26, 130; Russian occu-
   pations of, 205, 206, 207; trade of, with
   Istanbul, 120, 123; tribute paid by, 121-23;
   vassalage of, 67, 115. *See also* Danubian
   Principalities
Mongols, 10-11, 14, 18, 23, 57
Molière, 262
Moltke, Helmuth von, the Elder, 108
Monasteries (Romanian), 127, 136-37, 217-18
Monastir, 51, 73
Monophysites, 49
Montecucculi, Raimondo, 197
Morea, 16, 22, 28, 29, 30, 42, 66, 67, 92; Al-
   banians in, 197, 205, 222; anti-Catholicism
   in, 202, 203; local rule in, 237; revolt in,
   197; reconquest of, 203, 204; Russian naval
   attack on, 205; Venetians in, 199, 200, 202,
   203
Morlaks, 242. *See also* "Bandits"; *Hajduks*;
   Klephts; *Uskoks*
Morosini, Francesco, 197, 199
Moruzi, Alexandru, 141
Moscowy, 118
Mostar, 74
Mountains, 260
Mt. Athos, 129, 264, 265
Movilă family, 127
Mubaya, 125
Muhammad, 4, 5, 272
Muhtar, 75, 82, 83
Muhtesib, 82
Mukataa, 218. *See also Iltizam;* Tax farming
Mukayese, 125
Murad I, 16, 18, 20, 21, 23, 25, 27, 28, 39, 55,
   57, 252
Murad II, 16, 28, 29, 30, 39, 48, 57, 65, 66, 102
Murad III, 65, 190, 241
Murad IV, 56
Musa, Prince, 25, 26-27, 52
Muslims, 5, 6, 7; in the Balkans, 50-52; cul-
   tural life of, 252, 254; decline of birth rate
   of, 71, 222; in Dobrudja, 121; in Istanbul,
   50; majority of, in Ottoman Empire, 65;
   taxes paid by, 102; urbanization of, 222
Muslim calendar, 4
Muslim learning, 13
Muslim legal schools, 6
Muslim officials, 7
Mustafa II, 37n
Mustafa, Prince, the Elder, 28
Mustafa, Prince, the Younger, 28
Mücerred, 102
Müderris, 40, 43
Müfti, 7, 40, 43
Mülk, 96, 98, 211, 212; explained, 93
Mülkiye, 34, 36, 38
Mültezim, 36, 38, 100, 193, 215, 216, 218, 229;
   of Dubrovnik, 178; importance of, 210;
   hereditary position of, 217. *See also* Tax
   farmer

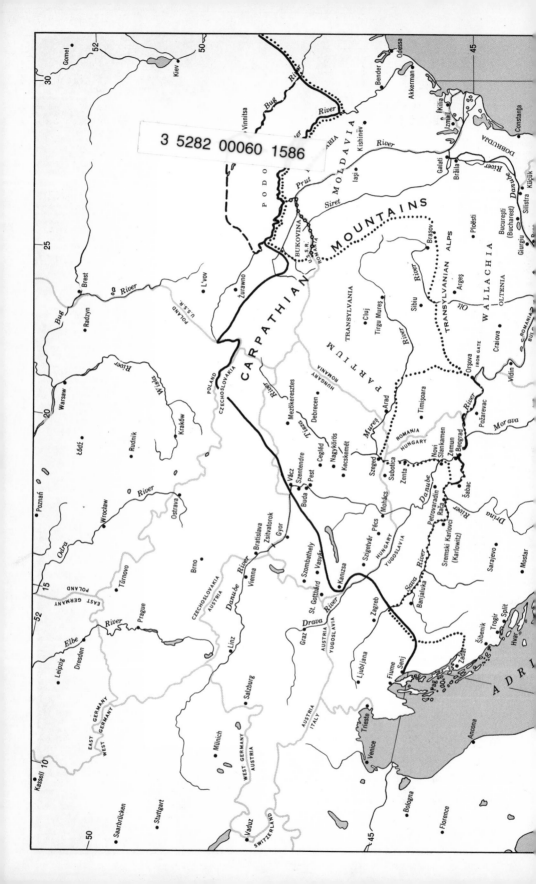